BUILDING THE RESPONSIBLE ENTERPRISE

BUILDING THE RESPONSIBLE ENTERPRISE

Where Vision and Values Add Value

SANDRA WADDOCK AND
ANDREAS RASCHE

STANFORD BUSINESS BOOKS

An Imprint of Stanford University Press
Stanford, California

Stanford University Press
Stanford, California

Special discounts for bulk quantities of Stanford Business Books are available to corporations, professional associations, and other organizations. For details and discount information, contact the special sales department of Stanford University Press. Tel: (650) 736–1782, Fax: (650) 736–1784

Printed in the United States of America on acid-free, archival-quality paper

Library of Congress Cataloging-in-Publication Data

Waddock, Sandra A., author.
  Building the responsible enterprise: where vision and values add value / Sandra Waddock and Andreas Rasche.
    pages cm
  Includes bibliographical references and index.
  ISBN 978-0-8047-8194-7 (cloth : alk. paper)
  ISBN 978-0-8047-8195-4 (pbk : alk. paper)
    1. Social responsibility of business. 2. Industrial management—Social aspects. 3. Industrial management—Environmental aspects.
  I. Rasche, Andreas, author. II. Title.
  HD60.W323 2012
  658.4'08—dc23
                                                            2011043524

CONTENTS

Preface   *vii*

Acknowledgments   *ix*

PART I   A CONTEXT FOR RESPONSIBLE ENTERPRISE

Chapter 1   Responsible Enterprise: A Systems Perspective   1

Chapter 2   In Search of Balance: Business, Politics, Civil Society, and Nature   20

PART II   DEVELOPING RESPONSIBLE ENTERPRISE

Chapter 3   The Role of Personal and Organizational Vision   55

Chapter 4   Values in Management Practice: Operating with Integrity   81

Chapter 5   Value Added: The Impact of Vision and Values   107

PART III   MANAGING RESPONSIBLE ENTERPRISE

Chapter 6   Stakeholders: The Relationship Key   131

Chapter 7   Managing for Responsibility   169

Chapter 8   Assessing Responsible Enterprise   188

Chapter 9   Sustainability and the Global Village   222

Chapter 10 Responsibility Initiatives and Guidance Documents   243

PART IV   REINVENTING CSR: CORPORATE SUSTAINABILITY
           AND RESPONSIBILITY

Chapter 11 Scanning the Future: Finding Pattern in Chaos   271

Chapter 12 Value Added for the Global Future   293

            Notes   311
            Index   351

PREFACE

This book aims to provide practitioners, academics, and students with a hands-on, yet theoretically based, introduction to corporate responsibility and responsible enterprise. Since the mid-1990s there has been a virtual explosion of interest in the issue of responsible enterprise, often labeled corporate responsibility. We adopt the term *responsible enterprise* to reflect the reality that responsibility practices go far beyond large multinational corporations; they are being implemented in small and medium-sized business enterprises, as well as in other newly emerging types of enterprises. Increasing attention to issues related to climate change and sustainability has only heightened the understanding of business's interdependence with the rest of society, its stakeholders, and the natural environment. In light of these major challenges, the goal of this book is to help those leading and studying responsible companies to understand the complex dilemmas that leaders face and the multiple perspectives embedded in every decision. The book also seeks to build awareness of the implications of managerial decisions for everyone they affect—the stakeholders and the natural environment with its manifold living beings.

In many respects the book reaches beyond the traditional literature on responsible enterprise. In discussing firms' social and environmental responsibilities, we rely on insights from other fields within the management domain (e.g., strategic management, human resource management, and organizational behavior) and on other academic disciplines (e.g., political science, philosophy, psychology, and sociology). The resulting reflections paint a picture of corporate responsibility that shows the field's embeddedness in other discourses, demonstrates its breadth, and, we hope, suggests its depth.

This book adopts a more personal tone than many other books on the subject. We do not want to provide yet another introduction to corporate responsibility/responsible enterprise without paying sufficient attention to the personal values and visions underlying the management of social and environmental issues. For us, managing a firm's responsibility is as much a personal journey as it is a management task. We hope that the discussions in this book reflect these more personal aspects and inspire readers to strive for change in companies and in themselves.

Let us be clear about two things. First, we do not believe that companies that start to address corporate responsibility will turn into paragons of virtue. Like human beings, every company makes mistakes. But responsible firms must be willing to deal with these mistakes and learn from them. Second, although we highlight the business case for responsible enterprise, we do not think that all corporate responsibility efforts will automatically create win-win situations. The existence of a business case for corporate responsibility depends a lot on what issues are addressed by whom and in what context.

Finally, we hope that readers will have as much fun reading the book as we had writing it!

Sandra Waddock
Andreas Rasche
Boston and Coventry
February 2012

ACKNOWLEDGMENTS

From Sandra Waddock: Intellectual debts are difficult to pay. To all the authors cited in this book and so many more in the field, I thank you for your ideas and vision and hope your ideas have inspired mine in ways that you find acceptable. There are a few people who deserve particular mention. I will be forever grateful to Jim Post of Boston University, mentor and friend for so many years, for his ideas and inspiration. Also to Brad Googins, former executive director of the Boston College Center for Corporate Citizenship, for his thought leadership and for providing ways for me to learn firsthand what responsible enterprise is all about; and to Ed Freeman for his friendship and all of his work on stakeholder theory. I also want to thank Malcolm McIntosh, co-author with me of *SEE Change: Making the Transition to a Sustainable Enterprise Economy*, for his intellectual courage and ability to speak truth to power, and to all the other "difference makers" and intellectual shamans whose lives and work are so inspiring. For those who have provided intellectual and other support over the years, particularly Dawn Elm, Jeanne Liedtka, Larry Lad, Judy Clair, and so many others, I am grateful.

The Boston area music community also deserves thanks for providing an outlet other than work—Summer Acoustic Music Week (SAMW), Ellen Schmidt and her open mikes and all the other open mike hosts, the Folk Song Society of Greater Boston, the Mystic Chorale (especially founder and director Nick Page), and the Boston Minstrels. To my good friends Priscilla Osborne, Pennie Sibley, Margaret Skinner, Tish (Schilling) Miller, Harriet Hart, and too many others to mention, thank you. For Ben Wiegner, my son, who inspires with his own very different passions, I am most grateful. Not least, in fact perhaps most, to Alan Rubin, who is steadfast through it all, my love and gratitude.

From Andreas Rasche: Many people have influenced my thinking about responsible enterprise over the years. Although any list of people would be incomplete, a few people deserve to be singled out. I am very grateful for the many insightful discussions I have had with my friend and colleague Dirk Ulrich Gilbert. I also express my gratitude to Colin Crouch at the University of Warwick (who taught me that responsible enterprise is much more about economic governance than I ever thought), Günther Ortmann at Helmut-Schmidt-University Hamburg (who helped me to understand the limits of thinking about responsible enterprise), and Ulrich Grimm at EBS Business School, Germany (who tolerated my interest in different academic discourses and thus allowed me to join this debate in the first place). I am particularly grateful to Sandra Waddock for choosing to collaborate with me on this project and for being a wonderful person to work with.

I am also much obliged to my family and friends for their enduring support, tolerance, patience, and most of all, true friendship. Last but not least, I am deeply grateful to Stephanie Rasche, my wife, who is a constant source of inspiration and love.

Finally, we both want to thank Margo Beth Fleming, our editor at Stanford University Press, whose support and encouragement enabled us to tackle this book at all, and Stanford University Press itself for publishing this book.

For all who would be responsible . . .
For all who make the world a better place . . .
For all who care . . .
We are grateful.

Part I

A CONTEXT FOR RESPONSIBLE ENTERPRISE

1 RESPONSIBLE ENTERPRISE

A Systems Perspective

> We have to choose between a global market driven only by
> calculations of short-term profit, and one which has a human face.
> Between a world which condemns a quarter of the human race to
> starvation and squalor, and one which offers everyone at least a
> chance of prosperity, in a healthy environment. Between a selfish
> free-for-all in which we ignore the fate of the losers, and a culture
> in which the strong and successful accept their responsibilities,
> showing global vision and leadership.
>
> Kofi Annan, former Secretary-General of the United Nations,
> in a speech at the World Economic Forum, 1999[1]

CORPORATE RESPONSIBILITY FOR SUSTAINABLE ENTERPRISE

The speech by former United Nations Secretary-General Kofi Annan quoted
in the epigraph above sparked a firestorm of interest among executives in
attendance. Only one year later the United Nations launched the UN Global
Compact as a formal organization. By its tenth anniversary in 2010, the UN
Global Compact was by far the world's largest corporate responsibility initiative, with over 8,600 signatories, 6,200 of which were businesses, including
many transnational corporations. Annan's words highlight an important and
often forgotten reality: business is integrally connected to both the social and
ecological contexts in which it operates.

With his statement, Annan signaled new recognition of an important shift
in the long-term relationships that businesses can expect to have with their
many constituencies—their stakeholders—and with how they treat the natural environment.[2] As businesses have grown larger and more powerful, their
attendant duty to be responsible wherever they operate has also grown. Indeed, some argue that the rise of the very term corporate responsibility since
the late 1990s came about in part because some companies in the process
of globalization began to assume responsibilities formerly assigned solely to
governments.[3] Today, expectations that businesses will play constructive and
responsible roles in creating an equitable and sustainable society are further

enhanced by worries about global climate change, the economic meltdown of 2008 and its ensuing social problems, and the continuing gap between rich and poor, North and South.

Consider the following: during the first ten years of the 21st century, the world was faced with a series of major business scandals and ethical abuses, including the collapse of Enron, a global financial crisis resulting from an increasingly dominant financial services industry that acted more like a gambling casino than your neighborhood banker, a collapsing housing market resulting from deceptive and problematic mortgage lending practices, and the recognition that climate change and a sustainability crisis were no longer impending but in fact present.[4] The gap between rich and poor globally grew wider, in some places resulting in revolution, and in others leaving billions of people to subsist in grinding poverty. Ecologists note that all major ecological systems are in decline—with overfishing, erosion of topsoil, desertification, clear-cutting of forests for timber, burning of rainforests for grazing and cropland, fertilizer polluting rivers, streams, and lakes, and species extinction at an unprecedented rate being only a few of the many ecological problems facing the planet.

Despite the Millennium Development Goals (MDGs) proffered by the United Nations with the intent of reducing poverty, increasing education, and enhancing sustainability in the world, nearly 3 billion of the 7 billion people in the world still live on less than $2.50 a day, 1.1 billion do not have clean water to drink or cook with, and 2.4 billion people have no sanitation facilities. Trust in business, according to many surveys, is at an all-time low—with other institutions not faring much better. The world's public authorities seem unable to move effectively to deal with the sustainability and climate change crises. Businesses are oriented toward short-term maximization of shareholder wealth. "Free"-market ideology has taken its toll on many nations and communities, which have lost jobs and the capacity to be self-sustaining as they tried to enter the global economy.[5] The litany could go on, but is it any wonder that some people doubt that it is even possible for business to be responsible in this context?

Calls for greater business and corporate responsibility—that is, more responsible enterprise: greater accountability, responsibility, transparency, and sustainability—from all types of enterprise are commonplace. Many companies have, in fact, developed significant initiatives around corporate "social" responsibility, which we define as explicit pro-social initiatives on the part of companies. Others have developed major sustainability initiatives or characterize their efforts as corporate responsibility, implying that they are attempting to be accountable, responsible, transparent, and sustainable in their business models and practices. We will say more about these ideas later, but the point is that there is a great deal of activity around responsible enterprise within companies—but still not enough to restore the public trust in business enterprise. Still not enough to ensure that there will be sufficient change to the system to guarantee necessary husbanding of planetary resources, care with social and human "resources," or safeguarding of financial resources.

With this book we offer a roadmap for those who wish to follow the path of responsible and sustainable enterprise; we provide frameworks and arguments for why doing so is not only good business but an imperative for all of us living on earth today. We are, in the end, all in this together.

DEFINING RESPONSIBLE ENTERPRISE

Responsible enterprise is an integral part of the whole corporation as it exists in whole communities and whole societies. Companies are increasingly being held accountable for respecting society and social rights (e.g., by not polluting or otherwise contributing to deteriorating environmental conditions, including global warming), for preserving individual or civil rights (e.g., by providing safe working conditions), and for respecting political rights (e.g., by not operating in countries with governments that do not uphold basic political and individual rights),[6] among many other responsibilities.

The embeddedness of corporations in societies—that is, their existence as socially constructed holons[7] in economic, political, societal, and ecological contexts—means that careful attention needs to be given to how they behave. Sustainability, not just of the company, but also of the earth's capacity to support human life, depends on a systemic understanding of corporations in society, which we develop throughout this book.

If we conceive of companies in terms of their relationships to stakeholders and the natural environment, then we can define responsible enterprise as follows:

> Responsible enterprise means that companies live up to clear constructive visions and core values consistent with those of the broader societies within which they operate, respect the natural environment, and treat well the entire range of stakeholders who risk capital in, have an interest in, or are linked to the firm through primary and secondary impacts. They operationalize their corporate responsibilities in all of their strategies and business practices by developing respectful, mutually beneficial relationships with stakeholders and by working to maximize sustainability of the natural environment. They are responsible, transparent, and accountable for their impacts.

Responsible enterprise by this definition involves far more than performing the discretionary tasks and duties associated with philanthropy, volunteerism, community relations, and otherwise doing "social good," which some people think is sufficient[8] and which constitutes corporate *social* responsibility.[9] This broad understanding of responsible enterprise means paying attention to how fundamental responsibilities—some of which are those traditionally assumed by governments, such as labor and human rights, environmental sustainability, and anti-corruption measures—are being met in all of the company's strategies and operating practices, as well as to the outcomes and implications of corporate activities. Responsible enterprise means developing a "lived" set of policies, practices, and programs that help the company achieve its vision and values.

Adopting such an integrative perspective on responsible enterprise implies not overemphasizing the role of (often isolated) corporate responsibility or corporate citizenship departments, executives, and reports. Real responsible enterprise starts where these measures end. Marc Gunther has made exactly this point by arguing that the traditional focus on the corporate responsibility infrastructure separates a firm's impact on the world from its core business activities.[10] We couldn't agree more! Our understanding of responsible enterprise highlights its embeddedness in the day-to-day practices of all people working for or with a firm. Isolating corporate responsibility may in fact imply also isolating its impacts.

One significant challenge, then, is to stop thinking of responsible enterprise as something that can be "fixed quickly" by adopting the "right" measures (which are usually the same as those adopted by everyone else). This challenge leads us to highlight two significant propositions underlying this book: (1) responsible enterprise is about inspired leadership and living espoused values in a company; and (2) responsible enterprise requires systems thinking—that is, the explicit recognition that businesses are shaped by and influence the larger social and ecological systems in which they operate.

THE CURRENT STATE OF CORPORATE RESPONSIBILITY: DO COMPANIES INTEGRATE?

Each year the UN Global Compact conducts an implementation survey of a subset of its participants throughout the world.[11] The survey is one of the largest and most comprehensive studies of corporate responsibility practices. The 2010 survey compiles more than 1,200 responses from 103 countries. It paints a global picture of corporate responsibility, including the voices of small and medium-sized enterprises (SMEs). The survey attempts to provide an overview of companies' efforts to integrate corporate responsibility into their everyday business activities, with particular attention to activities related to human rights, labor standards, environmental protection, and anti-corruption.

Although the survey reveals that companies perform at very different levels (mostly because of their large geographic diversity), it also shows that corporate responsibility practices are increasingly embedded into value and supply chain activities, particularly those related to the management of environmental issues and labor standards. For instance, almost half of all companies have developed management systems to monitor and evaluate performance in these two areas. Companies seem to have realized that just having policies or codes of conduct is of little consequence if these statements are not integrated into existing business processes. The Global Compact's survey, however, also shows that firms still have a lot to learn about corporate responsibility—in particular, human rights and anti-corruption issues are not yet adequately integrated into business practices. The survey also shows that company size has a significant effect on performance. While nearly 50 percent of larger companies have institutional frameworks for industrial relations in place, only

25 percent of SMEs have such frameworks. This insight also points to the fact that SMEs need more support and guidance when it comes to addressing social and environmental issues in their specific contexts. The study also finds that publicly traded companies perform more strongly in some areas (such as anti-corruption), possibly owing to government regulation of their operations.

The Global Compact survey shows that an isolated, project-based view of corporate responsibility is gradually being replaced by an integrated understanding. It is clear that firms are looking for more than philanthropic projects managed by corporate headquarters. The survey reports that 79 percent of firms are trying to spread their corporate responsibility practices to subsidiaries in order to connect company-wide policies to local issues and problems.

The decision to be a leader of responsible enterprise is, of course, voluntary; however, companies always bear responsibility for the ways in which they treat their stakeholders and nature—and are judged on their impacts—whether or not they proactively or interactively assume the role of responsible business leadership. Further, the imperatives of ecological sustainability, which have become apparent in recent years, mean that few companies or individuals today can afford to ignore the systemic consequences of a production system that is not focused on both ecological sustainability and responsible practice. Responsible enterprise has become institutionalized in the sense that it is perceived by many as a broadly accepted part of doing business driven by pressures from consumers, civil society organizations, investors, governments, and of course the self-interest of corporations.[12]

Given the preceding definition of responsible enterprise, we begin with a proposition: The core purpose of the corporation includes but goes far beyond generating shareholder wealth. Indeed, wealth and profits are simply important by-products of the firm's efforts to create a product or service for customers that adds enough value that customers are willing to pay for it. Value-added goods and services are produced through the efforts of employees, managers, suppliers, and allies, using a wide range of forms of capital. Management thinker Charles Handy puts the issue straightforwardly:

> To turn shareholders' needs into a purpose is to be guilty of a logical confusion, to mistake a necessary condition for a sufficient one. We need to eat to live, food

is a necessary condition of life. But if we lived mainly to eat, making food a sufficient or sole purpose of life, we would become gross. The purpose of a business, in other words, is not to make a profit, full stop. It is to make a profit so that the business can do something more or better. That "something" becomes the real justification for the business.[13]

Further, capital investments in businesses go way beyond those made by shareholders. Capital does, of course, include the important financial resources supplied by owners and shareholders. Equally important, capital encompasses the intellectual and human capital provided by employees, the trust and loyalty of customers that products or services will meet expectations and add value (for which they will pay), and various forms of social capital. Further, capital includes the infrastructure and social relations supplied by the communities and other levels of government in locations where the company has facilities. Capital encompasses the natural resources supplied by the ecological environment that go into the production and delivery of goods and services. It includes interdependent relationships developed among its business partners, suppliers, and distributors, and it exists in the social contract written or understood by a range of local, state, and national governments, which provide the social—and legal—contract and necessary physical infrastructure on which the firm's existence is premised. All of these capitals are supplied to the firm by stakeholders. In this sense, we understand responsible enterprise as the task of developing and operationalizing positive stakeholder relationships.

We differentiate responsible enterprise from corporate citizenship. Some scholars have used the term corporate citizenship to describe the discretionary activities that firms are undertaking to be perceived as good citizens in their society.[14] In this sense, corporate citizenship would be similar to the traditional understanding of corporate social responsibility as charitable giving and philanthropy. Other scholars have used the term corporate citizenship to describe the increasing political role of corporations.[15] Here, citizenship implies that companies can in some cases act like governments and influence the rights of people (particularly when governments are not willing or able to do so). The latter understanding of corporate citizenship often analyzes similar issues as responsible enterprise, however from a different (i.e., rights-based) perspective.

RESPONSIBLE ENTERPRISE AND GLOBALIZATION

The debate on corporate responsibility and responsible enterprise gained momentum as actors and problems became more globally interconnected. Today, the question "Why is there a need for responsible enterprise?" is often answered with reference to the intensified social and economic relations among actors in different geographic locations.[16] Globalization has many facets, although the increase in cross-border trade and investment (economic dimension) and the related liberalization of markets through the policies of intergovernmental organizations and political agreements are most frequently highlighted. Globalization also relates to the standardization of everyday life experiences throughout the world (e.g., with the Internet and social media) and the rise of mass consumption of largely standardized goods and services.[17]

The dominance of multinational corporations in the world has created a good deal of controversy about globalization and its impacts on civil society. One important critique of globalization (specifically, corporate globalization) identifies several problematic aspects for many nations, particularly those that are still developing, which are listed in Table 1.1. Pointing out that modern globalization is not inevitable, but rather a system designed by human beings, the nineteen authors of the critique note that the global system promotes free trade and consumerism over other societal values, including protecting the citizens of one's own country, in the belief that benefits will ultimately trickle down to the poor. Promoted by the Bretton Woods institutions (the International Monetary Fund, the World Trade Organization, and the World Bank), free trade is seen in this view to benefit largely the already-rich and corporations, leaving behind the poor as well as developing nations.[18]

Proponents of globalization make many predictions about the positive impacts that globalization will have on developing nations, among them poverty reduction, job creation, more foreign direct investment, and reduced inequalities.[19] Some analysts, however, suggest that these predictions do not necessarily hold in all cases, because globalization sometimes increases income inequality and decreases employment in developing nations. Too frequently companies aggressively seek out low-wage countries, leaving behind

TABLE 1.1 *Main Characteristics of the Current Globalization Model*

- Focus on unlimited growth and exploitation of social and environmental resources without adequate compensation.
- Deregulation of markets and privatization of public sector services and commodities.
- Standardization and homogenization of aspects of everyday life; rise of mass consumption (e.g., mass tourism).
- Rise of global financial markets and unrestricted movement of capital across borders.
- Transformation of some national economies into hubs for export-oriented production (creating negative social and environmental effects).
- Larger and more powerful corporations; high concentration of firms in some sectors.
- Increasing influence of (multinational) firms on traditional state-based, democratic governance.

SOURCE: John Cavanagh et al., *Alternatives to Economic Globalization: A Better World Is Possible* (San Francisco: Berrett-Koehler, 2002).

facilities in nations where wages have risen, creating what some observers call a "race to the bottom." This race to the bottom leaves the people in nations that have been left behind with lower social cohesion, fewer jobs, less political capacity, and fewer technological opportunities.

Over time, the globalization of society has affected many of the problems discussed in the context of responsible enterprise. For instance, the globalization of production and the related outsourcing of labor-intensive work to low-wage countries have significantly affected the discussion around working conditions. Some of the issues addressed within the sphere of responsible enterprise can even be characterized as genuinely global issues (i.e., issues that by their very nature affect the whole planet). Climate change, for instance, is a global problem because dealing with it effectively requires coordinated action across the globe. Although the increase of carbon dioxide in the atmosphere is largely the result of economic activities in a few countries (most of them in the global North), the consequences of a changing climate cannot be geographically isolated and are more likely to harm developing countries (e.g., through droughts and resulting decreases in agricultural productivity).

The increasingly borderless operations of corporations also challenge the underlying dynamics of regulation. Neither international organizations (whose regulations mostly reflect the lowest common denominator) nor nation-states (whose jurisdiction remains territorially bound) can adequately address global problems. Since a legally enforceable international regulatory framework for social and environmental problems remains a vision for the future, a variety of voluntary responsible enterprise initiatives have formed with the goal of regulating cross-border economic activities. The Forest Stewardship Council (addressing global deforestation) and Social Accountability 8000 (addressing labor conditions at supply factories), for example, have allowed corporations to voluntarily accept responsibility where nation-state regulation is largely absent and/or weakly enforced. Such "privatized governance" fundamentally redefines the role of business in the global economy, as it actively involves corporations and civil society organizations in the regulation of important social and environmental domains.[20]

One consequence of the rise of privatized governance is that it challenges the traditional division of labor between the political and economic spheres. Corporations are not just following the rules set by governments, but have turned into political actors themselves, going well beyond their traditional role as lobbyist for their own interests. Corporations have assumed responsibility for tasks that were once regarded as the domain of governments by contributing to public goods such as health and education programs, both in the developing and the developed world. Needless to say, the increasing political role of corporations raises the question of legitimacy. While most governments are democratically elected, corporations do not possess a political mandate but nevertheless influence the lives of people through their activities. For this reason, corporations must be held accountable for their judgments, actions, and omissions—a topic we will return to in Chapter 7.

THE FOREST STEWARDSHIP COUNCIL: AN EXAMPLE OF PRIVATIZED GOVERNANCE

Deforestation is one of the world's most pressing ecological problems. Although rates of deforestation differ from region to region, the nongovernmental organization (NGO) Conservation International reported in 2011 that the ten most endangered regions have already lost more than 90 percent of their original habitat.[21] The overwhelming driver of deforestation is the quest for agricultural land, which in turn is influenced by population pressure and weak economic and social conditions. The consequences of deforestation are both environmental and economic: the loss of trees that eliminate CO_2 from the atmosphere through photosynthesis may exacerbate global warming, and deforested land reduces agricultural productivity.

When governments were unable to commit to a binding international agreement regulating deforestation after the UN Conference on Environment and Development in Rio de Janeiro in 1992, businesses and civil society organizations responded by establishing the Forest Stewardship Council (FSC). According to Philipp Pattberg, "the FSC is a system of rules through which sustainable forest practices and products emanating from these practices are certified by accredited, independent organizations and made recognizable to consumers in the marketplace."[22] Currently, more than 143,299,840 hectares of land in seventy-nine countries are certified under the rules set by the FSC. To ensure that the rules of the global initiative are sufficiently adapted to local circumstances, the FSC has set up so-called National Initiatives in more than fifty countries. These initiatives anchor the FSC in local contexts by promoting its principles and developing national standards for certification.

The FSC's governance structure reflects its multistakeholder and global nature. Participants are divided into three "chambers" representing business, social, and environmental interests. Each chamber has equal voting power, while within each chamber no more than 50 percent of participants can represent the global North or South. This tripartite governance structure avoids capture of the initiative by any particular group of actors and strengthens its perceived legitimacy. A nine-member board of directors is elected from the three chambers for a three-year term.

The FSC is an important example of how corporate responsibility is increasingly managed through privatized governance. Although voluntary initiatives such as the FSC cannot substitute for effective regulation by governments or stronger intergovernmental agreements, they offer practical solutions to pressing global problems. It remains to be seen whether privatized governance can have large-scale impact. Currently, the FSC certifies only a small portion of the 3.9 billion hectares of forests covering the earth.

RESPONSIBLE ENTERPRISE AS AN EXAMPLE
OF SYSTEMS THINKING

Throughout this book we suggest that responsible enterprise should be approached from a systemic perspective, meaning that the different impacts of business activities should not be evaluated in isolation from each other. Businesses, as much as human beings, are influenced by and can influence numerous other systems, including the natural environment, the political system, and local communities. Understanding responsible enterprise in this way also prevents thinking about social and environmental problems from an isolated narrow philanthropic perspective. Systems thinking requires us to analyze responsible enterprise as not ending at the borders of the corporation. Instead, responsibility is determined by the interplay of different systems that are shaped by and shape business practices.

Western philosophy and Western science underpin the capitalist economic system in which we live today throughout much of the developed world. Western science, including the social science of economics, tends to approach its subjects by taking them apart and reducing them to their smallest elements—a linear process of atomization or fragmentation. Once the smallest elements or fragments have been understood, the Western approach is to reintegrate the parts and thereby figure out how they work as an integrated whole. This approach derives from thinkers such as Descartes, is premised on Newtonian physics, and is empiricist in its orientation in that it seeks observable evidence in coming to its conclusions; it tends to assume that linear cause-and-effect relationships exist and can be explained scientifically. But this reduction of things to their fundamental parts or atomistic elements also separates the material elements (body) from nonmaterial aspects of the world like consciousness, emotions, aesthetic appreciation, and spirituality.

In simple terms, Western thinking has largely separated and fragmented the mind and body, paying little attention to heart, spirit, community, or meaning, none of which is directly observable. It has, in some respects, done much the same thing to the environment, making some people forget (or ignore) our very human interdependence with the cycle of nature, a nonlinear set of relationships. In addition, technological advances have sometimes made progress seem inevitable, as if a solution to whatever problems arise is always just around the corner. The Western approach tends to lessen people's ability to think about the system as a whole, which also reduces their ability to think about systemic and ecological impacts of business actions.

SYSTEMS THINKING

A cloud masses, the sky darkens, leaves twist upward, and we know that it will rain. We also know that after the storm the runoff will feed into groundwater miles away, and the sky will grow clear by tomorrow. All these events are distant in time and space, and yet they are all connected within the same pattern. Each has an influence on the others, an influence that is usually hidden from view. Understanding the system of a rainstorm requires contemplating the whole, not any individual part of the pattern.

Business and other human endeavors are also systems. They, too, are bound by invisible fabrics of interrelated actions, which often take years to play out their effects on each other. Since we are part of that lacework ourselves, it's doubly hard to see the whole pattern of change. Instead, we tend to focus on isolated parts of the system and wonder why our most vexing problems never seem to get solved.

SOURCE: Peter Senge, *The Fifth Discipline: The Art and Practice of the Learning Organization,* revised edition (New York: Currency Doubleday, 2006), pp. 6–7.

The fragmented or atomistic approach has come under severe criticism in recent years, for reasons that management thinker Peter Senge highlights. Many people now believe that a more integrated approach, in part ecologically based and in part based on an integration of mind and body (or material and nonmaterial), better speaks to the long-term needs of human beings and the communities and organizations to which they belong (see the box on Systems Thinking). The systemic approach will be particularly critical in the technologically complex and ecologically resource-constrained future, where issues of climate change and ecological sustainability will very likely dominate important business decisions, and where an understanding of the impacts of one part of the system on the other will be increasingly necessary.

A systemic approach to responsible enterprise and sustainability has been fueled by the development of chaos and complexity theories, which shed light on the behavior of complex systems, a set to which human-created systems clearly belong. It has been further advanced by quantum physics, astrophysics, and biology's new understandings of the nature of matter and the interconnectedness of all living things, as well as between living and nonliving matter.[23] The emergence of economies with alternative points of view provides an interesting and important contrast to this atomization and fragmentation. Eastern philosophies and approaches tend to be more holistic in their orientation than Western ones, so the development of major economic powers like China (at this writing the world's second largest economy), India, and the other two BRIC nations (Brazil and Russia) portends significant change in the ways that economies are established and in their foundational principles.

Such developments have highlighted the need for a more integrated approach to understanding the impact of human beings, and the economic organizations they create, on the world and in particular on the natural environment. One seminal work emphasizing a systems approach to management is Peter Senge's influential book *The Fifth Discipline*.[24] Systems thinking emphasizes wholes, or more accurately, holons—whole/parts—and the interrelationships and interdependencies among them.[25] A holon is anything that is itself whole and also a part of something else. Thus, for example, a neutron is an entity, a whole, and it is also a part of an atom. A hand is an entity in itself and also a part of an arm, which is part of a body, and so on. In social systems, an individual (a whole) is part of a family (a whole), which is part of a community, and so on. In organizations, individuals are parts of departments, which are units of divisions, which are parts of the corporate entity, which is part of its industry, and which in turn is part of society. Holons are integrally linked to the other holons of which they are a part. When something shifts in one holon, the other holons are affected as well because all holons in a system are interdependent.

We can also think of holons as being nested within each other. Each holon is nested within the next level, ensuring their interconnectedness and interdependence. What this means in system terms is that anything that affects one part of the system also affects (at some level and in some way) the whole system. Thinking about systems in this way changes our perspective on the corporation's role in society. No longer can we pretend that a company has no impact on stakeholders, society, or nature. Because companies are part of the holon of communities, societies, and the global village in which they are nested, these systems must, by this way of thinking, impact each other reciprocally. Consider, for example, a company that has given money in the past to a nonprofit organization or paid a supplier in its supply chain. When the company withdraws funding—cuts the nonprofit off or decides to use another supplier—the company's leaders may believe that the decision puts an end to their impact or their responsibility. But the withdrawal of funding alters the financial stability of the nonprofit or the supplier and has multiple ramifications both within these enterprises and for the clients they serve. And while the funding company may believe that it is immune from these impacts, subtle shifts in its employees' morale or in important customer relationships will ultimately affect the business.

All actions within holons have impacts. Indeed, quantum physicists tell us that all actions have impacts on the whole system, though they may be subtle, and chaos theorists note that very small changes, or what Senge would call leverage points, can lead to large system shifts over time. Thinkers like Senge (and ecologist Thomas Gladwin, physicist Fritjof Capra, and theorist Margaret Wheatley, among many others)[26] propose that a holistic approach to enterprise should incorporate not only objective data but also the nonmaterial—that is, consciousness and conscience, emotion and feelings, meaning and meaningfulness, spirit and indeed spirituality.

An integrative and holistic systems perspective allows us to see our impact on the world and the world's on us. Companies, after all, are human creations that are nested within the larger social and even larger ecological systems of the world; they interact daily with government policies and, as has become increasingly obvious to companies under public scrutiny, with actors from civil society. No longer can a company act as if it were distinct and separate from these other aspects of our world or reasonably claim that "it's just business," when it violates ethical norms or when ecological issues arise. The interconnectivity provided by technology today links everyone on a global basis via the click of a mouse, the sending of a Tweet, or the posting of a Facebook note. We are also all influenced by factors today that seemed unimportant in yesterday's more static management world: the emergence of China, India, and other nations as serious competitors in the business and social arenas; a sustainability crisis that threatens all of us if responsible action is not taken; and the transparency that, in concert with the interconnectivity, makes us all stakeholders of the planet, and each other.

Responsible companies recognize this new reality and are responding appropriately. But there are still many companies and their leaders who are behind the curve. They are lagging behind the demands of many governments for triple bottom line (ecological, social, and economic) reporting in addition to financial reporting. They are lagging behind demands for greater transparency and interaction by nongovernmental organizations (NGOs), whose criticisms of company actions can stain hard-to-build and harder-to-restore reputations when things go awry, especially if companies do not engage with them before problems arise.

Understanding the many shifts in the external world of companies—and in how responsible management is practiced internally—is crucial to long-term success in such a dramatically changed climate. A systems approach understands the links between internal management practices that create a company's vision, underpin its values, and result in its value added. It understands the role of reputation—and how it is affected by accountability, transparency, and responsibility practices as companies interact with the many external stakeholders in the growing array of new institutions that demand responsible and sustainable practice. It requires thinking and leading in ways that understand how all elements of the system intersect, including the governmental or political system, civil society, and the natural underpinning of the ecological environment that supports human civilization. These intersecting elements of these spheres of human and natural activity are the topics of the next chapters, as we begin to explore what it means to be a responsible enterprise today.

HOW THIS BOOK IS STRUCTURED

The book consists of four parts, each highlighting different aspects of responsible enterprise. Part I starts by discussing the context in which responsible enterprise occurs. Our main goal is to show what enables and constrains managing for responsible enterprise. This chapter has already discussed the global dimension of responsible enterprise and introduced systems thinking as a new perspective for analyzing business's impact on social and environmental problems. Chapter 2 explores four interrelated types of systems relevant to the study of responsible enterprise: business, politics, nature, and civil society. We see this discussion as an inevitable precondition for understanding responsible enterprise, because social and environmental problems (and their solutions) depend on interactions between these systems.

Part II, "Developing Responsible Enterprise," consists of three interrelated chapters. Chapter 3 discusses the role of vision and leadership in integrating responsible enterprise into a company. Our discussion addresses vision at both the individual and the organizational level. We discuss what a vision is, how it relates to responsible enterprise issues, and why it requires strong leadership to bring a vision into reality. We reflect on how the vision can be lived within and beyond the organization, as an important building block for understanding how to systematically develop corporate responsibility activities.

Chapter 4 emphasizes the integration of values into the responsible enterprise. We first discuss how vision and values are intertwined and why values are an important part of enterprise strategy. We suggest that values are the very basis of managing responsible enterprise in different contexts. We introduce some of the core values related to different management concepts and to business operations in the global environment. Finally, we reflect on how to approach situations in which values are likely to conflict, both across cultures and between stakeholders. Chapter 5 rounds out the core vision of this book by discussing how integrating a responsibility vision and core values can add value. We discuss different "dimensions" of value, asking the reader to adopt a broad understanding of the concept that reaches beyond financial value. Our discussion also reviews the heated debate around whether there is a link between firms' social/environmental and financial performance. We discuss how firms with a clear vision and espoused values create value added by treating their employees, customers, and suppliers in a fair and principled way.

Part III highlights the actual management practices that enable enterprises of all sorts to achieve excellence in the context of corporate responsibility.

Chapter 6 first explores what we consider the relationship key: a company's stakeholders. After some initial reflections on what constitutes a stake and what kinds of stakeholder groups exist, we discuss how firms can succeed in managing relationships with their employees, customers, suppliers (and other partners), and local communities. Chapter 7 looks at practices associated with managing responsibly. We outline a system of responsibility management (RM) that is built around three components: (1) inspiration and leadership commitment to responsibility issues, (2) a change of day-to-day management systems and management practices, and (3) assessment of outcomes and the creation of learning and feedback loops. Our understanding of RM is built on the notion of continuous improvement—a well-known concept from quality management.

In Chapter 8 we discuss different approaches to assessing responsible enterprise. We start by reviewing assessment through a variety of principles (e.g., the UN Global Compact), certification initiatives (e.g., Social Accountability 8000), and reporting standards (e.g., the Global Reporting Initiative). We then discuss social investment and shareholder activism as ways to assess firms' responsible enterprise practices. We also discuss social investment through microlending initiatives. The chapter closes with thoughts on how various rankings are used to assess the performance of companies in the context of responsible enterprise.

Chapter 9 moves the conversation about responsible management to the debate around sustainability. We first consider the ecological dimension of doing business in a sustainable way. We briefly review some key facts about the nature and scope of environmental problems and, based on these, explore the need for achieving sustainability. We review ways to implement sustainable business practices within existing management processes and discuss how ecological problems affect developing countries in various ways. The chapter closes with a discussion of how sustainability reaches beyond the natural environment and how societies might reshape themselves in sustainable ways.

Chapter 10 takes a look at some important responsible enterprise initiatives and guidance documents. While Chapter 8 introduced standards, which can be used to assess corporate social and environmental performance, our discussion in this chapter focuses on selected initiatives and key guidance documents related to social issues (human rights and labor rights), anti-corruption, and environmental sustainability. We review and evaluate major human rights frameworks (the 2008 UN-backed "Protect, Respect and Remedy" guidelines), guidance on anti-corruption (Transparency International's recommendations to fight corruption), and selected sustainability principles (the Ceres Principles and the World Business Council for Sustainable Development).

Part IV focuses on reinventing Corporate Sustainability and Responsibility (or a "new" CSR). Looking into the future, we argue that a mere "technical" focus on CSR might not be enough—we need to start living responsible enterprise by realizing what is meaningful and important to create a balanced society. Chapter 11 explores the likely trends and forces that will shape how corporations address their responsibilities in the future. For instance, we review to what extent the UN's Millennium Development Goals (MDGs) have been achieved and how firms can support them. We also identify demographic trends, political changes, and advances in science and technology, all of which are likely to influence how CSR is understood in the future.

The last chapter discusses a vision for the corporation of the future—a corporation that looks different from the one we are all familiar with. We suggest that in order to address the scale and scope of current social and environmental problems, tomorrow's company will need to be based on a different understanding of how the economy, the political system, and civil society interact. Our discussion of the responsible corporation calls, above all, for a new attitude—one that respects the need to fundamentally shift our perspective on the changing role of business in society. In the end, this last chapter is a call to begin living responsible enterprise.

2 IN SEARCH OF BALANCE

Business, Politics, Civil Society, and Nature

> The [World Business Council for Sustainable Development's] 2050
> Project . . . developed a vision . . . in which the global population
> is not just living on the planet, but living well and within the
> limits of the planet. By "living well," we are describing a standard
> of living where people have access to and the ability to afford
> education, healthcare, mobility, the basics of food, water, energy
> and shelter, and consumer goods. By "living within the limits
> of the planet," we mean living in such a way that this standard
> of living can be sustained with the available natural resources
> and without further harm to biodiversity, climate and other
> ecosystems.
>
> World Business Council for Sustainable Development, Vision 2050[1]

What the World Business Council for Sustainable Development's Vision 2050 project is talking about in the epigraph above is balance, a better balance than exists today among the economic, governmental, and civil spheres of society, and between humanity and nature. Human civilization depends on a healthy ecological environment for its sustenance and maintenance; the environment or ecological system underpins all we do and are. But human society is itself a complex system that requires balance among several competing influences and activities, some of which today seem out of balance.

INTERSECTING SPHERES OF HUMAN CIVILIZATION, NATURE, AND ASSOCIATED VALUES

Modern business activities occur in an intensely competitive, even hyper-competitive, and globalized environment,[2] where issues related to ecological sustainability have only relatively recently begun to enter most managers' minds. Strikingly, ecologists have estimated that our earth can optimally support 1.5 to 2 billion humans.[3] Further, James Lovelock, author of the Gaia hypothesis, proposes that the world is actually a living system.

Lovelock suggests that climate change may result in a vastly reduced human population over the next century, in people surviving in far-flung locations and civilizations that are a fraction of their size today.[4] In our current business environment, change is a constant, and there is ever-increasing pressure for better productivity and performance. But the realities of climate change, ecosystem destruction, and population growth place new limits on business and other human activities—or are likely to do so in the foreseeable future.

Without diminishing the importance of competition—and competitiveness—for corporate success, we would add another perspective using a both/and (win/win) rather than an either/or (win/lose) logic. Consider that companies operate in a sphere or sector of activities we can call the economic (or market) sphere. This sphere has all of the imperatives of growth, efficiency, productivity, and competition that are inherent in the current capitalistic paradigm, which with the ascendance of developing or emerging nations, the rapid evolution of e-commerce, and the lack of a viable alternative is operating at some level in most free societies. We know, however, that the economic sector cannot operate independently of the rest of society, nor of its ecological underpinning. The economic system is a creature of society, and is one major sphere of influence.

There is, however, more to society than economics and business. Living well—that is, living the good life, by almost anyone's definition—must include important elements of long-term sustainability with regard to community health (in the civil society sphere) and ecological health (in the natural environment sphere). The good life also requires some form of governance or government (the public policy sphere) to function well. Each of these spheres intersects with, interacts with, and is interdependent with all the others; hence, they must be viewed together as a system, inextricably and unavoidably interwoven. The success of any one of the three human sectors requires that there be an appropriate balance of power and interests among all of them as well as with the natural environment or ecological sphere, which underpins everything, and on which everything depends. The key to long-term well-being and sustainability for humanity is finding that balance.

To complete this picture and provide for an integrated view of what is frequently called the global village (the world of communities in which we all live and to which we are all connected), we must first understand the critical role of the ecological or natural environment. The ecological environment or sphere is the essential foundation on which all else rests. Without the diversity inherent in the natural environment, without its sustaining resources, which provide raw materials for production, not to mention the air, water, food, and energy necessary for life, and without appropriate balance in human activities to protect those natural resources, industry and human societies quite literally cannot sustain themselves. In that sense we are all dependent on this foundation of ecology and the web of life that it supports for our very existence.[5] Likewise, being a responsible enterprise needs to be understood as a systemic issue characterized by ecological interdependence and mutuality among entities and institutions operating in all of the different spheres. The following are definitions for each of the spheres that form a core structure for understanding the context within which corporations' responsibilities are managed:

1. The *economic* sphere encompasses the businesses, profit-generating enterprises, and associated supplier/distributor relationships that produce the goods and services in markets on which human civilization today depends.

2. The *political* or *public policy* sphere encompasses government bodies at the local, state, regional, national, and global (international) levels that create the rules by which societies operate and establish what is meant (within and among societies) by the public interest or common good. Increasingly, other governance actors such as business associations and even corporations themselves enter this sphere.[6]

3. The *civil society* or civilizing sphere encompasses all other organized forms of activity, such as nongovernmental organizations (NGOs), nonprofit enterprises, schools, religious organizations, political organizations, unions, families, and civic and societal enterprises. This sphere generates the civilizing relationships and sense of community that characterize human society.

4. The *natural or ecological environment* underpins and supports all else, providing the raw materials that sustain human civilization and healthy

societies. A healthy ecology is essential to the long-term health of all of human civilization.

Each sphere operates with a different set of core values. In a pioneering work relating business values to biophysics and biochemistry, William Frederick outlined three important "value clusters," two of which dominate business or economic activities in the economic sphere.[7] The first and probably the dominant value for business corporations is *economizing*, or the prudent and efficient use and processing of resources needed to live well. Economizing is the primary purpose—and indeed the imperative—of business—that is, creating goods and services as efficiently as possible.

The second value cluster that Frederick says underpins business activity is power aggrandizing, or augmenting and preserving the power of managers and the organization itself.[8] Frederick notes that power-aggrandizing businesses (as well as other forms of organizations—governments in particular) have a tendency to accumulate and control resources and power over time, making themselves more and more influential. If we look at the broader societal system, we note that the major form of currency in the political sector is power, even more so than in business because of government's power to mandate or coerce. Activities in the government or political sphere tend to focus on the garnering and use of power because governments are in the business of setting the rules of the game for society. Power-aggrandizing values, which are also present in business and dominate the political (public policy) sphere, focus on maintaining hierarchy (bureaucracy) through a managerial decision-making capacity that helps to keep the power system stable or in equilibrium, and continued power enhancement.

These two value clusters are in some significant degree of tension with the third value cluster identified by Frederick, which is ecologizing. Ecologizing is the tendency of evolutionary and natural processes to "interweave the life activities of groups in ways conducive to the perpetuation of an entire community."[9] Ecologizing means using resources to sustain life and energy, meaning (as with nature) that nothing goes to waste. Natural processes are inherently cyclical and tend to waste nothing, suggesting that nature, which provides ecological underpinning for all of this human activity, is dominated by ecologizing values. Viewed ecologically, what is waste to one part of the system becomes, in effect, food for another part of the system. Increasingly, businesses are applying this type of ecological thinking to their production and service delivery processes as they think about creating sustainable enterprises.[10]

Civil society, in contrast, tends to focus on developing organizations and institutions that "civilize" society by building relationships and community. Thus, the values of the civil society sphere, which Frederick's model does not address, are more congruent with relationship and community building, and can sometimes conflict with both economizing and power-aggrandizing values. Civil society includes all of the social institutions other than business and government bodies that sustain the fabric of society. Civil society is dominated by values that emphasize the importance of building and sustaining relationships through what Nel Noddings calls an ethic of care—building connectedness and fostering civility through the building of community.[11]

Table 2.1 shows the major values associated with activities in each of the three spheres of human civilization plus nature, with what Frederick called X-factor value added. X-factor value is the value that each individual brings into an institutional or organizational setting. Further, human society has developed a set of technological values that have fostered industrial development over the past centuries. Technological values, which drive business activity, use various instruments to achieve their ends. In addition, according to Frederick, technologists learn to value "coordinative, integrative, and cooperative relationships among tool users." Also valued by technology users are technical expertise, honesty, and "participatory leveling," which is the tendency of advanced technology to create participatory and democratic environments.[12]

Economizing values, dominant within businesses, emphasize not only keeping the system whole, efficient, and economically sound, but also growing continually. Given these values, it is not surprising that businesses tend to focus on efficiency and growth at almost any cost. These emphases are the natural by-products of the business system that modern society has created. Further, it is the growth imperative that has created many of the ecological and sustainability problems facing our planet today. Finding ways to balance the drive for growth with sustainable development is a critical condition for

TABLE 2.1   *Dominant Values*

Business Sphere	Political (and Business) Sphere	Civil Society Sphere	Nature (Ecology)
Economizing values	*Power-aggrandizing values*	*Relationship values*	*Ecologizing values*
Economizing	Hierarchical (rank-order) organizing	Care	Linkage
(Efficiency)	Managerial decision power	Connectedness	Diversity
Growth	Power-system equilibrium	Community	Homeostatic succession
Systemic integrity	Power aggrandizement	Civility	Community
Technological values		*X-factor values (individual)*	
Instrumental pragmatics		Personal, idiosyncratic, role-conditioned values	
Cooperative-coordinative relations			
Technical expertise			
Public openness			
Participatory leveling			

SOURCE: William C. Frederick, *Values, Nature, and Culture in the American Corporation* (New York: Oxford University Press, 1995).

the long-term well-being of human civilization, as well as for the other creatures on the planet.

BUSINESS AS AN INSTITUTION IN SOCIETY

Many observers believe that business is the most powerful institution in society today. In 2009, 44 percent of the world's 100 largest (and 59 percent of the 150 largest) economic entities were not governments, but corporations.[13] These figures can be disputed because the basis on which they are calculated for countries and companies is different (comparing a country's GDP with a company's revenue); but they are informative to the extent that they give an indication of the relative size and clout of modern multinational enterprises.

At the core of today's dominant economic model is the values cluster of economizing—that is, "prudent, careful, sometimes deliberately calculated, rational-where-possible actions of individuals, groups, and organizations that are intended to produce net outputs or benefits from a given amount of resource inputs."[14] Economic development is an important contributor to the welfare of societies. The positive side of economic development is that it brings goods, services, and jobs to consumers throughout the developed world. Although some critics decry the materialism inherent in such a consumerist approach to the global economy, the competitive dynamic on which it rests is undeniable. Rapid change, intensifying competition, multiple new competitors in most product and service domains, and global connectedness have reshaped the economic—and social—environment in which people in the developed world live today. These shifts have also put into stark contrast the conditions of poverty and deprivation that two-thirds of the world's population live in.

At the same time, management theorists C. K. Prahalad and Allen Hammond argued that many new opportunities are to be found in businesses—both large and small—serving the world's poor through what Prahalad termed "bottom of the pyramid" business development strategies.[15] Noting that 65 percent of the world's population, or some 4 billion people, earn less than $2,000 annually, these authors say that there is a "fortune at the bottom of the pyramid."[16] In what has generated a global search for profitable business opportunities that serve the world's poor, bottom-of-the-pyramid strategies are used by both large and small businesses to develop products and services that can be afforded by people of limited means and thereby improve their standard of living. Prahalad said that the poor should not be treated as victims or as a burden, but rather from an asset-based point of view, as potential entrepreneurs and consumers.[17]

Another scholar, Aneel Karnani, criticizes the economic underpinnings of the bottom of the pyramid, claiming that there "is little glory or fortune at the bottom of the pyramid," that is, that the market is actually quite limited, that the poor are (for obvious reasons) quite price sensitive, and that Prahalad overestimated the purchasing power of the poor.[18] While Karnani acknowledges that there is potentially some money to be made by serving the poor as consumers, he suggests that a better approach is to view the poor as potential producers—and help them enhance their productivity and thereby the means to improve their situations.[19] Whichever perspective is more accurate, however, the concept of bottom of the pyramid strategies has begun to be adopted by large and small companies, as well as by explicitly social enterprises, as another tool in the arsenal of economic development.

Not in Balance: The Capitalist Market System Today and in the Past

Corporate responsibility originates in the corporate form itself, which is based in a legal charter granted wherever a company operates. These government-granted charters or papers of incorporation give companies the right to do business and receive certain legal benefits. Today incorporation means that the corporation itself is treated as a person in that it can be sued, sign contracts, and act in other ways that a person can. In addition to the corporation itself being viewed as a person, individual managers are now increasingly being held liable for corporate acts. For example, in the wake of numerous corporate scandals in the early 2000s, the U.S. government passed the Sarbanes-Oxley Act of 2002, which requires chief executive officers (CEOs) to certify that audited financial statements of the company are accurate, provides for an oversight board and new rules for the accounting industry, imposes strict penalties on executives and companies that commit fraud, and protects whistleblowers (those who make wrongdoing public). It also demands that public companies include independent audit committees on their corporate boards, requires companies to assume responsibility for their financial reports and avoid improperly influencing audits, and other requirements to hold companies accountable for their statements and internal practices, particularly as they relate to the governance of the company.[20]

In the United States, early corporations were granted charters through state legislatures for only limited periods and with restricted powers; indeed, early corporations were supposed to stay in business only as long as they served the social benefit and until they accomplished a specific purpose.[21] Charters were considered "legal fictions with no claim to a natural place in the order of things or in the spontaneous associations or contracts of private parties."[22] Over time, however, U.S. courts made decisions that granted to companies the rights of a legal person. These rights include the right to free speech, which is powerfully used not only in advertising and the media but also by corporate political action committees (PACs), entities established by corporations to lobby legislators and take other political actions on the organization's behalf. In the United States, a 2010 Supreme Court decision in the Citizens United case now allows businesses to make unlimited (and unreported) contributions to political campaigns.[23]

Capitalism Today   Today's capitalist market system—which dominated economic thinking from about 1980 until the economic meltdown of 2007–2008 at least began raising some questions about it, albeit not changing it much— is frequently termed "free-market capitalism." This approach is based on the neoclassical (or Chicago School) economic model and is sometimes called neoliberalism. Derived from the ideas of Adam Smith, and vociferously supported by the late Milton Friedman and his followers, the concept of a free market is premised on the notion that a multitude of small buyers will demand goods and services from a multitude of small producers. No one buyer or supplier will, under this model, be able to command a significant portion of the market or influence the market price. Over time, with many transactions, demand and supply will reach a point of equilibrium.[24]

Another assumption of the neoclassical model is that information is readily available to all participants in the market (i.e., there are no trade secrets or proprietary knowledge). Further, sellers bear all the costs of producing goods and services; that is, such costs are internalized rather than externalized. If this were reality, full-cost accounting—which fully accounts for all of the costs associated with the production of goods and services, including those costs today not typically included, such as the cost of using up raw materials or creating pollution—would be employed (though it is not). When costs are not included in a full costing system, they are typically externalized to society and paid by the public through taxes or reduced quality of life. With externalization, costs remain in the system somewhere, but they are borne by taxpayers, not by the organization that produces them. In addition, the free-market model of neoclassical economics assumes, following David Ricardo's theory of comparative advantage, that investment capital remains within national borders and international trade is balanced. Finally, the model assumes that savings are invested in productive capital.[25]

Failed Assumptions of Neoclassical Economics   The problem with the assumptions of neoclassical economics is that few of them actually apply to today's economies, which means that to some extent the balance implied in the term *free market* is mythical in the complex global economic arena. Most modern industries, rather than being made up of numerous small buyers and sellers, are oligopolies comprising a few very large corporations, some of which are larger than whole countries' economies. There are lots of intersections between business and government. This reality was made evident when governments rescued failing financial institutions during the 2008 economic crash, which was caused by free markets run amuck, and was particular evident in the housing industry where deceptive and even fraudulent practices evolved in a race for profits that caused many people to assume home mortgage loans they could not afford. Much of the conversation around saving some of the financial entities was that they were "too big to fail"—that is, too interconnected with the rest of the world—suggesting oligopolistic (if not near monopolistic) tendencies. In other words, some companies do, in fact, command significant portions of the market and are quite capable of influencing the market price.

Further, most large corporations today have numerous trade secrets and much closely held proprietary information that they use to their competitive advantage. Indeed, trade secrets are often the very source of competitive advantage (in addition, of course, to the knowledge capital of employees). Many costs are externalized. In fact, the whole thrust of the economizing value articulated by William Frederick and discussed earlier, which is the core business imperative, is to foster as much externalization of costs as possible in order to preserve efficiency and enhance productivity. But because the costs are in the system somewhere, they must be paid for somewhere, typically by taxpayers, as the 2008 rescues made clear.

Finally, since the early 1980s, there has been an almost obsessive attention on the part of financial analysts—and hence by corporate managers—to increasing shareholder wealth with little regard for the other stakeholders who are necessary to the success of the business. This orientation is decidedly a short-term one, and often works to the disadvantage of companies that wish to plan for the long term.[26] Most shareholders in modern large corporations are distantly removed from strategic or operational details and manifest their "ownership" through the lens of some sort of institution (pension, index, or money market funds, for example); hence they may not even be aware of what they own, or only "own" their shares for very short periods of time because of the churn associated with stock turnover and associated speculation. Further, most shareholders hold only a small fraction of the millions of company shares outstanding and thus have little real voice in or impact on corporate affairs, even if they were allowed to participate in company affairs, which, for the most part, they are not. Such shareholders are, as iconoclastic management thinker Charles Handy has pointed out, not really owners in the true sense of the word, but rather distanced investors who deserve a fair return on their investments.[27] Unfortunately, the emphasis on maximizing shareholder wealth means that too frequently corporate resources are used to generate short-term improvements in share price, while long-term business (and societal) needs are put aside, bringing us back to the question of balancing societal with economic and ecological imperatives. The shareholder wealth or finance capitalism model thus pays little regard to building productive assets in the underlying business, in part because accountability for corporate actions is limited and corporate power is high.[28]

Robert Reich, who served as secretary of labor in the Clinton Administration, has argued that it is both investors' desire for high returns (e.g., through pension and mutual funds) and consumers' desire for low prices that have created the "supercapitalism" of today's global markets.[29] It is that supercapitalism whose foundations were shaken during the economic collapse and ensuing recession of 2008, and that has caused a global reconsideration of the need to regulate financial markets and the so-called free market. Although new regulations have been passed, much of what is still going on in financial markets looks like business as usual for speculators in what some have called a global gambling casino.

Public and Private Responsibilities in the Context of the 2008 Global Financial Crisis

There is an alternative perspective to the neoclassical economics view of the firm which suggests that companies have public as well as private responsibilities. In some respects, the business system itself can be viewed as an ecological system, without clear boundaries between one type of enterprise and the next, interconnected and interdependent, and working as much from collaboration as from competition.[30] The role of business in society was brought into stark relief by the global financial crisis of 2008: the financial sector and financial interests (e.g., maximizing shareholder wealth at the expense of every other stakeholder's or nature's interests) had gained dominance over the so-called real economy in the United States and other global economies. Indeed, some observers suggest that instead of being the "servant" of the economy, the financial sector had become the major force fueling the economy in the years before the market crashed, which indicates a shifting of priorities to what years ago was called "paper entrepreneurialism,"[31] as opposed to real entrepreneurialism that produces new and needed goods and services.

The laissez-faire or free-market system that had been strongly advocated, particularly by the United States and by the Bretton Woods institutions, since the Reagan-Thatcher "revolution" of 1980 has created a situation that many observers believe is unsustainable socially—and certainly ecologically. Economists Paul Volcker (former chairman of the Federal Reserve System in the United States) and Robert Kuttner both argue that the creating and trading of abstract securities, removed from any real economic activity during the thirty-year period before the economic crash, added no economic value. (Indeed, Volcker has claimed that the only value-adding activity of the financial sector during that period was the automated teller machine [ATM]!) Among the excesses of the economy, particularly in the United States but also around the world, in the run-up to the 2008 market meltdown were excessive CEO compensation and uncontrolled financial instruments, called derivatives, that created significant market risk (and great wealth for the hedge fund managers who sold them, with the top twenty-five hedge fund managers reaping the princely sum of $11.6 billion in pay in 2008—and as much as $22.6 billion in 2009).[32] The imperative of shareholder returns also drives many executives to make short-term "strategic" decisions for their companies that actually work against the long-term interests of the firm and its many stakeholders by focusing firms on share price rather than true strategic needs or interests. It could be said that such short-termism drives irresponsible decision-making rather than more responsible decisions.

Economist Joseph Stiglitz, who headed up the U.S. Commission on the Measurement of Economic Performance and Social Progress,[33] argued that the economic meltdown of 2008 exposed "the moral bankruptcy of the pre-vailing (neoclassical) economic model" in an article in *Mother Jones* maga-zine.[34] Stiglitz notes that markets shaped not only the economy but also soci-ety—and that may not be such a good thing, since "materialism overwhelms moral commitment." According to Stiglitz, the dominance of economics has eroded any sense of community or commitment to the whole, as well as shifting the social contract toward the radical version of neoclassical eco-nomic theory begun in the Reagan-Thatcher revolution of 1980. The impact of business on society is made clear by these shifts, as well as in the level of consumption and materialism that now pervades the developed world—and is quickly seeping into the rest of the developing world.

THE COLLAPSE OF BEAR STEARNS AND LEHMAN BROTHERS

On Friday, March 14, 2008, the world watched in horror as the once vaunted financial house Bear Stearns began a precipitous collapse that ended on Sunday with the com-pany, which only a year earlier had been valued at $170 a share, being acquired by J. P. Morgan Chase, backed by the U.S. government, at the bargain-basement price of $2 per share for a total of only $236 million. *BusinessWeek* claimed that only the com-pany's new building allowed it to garner even that pitiful amount.[35] Bear Stearns's fall from grace sent shudders through the financial community—and the rest of the economy—because the company's collapse stemmed from an even broader set of issues associated with the erosion of the subprime housing market—and also from issues associated with Bear Stearns's reputation in the financial markets.

BusinessWeek made the following assessment of the situation:

> The quick collapse of Bear is a sober reminder of just how quickly a Wall Street firm can lose the confidence of investors, traders, and other institutions. A week ago, Bear executives were talking about how the firm was poised to report a profitable first quar-ter, after the firm posted its first quarterly loss in its history in the fourth quarter. But in the span of seven days, Bear went from being Wall Street's fifth largest firm to another in a long line of investment firms to bite the dust.[36]

The causes of Bear Stearns's dramatic fall sent financial markets around the world on a roller coaster ride over the next days, because the collapse hinged on the firm's position in the subprime mortgage crisis already looming large in the United States, and few knew the extent of damage that the larger underlying crisis would actually have. The subprime mortgage market had sucked in many individual investors, and even sophisticated financial houses put themselves at risk because they failed to understand the systems logic that meant that housing prices—on which subprime mortgages were based—could not logically continue to rise forever.

A long litany of events and poor decisions resulted from a failure to think about the whole system underpinning the Bear Stearns debacle. When housing prices were seemingly going up endlessly, some 6 million people in the United States were able to borrow nearly 100 percent of their house's value in the subprime market.[37] Lenders then consolidated these high-risk mortgages into bonds called mortgage-backed securities and sold them to other financial institutions, with a low credit rating from credit ratings agencies, effectively making them too risky for most professionally managed funds. But to overcome this risk, at least on the surface, investment bankers then divided the risky securities into tranches called collateralized debt obligations, by combining them with other, less-risky debt obligations.

As the financial crisis was unfolding, another investment bank, Lehman Brothers, declared bankruptcy on September 15, 2008. The causes were very similar to those that led to the collapse of Bear Stearns. Lehman suffered significant losses from the ongoing subprime mortgage crisis. In the second fiscal quarter of 2008 alone, Lehmann reported losses of $2.8 billion, leading its stock price to decrease by 73 percent. After Lehman's collapse, investigations by the U.S. government revealed that there was a lack of accountability across the company. Just before the collapse of the bank, executives at Neuberger Berman (a money management subsidiary of the bank) sent an e-mail to Lehman's executive committee suggesting that "top management should forgo bonuses this year"[38] in order to accept accountability for the firm's poor performance. The proposal was quickly rejected, with one executive of Neuberger Berman apologizing to Lehman's executive committee that this matter was raised.

These trends underlie the unsustainability of the current linear economic and production systems of the world,[39] and many worry that they threaten the underpinnings of democracy itself. With the 2010 U.S. Supreme Court's Citizens United decision, which allows companies to contribute as much money as they want to political campaigns, the concern is that "institutional corruption" as Lawrence Lessig calls it will become even more endemic than it already is, and that corporate interests will consistently be placed over the long-term (or even short-term) interests of the citizenry. Institutional corruption is not explicitly corruption, as, for example, bribery is. But by considering corporations to have the full free speech rights of actual persons, this decision allows companies to spend unlimited amounts to support political campaigns, which creates not a direct form of bribery, but rather what Lessig describes as a sort of "sleaze factor" that starts to align corporate interests with the "public good," to the detriment of what the general populace might view as the actual public good.[40]

As a sign of some hope in the United States, however, two years after the crisis occurred, the U.S. Congress passed financial regulatory reform in an effort to curb some of the worst abuses and restore American financial stability. The Dodd-Frank Wall Street Reform and Consumer Protection Act of 2010 was designed to accomplish a number of things, including creating a consumer protection agency that will ensure that consumers get sound information about financial products, end the era of "too big to fail" institutions that ask taxpayers to bail them out when they get in financial trouble, create an advance warning system around issues of systemic risk, eliminate loopholes for exotic financial instruments and derivatives, provide supervision of the federal banking system, and give shareholders a nonbinding "say on pay" vote on executive compensation, among other changes.[41]

THE POLITICAL SPHERE: GOVERNMENT, THE CORPORATION, AND THE COMMON GOOD

The public interest is defined as the particular standards and values that most people in a society agree are in the best interests of that society. In most democratic nations, the common good is underpinned by such values as social justice, equity and fairness, and human dignity. Governments create and implement the rules of societies through what is called the public policy process. According to Preston and Post, "Public policy refers to widely shared and generally acknowledged principles directing and controlling actions that have broad implications for society at large or major portions thereof."[42] A nation's political structure and constitution determine the public policy process

the 1960s that resulted in the passing of protective laws and regulations. And new needs arise because information availability raises consciousness about issues of public concern, or because things go wrong, as evidenced by the passage in the United States of the Sarbanes-Oxley Act of 2002 and the Dodd-Frank financial regulatory reform act of 2010.

One of the problems associated with corporate political activism relates to the fact that companies with significant economic resources use those resources to present and argue for their positions. Their power becomes especially apparent when companies create PACs, hire lobbyists, or provide public officials with industry-biased information. Some political observers claim that corporate influence is corrupting democracy by creating too close ties between business and government. In his book *Supercapitalism*, Robert Reich argues that the power that companies wield in the U.S. public policy process by hiring lobbyists with close ties to politicians and contributing vast sums to political campaigns subverts the democratic process to the interests of the economy.[48] Reich claims that instead of focusing on issues and social values, too much government today is focused on issues in which an industry sector's (or even a business's) interests will prevail:

> The predominance of corporate-financed "experts" in policymaking, in effect, leads the public to assume the only issues of any importance are those that bear on the welfare of consumers and investors, rather than on the well-being of society or the planet as a whole. [In this system . . .] public policies are to be judged by a utilitarian calculus of whether they improve the efficiency of the economy. They are presumed to be wise if consumer-investor benefits exceed consumer-investor costs if the opposite holds.[49]

Reich goes on to argue that:

> Absent from any such calculus is consideration of whether the resulting distribution of benefits further widens inequality among citizens or reduces it, provides more or fewer opportunities to the nation's or world's less fortunate, offers more or less economic security to people now lacking it, respects or undermines civil or human rights, promotes or undermines public health and domestic tranquility, fosters or detracts from community, generates a cleaner or dirtier environment, advances or sets back the cause of tolerance and global peace, or, more generally, strengthens or weakens democracy.[50]

Communities, activists, and individuals may have significantly fewer resources at their disposal than do many corporations. Hence the voices of citizens and even organized NGOs can be drowned out when corporate interests are at play in the public policy process. Some people question whether sufficient public voice is available to less-powerful or less-resource-rich parties in the public policy arena to ensure equitable outcomes.

Shifting Public Issues: The Issue Life Cycle

Attention and activity in the public policy arena shift over time with the shifting of competing interests, as well as with the relative amount of power and voice contesting parties have. Social problems exist in all societies, but they become public issues when sufficient public attention is devoted to them. Public issues tend to go through a typical life cycle as they emerge from obscurity, indifference, or simple inattention and make their way onto the public policy agenda (see Figure 2.1). Not all issues follow exactly the same cycle, and not all are resolved through the public policy process. In fact, many companies have established issue management, public relations, and public affairs units in the hope that they can work cooperatively with government and community stakeholders or forestall actions before issues are resolved legislatively or in the court system.

First, public issues are in the public arena, possibly subject to public policy or nonpublic resolution.[51] Public issues usually rise to prominence as a result of unmet expectations.[52] A gap between what is and what ought to be draws attention to the issue from one or more stakeholders, who begin to shape or frame the issue in ways that reflect their interests and perceptions. Often this gap develops when society is changing, with resulting changes in public expectations. The contest arises particularly when there are multiple opinions (often of people or groups of equal goodwill) about how best to resolve the problem. Further, unless the gap between what is and what ought to be creates a significant perceived present or future impact on an organization, society, or stakeholder, it is unlikely to become an issue. Frequently, issues arise when there is a question of legitimacy or when there is controversy about what the costs and benefits of issue resolution are.

For example, use of DDT as a pesticide was largely uncontroversial until the 1963 publication of Rachel Carson's *Silent Spring*, which galvanized

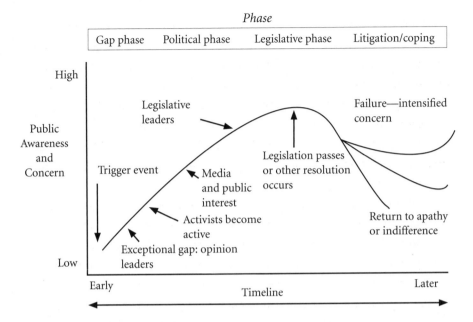

Figure 2.1: Public Issue Life Cycle

environmentalists into action.[53] Similar trigger events include the publication of the surgeon general's report on smoking and health in the 1960s, which generated a great deal of antismoking activism. More recently, sweatshop conditions in less-developed countries from which clothing and shoes are sourced have drawn outrage from the public when revealed by activists or international bodies such as the International Labour Organization (ILO). During the first, or gap, stage, only a few people or groups, typically activists or opinion leaders, may be interested in an issue, but once their activities begin to attract wider attention, the issue enters the second stage of its life cycle.

The second, or political, stage of the issue life cycle occurs when the issue, as framed by one or more of the interested stakeholders, begins to draw public attention and concern, typically through the media or various forms of activism. In this stage, the new expectations have become more widely recognized and the issue itself may become politicized.[54] As Figure 2.1 suggests, public awareness increases rather dramatically during this stage, and more stakeholders are likely to become involved in the effort to frame the issue in a way that benefits their own point of view. In this stage, the contest of different values is in full swing.

Government or political actors become involved as the issue progresses to the third, or legislative, stage of the life cycle. These actors investigate and determine how and where the issue should be dealt with legislatively, if that is an appropriate outcome. Once an issue has entered the legislative phase of its life cycle, public debate and contested framings of the issue are likely. During this phase business leaders and others may be called to testify before the relevant legislative body. Corporate lobbyists and industry stakeholders become proactive in getting information to legislators and other decision makers in the hope of influencing the outcome in their favor.

Assuming legislation is passed, the issue enters a fourth stage, called litigation or coping, in which stakeholders are expected to comply with the new legislation. If they disagree with the outcome, they might fight it through the court system by means of litigation. If legislation does not pass or is unsatisfactory to some powerful stakeholders, the issue can take on new life. This is what happened with the environmental movement in the 1980s when it became clear that existing regulations were insufficient to solve newly recognized ecological problems like acid rain, rain forest depletion, and the shrinking of the ozone layer. Renewed environmental activism ensued in an effort to pass stricter laws protecting the environment. In 1992 in Rio de Janeiro, the United Nations sponsored the first global conference to address the increasingly global nature of environmental problems generated by population growth and processes of industrialization. This conference produced the so-called Rio Agenda and the Rio Declaration on Environment and Development (or Agenda 21).[55] Today the issue has resurfaced yet again under the rubric of sustainability.

Generally speaking, the government is one of at least three primary stakeholders in any public issue that affects business. (Not all public issues affect businesses directly.) The other two are corporations or the economic community, and the particular activist or issues group interested in resolving the issue.[56] A comprehensive understanding of any issue therefore requires a capacity to hold the multiple perspectives of at least these stakeholders simultaneously and to see where their interests diverge and where they converge. This is normally the task of policymakers as they attempt to determine what outcome at a given time would be in the public interest. And, in their quest to determine the public interest, policymakers' ideas and perceived solutions are shaped, as are all members of a culture, by the national or community ideology.

THE CIVIL SOCIETY SPHERE

Civil society is fundamentally associational society. Civil society comprises entities and organizations that develop civility and coherence through the long-term building of civilized community and social capital, the capital of relationships. The organizations and associations of a civil society constitute community at whatever level of analysis is being considered. Civil society includes families, religious institutions, nonprofit organizations and other nongovernmental organizations (NGOs), educational institutions, health care institutions, voluntary organizations, civic and political organizations, and associations of all types. The exact number of NGOs in the world is unknown, but what is known is that their numbers have dramatically increased in the past half century, in part as a response to the growth of corporate power and in part because they offer a more effective way of having the "voice" of civil society heard by international agencies like the United Nations.[57]

In one sense, civil society is everything outside the economic and political spheres of activity, or as political scientist Alan Wolfe puts it, "those forms of communal and associational life which are organized neither by the self-interest of the market nor by the coercive potential of the state."[58] In its positive and constructive sense, civil society includes those enterprises and associations that promote what is thought to be the common or collective good in societies. That is, we would like to be able to exclude from our definition of civil society any negative associational entities, such as terrorist organizations or radical groups bent on destroying society, since these entities' purposes are decidedly and determinedly uncivil in their intent and impact. Such uncivil groups would include the terrorists who used airplanes to attack the World Trade Center and the Pentagon on September 11, 2001, and who continue their terrorism in vulnerable spots around the world.

The fundamental purposes of civil society are to construct relationships among social institutions and peoples that give meaning to the terms civility and community. Hence, the fundamental values of civil society are those of relationship, civility, and community. As Alan Wolfe notes in his seminal book *Whose Keeper?*, the basic values of any society are those that constitute its ideology.[59] In contrast to the economizing or power-aggrandizing values of the economic and political spheres, these are the values that are encompassed in art, friendships, loyalties, love, and other personal values that build relationships. These values are the X-factor values that individuals and some groups bring to all of their activities, and they are also deeply embedded in the meanings that we associate with community.[60]

Just as there is a need for a healthy ecosystem to support human civilization, so there is a need for a healthy and effective civil society to provide the values and social capital to support economic and political activities. As the structure and rules that government constructs provide a foundation for enterprise, so the relationships of trust and civility allow the economic system to operate effectively. Civil society provides a foundation of connectedness that gives people a sense of place and community. Civil society is where shared norms and values (the ideology that shapes political and governmental activities) emerge in the first place. Civil society provides the human in human civilization.

The humanization that comes from positive social capital occurs because links within a given community create a network of reciprocal relationships and mutual obligations among individual members of that community. Community members also exchange information, which helps them build a shared sense of identity and common set of values. In turn, these values generate norms of behavior and appropriate practices that provide sanctions where appropriate and rewards where feasible.[61] Overall, when social capital diminishes there is less sense of community, less common good, because people have less in common and less of a sense of shared identity.

Through their development of trust, shared identity, and sense of community, healthy civil societies develop proactive and capable citizens.[62] In democracies, an active citizenry is capable of solving its own political and economic problems. In contrast, the uprisings in Egypt in 2011, which were quickly followed by protests in other Arab nations, suggest what happens when civil society's needs are suppressed. Active citizens are also capable of placing restraints they believe to be appropriate on enterprises and activities in both of the other spheres of activity, as well as in civil society itself. These restraints occur through political action as well as through the activism associated with a range of causes of concern to different citizen groups when they share a common set of values and goals. Active citizens are capable of mobilizing themselves and the other spheres to deal with problems as they arise, as citizens in the United States did in 2011 through the "Occupy Wall Street" (and elsewhere) movement. On the other hand, citizens who feel little connectedness to or shared interest with the communities they operate in may remain passive, with problems going unresolved. It is because of the possibility of the erosion of social capital in democratic regimes that some observers are concerned about the institutional corruption discussed above.

Today the impact of many activities in the economic sphere on civil society are uncertain. Responsible companies may need to be rooted in the identity of the localities in which they operate if they hope to be successful in the long run, because that is where values and norms develop and where meaning is generated. A strong civil sphere provides a necessary counterpoint (balance) to the otherwise dominating power of the multinational corporation with its individualistically oriented values focused on material goods and consumption of increasingly scarce resources. Having a strong civil society creates public goods that can then be shared by all members of the relevant communities.

THE ENVIRONMENTAL SPHERE: THE NATURAL ENVIRONMENT

Why do some companies move toward sustainable ecological practices in addition to recognizing the importance of stakeholders throughout their supply, production/service delivery, and distribution chains? Let us examine the larger system in which businesses operate: the natural environment. Research by the Global Footprint Network indicates that humanity is already in significant and problematic "ecological overshoot." Each year humanity consumes considerably more resources than the earth can renew (like running on a deficit budget, this is possible for a short period of time, but not forever). The frightening estimate is that, as of 2011, each year it takes the earth a year and six months to regenerate the (renewable) resources that humanity now uses in a single year.[63]

In 2007 the Intergovernmental Panel on Climate Change (IPCC) released its Synthesis Report,[64] which warned that the scientific consensus is that "warming of the climate is unequivocal," and that all natural systems are being affected by this and other changes, which they attribute to humanity's impact on the natural environment. The IPCC report gives five important reasons for concern about climate change. First, there are risks associated with unique and threatened systems, including polar and high mountain ecosystems, as well as increased risk of species extinction and coral reef damage. Second are risks of extreme weather events, such as droughts, heat waves, and floods, which can affect large geographical regions.

The third reason has to do with the distribution of impacts and vulnerabilities, for as IPCC notes, there are big regional differences in climate change impacts. The most vulnerable groups, like the poor and elderly, are likely to be worst affected, as well as populations in low-latitude, coastal, and less-developed regions. Further, there are aggregate impacts of climate change on economic stability and conditions. Consider the costs of cleaning up after Hurricane Katrina in the United States in 2005 and the global impact of the earthquake and subsequent tsunami on Japan in 2011. The fifth reason is that global warming over centuries might result in higher sea levels as glaciers melt. With vast swaths of humanity now living in coastal areas, rising sea levels will prove costly in many different ways.

One organization that has taken a creative and systemic approach to understanding ecological sustainability and business's role in it is the Swedish nonprofit organization The Natural Step (TNS).[65] TNS highlights some of the problematic aspects of human economic development on the ecology. Because of the impact of the nearly 7 billion people currently alive on earth, multiple ecological systems—including croplands, wetlands, the ozone layer, rain forests, fisheries, and groundwater—are facing serious challenges. Garbage is filling up landfills, while pollutants accumulate less visibly in the atmosphere. The depletion of the rain forests is having an almost unimaginable impact on world ecology, for rain forests not only provide fresh water but also cleanse the atmosphere.

TNS's framework offers a set of system conditions that, according to scientists, will be needed to prevent the planet from hitting a wall of unsupportable

TABLE 2.2   *Four System Conditions for Sustainability*

The Four System Conditions	... Reworded as the Four Principles of Sustainability
In a sustainable society, nature is not subject to systematically increasing: 1. Concentrations of substances extracted from the earth's crust; 2. Concentrations of substances produced by society; and 3. Degradation by physical means; 4. And, in that society, people are not subject to conditions that systematically undermine their capacity to meet their needs.	*To become a sustainable society, we must...* 1. Eliminate our contribution to the progressive buildup of substances extracted from the earth's crust (for example, heavy metals and fossil fuels); 2. Eliminate our contribution to the progressive buildup of chemicals and compounds produced by society (for example, dioxins, PCBs, and DDT); 3. Eliminate our contribution to the progressive physical degradation and destruction of nature and natural processes (for example, overharvesting forests and paving over critical wildlife habitat); and 4. Eliminate our contribution to conditions that undermine people's capacity to meet their basic human needs (for example, unsafe working conditions and not enough pay to live on).

SOURCE: The Natural Step, http://www.naturalstep.org/the-system-conditions.

demands on the natural environment. These four system conditions or principles of sustainability would allow humanity to create sustainable societies (see Table 2.2).

The aim of sustainable development is to balance the interests of humanity with those of other creatures and systems on the planet. Sustainable development was originally defined by the Brundtland Commission in 1987 as "Development that meets the needs of the present without compromising the ability of future generations to meet their own needs."[66] Sustainability can also be seen as "a process of achieving human development . . . in an inclusive, connected, equitable, prudent, and secure manner," according to ecology scholar Thomas Gladwin and his colleagues.[67] Gladwin has defined these five elements—inclusiveness, connectivity, equity, prudence, and security—as representing a set of constraints on human development, similar to those for the material world that TNS produced.

Inclusiveness connotes an expansive view of the space, time, and component parts of the observed ecology, embracing both ecological and human conditions in the present and the future. Connectivity means understanding the inherent interconnectedness and interdependence of elements of the world and problems in the world. Equity means a fair distribution of resources and property rights within and between generations. Putting connectivity and equity together suggests greater comprehension of the unavoidable links between, for example, creating better ecological health and efforts to reduce poverty or the gap between rich and poor. Prudence means taking care of the resources of the world, as suggested by the TNS constraints. In practice, being prudent means keeping ecosystems and socioeconomic systems healthy and resilient; avoiding irreversible losses of ecological or other resources; and, again as the TNS constraints indicate, keeping human activities within the earth's regenerative capacity. Finally, security focuses on the sustainability of human life, that is, ensuring "a safe, healthy, high quality of life for current and future generations."[68]

The element of connectivity in Gladwin's framework is particularly relevant from the perspective of systems thinking. Because most of the problems underlying the sustainability agenda are connected with each other, neither businesses nor policymakers should approach these problems in isolation. Climate change, for example, is likely to increase child labor and reduce levels of education as the effects of global warming (e.g., severe droughts) lead to higher food prices and hence more poverty, and make it necessary for more children to help support their families and difficult for them to attend school.[69] This is only one small example of the interconnected nature of problems and their underlying systems.

Thinking about ecological sustainability may mean complementing traditional Western ways of viewing human beings' relationship to the natural world with more holistic perspectives. It may even mean going beyond an ecocentric (ecological) worldview.[70] It may mean moving toward a wholly integrative approach to economic development focused on sustainability that is earth-centric rather than human-centric. A fully integrated perspective would synthesize the three critical spheres of civilization (economic, political, and societal) with the ecological, and would also integrate the subjective and intersubjective elements of emotions, intuition, aesthetics, and culture into our perspective. The result would be a better understanding of the values that underpin each sphere of activity.

Just as nature requires a balance among elements to sustain any healthy ecological environment, we must think about responsible enterprise as part of the social ecology. Mastering systems thinking is a critical element of creating enterprises that learn and improve continuously.[71] An integrative systems approach is essential to the sustainable operation of businesses, governments, and civil society enterprises, giving due consideration to the seventh generation out, as our Native American ancestors believed was necessary for any decision with potential intergenerational impacts. We will return to the issues facing the natural environment in Chapter 9.

BLURRING BOUNDARIES

Although we have described activities within each sphere of society as if they were easily separable, it is clear today that some of the boundaries among these different types of organizations are blurry at best. For example, there has been a considerable rise in the number, focus, and extent of cross-sector collaborations and partnerships since the early 1980s, when they first became popular. Strategic alliances, multistakeholder initiatives, and global action networks (GANs) have become commonplace among and between businesses, as well as between businesses and other actors in civil society and public policy.

The blurring is further fostered by technology, in particular by the Internet, and the wide availability of data to actors from different spheres. Google, for example, has created what in essence is a public good by making access to data and information virtually instantaneous globally. Its crossing of sectoral boundaries became problematic for the company in China when the Chinese government wanted to restrict its citizens' access to information, a move that prompted Google to redirect its users to its Hong Kong site (where there is no censorship). Google revoked this decision, however, when its license to operate in China was about to expire, and the Chinese government renewed Google's license to operate in 2010.

Google and other corporations are increasingly adopting the role of political actors, influencing the rights of people, as their power and reach increase. In other parts of the world, corporations act as political actors because governments fail to protect the rights of their citizens. Labor monitoring in global supply chains, for example, is necessary because some governments have failed to protect workers' basic rights. The de facto political role of the corporation raises questions around missing democratic accountability. If corporations influence the rights of people, they also need to be answerable for their actions, judgments, and omissions, which is to say they need to be accountable.

Many companies are blurring the relationships among stockholders and stakeholders through employee stock ownership plans (ESOPs). ESOPs typically offer employees stock and some degree of participation as owners in the company, thereby converting them to owner-employees. Further blurring occurs because a huge proportion of employees' retirement money is invested in equity (stock) funds, which gives many employees an often unrecognized ownership stake in long-term corporate performance.

The rise of what are termed social enterprises run by social entrepreneurs—businesses that attempt to earn a profit while simultaneously working to solve social problems—has made sectoral distinctions less clear. Some social enterprises that were previously considered to be fully in the civil society sector are now engaged in profit-making activities to provide a sustainable business model for themselves. Likewise, many large corporations, while still primarily pursuing economic ends, have begun developing social entrepreneurial or "bottom of the pyramid" businesses aimed at improving societies and the lives of people within them.

Social entrepreneurs are individuals who start businesses—either as a part of a large corporation or as a new venture—that attempt to meet a social need while simultaneously making a profit—that is, doing well and doing good. The most widely cited definition of a social entrepreneur is that of Gregory Dees, who says:

> Social entrepreneurs play the role of change agents in the social sector, by:
> • Adopting a mission to create and sustain a social value (not just private value),
> • Recognizing and relentlessly pursuing new opportunities to serve that mission,
> • Engaging in a process of continuous innovation, adaptation, and learning,
> • Acting boldly without being limited by resources currently in hand, and
> • Exhibiting a heightened sense of accountability to the constituencies served and for the outcomes created.[72]

Sandra Waddock's work in identifying a group of individuals called *difference makers*, who have built today's infrastructure around corporate responsibility as social and institutional entrepreneurs, suggests that social entrepreneurs have distinctive qualities. They are visionaries who aren't afraid to see a problem, name it, and think about what kinds of institutional organizational pressures, market forces, activism, or innovations are needed. They tend to be values-driven—oriented toward wanting to do their part to build a better world—and are willing to take considerable risks to solve the problems they feel strongly about. They are able to gather resources, though most started with very little; they tend to start small while thinking big and being politically savvy, knowing that they need to work incrementally. They have persistence and courage in the face of obstacles and think systemically about the problems they are dealing with, articulate and frame the issues so that others can understand them while they build networks of allies that help foster legitimacy for their efforts in what is often a dialectical and circular, rather than linear, process of change.[73]

GRAMEEN DANONE FOODS LTD.—SOCIAL ENTREPRENEURSHIP IN ACTION

One of the best-known social enterprises emerged from a collaboration between the Grameen Bank (a microfinance organization that, with its founder Muhammed Yunus, was awarded the Nobel Peace Prize in 2006) and Groupe Danone.[74] Launched in 2006 in Bangladesh, the social business produces a special yogurt, called Shakti Doi (meaning "yogurt to give strength") that contains important vitamins and proteins to meet the nutritional requirements of children. The yogurt is priced affordably—one cup of yogurt (60g) costs 6 taka (approximately $0.08). The business is operated as a profit-making enterprise, although both Grameen and Danone agreed to reinvest all earnings into further employment opportunities for the poor. This "no loss, no dividend" operating model reflects the unique positioning of social enterprises: they are neither full members of the business sphere (because dividends are not paid) nor fully nonprofit organizations (since the business needs to be self-sustaining).

This social enterprise is interesting for several reasons. First, it unites the charismatic leadership of Muhammed Yunus, a social entrepreneur, with Groupe Danone's expertise in producing food. Second, it tackles the most pressing problem in Bangladesh: poverty. Approximately 40 percent of the 162 million people living in Bangladesh live below the national poverty line.[75] Malnutrition is a direct consequence of poverty and also reinforces it. Hence, selling low-priced, high-nutrition yogurt is an effective way to address this problem. Third, Grameen Danone Foods Ltd. employs local people and sources its raw materials from local farmers. This business design creates additional opportunities for the development of the local economy. For instance, the yogurt is distributed primarily through a network of "sales ladies" who introduce the product into their local communities.

According to Muhammed Yunus, there are two types of social enterprises. The first type, which is reflected by Grameen Danone Foods, explicitly addresses pressing social or environmental problems by providing a particular product or service. The second type is directly owned by the poor, but does not necessarily address social and environmental problems. The idea is that poor people raise their standard of living by profiting from the dividends (or other benefits) that the business creates. Whatever form a social enterprise takes, the underlying principle is that it is possible to reconcile the advantages of a for-profit business (such as efficiency) with the need to address selected social and environmental problems.

However, the Grameen Danone enterprise has also demonstrated that managing a social enterprise can raise unique challenges. In 2008, the swiftly emerging global food crisis hit the social enterprise particularly hard. Since the business was not yet making a profit, it had to pass the higher prices of raw materials on to its customers. The price for a cup of yogurt increased by almost 60 percent within a short period of time and demand dropped sharply. Although Grameen Danone was able to recover from this crisis (by introducing smaller cups and revising its formula to maintain nutrition levels), this experience shows that managing social enterprises can pose quite different challenges than managing traditional businesses or even managing corporate responsibility in for-profit companies.

Another view is that there are at least three kinds of social entrepreneurial entities: enterprises that support themselves with income-generating activities rather than donations; enterprises that serve a social purpose and earn a profit; and enterprises that are built from (typically larger) for-profit business. Social entrepreneurs face challenges that differ from those of traditional for-profit entrepreneurs. These include managing accountability, because there are at least two bottom lines to account for (financial and social) as well as additional stakeholders. Because social enterprises are hybrid organizations, social entrepreneurs must contend with sometimes complex identity issues, which can create problems between the commercial and social sides of the business.[76] A social entrepreneurial venture may emerge from within a large corporation, where a champion in the company sees a new market opportunity. Other ventures begin small with an explicit dual- or multiple-bottom-line orientation.

Part II

DEVELOPING RESPONSIBLE ENTERPRISE

3 THE ROLE OF PERSONAL
AND ORGANIZATIONAL VISION

For me the fundamentals start with a set of deep capacities [that] few in leadership positions today could claim to have developed: systems intelligence, building partnership across boundaries, and openness of mind, heart, and will. To develop such capacities requires a lifelong commitment to grow as a human being in ways not well understood in contemporary culture. Yet in other ways, these are the foundations for leadership that have been understood for a very long time.

Peter Senge, "Systems Citizenship: The Leadership Mandate for this Millennium"[1]

VISION: THE POWER OF IMAGINATION

Successful companies achieve value added—that is, profitability for shareholders and successful engagement with and for their other stakeholders—through a sustained effort to develop high-quality products and services that meet the needs and interests of their customers. Such companies typically have a vision that is underpinned by values. This and the following two chapters build the systems case for that statement. Vision provides a way for stakeholders to identify with an enterprise, and vision gives the enterprise meaning, thereby creating the potential for a lasting, productive bond.

The word vision has connotations that provide helpful insights into the links between the spheres of society. Of course, a vision is something that is seen, but it is also more than that: vision is also the power to perceive what is not actually present: possibilities and potential. Used constructively and positively, a vision is a picture or an idea that taps the imagination and allows it to soar. In *The Fifth Discipline*, Peter Senge defines vision as a picture of the future that we seek to create.[2] To the extent that a vision is a picture, it helps us to quite literally see where we want to go and make choices about how to get there.

Visions, of course, can be destructive, oppressive, or autocratic, like those of Hitler and Stalin. In contrast, the vision of a responsible enterprise is based on positive values that inspire the human spirit and are the foundation for building a better world.

Visions are created by foresighted individuals or by groups in organizations working collaboratively to achieve some higher purpose. In the past many corporate visionaries were viewed as impractical dreamers out of touch with reality. Today, however, it is well recognized that successful organizations benefit from the inspiration of visionaries who can help motivate action, commitment, and connection, especially among critical stakeholders like employees. In this positive sense, visionaries are, first of all, those who see what is, clearly and unrelentingly. They are realists, willing to grapple with the hard facts, figures, and relationships that constitute organizational life. Second, and equally important, visionaries are able to imagine a possible or hoped-for future—and to represent that future to others in ways that capture their imaginations and help guide them toward its realization. In difficult times, we believe that we need visionaries more than ever.

VISIONS: CREATING MEANING AND FOSTERING PURPOSE

Visions help businesses establish meaning and purpose and help others to make connections between their own actions and values and the purposes of the enterprises in which they are involved. Visions become organizationally real when they are widely held and widely shared. Visions tap people's spirit and soul; they draw out feelings and emotions. In short, visions inspire. A shared vision, one not foisted on people but built by them collectively, reflects individuals' personal visions and simultaneously creates meaning for the group. Shared visions provide opportunities for individuals to live out a dream through productive organizational work that calls for personal commitment and engagement and allows individuals to see that they make a difference or a contribution.

Clear visions in organizations are created by developing, implementing, and sustaining what scholars James Collins and Jerry Porras termed core ideology in their book *Built to Last*. A company's core ideology consists of its vision or purpose and a set of core values that sustain it even through bad times.[3] And all companies face bad times. The key to maintaining a vision and the values that guide action or practice is to hold true to the underlying core ideology and to make sure that it is positive and meaningful to everyone involved with the firm. At the same time, companies need to make the changes that are necessary to sustain themselves strategically and competitively and as the internal and external context demands. The same dynamic holds true for individuals.

Visions are implemented through practices that operationalize core values in day-to-day initiatives. Values are demonstrated in how relationships are developed with stakeholders, including employees, customers, community members, owners, local authorities, and nature. In other words, visions are implemented through the processes, policies, and procedures—in sum, the practices—that organizations develop. By creating visions that inspire commitment, loyalty, meaning, and a sense of community among primary stakeholders—and by implementing practices that sustain positive interactions with them—firms can achieve high levels of performance over time.

Why Vision?

Clearly articulated visions guide action and decisions. Vision helps individuals and organizations evaluate just what actions and decisions make sense in a particular context. Clear and constructive visions help determine what kinds of actions should not be taken, when those actions are unnecessary, will deter achievement of the vision, or are inconsistent with the vision or its associated values. Constructive visions guide participants in an enterprise toward the achievement of shared goals and toward productive ways of interacting. Visions are enacted through organizational norms and cultures—that is, the shared set of practices and beliefs that tell people "how things are done here," as well as what the company stands for. Visions provide, both figuratively and literally, a picture of where the company is going and how it is going to get there.

Vision inspires in multiple ways, not least of which is by motivating people to make a difference in the world. It is the sense of making a difference that creates meaning. Vision can create aspirations; it can enhance the pursuit of a larger purpose, something outside of and bigger than oneself or one's own purpose. Constructive and positive visions can exhilarate, encourage, and connect people in their pursuit of a common purpose. Visions help to create a sense of "we" rather than "us versus them" in an organization, as well as a sense of belonging to a community that is doing important work. Shared visions can also foster creative risk taking and experimentation, which are necessary for innovation and entrepreneurship even within large corporations. And vision helps managers overcome a short-term orientation by focusing their attention on long-term achievements.[4] These outcomes of vision are critical if companies are to become companies and their managers are to be perceived as responsible and trustworthy.

Visionary Leaders: Imagination and Leadership

Some individuals can see what others cannot. They make links that others don't. They are more aware of their surroundings. They understand connections and see the dynamics of situations. They are systems thinkers who understand the relationships among different facts, events, and opportunities. They see through the chaos of daily life to find possibilities, potentials, and meanings—and they can articulate those possibilities in ways that make sense to others. It is the awareness of those possibilities, potentials, and meanings that inspires others to join in efforts that link people in common endeavors, whether in a community or business or for social change. We all know some of these people. We call them visionary leaders.

Leadership, even visionary leadership, is not some arcane undertaking available only to the select few. Indeed, Joseph Raelin has articulated a concept he calls "leaderfulness," leadership coming from all parts of the organization, which he says is essential for the success of today's complex businesses and other organizations.[5] By exploring what is important in his or her life, any person can develop awareness of self and others, awareness of impacts, and awareness of the profound values that underpin actions and decisions. Such awareness helps the person understand his or her impact in a given context, know where significant changes can be made either internally or with others, and develop personal vision that can, in turn, inspire organizational vision. Personal and organizational visions inspire work, life, and play. Inspirational organizational visions embed responsibility, higher purpose, and meaning in the enterprise to provide a basis for working on something together. Crafting a positive and inspirational vision, whether

personal or organizational, therefore involves determining what is meaningful, what provides purpose, and what goals will inspire oneself or others to
action.

Individual Awareness and Reflection

Consciousness or awareness, particularly self-consciousness, is an important
component of what distinguishes human beings from other sentient beings.[6]
Humans are the only beings (that we yet know of) that are truly conscious
of their own existence and have the capacity for reflection.[7] Reflection is a
capacity that allows us to continue to learn and develop cognitively.[8] But
there's more. The capacity to reflect also provides for growth and maturing
processes in other domains. In organizational life, moral and emotional development is also essential for responsible behavior. Such development is, in
particular, a necessary condition for working effectively with stakeholders,
the key ingredient of responsible enterprise.

Consciousness is intricately tied to language, as the biologists Humberto
Maturana and Francisco Varela pointed out.[9] The close link between the development of consciousness and awareness of language suggests that human
beings are inherently social creatures, creating through their interactions not
only individual meaning and purpose but also communities. Communities
are shaped by cultural, spiritual, and economic bonds that result from human interactions. Because humans are social creatures necessarily embedded
in communities, and because "self-awareness is at the core of being human,"[10]
creating shared meanings through awareness, vision, and reflection is a fundamental part of the human experience and, when generatively embedded in
organizations, a core of responsible enterprise.

The communal nature of human society, which Frans de Waal has also
documented among our primate progenitors, gives rise not only to language
and meaning, to common purpose and shared identity, but also to notions
of right and wrong—that is, to ethics.[11] Organizations in the economic and
other spheres are a part of this communal nature; hence, their modes of operation and the shared meanings that their purposes allow them to fulfill are
inherently and fundamentally premised on ethics and values as well. Individuals in key decision-making capacities within organizations—leaders and

managers—need to understand how to create purpose and shared meaning through the visions they engender. Only then can they develop organizations that embody positive visions that contribute constructively to society in ways that enhance work in the other spheres and treat the natural environment respectfully.

Transformation: From Managers to Leaders

There is a long-standing debate about whether leaders are born or made. It appears, however, that the capacity for leadership can be nurtured as an individual matures, particularly as his or her cognitive, moral, and emotional capacities develop. Higher development in these three arenas means that leaders are more aware of their impacts and can think through and develop better relationships, all skills critical to responsible enterprise.

Management scholar Russell Ackoff said that wisdom "is the ability to perceive and evaluate the long-run consequences of behavior."[12] This capacity of what we shall call mindfulness is "associated with a willingness to make short-run sacrifices for long-term gains."[13] The notorious short-sightedness of corporations, not to mention the sorry state of relationships that many companies have with some of their stakeholders, suggests that mindfulness is in woefully short supply among corporate leaders, and that the system itself fosters short-sightedness.

Certainly mindfulness and wisdom require a degree of maturity and insight that not every leader finds easy to attain. Being mindful demands that individual decision makers who are acting on a company's behalf function at relatively high developmental levels, not only cognitively but also morally and emotionally. If responsible enterprise demands building relationships with stakeholders, it also demands insightful understanding of those stakeholders' perspectives—and such understanding requires a fairly high cognitive capacity as a starting point. Seeing the consequences and implications of one's actions, one of the requisites of integrity, marries cognitive with moral development at a relatively high level. Thinking through consequences demands systemic thinking, and also requires leaders to be well aware of how other stakeholders will perceive and understand their actions and practices. Moreover, leaders have to be willing to reflect honestly about their understanding, about their relationship with other stakeholders, and about their own roles within the company.

To develop these skills, leaders need both the cognitive capacity to "perspective-take" and the moral capacity to understand how their decisions affect others (which is the essence, after all, of ethics). Further, because sound relationships are essential to the stakeholder-based definition of responsible enterprise, leaders also need emotional intelligence sufficient to build lasting relationships with critical stakeholders. Below, we explore these three core aspects of responsible leadership.

LEADERS' COGNITIVE, MORAL, AND EMOTIONAL DEVELOPMENT

Research on personality, cognitive, moral, emotional, and even spiritual development suggests that individuals go through stages as they mature. Developmental theorists now believe that most individuals move through these stages in order, progressing from the less to the more developed—and typically more encompassing—stage, without regressing.[14] Although these developmental stages are associated with the physical maturing that is part of the aging process, people do not always experience the stages at the same age, and each stage is not necessarily associated with any particular age.

Cognitive Development

Howard Gardner (who researches multiple intelligences), Lawrence Kohlberg (who studied moral development), and Jean Piaget (who studied child development), among many others,[15] all posited that three waves or stages constitute a generic stage framework: preconventional, conventional, and postconventional.[16] Many developmental theorists agree on these three general stages of development, which have analogs in multiple arenas.

- *Preconventional reasoning* means operating without an understanding of society's expectations and rules and with a fear of punishment if rules are broken or when acting with self-interest.[17]
- *Conventional reasoning* means "conforming to and upholding the rules and expectations and conventions of society or authority just because they are society's rules, expectations or conventions."[18]

- *Postconventional reasoning* means understanding and accepting that society has rules and realizing that principles underlie those rules and that one can apply those principles in different situations.[19]

To the extent that these stages apply to many forms of development, they represent a useful framework for understanding cognitive, moral, and emotional development.

Further, many developmental theorists argue that stages are nested. That is, each later stage encompasses all of the capacities of the earlier stages. New ways of understanding (e.g., the capacity to take another's point of view) are incorporated at each stage, making regression to an earlier stage unlikely. Robert Kegan, a Harvard psychologist who has studied adult development, argues that the complexity of the modern world is such that people need to move beyond conventional levels of thinking to postconventional levels.[20] Kegan points out that it takes time (maturity that comes with age) as well as real work to develop these capacities. Not many individuals yet reach postconventional stages of development, according to research by William Torbert and his associates.[21] But that level of development is, in fact, what the modern world demands of us cognitively—and also, we argue, morally, particularly for leaders who want their companies to act responsibly. Dealing with complex problems, testing assumptions, inquiring about rationales behind decisions, and engaging in dialogue with others, including stakeholders very different from corporate leaders, can be helpful ways of developing these capacities, and they are valuable behaviors in today's business world.

Responsible enterprise is based on developing stakeholder relationships, so understanding multiple stakeholders' perspectives is one key to success. One way to advance cognitive development is through techniques that involve conversation and dialogue in which different parties to an argument or discussion express their points of view. Other ways include tackling unstructured problems where "problem finding" rather than simply problem solving is necessary, working collaboratively with others to devise joint solutions, and engaging in ongoing reflective practices both personally and in groups.[22]

Cognitive development can also be advanced, as management scholar Chris Argyris argues, by having individuals explore the reasoning behind behaviors and decisions, both their own and others'. Other scholars, such as Torbert and colleagues,[23] suggest that individuals should undertake personal experiments involving inquiry—for example, seeking out the perspectives of others—in order to move from one stage of development to another. Torbert has developed a framework for "action inquiry," in which managers enter into difficult conversations or conversations where perspective taking is needed. Action inquiry entails first framing the situation, then illustrating the other person's point, advocating a position, and finally (and perhaps most important) openly inquiring about the perspective, position, and rationale of the other person.[24]

Responsible companies that want to develop the cognitive capacities of their employees can use action inquiry, as well as the dialogue processes recommended by William Isaacs, in training and development programs throughout their organizations, as well as in the ways that the business itself operates.[25]

Moral Development

The second developmental arena critical to responsible enterprise is moral development. To operate responsibly and with integrity, corporations need leaders who understand how to reason from principles rather than simply assuming that "anything goes" because "it all depends." Lawrence Kohlberg, who studied moral reasoning in males, found that there is a clear link between the development of the capacity to reason abstractly at the level Piaget calls "formal operational thinking" and the capacity to think in moral terms. Moral development, in fact, depends on the development of sufficient cognitive capacity to reason in more advanced ways—that is, at least the third stage of Kegan's framework. According to Kohlberg, an individual who is at any given stage of cognitive development cannot reason morally at a higher stage of development.[26]

Kohlberg identifies six stages of moral development, two within each of the generic developmental levels discussed above. In preconventional reasoning, stage 1 individuals focus on obedience and punishment. They reason that it is wrong to break rules because rule breakers are likely to be punished. The motivation for doing the right thing at this stage is to avoid being punished or to follow the rules because higher authorities say you should, not because you recognize that there may be a better way of doing something. Stage 2, also preconventional, focuses on instrumental purpose and exchange. Individuals at this stage act morally to further their own interests, focusing on individualism, instrumental purpose, and exchange, and following rules because it is in their self-interest to do so.

In conventional levels of reasoning, individuals use a reference system for their moral guidance. For example, at stage 3, which Kohlberg calls interpersonal concordance, individuals act to meet the expectations of their immediate peers and close groups. Individuals at this stage (often teenagers) believe that what is right is what some important reference group expects, and they understand the need to develop ongoing relationships through trust, loyalty, respect, and gratitude. Stereotypes and reference to the Golden Rule ("Do unto others as you would have them do unto you") dominate this type of reasoning. The perspective is one of the individual in relationship to other individuals, with an emerging capacity to take the other's point of view. At stage 4, social concordance and system maintenance, individuals act to meet social expectations that are articulated in the laws and rules of society. At this stage individuals begin to understand the system as a whole and recognize the need for rules and obligations to keep the system healthy. They can differentiate their own point of view from that of society as a whole and can place themselves within the larger context. Most adults are at this stage of development.

Postconventional or principled reasoning is the type of reasoning most useful in today's complex, dynamic global economy, where many companies have to contend with multiple cultures and different moral frameworks. At postconventional stage 5 reasoning, individuals refer to the social contract and act to achieve social consensus and tolerance on contentious issues with system integrity in mind. Individuals at this stage are aware that people hold numerous values and opinions that are relevant to their own groups. But they also begin to recognize that some nonrelative values or principles, such as respecting human dignity, should be upheld in all circumstances. Business ethicists Thomas Donaldson and Thomas Dunfee have called such principles "hypernorms."[27] Doing right at this stage means respecting the law because the social contract exists for the benefit of all. The dominant form of ethical reasoning at this stage is utilitarian analysis, or "the greatest good for the greatest number."

The highest stage of development identified by Kohlberg is a postconventional stage in which individuals act consistently according to self-selected moral principles. At this stage, individuals emphasize universal ethical principles, following self-chosen guidelines. They recognize that the social contract is valid because it rests on valid principles such as justice, equality of human rights, and human dignity. Doing right here means living up to one's own principles. The moral point of view at this stage is that all persons should be treated not as means to some end but as ends in themselves.

Kohlberg's research has been criticized because it was conducted entirely with men. Carol Gilligan studied moral development in women (though, unfortunately for the scientific validity of her work, only in women) to see if they reasoned morally using the same principles that men use at later developmental stages. Gilligan found that, in contrast to men who reason (at the higher levels) from principles, women perceive themselves—and their moral obligations—as embedded within a network of relationships, a perception that Gilligan called an "ethic of care."[28]

Strikingly, however, the women studied went through developmental phases in their capacity to role-take that were similar to the phases Kohlberg identified for men. In the preconventional stage, women's reasoning is based on caring about self and thinking about survival; that is, they do not take the perspective of others. They begin questioning their self-emphasis as they develop a capacity to role-take, or see the perspective of others, which translates in the conventional stage into caring for others without concern for the self. The transition to postconventional reasoning is characterized by a recognition that it is illogical to care only for others without regard for self, thus precipitating a need to reconcile competing views for the good of the system as a whole. Postconventional reasoning, like other stages of postconventional development, is one in which multiple perspectives or points of view are held simultaneously, based on an understanding of the interconnectedness of those embedded in the relevant relationship web.

These findings about the moral development of women and men of course represent norms, not absolutes. The studies find that men tend to reason from principles at the higher stages of development, while women tend to reason from an ethic of care or relationships. But these tendencies do not mean that men never reason from care or that women never reason from principles, merely that the genders have tendencies in these directions.

Kohlberg's and Gilligan's work suggests that one important means of enhancing moral development is through social interaction, the opportunity for dialogue and exchange, which helps an individual gain insight into the perspective of others. Such role-taking is essential to moral development at the higher levels.[29] Role-taking is particularly important for understanding the multiple contexts and issues that stakeholders of responsible enterprises bring to managers' attention for action. But, as we shall see next, a third set of developmental capacities—based on emotional maturity—is also necessary for effective leaders.

Emotional Development

Emotional intelligence in leaders, according to Daniel Goleman, who has pioneered development of this concept, consists of five major elements. Core to a realistic sense of self is self-awareness, which allows one to reconcile decisions with one's deepest values and purposes, and provides a base of self-confidence for listening to one's conscience ("inner voice") and recognizing the right thing to do or say. Second is the ability to control impulses and manage emotions such as anger, sadness, and anxiety; these self-control skills are a core basis of integrity, conscientiousness, and trustworthiness, according to Goleman. Third is the capacity to motivate others, often through optimism, which helps change how a given situation is seen (and is related to vision). The fourth element of emotional intelligence is the ability to empathize or read emotions in others, thereby ensuring that respect for and resonance with others is present even in difficult situations. The fifth element is the ability to stay connected with oneself and with others, exhibit enthusiasm, and convey positive energy (which is contagious, as is negative energy).[30] Emotional intelligence makes it possible for leaders to engage productively and positively with stakeholders and take actions that respect stakeholders' interests, while still achieving their own interests.

Goleman documents that individuals mature emotionally as they age, though he does not use the same kind of developmental theory we have been discussing above.[31] Nonetheless, emotional intelligence (or development) is essential in working with others, as well as in gaining a realistic perspective on the self.

All of the skills of emotional intelligence are crucial to successful leaders and, ultimately, to the success of the enterprises they manage. One study suggests that intuition is related to emotional intelligence; authors Kurt Matzlon, Franz Bailon, and Todd Mooradian define intuition as a "highly complex and highly developed form of reasoning that is based on years of experience and learning, and on facts, patterns, concepts, procedures and abstractions stored in one's head."[32] Self-awareness is the key to developing a vision that is personally meaningful and, when tied with the other skills of emotional intelligence, can produce leaders with vision whose organizations have purpose and meaning that are widely shared. When people work in environments where meaning is not developed and shared, they may feel that their work is meaningless or of little value and makes no contribution to anything but their own household's subsistence (useful, of course, but not sufficient to create a meaningful life).

Managing emotions, being aware of one's environment, and having self-control provide a sense of self- or personal mastery.[33] Senge says that personal mastery involves "approaching one's life as a creative work, living life from a creative as opposed to a reactive viewpoint."[34] Individuals who can manage their own emotions are more likely to be in balance and harmony with themselves and the rest of the world, and able to express their feelings in ways that are appropriate to the circumstances.

Implementing a vision to set the context for responsible enterprise requires leaders and leadership. Effective leadership, however, depends on cognitive, moral, and emotional development. Developing and realizing a vision requires leaders to adopt the perspective of other, often neglected, stakeholders (cognitive development), demands that they understand how implementing this vision will affect those stakeholders in positive and negative ways (moral development), and involves building long-term relationships with them (emotional development).

COCA-COLA AND WATER STEWARDSHIP—FROM VISION TO REALITY

Coca-Cola is the world's leading beverage company, using in 2009/2010 about 309 billion liters of water in the production of its beverages. Not all of this water was used in the beverages that Coca-Cola sold. The company needs about 2.36 liters of water for every liter of beverages that it produces.[35] Coca Cola relies on access to adequate water resources for most of its major products. It began to recognize how seriously these resources were being depleted after it came under fire from activists for the impact of its water use on developing countries. The company has been charged with "swallowing up" local clean water in villages in India and elsewhere, adding to the complexity of attempting to manage its resources appropriately—and in the context of its attempts to manage its corporate responsibilities.[36] Not surprisingly, water sustainability is one of the key issues the company has chosen to address.

In 2006, Amit Srivastava of the Indian Resource Center made the claim that not only did Coca Cola have a "dismal record of protecting water resources," but that it also was depriving thousands of people in India of a livelihood in agriculture by using water that their communities need to sustain themselves. Srivastava noted that lack of access to clean drinking water is problematic for as much as 20 percent of the world's population (or about 1.3 billion people).[37] Other criticisms around water use also plagued the company; in March 2004, for instance, Reuters reported that Coke's premier water product, Dasani, is like many other bottled waters: nothing more than purified tap water.[38] Mere weeks later, the company was forced to recall all of its British Dasani because of contamination by potentially cancer-causing bromates.[39]

After being lambasted by such criticisms for years, in July 2007, Coca-Cola announced that it would reduce and recycle water used in production and replenish water it takes from communities and from nature.[40] This endeavor is in line with the company's stated vision and values:

Our vision . . . guides every aspect of our business by describing what we need to accomplish in order to continue achieving sustainable, quality growth.

- People: Be a great place to work where people are inspired to be the best they can be.

- Portfolio: Bring to the world a portfolio of quality beverage brands that anticipate and satisfy people's desires and needs.
- Partners: Nurture a winning network of customers and suppliers, together we can create mutual, enduring value.
- Planet: Be a responsible citizen that makes a difference by helping build and support sustainable communities.
- Profit: Maximize long-term return to shareowners while being mindful of our overall responsibilities.
- Productivity: Be a highly effective, lean and fast-moving organization. . . .

Our values serve as a compass for our actions and describe how we behave in the world.

- Leadership: The courage to shape a better future
- Collaboration: Leverage collective genius
- Integrity: Be real
- Accountability: If it is to be, it's up to me
- Passion: Committed in heart and mind
- Diversity: As inclusive as our brands
- Quality: What we do, we do well[41]

The Coca-Cola Company's vision statement is an important step toward realizing the vision of the company and living its values. Coca-Cola's "Water Conservation Pledge," which is based on a partnership with the WWF (World Wildlife Fund), is one specific way to embed vision into values and put values into reality:

Our pledge to replace the water we use has three core components: reduce, recycle and replenish.

Reduce: We will set specific water efficiency targets for global operations by 2008 to be the most efficient user of water among peer companies.

Recycle: By the end of 2010, we will return all the water that we use for manufacturing processes to the environment at a level that supports aquatic life and agriculture. At Coca-Cola, we have water treatment standards that are more stringent than many local standards and nearly 85% of our manufacturing facilities have implemented these standards, again reflecting the commitment of our bottlers to water stewardship. We are committed to 100% alignment among our manufacturing facilities with our Company's stringent water treatment standards.

Replenish: The water that leaves our plant in our finished products fulfills the basic human need for hydration. If that need were not met by our products, it would be met by other means. Our commitment to replenish means that on a global basis we will give back by supporting healthy watersheds and sustainable community water programs to balance the water used in our finished beverages. We will do this by working on a wide range of locally relevant initiatives, such as watershed protection, community water access, rainwater harvesting, reforestation, and agricultural water use efficiency.[42]

The company employs a variety of water use and efficiency measures to monitor its progress on these goals. Although the firm's 2009/2010 Sustainability Review still lists the recycling of all water used in manufacturing processes as a goal to be reached by the end of 2010 (and not as an achievement), it is clear that Coca-Cola continues to address the critical issue of water use. Like many other businesses, Coca-Cola partners with a variety of organizations (such as the United Nations Development Programme) to address water challenges in the local environments in which it operates. Coca-Cola's efforts in the context of water management demonstrate the integration of corporate responsibility with the company's value and supply chain and local needs.

DEVELOPING A VISION AND UNDERSTANDING STAKEHOLDERS

Motivating oneself means taking initiative when appropriate opportunities arise and working toward goals. Leaders need this capacity to energize themselves before they can help energize others toward pursuit of common goals. Research in cognitive psychology suggests that optimism—setting high but achievable goals—and thinking positively (i.e., visioning) can be powerful motivational tools. A feeling of self-efficacy, or the belief that one can control events in one's own life, is another key to self-motivation.

Although one would never know it from the headlines and cover stories in the business press that glamorize the tough and even abusive boss, truly successful leaders have a great capacity to empathize with others—and that capacity is essential in dealing with stakeholders and a complex external environment. Empathy means putting oneself in the place of others and understanding what they are feeling. As we noted above, the cognitive capacity to role-take is essential to developing this emotional capacity. Indeed, some research suggests that charismatic leadership is associated with three components similar to those we have been discussing: envisioning, empathy, and empowerment of others.[43]

Being a responsible enterprise today means developing positive relationships with the many stakeholders who influence or are influenced by a company's activities. Doing this well means developing the capacity to effectively manage interpersonal relationships and a willingness to share power and work collaboratively with others. Goleman says that what is really needed to humanize modern organizations and make them stakeholder-friendly is the capacity to "manage with heart."[44] Managing with heart means taking a positive—and visionary—approach to managing. It is both inspirational and aspirational and it helps inspire others to achieve. The keys to emotional health are confidence, curiosity, intentionality (wishing and having the capacity to have an impact), self-control, relatedness (an ability to engage with others), communication skills, and cooperation.[45] These are capacities that very young children who are treated well have. Such attributes are also critical in organizational life today. They can be enhanced by the development of personal vision.

Developing a personal vision—and translating it into a shared organizational vision—is one way to begin to understand what is really important in life. It is also important for building collaborative relationships with stakeholders that are based on a sense of common purpose or meaning in the enterprise. Having a sense of purpose, of what is meaningful, is one of Stephen Covey's seven habits of highly effective people, and also an essential element of what Senge calls personal mastery.[46] How, after all, can someone effectively lead an organization or group, or build effective relationships with stakeholders whose perspectives are very different, if she is unaware of herself and what she stands for? We will see in Chapter 4 how important self-knowledge is to the types of constructive values that underpin successful corporations and generate a sense of shared meaning in an organization.

Being as mature morally and emotionally as one is cognitively is an ideal to strive for, but there is ample evidence that even highly developed individuals in one area may be significantly less developed in other areas. For example, a scientist who has a highly developed cognitive capacity may still be emotionally or morally immature and therefore not always get along well with others or think through the ethical consequences of developing a new technology. Cognitive development appears to be a necessary, but not sufficient, precondition for other types of development.[47]

Highly developed cognitive, moral, and emotional capacities allow people to understand issues that stakeholders raise from other stakeholders' perspectives as well as their own. The way issues are raised has to do with the way an individual or institution frames them. Frames are the underlying structure of beliefs and perceptions.[48] All issues, policies, and perceptions are necessarily viewed through some sort of lens or frame. Understanding this reality means that one has acquired the ability to understand others' points of view. Having the reflective understanding that most of the frames that people use are tacit—that is, unarticulated rather than explicit—helps stakeholders analyze situations more incisively and find resolutions more readily when multiple frames are at play.

The consequences of a lack of cognitive, moral, or emotional maturity may include significant harm to an organization's relationship with key stakeholders and to its capacity to develop a shared sense of meaning and responsibility for its own actions. Thus:

> Leaders are individuals who achieve personal vision, work effectively in organizations to create shared meaning and constructive vision and values, and are able to reflect on and understand the perspectives of a range of stakeholders and the implications of their actions and act ethically in the circumstances.

Visionary Responsible Enterprise

In responsible companies the development of mutually beneficial relationships with stakeholders is underpinned by corporate vision and values. In their important book *Built to Last*, James Collins and Jerry Porras explain that what makes companies great is a well-conceived and shared vision.[49] This view was more recently confirmed by authors Rajendra Sisodia, David Wolfe, and Jagdish Sheth in *Firms of Endearment*, who found that companies that treat their stakeholders well, with passion and purpose, also achieve excellent results.[50]

Vision in a firm consists of an articulated core purpose, a sense of how the world will be different because of the firm's work, supported by core values that guide it over hurdles. Vision and values, which Collins and Porras call "core ideology," are combined with clear strategies for achieving "big, hairy, audacious goals" (BHAGs). In visionary companies, core ideology remains relatively immutable and stable over time, and the strategies underpinning BHAGs change as conditions warrant. Sisodia and his colleagues similarly found that companies operating with passion and purpose create multiple forms of value for their stakeholders—emotional, experiential, social, and financial—because they view doing so as a source of long-term competitive advantage.[51]

PROCTER & GAMBLE'S SUSTAINABILITY VISION

Vision gives a company's corporate responsibility efforts direction and purpose. In 2010, Procter & Gamble (P&G), the largest consumer packaged goods company in the world, gave its efforts direction by introducing its "sustainability vision." P&G's vision contains several long-term objectives designed to inspire more precise operational actions and serve as an inspirational framework for building positive stakeholder relations:

Our Long-Term Product End-Points:
- Using 100% renewable or recycled materials for all products and packaging
- Having zero consumer waste go to landfills
- Designing products that delight consumers while maximizing the conservation of nature

Our Long-Term Operational End-Points:
- Powering our plants with 100% renewable energy
- Emitting no fossil-based CO_2 or toxic emissions
- Delivering effluent water quality that is as good as or better than influent water quality with no contribution to water scarcity
- Having zero manufacturing waste go to landfills[52]

While P&G admits that parts of this vision may take decades to realize, critics have argued that some of the statements contained in the vision are near utopian (e.g., having zero customer waste go to landfill).[53] To link vision and reality, P&G has translated this vision into more precise short-term goals (e.g., powering its operations with 30 percent renewable energy by 2020) and will report progress on these goals in its annual sustainability report. The P&G story shows that visions need to have the right mix between ambitious and achievable long-term targets. Visions that are too ambitious will quickly lose credibility (or never gain it in the first place), while visions that lack ambition do not fulfill their purpose; they neither inspire nor mobilize people to initiate specific activities. Translating the vision into more specific objectives, as P&G has done, is thus important in order to fully reap the benefits of guiding a firm's corporate responsibility activities.

Interestingly, P&G's vision has a strong collaborative dimension. On the one hand, the vision was developed through extensive consultations with the company's internal and external stakeholders. Employees at all levels and from all functions were involved in the year-long development process. On the other hand, the vision sets the ground for developing more intense collaborations and partnerships with stakeholders. One partnership, for instance, aims at intensifying the relations between P&G and the World Wildlife Fund to address issues related to sustainable production and sustainable consumption. In this way, visions enable and deepen existing stakeholder relationships and also help to form new ones.

Collins and Porras identify some of the factors that have resulted in successful results for visionary companies. They say that visionary companies have successfully made the link between rhetoric and reality, closing the gap between what they say they are going to do and what they actually do in day-to-day practice. In other words, visionary companies are like individuals who are cognitively, morally, and emotionally mature; they are self-aware and self-reflective; and they are willing to acknowledge their faults and work to improve performance. Many, perhaps most, companies fail to create and implement visions and may be hard-pressed to live up to their potential for financial, market, and other measures of success. Most never achieve alignment between vision and values and their day-to-day operating practices, particularly with respect to treating stakeholders well. And as the failures of many formerly visionary companies attest, sustaining vision over long periods of time in turbulent conditions is very difficult. Responsible companies understand this reality and work hard to develop and sustain their visions.

Sisodia, Wolfe, and Sheth build on stakeholder theory to argue, based on evidence from companies, that firms that pay attention to all of their stakeholders will dramatically outperform companies that do not. They write that we live in an age of transcendence in which the search for meaning is "changing the very soul of capitalism."[54] If they are correct, companies that recognize that it is no longer "share of wallet" that matters to different stakeholders—but rather "share of heart"—are the ones that will succeed in the future. They claim that companies that can inspire emotions such as affection, joy, love, authenticity, empathy, compassion and soulfulness—in short, terms of endearment—will be the ones who succeed in today's complex and challenging environment. And they will accomplish this goal by treating all their stakeholders well, connecting with them on an emotional plane that most other companies do not.

The study's authors found that firms of endearment focus on five stakeholder groups with the acronym SPICE: Society (local and broader communities, governments, and NGOs); Partners (upstream partners like suppliers, allies, and downstream partners like distributors and retailers); Investors (both individual and institutional, as well as lenders); Customers (of all types, present, future, and past); and Employees (current, future, and past, including their families). Combined, these sets of stakeholders form a cohesive community around the company and interact with it regularly. The results of being a firm of endearment: better financial performance than companies that do not treat their stakeholders so well.

Like individuals, then, responsible corporations need to develop a shared vision through a capacity for self-awareness and reflection on the implications and consequences of their actions and decisions. This consciousness comes about through dialogue and interaction, through a sharing of assumptions and rationales, and through efforts to work collaboratively toward common goals.

Stages of Corporate Responsibility or Citizenship and Responsible Enterprise

Companies, like people, go through developmental stages associated with their corporate responsibility. Philip Mirvis and Bradley Googins have identified five stages of corporate citizenship, which like the stages of human development, are increasingly complex, integrated, and encompassing as companies develop: from elementary to engaged, innovative, integrated, and transforming.[55] The conception of corporate citizenship differs at each stage (see Table 3.1 for a summary). Unlike human development, which is relatively stable once a new level of development has been achieved, company development can regress if leadership or circumstances change for the worse, if competition dramatically increases, or if external challenges cause the company to narrow its focus.

The first stage identified by Mirvis and Googins, which they call elementary, is basically a "business as usual" stage that is aligned with the thinking of Milton Friedman discussed in the previous chapter; at this stage the corporation views its only responsibility as compliance with the law, providing jobs, paying taxes, and making money. The company focuses its strategic intent on legal compliance, and its leadership tends to be out of touch with stakeholders, paying lip service to corporate citizenship. There tend to be few if any corporate responsibility staff, and those who are present are marginalized. The posture of the company tends to be defensive, and it communicates unilaterally with stakeholders, if at all. The major challenge facing the company is establishing credibility.

As companies begin to realize that they need to pay more attention to their external environments and stakeholders, they enter the "engaged" stage. Their concept of citizenship evolves to include participation in philanthropic or charitable contributions and volunteer programs, and they may begin to focus on environmental protection through environmental management programs. Their strategic intent at this stage is to protect their "license to operate"—that is, the social contract they have entered into with society. Leaders tend to be supportive of these initiatives, which manifest themselves as public affairs management, corporate community relations, and other boundary-spanning functions. They respond to most external issues

TABLE 3.1 *Stages of Corporate Citizenship*

	Stage 1 Elementary	Stage 2 Engaged	Stage 3 Innovative	Stage 4 Integrated	Stage 5 Transforming
Citizenship concept	Jobs, profits, taxes	Philanthropy, environmental protection	Stakeholder management	Sustainability or triple bottom line	Change the game
Strategic intent	Legal compliance	License to operate	Business case	Value proposition	Market creation or social change
Leadership	Lip service, out of touch	Supporter, in the loop	Steward, on top of it	Champion, in front of it	Visionary, ahead of the pack
Structure	Marginal— staff driven	Functional ownership	Cross-functional coordination	Organizational alignment	Mainstream, business driven
Issues management	Defensive	Reactive, policies	Responsive, programs	Proactive, systems	Defining
Stakeholder relationships	Unilateral	Interactive (actively "managing" stakeholders)	Mutual influence	Partnership	Multi-organization alliances
Transparency	Flank protection	Public relations	Public reporting	Assurance	Full disclosure
Challenge	Gain credibility	Build capacity and sustain energy	Create coherence	Deepen commitment	

SOURCE: Philip Mirvis and Bradley Googins, "Stages of Corporate Citizenship," *California Management Review* 48, no. 2 (Winter 2006): 104–26. © 2006 by the Regents of the University of California. Reprinted with permission from the University of California Press.

reactively. Although Mirvis and Googins say that they may reach out to some stakeholders, for the most part companies attempt to steer the agenda and dominate or "manage" their stakeholders and the external stance of the corporation through public relations (often seen as "window dressing"). The major challenges of the engaged stage are to sustain the energy and commitment to the corporate social responsibility programs the company has developed and to build capacity.

The third stage, according to Mirvis and Googins, is the "innovative" stage, in which stakeholder relationship management begins to take center stage—that is, the company begins to recognize the importance of stakeholders to its long-term productivity and success. In this stage, the strategic intent—and a lot of the language—revolves around making the "business case" for responsible enterprise, which means trying to show how being a better corporate citizen contributes to the bottom line. Leaders begin to view themselves as stewards, for example, of the environment and the community. Boundary-spanning functions developed in the engaged stage now begin to be integrated cross-functionally and a more proactive (mutually influenced) stance begins to emerge, so that programs and approaches to external issues are more responsive. At this stage, companies may begin developing external reports about their social and environmental programs and policies, known as multiple- or triple- (environmental, social, and economic) bottom-line reports and by various other names, such as social and environmental reports. The challenge in the innovative stage is to create coherence among the programs that have evolved, as part of the business practice.

A more "integrated" stage can emerge in progressive companies following the innovation stage. Integrated companies recognize the imperative of focusing on sustainability (for the company as well as the natural and social environments) and begin to emphasize the value proposition associated with being more responsible. Companies at this stage frequently take the risk of being out in front of the responsible enterprise agenda—as General Electric is attempting to do with its "Ecomagination" program, and Wal-Mart with its sustainability initiatives. In the integration process companies attempt to structurally align their initiatives with the business model and corporate vision, working proactively and interactively with stakeholders, collaboratively across boundaries both internally and externally, and focusing on assuring external stakeholders that they are doing what they say they are doing. The challenge at the integrated stage is to deepen commitment throughout the enterprise by aligning corporate objectives with sustainability objectives.

The final stage identified by Mirvis and Googins, which few companies have yet achieved, is "transforming," which entails attempting to change the game entirely. The carpet manufacturer Interface is trying to do this with its sustainability agenda, and Unilever is trying to do it with some of its bottom-of-the-pyramid strategies. The strategic intent is to create new markets for social change. Leadership is out in front and on many issues "ahead of the pack." Responsibility issues are mainstreamed into the core of the business, with issues to some extent defining the nature and practice of the business. The organization has multiple alliances and an orientation toward full transparency. The Gap exhibited some of these game-changing qualities in 2005 when it published a multiple-bottom-line report that identified some of the problems in its supply chain; a year later Nike published a full list of its suppliers on its website. Still, few corporations have actually achieved the transforming change fully, and it is common knowledge that The Gap and Nike still have significant supply chain issues to deal with. The clarity provided by integrating business purposes with the needs and interests of society helps to guide decision-making processes and also helps a company build ways of engaging interactively with stakeholders to determine their needs and interests (rather than assuming that they already know what their needs and interests are). In this interactive mode of engagement, mutual learning and mutual change and accommodation can take place and potentially bring about a balance of interests among the three spheres of activity in human societies.

CHALLENGES OF VISIONING

Thinking about the role of individual and corporate vision in creating a world that we can all live in may be essential to building a better future. In this chapter we have looked at three types of development that leaders need to work on if they hope to create corporate visions that improve, rather than harm, societies. By consciously choosing visions that create common and inspirational purposes that focus on building a better world, leaders can begin the long-term process of working productively and interactively with stakeholders. This interaction is necessary to building the successful stakeholder relationships required in our complex world.

And to do it well, leaders need to work on knowing themselves and their own purposes—or visions. They need to build learning opportunities for themselves and others in their organizations. Only by constantly working to raise both individual and corporate awareness can individuals gain a necessary grounding of mindfulness and wisdom, necessary not just for corporate success but for the well-being of society and nature. Developing higher levels of awareness and mindfulness means taking time to reflect on the implications of decisions for the company's many stakeholders. It also means making time for dialogue with those stakeholders to ensure that their points of view are understood and incorporated into the company's plans. These activities can advance leadership development in corporations so that those businesses will be able to avoid "getting in over their heads," to use developmental psychologist Robert Kegan's term. Leaders must think systemically about their companies' actions and their own, and understand the implications of those actions on communities, employees, customers, and others who rely on and trust their companies to act in good faith.

The arguments made above suggest that it is better for companies to be interactively engaged with stakeholders in a dialogue than to be in mere compliance, and that companies should move toward integrating and ultimately transforming their relationships with society, stakeholders, and nature. Such interaction helps companies and stakeholders determine the best ways to meet their mutual needs and interests.

Progressive companies known for their responsible practices not only understand the visions and values on which their activities are built but also work toward the higher stages of interacting. In this way they both add value for relevant stakeholders and uphold the values that they have articulated and thereby doing the right thing by all stakeholders.

4 VALUES IN MANAGEMENT
PRACTICE

Operating with Integrity

The Earth Charter

We stand at a critical moment in Earth's history, a time when
humanity must choose its future. As the world becomes
increasingly interdependent and fragile, the future at once holds
great peril and great promise. To move forward we must recognize
that in the midst of a magnificent diversity of cultures and life
forms we are one human family and one Earth community
with a common destiny. We must join together to bring forth a
sustainable global society founded on respect for nature, universal
human rights, economic justice, and a culture of peace. Towards
this end, it is imperative that we, the peoples of Earth, declare our
responsibility to one another, to the greater community of life,
and to future generations. . . .
      The Earth Charter Preamble, 2000

INTEGRITY: HONESTY AND WHOLENESS

The words of the preamble to the Earth Charter suggest growing global recognition of the imperative for a common human set of values and ethics that
can lead to global system integrity—an integrity now lacking. This recognition implies the need for a new approach to the economy that sustains both
the natural environment's capacity to support human civilization and the
well-being and health of societies themselves, in addition to productive enterprise. These values would emphasize a reorientation toward integrity—system integrity as well as organizational and individual integrity. Companies
that are responsible know that an important key is operating with integrity
and avoiding the ethical scandals and responsibility problems that are plagu-
ing so many companies and whole systems today.

Responsible companies have missions, goals, and strategies that orient
them to a vision for how their activities can improve the world. This vision
needs to be underscored by core values that are clear and compelling enough

to influence company decisions and actions. Companies, especially those that are most successful over the long run, do in fact act with integrity in both good and bad times. That said, it is important to be clear about the meanings of integrity. There are two primary definitions. First is soundness of moral principle or character: honesty. People—and organizations—have integrity when they are honest. They mean what they say, they say what they mean, and their behavior is consistent with stated values. Companies with integrity work hard to live up to the principles and values they articulate; they are trustworthy, and they respect others.

The second meaning of integrity is wholeness or completeness. By this definition, integrity exists when the system is whole rather than when it is fragmented or atomized. Companies operating with this second meaning of integrity in mind recognize that they represent a system within society; they are holons, that is, both whole within themselves and also a part of a whole that is larger and more developed than themselves.[1] As wholes, companies are complete systems operating within the larger social system, whose integrity is increasingly questionable from sustainability, human security, and equity perspectives. In any system what happens in one arena influences what happens in other arenas. By implication, in a company, the way that one stakeholder is treated affects the way that stakeholder perceives and interacts with the company and has ripple effects to other stakeholders within the system. As embedded elements of larger systems, responsible companies recognize their interdependence with society and with nature. They recognize that what they do has numerous consequences, both expected and unexpected, on their stakeholders and on the company itself, as well as on society and nature.

Responsible companies that understand integrity as wholeness also know that they exist in the multiple domains of both the individual and the collective, with subjective and objective aspects to their existence. They find ways to incorporate these domains into all that they do. Organizations with integrity find ways to treat their stakeholders according to the principles and values that they have established so that they too can remain successful and healthy. They engage not only the traditional financial bottom line that has assumed so much dominance in recent years, but also the softer bottom lines associated with other stakeholders.

Values and Integrity

Values are the basis of any organization's ability to operate with integrity and responsibility. Companies that wish to operate with integrity must articulate positive and constructive values to guide their behavior. The best vision and mission statements are underpinned by what leadership theorist James Mac-Gregor Burns termed end values, while simultaneously establishing a series of modal values to guide practice.

End values describe desirable end states, or collective goals or explicit purposes, establishing standards for making choices among a set of alternatives. Thus, end values combine two meanings: goals and the standards by which those goals will be met.[2] Modal values, in contrast, define modes of conduct or, in the corporate context, managerial practice. Burns described modes as the means by which human enterprise should be conducted, although they are sometimes goals in themselves. Modal values include such things as honor, courage, civility, honesty, and fairness. Some modal values are intrinsic, in that they are ends in themselves (i.e., worth achieving simply because they are worth something), thus serving as both ends and means. Others are extrinsic or instrumental in that they help us achieve a goal or end value.[3]

Operating with integrity means consistently operating with end values clearly in mind. Operating with integrity requires leaders who are highly developed cognitively, emotionally, and morally so that they can inspire others to support and adopt the enterprise's goals. A shared set of end values helps all stakeholders in the enterprise develop their own meaning about the purposes of their work and their involvement in that work. If implemented properly, core values help stakeholders identify with the broader and higher purposes articulated by the company and sustain individual growth and development. They enhance the development of a collective spirit among stakeholders, particularly employees, who see themselves as a part of the firm.

The downside risk, of course, of having inspiring and meaningful end values that generate commitment and loyalty from employees is the risk of creating a cult. Indeed, researchers James Collins and Jerry Porras pointed out that the visionary companies they studied do indeed sometimes have cult-like cultures.[4] Organizations with too-powerful cultures can overshadow individuals in their zeal to have everyone conform to the organization's vision. Thus, in establishing the core values by which an enterprise is to be guided, leaders must consider the behavioral implications of those values. Looking specifically at the kinds of values that responsible enterprise inspires, as we do next, will help companies avoid this problem and empower their stakeholders.

VISION AND VALUES

Responsible enterprise fundamentally involves developing a constructive, positive vision that inspires and connects people to it and the enterprise. To be fully lived, the vision needs to be underpinned by a set of end values that guide policy development and implementation, as well as the stakeholder relationships on which a company is built.[5] Being a responsible corporation is not about becoming a paragon of virtue; all companies, as human systems, make mistakes, and those mistakes have consequences. Rather than aiming to be a paragon of virtue, the responsible corporation honestly commits to and engages in the ongoing and authentic struggle to live up to an aspirational vision and set of core values. This struggle is both a process and an end in itself, just as modal values can be both means (processes) and ends.

The end values embedded in an enterprise's core ideology are typically articulated in a mission, vision, or values statement and sometimes in a code of conduct. The "living up to" is done through the development and implementation of operating policies, procedures, and programs—that is, the practices that define "the way business is done here." Implementing values through managerial, employee, and other stakeholder-related practices, such as customer relations, supplier relations, or governmental relations, is ongoing: new developments and conflicts will arise as the external context changes, as new decisions are made internally, as new competitors arise, and as technology changes. Assessment and evaluation of outcomes is essential to this process, so that companies can benchmark their progress—and equally important, how far they have to go.

One key to responsible enterprise, particularly at the global level, is finding a set of core values that are both constructive and meaningful within the internal and external context of the firm, and yet resonate globally as well. Recent initiatives—the Earth Charter; the United Nations Global Compact;[6] the OECD Guidelines for Multinational Enterprise;[7] the "Protect, Respect, and

Remedy" Framework on Business and Human Rights;[8] and numerous others—reflect a growing international consensus around certain core values that relate to business practice. Responsible corporations are in the business of doing something well—and something good. Their natural tendency to economize needs to be balanced by constructive values that emphasize responsibility to society, despite the pressures to also increase profitability. Unfortunately, far too many corporate mission, vision, and values statements are left to moulder in drawers or are framed and hung on walls and then forgotten. Perhaps they go unnoticed—and not lived up to—because they have been developed without enough thought as to whether the values they embody are actually alive within the corporation, through the practices and strategies that constitute the way the organization implements its business model.

A second key to responsible enterprise at the global level is having managers, leaders, and employees who are highly personally developed cognitively, emotionally, and morally/spiritually, and can lead from that place. Individual development, when shared across an organization and incorporated into reward and other management systems, creates a climate or culture that allows for ongoing learning and expanding awareness. Learning entails becoming aware of the impacts that actions have and understanding the system dynamics that cause problems; understanding the interconnectedness among the organization, its stakeholders, and the natural environment; and growing the capacity to do what is necessary even in changing circumstances. Learning is essential to an organization that has any hope of succeeding in today's rapidly changing competitive environment.

WAL-MART: LIVING ITS VALUES?

Wal-Mart Stores Inc., the largest retailer in the world with more than 8,500 stores in fifty-five countries, is a company with two faces. Wal-Mart has a well-known strategy of driving down prices for customers to achieve its strategic intent: offering products at the lowest possible prices. It accomplishes this by pressuring its suppliers for more efficiency (i.e., economizing) and squeezing out inefficiencies in all of its operations, creating both stunning success and controversy. *Fortune* magazine has described the two faces of Wal-Mart as follows:

There is an evil company in Arkansas, some say. It's a discount store—a very, very big discount store—and it will do just about anything to get bigger. You've seen the headlines. Illegal immigrants mopping its floors. Workers locked inside overnight. A big gender discrimination suit. Wages low enough to make other companies' workers go on strike. And we know what it does to weaker suppliers and competitors. Crushing the dream of the independent proprietor—an ideal as American as Thomas Jefferson—it is the enemy of all that's good and right in our nation.

There is another big discount store in Arkansas, yet this one couldn't be more different from the first. Founded by a folksy entrepreneur whose notions of thrift, industry, and the square deal were pure Ben Franklin, this company is not a tyrant but a servant. Passing along the gains of its brilliant distribution system to consumers, its farsighted managers have done nothing less than democratize the American dream. Its low prices are spurring productivity and helping win the fight against inflation. It is America's most admired company.

Weirdest part is, both these companies are named Wal-Mart Stores, Inc.[9]

Wal-Mart has been listed by *Fortune* as one of the most admired companies in the world (it was ranked eleventh globally in 2011).[10] The company describes its own values as follows:

1. *Respect for the Individual*: We're hardworking, ordinary people who've teamed up to accomplish extraordinary things. While our backgrounds and personal beliefs are very different, we never take each other for granted. We encourage those around us to express their thoughts and ideas. We treat each other with dignity. This is the most basic way we show respect.

2. *Service to our Customers*: Our customers are the reason we're in business, so we should treat them that way. We offer quality merchandise at the lowest prices, and we do it with the best customer service possible. We look for every opportunity where we can exceed our customers' expectations. That's when we're at our very best.

3. *Striving for Excellence*: We're proud of our accomplishments but never satisfied. We constantly reach further to bring new ideas and goals to life. We model ourselves after Sam Walton, who was never satisfied until prices were as low as they could be or a product's quality was as high as customers deserved and expected. We always ask: Is this the best I can do? This demonstrates the passion we have for our business, for our customers and for our communities.[11]

While these values emphasize the company's positive relations with its stakeholders (in particular customers and local communities), critics say that there is not much to admire about this company. Yale University's Jeffrey Garten wrote in *BusinessWeek* that Wal-Mart stores leave the "local community with empty structures and huge shortfalls in public revenues."[12] Many downtowns have been decimated when locally owned and managed stores had to fold because they were unable to compete against Wal-Mart's efficiency machine.

Wal-Mart also faces criticism from labor and human rights activists for its sourcing practices. In 1997 the NLC exposed Wal-Mart's labor violations in Central America with respect to products that carried the name of television celebrity Kathie Lee Gifford. The real issue highlighted by the NLC report, in some respects, is the difficulty of uncovering even dramatic worker exploitation and mistreatment. The company also faced a major sex-discrimination class action suit alleging systematic mistreatment of its female employees. Among other charges, the suit claimed that Wal-Mart pays women less than men in the same jobs, prevents them from advancing by denying them training, and prevents them from applying for management positions by failing to post them. Bolstering the charges was the allegation that women were not adequately represented in management positions (e.g., store managers). Although the class action suit was thrown out by the Supreme Court in 2011, largely because the women could not point to a discriminatory policy affecting all of them, the decision still allows for smaller lawsuits based on discriminatory practices in single stores.[13]

All of these complexities led Jeffrey Garten to query: "If Wal-Mart succeeds with its low-price-at-any cost strategy, what kind of message does this send about the ability of U.S. companies to be good corporate citizens? What kind of backlash against international trade and investment would it eventually provoke?"[14]

ENTERPRISE STRATEGY: WHAT DO WE STAND FOR?

Responsible corporations, in articulating their values and their fundamental purposes in society, clearly indicate what they stand for. A company whose values are alive lets all its members know what those values are, and how (and how well) they are being implemented. Such values become a critical part of what authors R. Edward Freeman and Dan Gilbert called "enterprise strategy," in which the organization and the individuals within it ask the fundamental question, "What do we stand for?"[15] Freeman and Gilbert suggest that companies should simultaneously ask this question along with the fundamental strategy question, "What business are we in?"

The answers to these questions will identify the values that should become an integral (integrated) part of the practice of daily management. Rather than merely being added on to practices that already exist, these core values are an essential aspect of the company's practices: they are the system that the company develops to operationalize its vision, implement its values, and act with integrity. The enterprise strategy question focuses on how the company and its participating stakeholders will operate and treat each other as they conduct their business. By articulating and implementing core values through their day-to-day operating practices, particularly those that support a systemic and integrated management approach, companies can help create a meaningful context for stakeholders and build a values base into their strategies and operating practices.

Business success is built on constructive values that generate a sense of community and a context of meaning within the corporation. Corporations are more than profit-generating machines: to succeed, they require community, integrity, and the trust of stakeholders. They also require the production of a good or a service that people believe is valuable enough to purchase. Businesses are also social actors with effects on numerous types of stakeholders and the natural environment, and hence on the communities and governments with which they interact. To think otherwise is simply short-sighted and ignores the fact that companies exist in societies, which depend on them for jobs, tax payments, and key elements of the social structure.[16]

Freeman and Gilbert argue that one possible outcome of fully implementing an enterprise strategy would be to allow individual employees to pursue personal projects within the context of their jobs. They would work on a personal goal while simultaneously operating in the context of a community within a corporation, assuming that the project did not interfere with the rights and dignity of others or detract from the achievement of the company's purposes. If a company is generating an inspirational vision and corresponding set of values, then stakeholders, particularly employees, might find ways to pursue their own personal projects in the context of the company's goals.

VALUES THAT ENHANCE INTERNAL OPERATIONS

Business scholars and managers alike have developed management techniques to help organizations succeed in the turbulent global arena. Starting with the participative management theories of the 1970s, and including more recent corporate innovations—such as collaboration, strategic thinking, re-engineering, total quality management, and the learning organization—corporations have adopted new approaches to managing in their quest for ever better performance.[17]

Management scholar Jeanne Liedtka writes that many well-known management concepts have a common set of values that, if fully implemented (always the sticking point), would constitute a progressive and constructive "ethic of practice." These common values allow companies to develop unique and individual strategies to compete effectively, while treating internal stakeholders fairly.[18] Work by Collins and Porras and by Sisodia and co-authors supports Liedtka's argument that these companies' success is a function of their capacity to sustain and implement their visions and associated core values. Visionary companies have both sustaining and relatively immutable core ideologies, comprising vision and values, combined with vivid descriptions that bring the strategies to life as the situation warrants.[19]

Liedtka, drawing on the work of Alisdair MacIntyre,[20] defined the essential elements of a practice. A practice is (1) a cooperative human activity, (2) with intrinsic goods or outcomes related to the performance of the activity itself, (3) and a striving toward excellence both in the ends and the means, providing (4) a sense of ongoing extension and transformation of goals.[21]

We are all familiar with the management fads that many companies have adopted over the years in an effort to improve performance.[22] Fads are for managers unwilling to look deeply within and make serious transformational, or systemic, changes across the whole enterprise. Using the ideas espoused by Peter Senge (the learning organization),[23] W. Edwards Deming (total quality management),[24] and Michael Hammer and James Champy (reengineering),[25] Liedtka argues that successful approaches to improving organizational performance are best applied systemically—that is, throughout the enterprise—as a means of transforming the entire enterprise in order to achieve the goals of economizing, while living within nature's constraints.[26] When a new approach is simply laid over an existing management system, elements like organizational structure, rewards, culture, and power relationships can and usually do remain essentially unchanged. Liedtka's insight is that the values-based management approaches she studied are founded on values that would allow for transformational change that could foster responsible enterprise if fully implemented. Any one of these approaches, applied systemically by embedding it fully into the operating practices of the firm, would very likely improve performance. Table 4.1 illustrates the values common to these approaches.

The first value common to the values-based management practices is creating shared meaning. The effort to create a shared meaning, and its accompanying vision, links the individual to the organization. Meaning and vision tap into the soft (and even spiritually significant) side of business. It is the inspiration provided by vision and related values that can make working in an organization not just a job, but a calling.[27] Meaning-making focuses on people's needs to identify with an organization, to find personal meaning (or personal projects that allow individuals to develop their own work-related meanings)[28] in the larger context of doing something to make the world a better place, which arguably all individuals desire.[29] Of course, as anyone who has ever managed knows, the so-called soft stuff is really the hard stuff. Bringing the systemic and meaning-making elements of management into reality is among the hardest—and most important—managerial tasks.

The second common value is developing a systems perspective among organizational members, highlighting the place of the individual or group within the larger system. This perspective helps participants see the system as a whole and from the perspective of different stakeholders. This capacity, which Mintzberg calls strategic thinking and Senge calls systems thinking, is a critical element of creating a stakeholder-friendly environment, and developing the capacity for it is a major focus of this book.[30]

TABLE 4.1 *Values-Based Management Practices in Systems Approaches to Managing*

Convergent Themes	*Values-Based Business Practices*
Create a shared sense of meaning, vision, and purpose that connects the personal to the organizational.	• Values community without subordinating the individual. • Sees community purpose as flowing from individuals.
Develop a systems perspective, views individuals hold of themselves are embedded within a larger system.	• Seeks to serve other community members and ecosystem partners.
Emphasize business processes rather than hierarchy or structure.	• Believes work itself has intrinsic value. • Believes in quality of both ends and means.
Localize decision-making around work processes.	• Emphasizes responsibility for actions. • Gives primacy to reach, with needed support.
Leverage information within the system.	• Values truth telling (honesty, integrity). • Provides full access to accurate and complete information.
Focus on development, at both personal and organizational levels.	• Values the individual as an end. • Focuses on learning and growth, at both individual and organizational levels.
Encourage dialogue.	• Allows freedom and responsibility to speak and to listen. • Encourages commitment to find higher ground through exchange of diverse views.
Foster the capacity to take multiple perspectives simultaneously.	• Strives to understand and work with the perspectives of others, rather than imposing own views.
Create a sense of commitment and ownership.	• Emphasizes promise keeping. • Instills a sense of urgency. • Encourages engagement rather than detachment.

SOURCE: Jeanne Liedtka, "Constructing an Ethic for Business Practice: Competing Effectively and Doing Good," *Business and Society* 36, no. 3 (September 1998): 254–80, © 1998 (SAGE). Reprinted with permission from SAGE Publications.

The third commonality is that these theories all emphasize processes rather than hierarchy or structure. Process approaches allow for continuous learning, growth, and development, which is necessary because organizational and social change are themselves continuous.[31] Companies that value processes as well as products or outcomes do not tend to get stuck on issues of power and politics and can move forward when circumstances warrant without being threatened by the process of change itself. As Liedtka noted, such a system requires—and develops—a sense of commitment and ownership among members of the organization, and sometimes even engages external stakeholders interactively.

Localizing decision-making around work processes allows for participants in an organization to "own" their work and its associated outcomes. Ownership fosters pride in a job well done, as well as organizational commitment, loyalty, and a sense of place or belonging, which are essential components of community and spirit.[32] Leveraging information within the system is particularly important in today's knowledge-based enterprises, where knowledge is a, if not the, critical source of competitive advantage.[33] If organizations are to change continually, if individuals are to grow within them, and if stakeholder relationships are to be developed positively, then all must share information honestly and with integrity.

Paying constant attention to personal and organizational development is another values-based practice in management. Only if people—and the organizations they operate within—can achieve higher levels of development will they be able to engage in the difficult struggle that implementing these values systemically entails. Only then can they continue to adapt and change in their complex environments.

Both external and internal stakeholders continually pressure companies to perform better for a variety of reasons, in part because organizations are human systems imbued with human failings. Stakeholder dialogue helps create "good conversations" that can result in new solutions to intractable problems, unearth ethical issues that might otherwise go unnoticed, and create innovations that help everyone involved.[34] In general, good conversations or stakeholder engagements make room for the articulation of assumptions, the discussion of issues that might otherwise be undiscussable,[35] and help move understanding toward what Buddhists call third-way thinking—that is, new understandings that evolve in dialectical fashion from preexisting understandings of participants in the conversation. The capacity to understand multiple perspectives, another common characteristic of the systems Liedtka discussed, is essential to generating such new understandings and innovative potential.

Openness is the key to encouraging dialogue. In an open conversation, people are free to speak their minds and are also willing to challenge their own thinking. With openness comes the potential for new ideas, innovations, and new relationships that create entirely new possibilities for the organization. Combined with a capacity to make decisions locally, especially decisions that affect employees' own work, openness generates, finally, a sense of ownership and commitment to the enterprise.

Together the themes and practices listed in Table 4.1 create an internal management system with integrity in all meanings of the word. Such a systemic approach, properly implemented through values-based managerial practices, provides a basis for the articulation of enterprise strategy. In other words, it answers the "What do we stand for?" question. As we discuss in the next section, the rise of global enterprise has made understanding common values across cultures an imperative for both external relations and internal practices.

GLOBAL VALUES THAT ENHANCE INTEGRITY

To cope successfully with external stakeholders in other sectors and other parts of the world, companies need to understand the values that are held in common across cultures.[36] Responsible companies need to endeavor to live up to "foundational values" in the global arena as well as at home. The concept of foundational values—called "hypernorms" by business ethicists Thomas Donaldson and Thomas Dunfee—suggests that, contrary to what some people believe, ethics are not all relative to one's culture or belief system.[37] In fact, Donaldson and Dunfee say that businesses exist in society because of a basic social contract, underlying which there are some core principles common across the world's many belief systems and cultures.

Foundational values or hypernorms are manifest in international documents and treaties, especially those generated by the United Nations, which holds a special place in the world as a global authority (with currently 193 member states)—and also a moral authority, because so many nations have signed such a large number of treaties, signaling nearly universal agreement. Hypernorms "entail principles so fundamental to human existence that they serve as a guide in evaluating lower level moral norms."[38] As demands for greater accountability and responsibility grow, corporations are increasingly being held accountable for the implementation of such agreements and foundational values.[39]

Foundational values are built on the need for system integrity, trust, and mutual respect. According to Donaldson and Dunfee, three basic principles of respect are useful in determining foundational values: respect for core human values, including the absolute moral threshold for business activities; respect for local traditions; and respect for the belief that context matters in deciding right and wrong.[40] These guiding principles result in three core values: "human dignity; basic rights; and good citizenship (working together to support and improve institutions on which the community depends."[41]

In the global community, several major treaties form the basis of a guiding set of principles articulated in 1999 by Kofi Annan, former Secretary-General of the United Nations, in the UN Global Compact. The Global Compact represents an agreement between the UN and businesses to live up to ten core principles. Drawn from documents such as the UN Universal Declaration on Human Rights; selected core conventions of the International Labour Organization (ILO); the 1992 Rio agreement, called Agenda 21; and the UN Convention Against Corruption, these ten principles cover human rights, labor rights, environmental sustainability, and anti-corruption. As of July 2011, nearly 8,700 organizations, mostly corporations, had signed on to the Global Compact.

The UN Global Compact's human rights dimension includes rights to freedom of physical movement, ownership of property, freedom from torture, a fair trial, nondiscriminatory treatment, physical security, freedom of speech and association, minimal education, political participation, and subsistence.[42] Labor standards in the UN Global Compact include just and favorable working conditions, requirements against child labor, nondiscrimination in the payment of wages and the right to equal pay for equal work, freedom from forced labor, and freedom of association (e.g., to form a union and bargain collectively).[43] All of these values can be found in the ILO's core conventions, signed by most nations of the world.

The ecological sphere of the UN Global Compact is, of course, guided by the fundamental principle of sustainability or "ecologizing": what is waste in one system is food in another.[44] The UN's Agenda 21 emphasizes the following foundational values: taking a precautionary or preventive approach to environmental challenges (i.e., being cautious even when the scientific evidence does not yet fully confirm that something is problematic); responsible and ethical management of products and processes; and development and diffusion of environmentally sound technologies.

A tenth principle, which was added in 2004, emphasizes the problems related to corruption and shows the relevance of the anti-corruption work of Transparency International (TI). TI was founded in 1993 to fight corruption internationally, and issues an annual country-based corruption perception index. It is also important to note that in 2003 the Organization for Economic Cooperation and Development (OECD) Convention on Combating Bribery of Foreign Officials in International Business Transactions was ratified by thirty-four signatory countries, which together account for three-fourths of global trade. It was this treaty that made possible the tenth anti-corruption principle of the UN Global Compact.

GOOGLE'S "DON'T BE EVIL" DILEMMA

Internet search engine and high-tech giant Google has come under considerable fire for what some see as a violation of its own core value: "Don't be evil." In early 2006, Google announced that it would censor the Chinese version of its search engine by blocking content the Chinese government found objectionable.[45] Google's history in China had already been somewhat rocky. By 2002, Google had achieved a 25 percent share of the Chinese search engine market, but then on September 3, 2002, Google disappeared. The Chinese government, which until then had been reluctant to ban the website because of its popularity, blocked all Google searches in what became known as "The Great Firewall of China."

What caused this swift crackdown? According to some, including various American Internet executives, a competitor of Google may have decided to take advantage of covert government intervention, and many point the finger at Baidu, a Chinese search engine, although the claim has never been substantiated. Baidu, which at this writing has approximately 75 percent of the search market, had a mere 3 percent of the Chinese search market at the time of the Chinese government's crackdown on Google. Baidu denies that it had anything to do with the ban on Google, and attributes its success to the fact that it, as a Chinese company, can better understand the Chinese market.

Whatever the truth, Google's situation demonstrates the intricate web of possibilities that companies must deal with in the Chinese search engine market. Faced with the choice of providing intermittent and precarious service or cooperating with the Chinese censorship authorities, Google decided to create a Chinese version of Google, "Guge." Andrew McLaughlin, who is senior policy counsel at Google, wrote:

> This problem [of poor service] could only be resolved by creating a local presence, and this week we did so, by launching Google.cn, our website for the People's Republic of China. In order to do so, we have agreed to remove certain sensitive information from our search results. We know that many people are upset about this decision, and frankly, we understand their point of view. This wasn't an easy choice, but in the end, we believe the course of action we've chosen will prove to be the right one. . . . For several years, we've debated whether entering the Chinese market at this point in history could be consistent with our mission and values. . . . We ultimately reached our decision by asking ourselves which course would most effectively further Google's mission to organize the world's information and make it universally useful and accessible. Or, put simply: "How can we provide the greatest access to information to the greatest number of people?" . . . Filtering our search results clearly compromises our mission. Failing to offer Google search at all to a fifth of the world's population, however, does so far more severely.[46]

Other high-tech companies faced similar problems in China. Yahoo! surrendered information on at least two e-mail customers who were later jailed for disclosing state secrets. Microsoft, another major player in China, has also agreed to censor individual blogs at Beijing's behest. Human Rights Watch lambasted all three firms, maintaining that if they were to collectively boycott the China market they would have enough leverage to dissuade the Chinese government from its censorship policies. However, it remains contested how much power companies like

Google, Yahoo!, and Microsoft really possess in China (especially considering the rapidly growing domestic competition).

In early 2010, after Gmail accounts of Chinese human rights activists were hacked, Google announced that it would no longer censor search results. Even though Google did not directly blame the Chinese government in this attack, the company started to redirect all search queries coming from Mainland China to its Hong Kong–based server (Hong Kong is not subject to most Chinese laws, including censorship laws). A few days later, the Chinese government banned all Google search sites from Mainland China. Although the ban was lifted after about twenty-four hours, the incident clearly showed the power of the Chinese government in regulating the Internet. A few weeks later Google decided to stop its automatic redirection to its Hong Kong–based server (but instead placed a link to its Hong Kong–based site on Google.cn). One reason Google changed direction was that it feared having its Internet Content Provider (ICP) license revoked. Google's ICP license was renewed in July 2011.

STAKEHOLDER RELATIONSHIPS AS PRACTICE: IMPLEMENTING CONSTRUCTIVE VALUES

Responsible enterprise, when handled holistically, integrates the needs and interests of all of its stakeholders into the core purposes of a company and engages their commitment through the ongoing strategies and practices core to managing the enterprise. These practices can positively influence the traditional bottom-line indicators related to financial performance. They also engage the spirit and hearts of stakeholders in constructive ways that help to build a positive and proactive corporate culture and set of operating practices. That is, they integrate the whole person.

Embedded within the implementation of practices is the "both/and" logic that Collins and Porras discovered in visionary companies, and that Sisodia and his colleagues later found to be true of their "firms of endearment."[47] Responsible corporations value both individuals and communities, both internally and externally; they are both profitable and values-driven. Similarly, individuals embedded in such systems show strong evidence of reciprocity rather than one-sided self-interest.

By focusing on business processes, rather than simply products or outcomes, visionary companies and their managers signal to employees that the nature of the work has inherent or intrinsic value. People in visionary companies tend to be motivated by the nature of the work and the achievement of the core purpose, and only partially by extrinsic factors such as money or other rewards.

Key ethical practices associated with the common themes are respect and human dignity. These ideas can be operationalized as valuing the individual as an end rather than as a means to an end, which the philosopher Immanuel Kant proposed as the foundation for ethical behavior; that is, one should always value human beings as ends in themselves, not as mere instruments for achieving other ends.[48] If companies take this practice and the values that underpin it seriously, then they will treat all of the people who interact with them, in whatever capacity, with dignity and respect. This respect extends to customers, who deserve good products that serve useful and necessary purposes. It also extends to employees, including laborers in less-developed countries who, though national standards may differ, deserve fair wages, labor rights, and adequate and safe working conditions. (We return to this aspect of stakeholder relationships later in the book when we discuss corporate relationships with different stakeholder groups.)

Other aspects of generating integrity within firms include fostering higher levels of human and organizational development. Highly developed firms can encourage freedom and responsibility because they know that engaged stakeholders are committed to the purposes of the firm and will work to achieve them. They also encourage freedom of speech and association (fundamental labor rights according to the International Labour Organization) and the responsibility to listen and speak out when things go wrong (as well as when things go right, so that they are noted and appreciated). The capacity to take multiple perspectives demands a postconventional level of cognitive and moral development. Companies pursuing the path of integrity foster such development among employees, managers, and other stakeholders. They are not threatened by the questioning of assumptions, the need to take full responsibility for their actions, or demands for accountability. Such responsibility is the basis for solid long-term organizational performance.

Responsibility at all levels—individual, group, and whole organization—is characteristic of the responsible corporation. If companies expect employees, for example, to be responsible for entrepreneurial and innovative efforts within their own domains, as many do these days, then they need to foster a supportive environment for doing so. Supportive actions would include devolving responsibility to the appropriate level where action can be taken, providing access to complete and accurate information, being consistent in word and deed (being honest, keeping promises), and remaining engaged in the work of the enterprise. Further, the reward system must support the behaviors that are desired—because behaviors that are rewarded are often the ones that happen!

Such enterprises are likely to foster an emotional commitment, a loyalty, and sense of connection and community among stakeholders. Thus, one implication of fully implementing the type of system that generates corporate integrity is that such companies are willing to acknowledge the importance of human, or soft, investments as well as the more objectively measurable results.

LIVING VALUES AND NEGOTIATING DILEMMAS

The combination of the enterprise strategy question, "What do we stand for?" with the articulation and implementation of values helps companies to step back from problematic situations and ask another important question. That question is not just "What can we do?"—which really asks what can feasibly be accomplished—but more fundamentally, "What should we do?"

Not all situations facing companies are easy to resolve ethically. Managers often face ethical dilemmas—that is, problems for which there is no clear or ready answer and for which any decision will create tension or conflict. A dilemma, by its very nature, is a challenge to the decision maker. How can individuals and organizations operate with integrity in the face of such dilemmas? If the decision maker—and the organization in which he or she works—has no guiding principles or values, then decision-making is even tougher. Guiding principles "guide" when decision makers face dilemmas, and they help the company get back on track when mistakes are made, as they inevitably will be.

One way to resolve a dilemma is to reframe it so that it is not an either/or proposition with negative consequences. Managers should strive to see whether, using "third-way thinking," they can formulate a win-win proposition. Sometimes a both/and or a win-win proposition can be developed by moving the thinking up one level of analysis from where the problem seems to reside. At other times, the difficult decision has to be made despite the dilemma.

When one is confronted with an ethical dilemma, it is not always sufficient to use only one type of reasoning. For such situations business ethicists Gerald F. Cavanagh, Manuel Velasquez, and Dennis Moberg have provided a helpful framework based on four major philosophical traditions in ethics.[49] Although complexity remains, the best ethical decision can be made by using all four of the following bases for ethical decision making: the norm of rights and duties, the norm of justice, the norm of utilitarianism (or the greatest good for the greatest number), and the norm of caring.

Rights and Duties

Rights are important, normative, justifiable claims or entitlements. Rights derive from the basic premise that each person is unique and deserving of human dignity. Individuals have a moral right to pursue their own interests, as well as corresponding duties, obligations, requirements, or prohibitions. Legal rights are those written into specific laws, judicial decisions, or a constitution.[50]

In the United States, for example, the Bill of Rights (the first ten amendments to the Constitution) spells out what are considered to be the essential rights of a U.S. citizen, including freedom of speech and freedom of religion. In the international arena, the International Labour Organization has spelled out rights and principles for individuals at work that include freedom of association (i.e., freedom to practice collective bargaining), freedom from forced labor, the abolition of child labor, and freedom from discrimination in labor. Most nations of the world have agreed to uphold these rights.

If we think of rights as one side of a coin, then we know that there is another side: duties or obligations. All rights come with a set of corresponding duties that need to be upheld if the right itself is to be sustained and societies are to be kept healthy. One question to ask when faced with a moral dilemma, then, is "Does this act respect the rights and the duties of the individuals involved?"

Justice

In addition to considering whether rights are abrogated or supported in making a decision, the decision maker must consider the implications of the decision for justice. Justice requires that people be guided by fairness, equity, and impartiality, emphasizing in particular a fair distribution of societal benefits and burdens, fairness in the administration of laws and regulations, and fairness in sanctioning wrongdoing or compensating for wrongs suffered.[51]

Standards of justice, for example, prohibit discrimination and enormous inequalities in the distribution of goods and services within a society. Justice speaks to the issue of what philosopher John Rawls called "distributive justice," which has as its fundamental principle that "equals should be treated equally and that unequals should be treated in accord with their inequality."[52] Rawls also said that societies and the distribution of goods and services within them should be constructed using a "veil of ignorance." That is, when we are responsible for a decision that will affect a system, we should make that decision as if we did not know where in the system we would end up. By doing this, we will make a decision that is fairest to all and allows us to overcome our own biases.

A second question to ask in the face of a moral dilemma is: Is this decision consistent with the canons of justice? Would I make the same decision if I could end up anywhere in the system after its impact has been felt?[53]

Utilitarianism

The third basis for addressing ethical dilemmas is called utilitarianism, which is usually expressed as "the greatest good for the greatest number." Utilitarianism, which is the reasoning used in systems of cost-benefit analysis, is the most common kind of managerial reasoning. It does not necessarily mean that majority rules but rather that the harms and benefits of an action need to be considered from all perspectives. Making a decision requires calculating the degree of both harm and benefit that would result. Utilitarian outcomes need to be considered along with both justice and rights.

The concept of the greatest good for the greatest number, while difficult to operationalize quantitatively, proposes that the best action is the one that results in the best overall good—that is, the best outcome for the most people affected by that decision. Thus, when weighing a decision that has both positive consequences for some groups and negative ones for others, it is important to consider where the most good can be accomplished as well as where the most harm will be done. Decision makers need to weigh such considerations as how many people will be affected either positively or negatively, and the extent of the good or the harm done to each group (assuming these can be known in advance and quantified, which are two of the problems with utilitarian analysis).

So, a third question to ask in dealing with ethical dilemmas is: Who will be harmed or benefit from this decision, and how much?

Caring

As noted earlier, research suggests that women's moral development may proceed somewhat differently than men's and that women (as well as many men) may use a different basis for making ethical judgments than the principles of rights, justice, or utility. Women are, according to Carol Gilligan, Mary Belenky and colleagues, among others, focused more explicitly on what has been termed an ethic of care.[54] In business situations, as well as in life situations according to this ethic, emphasis on principles can be balanced effectively by considering how the decision will affect people and the relationships among them.

The ethic of care argues that we exist within a network of relationships that are affected by the implications of ethical decisions. In making decisions according to an ethic of care, we consider the effects on those relationships and the people who are in the network. As Cavanagh points out, the definition of care is left somewhat vague in feminist ethicists' writings, but one can think of caring as an obligation that varies according to the closeness of the relationship and the particular roles embedded in the relationship. That is, a mother has a clear and strong obligation to care for her child, whereas she has less of an obligation to care for an acquaintance. The obligation to care also exists only in accordance with one's capacity to give it.

It is interesting to note that an ethic of care seems to be more common in countries that have a more collectivist—or communitarian—orientation than in individualistic countries like the United States. Thus, in business situations in Japan and Korea, for example, this ethic seems to be foundational for extended networks of companies, known as keiretsu in Japan and chaebol in Korea, that share mutual obligations to help and support each other before doing business with "outsiders." Indeed, in some Asian countries, the concepts of rights, justice, and utilitarianism as the basis of ethical thinking might seem strange indeed; the far more important consideration would be the impact of any given decision on important relationships.

Thus, an ethic of care suggests that when weighing a decision one needs to ask, "How will this affect the people that I care about?" in addition to the other questions and, from a virtue ethics or character perspective, "What does this decision say about me as a person (or as an organization)?"

RESPONSIBLE MANAGEMENT AND CULTURAL DIFFERENCES

Cultural differences also influence how companies can and do operate responsibly in different nations around the world. These differences, of course, complicate an analysis of the ethics of a given situation; however, understanding the bases of some of these differences makes doing business somewhat easier. Many of the models of responsible enterprise have been developed in the United States or Western Europe. Businesses in China, India, and Japan, and in many Latin American companies, tend to view their responsibilities less in the more fragmented ways that are popular in the United States, and more holistically through an implicit stakeholder or relational lens. In other words, some companies tend to view their responsibilities as part and parcel of the way they do business day-to-day, the way they treat customers and employees, and how they relate to their government and the public interest as defined by government.[55]

Operating responsibly and with integrity in different cultures means understanding important differences that exist in different contexts. Responsible companies need to understand these differences. Readily recognizable, of course, are differences in language, including different structures, vocabularies, and word meaning.[56] Other relevant differences, discussed by Mary

O'Hara Devereaux and Robert Johansen in their book *GlobalWork*, are differences in context, perceptions of time, equality/power, and information flow. These differences can lead to misunderstandings even between individuals who view themselves as operating with integrity within their own cultures and contexts.

What sociologists call context involves the elements that surround and give meaning to communication. People in low-context cultures, such as the United States, Germany, and the Scandinavian nations, rely largely on objective communication (i.e., the words or physical gestures). In contrast, people in high-context cultures, such as Japan, China, and Mexico and many countries in the global South, take their cues about meaning as much from the situation and the relationships of all the people involved as from the words themselves. That is, the meaning of words is affected by the context in which they are said.

Relationships are significantly more important in high-context cultures than they are in low-context cultures. It takes longer to develop business opportunities in, say, China or Japan, than in the United States. For U.S. executives, having a written contract may be enough to establish an alliance that can successfully operate in a way that pleases both partners. In many Asian countries, however, long-term relationships are essential to building trust, connection, and a shared sense of what is needed to make the alliance work. Anyone trying to establish a contract in a first meeting would be likely to be viewed as untrustworthy—operating without having established the necessary context of a relationship and therefore without integrity.

Other cultural differences can be found in the perception of time. Some cultures are essentially monochronic: people pursue one event, action, or activity at a time. Others are polychronic: people may pursue multiple activities simultaneously. For people in polychronic cultures, time is a state of being and activities are viewed as cyclical and iterative, while people in monochronic cultures view time as a scarce resource to be measured and managed carefully. Thus, for a monochronic U.S. manager, dealing with one customer at a time means treating him or her respectfully and with integrity. In contrast, a polychronic Mexican manager or employee dealing with a customer from the same culture would be surprised if a customer were insulted because the manager was answering the phone, writing out a second customer's order, and simultaneously waiting on a third customer. Handling multiple activities at once is what is expected in Mexico.

Cultures also differ in the ways people handle power and equality across organizational and social levels. In the United States and Northern Europe people assume a lower "power distance" and are relatively accepting of the idea that all people are created equal (at least in principle). Most nations of the world, however, have more hierarchical power relationships; they accept inequalities and hierarchical arrangements more readily, including uneven application of rules, as a way of life. Misunderstanding these differences in the way power is handled and how people are treated can lead to conflicts and concerns over whether corporations operating cross-culturally are living up to their values or operating with integrity.

Cultural differences related to information flow are also important—specifically, whether information is sequenced or looped in more cyclical fashion. Generally speaking, businesspeople in low-context cultures like the United States tend to get straight to the point. Information flow involves both the path and speed of communication, which U.S. managers like to be both direct and speedy. Managers from high-context cultures, where relationships affect business conduct, and in polychronic cultures where time is viewed more cyclically and less linearly, tend to see information as looped and connected with processes that are not directly relevant to a given transaction.

Of course, these descriptions of cultural differences are not absolutes. Being informed about them can be of great use when analyzing how a national culture might influence a corporate responsibility problem. It should be noted, however, that studies of cross-cultural behavior rest on comparisons of national averages; they do not take account of individual behaviors or subcultures within a country or region.

OPERATING RESPONSIBLY WITH INTEGRITY

Companies (and individuals!) must have a clear and inspiring vision embedded with positive values if they hope to operate with integrity. The challenges of operating with integrity are many, and leaders need to develop personal awareness and mindfulness of the impacts of their decisions on other stakeholders. These challenges go beyond simple bottom-line benefits and speak to the moral issue of operating with integrity. Robert Reich, among others, has identified how hard it is for companies to serve social and profitability purposes simultaneously. Given the emerging notion that the fundamental purpose of the corporation may need to be rethought to better meet 21st-century needs, it seems that the integrity imperative is more important than ever and another important facet of building responsible enterprises.[57]

Mindfulness demands personal presence.[58] Leaders must recognize that the same person who makes business decisions is the one they must face in the mirror in the morning. There can be no disconnect between business judgments and personal integrity if managers are aware, conscientious, and ethical. And, of course, common sense is paramount, especially in applying the simple test of "What would I do if I knew this decision were going to be broadcast on TV tomorrow?" At the same time, while it is important to base decisions that affect stakeholders on principles, responsible companies need to take into account culturally based attitudes toward time, relationships, and information, or problems will multiply needlessly.

5 VALUE ADDED

The Impact of Vision and Values

> Our understanding of both investment and return is founded
> upon a traditional separation in the creation of social versus
> economic value. It is logical. It is the common understanding of
> the world. It is also inherently wrong. . . .
>   The buzzing in our ears is the Zero-Sum Dissonance of a
> traditional artificial market that only considers and values
> financial returns . . . In truth, the core nature of investment and
> return is not a trade-off between social and financial interest but
> rather the pursuit of an embedded value proposition composed of
> both.
>
>   Jed Emerson, "The Blended Value Proposition: Integrating Social and
>   Financial Returns"[1]

VALUE ADDED

Companies are in the business of adding value through their economizing efforts and through the productive activities they undertake and the goods and services they provide. Most of the time we measure that value as financial value or shareholder wealth; however, recent attention to what is called the triple bottom line of economic, social, and ecological returns (sometimes framed as ecological, social, and governance, or ESG, returns) has highlighted the reality that there is more than one type of value—and that multiple values contribute to the generation of value added.[2] It is the merging of these values that Jed Emerson calls the blended value proposition.[3]

There is a close relationship in the responsible corporation between good stakeholder-related practices, environmental sustainability, social cohesion and equity, and value added. Together they represent a blended value orientation to performance. In addition, there is a growing societal need for companies to consider the full costs of doing business from what some observers call "cradle to cradle" (that is, regenerative, rather than from cradle to grave, which implies waste and loss).[4] Further, there is significant risk and waste involved in problematic stakeholder relationships and environmental practices, not just the obvious ones that are typically measured. All of these factors indicate the need for a new approach—the value-added approach—to assessing company performance.

Indeed, the combined impact of the global financial crisis of 2008 and the prospect of a significant sustainability crisis has made clear the limitations of some of our current ways of measuring economic activity, value added, and progress, both at the company level and more broadly. For example, the flaws of the economic measure, gross domestic product (GDP), have been known since its inception. GDP measures economic activity and cash flows, as if all such flows resulted in positive outcomes. In this system, strip mining, clear-cutting of a forest, a hospital stay or an illness that provides revenue to a doctor, expenditures on war, and cleaning up a polluted river contribute as much to GDP as economic activities associated with more positive endeavors.

GDP was never intended as a measure of quality of life, but that is how it has been used and interpreted for many years.[5] Even when it was proposed to the U.S. Congress in 1934, its proponent, Simon Kuznets, noted that certain critically important economic (never mind noneconomic) activities were missing—for example, the work of stay-at-home parents, philanthropy, earnings from "owned durable goods," odd jobs, and a whole panoply of illegal activities that have economic impact.[6] What is actually needed today and as we move toward a more resource-constrained future in a world whose population has quadrupled since 1900 is a measure of well-being, not just sustainability.

Two indicators that attempt to measure well-being at the societal or national level are the Happy Planet Index and the Genuine Progress Indicator (GPI). The Happy Planet Index measures "the ecological efficiency with which human well-being is delivered around the world," by taking into account the relative efficiency with which nations use their ecological resources and how those resources translate into their citizens' productivity and longevity.[7] So far, the Happy Planet Index shows an "unhappy" planet on the basis of three measures: life expectancy, life satisfaction, and a nation's ecological footprint, with no nation scoring highly on all three indicators.[8] Indeed, the United States has a "blood red" footprint (not a green footprint) on this indicator, with two components rated as poor.

The Genuine Progress Indicator or GPI is being used in some parts of the world in an effort to "measure what really matters to people—health care, safety, a clean environment, and other indicators of well-being," with the ultimate goal of shifting public policy toward more sustainable practices.[9] Developed in 1955 by an organization called Redefining Progress, it is adjusted positively for factors like relatively equal income distribution and incorporates household and volunteer work; it is adjusted negatively for factors like high crime, resource depletion, high costs of defense and war, environmental problems, and loss of leisure time. Interestingly, Redefining Progress suggested that GDP "confuses" value provided by consumption with the total amount spent, thereby obscuring losses in well-being that come with planned obsolescence. The GPI attempts to overcome this problem by costing out capital items and considering their value through the years as a benefit, applying this approach both to private and public (e.g., infrastructure like roads) purchase. GPI also counts dependence on foreign assets that reduce a nation's capital stock (e.g., national debt) as detrimental to well-being, and national capital investments (e.g., in infrastructure) and the reduction of national debt as beneficial to well-being.[10]

These indexes measure well-being at the national level; however, companies too are increasingly being measured according to indicators that are not strictly financial. Thinking about value added beyond traditional financial measures is critically important in an era when social activists, community leaders, and politicians are demanding more accountability, responsibility, transparency, and sustainability—the ARTS of responsible management. Likewise, environmental, social, and governance (ESG) issues are often used as a multiple-bottom-line designation for businesses as they assess their impacts on stakeholders, society, and the natural environment. Broadening the definition of value also matters in a knowledge-, information-, and Web 2.0–based economy, where the sources of value added and wealth generation are shifting dramatically.

Some two-thirds of the value of many corporations today lies not in their tangible assets, but in their intangibles.[11] The word intangibles covers a multitude of nonfinancial but highly valuable resources in any modern organization: human, intellectual, social, and structural capital, as well as goodwill and reputation. Further, intangibles have been demonstrated to improve a company's financial performance.[12] Stakeholder relationships (including those with employees), organizational culture, innovations that come from committed stakeholders who trust the enterprise enough to share them, and the human assets and abilities that people bring with them are all part of this mix.

Developing the basis of trust that allows intangible forms of capital to emerge is the very essence of good stakeholder relationships. Social capital, as scholars call these forms, is a core ingredient of responsible enterprise. Intangible assets are built on trust. Trust is lost when companies and other types of organizations fail to operate with integrity. In contrast, when trust is present, there is potential for excellent productivity and performance; for contributions from a multitude of stakeholders; and (no small thing), for the avoidance of fines, regulations, and other hindrances to doing business. And these gains do not even take into account the retention of customers and employees, and investments from all types of investors, including those interested in responsible enterprise. A further consideration today is digital connectivity, particularly through interactive Web 2.0 technologies that provide for (sometimes unwanted) transparency, and the ability of stakeholders to engage with companies and each other on a wide variety of issues. It is building strong relationships through constructive stakeholder and environmental practices—and their link to value added—that are the focus of this chapter.

MAKING A DECISION TO OPERATE WITH INTEGRITY

There is a long-standing debate among scholars about whether it pays to be responsible; that is, is there a positive relationship between responsibility and financial performance? A positive relationship is sometimes called the "business case" for responsible enterprise or labeled as "doing well by doing good." In other words, the business case is that there is a positive link between corporate social/environmental performance and financial performance. Though there is some empirical evidence to support that view, particularly with respect to employees and eco-efficient technologies, the relationship between social/environmental and financial performance appears to be neutral;[13] that is, there is no apparent gain in performance for acting responsibly, though arguably, from an entirely different perspective, acting responsibly does produce notable moral rewards.

The question whether there is a business case for being responsible has led scholars, social investors, and skeptics alike to seek out a profitability (versus a moral or normative) rationale for companies to be responsible and accountable. What is clear is that companies—and their managers—have a fundamental choice to make: to operate responsibly or not. And it is also clear that the decision to operate with integrity should be made independent of bottom-line results. As Matthew Kiernan, former CEO of Innovest Strategic Value Advisors, once asked: "Why on earth should one need to make a 'business case' for doing the right thing?"[14]

There is, however, some evidence that the "both/and" of effectiveness and efficiency, integrity and economizing, doing things right and doing the right thing, brings about long-term success. One can make "business case" arguments along a number of critical stakeholder and natural environment dimensions, but these dimensions do highlight the stark choice executives face. Companies' leaders can choose to operate with only the interests of economizing and power aggrandizing in mind. Or they can articulate their own values, understand what they stand for in a positive and constructive way, and operate with integrity, sometimes even when there is a short-term cost to doing so. Either way, they will be held responsible—and increasingly accountable—for their actions by a growing array of interested stakeholders.

The choice is thus fundamentally a moral one that involves an important distinction between the concepts of effectiveness and efficiency. In the words of the management theorist Russell Ackoff, citing the management guru Peter Drucker:

> Peter Drucker once made *a distinction between doing things right and doing the right thing. This distinction is the same as that between efficiency and effectiveness.* Information, knowledge, and understanding contribute primarily to efficiency but provide little assurance of effectiveness. For effectiveness, wisdom is required.[15]

Responsible companies seek wisdom in their choices and the impacts of those choices. Thus they have to be efficient *and* effective, do things right, economize appropriately so that little is wasted and their activities and the communities that support them are sustainable. *And* they need to do the right thing so that they can operate with integrity and respect for the dignity of their stakeholders, as well as the health of the natural environment. Here we are faced with implementing decisions using the logic of both/and rather than the less progressive logic of either/or.

Operating with integrity and respect can sometimes mean internalizing costs that might otherwise be externalized. Sometimes it means putting a code of conduct or a set of operating principles in place—and sticking to them even when there is a temptation to lapse, even when governments fail to enforce local regulations and laws. It is in these circumstances that companies must act to ensure the rights of citizens, sometimes in the place of governments.[16] Sometimes it simply means thinking through the consequences of operating practices and choosing those that do the least harm or help stakeholders the most.

For example, companies can develop employee policies that make recruitment difficult and turnover high, and that treat employees more as cogs in the machine of business than as people, discarding them through layoffs when the going gets rough. Or they can choose policies that retain skilled and knowledgeable workers to improve productivity in the long term, even when times are difficult. They can be careless about product and packaging design, generating waste and harmful by-products, or they can carefully design products to minimize packaging and waste and move toward sustainability.

Companies can develop shoddy products that sell quickly but ultimately destroy goodwill among customers, leading to fewer repeat sales; or they can pay attention to quality and value added for the customer, leaving customers satisfied and willing to purchase again. They can seek the materials from suppliers at the lowest possible cost, stretching the suppliers' resources to the maximum and inhibiting their survival. Or companies can work in alliance with their suppliers to build a healthy network of relationships and allow the supplier enough in profits to make appropriate and adequate investments in R&D, infrastructure, human resources, and equipment to meet long-term demand.

Further, companies can treat their local communities and the natural environment as temporary stopping (or more accurately, stomping) grounds, grabbing tax breaks and infrastructure development from the community, or externalizing pollution, without recognizing the long-term costs to the community. Or they can recognize the mutuality of the corporate–community relationship and become a neighbor of choice, instilling goodwill and positive long-term commitment that enhances the well-being of community and the natural environment.[17] Responsible enterprise means that companies take positive actions simply because they are the right things to do, not when they are forced to do so by public or stakeholder pressures, laws and regulations, or media scrutiny.

There seem to be few negative by-products of operating responsibly, at least when many companies are studied together. And increasingly, a fiduciary responsibility case is being made for responsible practices as a part of a company's normal risk-management activities. More important, much of the research suggests that there are positive benefits to acting responsibly. The rest of the chapter explores some of the evidence for the link between effectiveness and efficiency, doing the right thing and doing things right—and, ultimately, operating with integrity.

RESPONSIBILITY AND PERFORMANCE

Financial performance can be influenced by intangible factors such as vision, social performance, and different kinds of stakeholder relationships, including risk management.

Vision and Performance

One of the more striking studies of the impact of vision can be found in the work of James Collins and Jerry Porras, which was discussed in Chapter 3. In their book *Built to Last*, Collins and Porras report on studies of thirty-six companies, eighteen classified as visionary and eighteen runners-up, which were not necessarily companies lacking vision but exhibited fewer of the qualities of visionary companies.[18] The critical finding of Collins and Porras's study was that the impact of vision on long-term performance was dramatic. Although the visionary companies exhibited elements of their human (and therefore fallible) origins in some of the strategic and performance bumps and hurdles they crossed over the years (and they were all long-lived companies), the visionary companies markedly outperformed the comparison companies. The visionary companies, guided by their core ideology and meaningful sense of purpose, displayed what Collins and Porras termed "remarkable resiliency," or the ability to bounce back from adversity:[19]

> Visionary companies attain extraordinary *long-term* performance. Suppose you made equal $1 investments in a general-market stock fund, a comparison company stock fund, and a visionary company stock fund on January 1, 1926. If you reinvested all dividends and made appropriate adjustments for when the companies became available on the Stock Exchange, your $1 in the general market fund would have grown to $415 on December 31, 1990—not bad. But your $1 in the visionary companies' stock fund would have grown to $6,356—over six times the comparison fund and over fifteen times the general market.[20]

Collins and Porras draw several conclusions that debunk management myths:

> Contrary to business school doctrine, "maximizing shareholder wealth" or "profit maximization" has not been the dominant driving force or primary objective through the history of the visionary companies. Visionary companies pursue a cluster of objectives, of which making money is only one—and not necessarily the primary one. Yes, they seek profits, but they're equally guided by a core ideology—core values and sense of purpose beyond just making money. Yet, paradoxically, the visionary companies make more money than the more purely profit-driven comparison companies.[21]

The key to understanding Collins and Porras's findings is to understand that *profitability is a by-product of doing something well, not the end in itself.* Equally striking results were more recently obtained by Sisodia, Wolfe, and Sheth in *Firms of Endearment.* The twenty-eight companies they studied, which are loved by their stakeholders and who love them in return, outperformed the S&P 500 almost tenfold over the same ten-year period: 1,025 percent to 122 percent. [22]

TREATING EMPLOYEES WELL AT COSTCO

Even though Wall Street analysts don't always like to believe it, treating employees well can be a winning strategy, and Costco offers living proof. Touted by *Fortune* as

"The Only Company Wal-Mart Fears," Costco is 20 percent of Wal-Mart's size, but in *Fortune*'s words "has made a monkey of the 800-pound gorilla" in the warehouse club niche.[23] Costco outperforms its direct competitor Wal-Mart in many ways: it has a higher rate of employees covered by health insurance and a lower annual worker turnover rate, pays workers a higher average hourly, and generates more profit per employee.[24]

Despite these figures, and a 25 percent gain in profits in the first quarter of 2004, Costco's stock price dropped by 4 percent right after the profit was announced. *BusinessWeek*, taking the analysts to task, stated:

> The market's view of Costco speaks volumes about the so-called WalMartization of the U.S. economy. True, the Bentonville (Ark.) retailer has taken a public relations pounding recently for paying poverty- level wages and shouldering health insurance for fewer than half of its 1.2 million U.S. workers. Still, it remains the darling of the Street, which, like Wal-Mart and many other companies, believes that shareholders are best served if employers do all they can to hold down costs, including the cost of labor.[25]

According to *BusinessWeek*, the strategy of paying employees well has multiple benefits:

> We found that by compensating employees generously to motivate and retain good workers, one-fifth of whom are unionized, Costco gets lower turnover [6 percent to Wal-Mart's 21 percent] and higher productivity. Combined with a smart business strategy that sells a mix of higher-margin products to more affluent customers, Costco actually keeps its labor costs lower than Wal-Mart's as a percentage of sales [9.8 percent to 17 percent], and its 68,000 hourly workers in the U.S. sell more per square foot.[26]

CEO Sinegal, according to the *New York Times*, "rejects Wall Street's assumption that to succeed in discount retailing, companies must pay poorly and skimp on benefits, or must ratchet up prices to meet Wall Street's profit demands." He notes, "Good wages and benefits are why Costco has extremely low rates of turnover and theft by employees," he said. "And Costco's customers, who are more affluent than other warehouse store shoppers, stay loyal because they like that low prices do not come at the workers' expense. This is not altruistic," he said. "This is good business."[27]

Social and Financial Performance

The typical assumption, particularly in financial circles, is that there is a necessary trade-off between social and financial performance. This assumption
implies that social and ecological responsibilities are discretionary, which we
have argued they are not. Instead, we believe that such responsibilities are integral to determining a company's overall performance—in a blended value
sense. The fear embedded in this assumption is that the more responsible
companies will place themselves at a competitive disadvantage because they
are incurring more costs than other companies. Certainly some responsibilities do require investment; however, there is significant evidence that—when
viewed as an investment—responsible behavior shows returns much like any
other type of investment.

A meta-analysis (study of studies) done by Joshua Margolis, Hillary Elfenbein, and James Walsh concludes that the relationship between financial
performance and responsibility is slightly positive, but so slight as to be essentially neutral.[28] This team integrated the results of 167 papers looking at
the social-financial performance relationship over a thirty-five-year period
and found that while better responsibility does not destroy value—i.e., has
no competitive disadvantage—neither does it add much to value. Margolis
and Elfenbein, writing in the *Harvard Business Review*, draw several conclusions: (1) corporate misdeeds are costly to companies—if people find out, but
(2) doing "good" will probably not hurt shareholders' returns, and, as noted
above, (3) greater profits should not be the main reason companies engage in
corporate responsibility activities.[29]

Other research has altered this picture slightly by finding only an indirect relationship, which relies on the mediating effect of intangible resources,
between firm performance and corporate responsibility.[30] Still different research has found that unusually high social performers achieve outstanding
long-term financial performance, while unusually poor social performers
achieve high short-term financial performance.[31] Although the evidence of
a positive relationship between corporate social and financial performance
remains mixed to date (also depending quite significantly on the study context), there is no reason to assume that there is a negative relationship. In
other words, the still widely held belief that there is a trade-off between good

social and financial performance is not supported. As it becomes harder and harder to believe that there are financial drawbacks to behaving more responsibly, the moral argument grows stronger.

Stakeholder Relationships and Performance

Responsible enterprise is fundamentally about integrity, responsibility, and accountability for the company's impacts on stakeholders and on nature. Below we explore how this principle operates in practice.

Responsible (Ethical) Investing   One question that investors, considered as owners, seek answers to (in the old either/or logic) is whether there is a penalty for investing in businesses that choose to operate in a responsible manner. Socially responsible (or ethical) investors care about the uses to which their money is put. Broadly speaking, investors use three social investment strategies: they (1) screen companies against certain criteria, (2) use their shareholder resolutions to actively seek changes from management, or (3) accept lower returns for specific types of community-based investments aimed at doing social good.

The U.S. Forum for Sustainable and Responsible Investment (US SIF) estimates that some $3.07 trillion out of $25.2 trillion total is now invested in professionally managed portfolios that use one or more of those criteria.[32] In its latest report at this writing (2010), US SIF found that social investment had grown 13 percent from 2007 to 2010 and that nearly one in eight investment dollars under professional management (about 12.2 percent) was included in that total.[33] US SIF estimates that in 2010 there were some 250 socially screened mutual funds in the United States holding about $316.1 billion in assets, and that the fastest growing area was the community investment segment.[34]

As with financial performance discussed above, it appears that the market performance of socially screened funds (i.e., the stock price) is either about the same as or slightly better than that of traditional funds, with possibly somewhat higher volatility. The longest running socially responsible investment (SRI) index is the FTSE KLD 400, started in 1990, and it has performed competitively with other major indexes, such as the S&P 500 (e.g., returning 9.51 percent from 1990 to the end of 2009 versus 8.66 percent for the

S&P 500).[35] Scholars who studied the performance of screened companies for five years found that the mean financial performance of large responsible companies is significantly better than that of other large companies.[36] Results of that 2003 study using a metric called market value added (MVA), which measures long-term value added for shareholders since the inception of the company, demonstrate that responsible corporations generate two to four times more long-term wealth for shareholders than the remaining companies in the S&P 500.

Taken together, the research indicates that there is no apparent trade-off in financial performance for better corporate responsibility. In fact, some suggest that more responsible companies reduce overall risk for investors. A study by Darren Lee and colleagues, for example, finds that greater screening intensity of social and environmental issues reduces funds' overall systemic risk.[37] Further, investors may actually benefit from the better management practices and stakeholder relationships associated with responsible enterprise. At the very least, it appears that the relationship is a neutral one. Since there is a choice to be made—and the choice is fundamentally, as we pointed out above, a moral one—it makes sense to invest in more responsible companies.

One knowledgeable observer, thinking about the future of responsible investing, argues that in the future the focus will be primarily on sustainable investing, rather than socially responsible investing. That observer, Joe Keefe, president and CEO of PAX World, said in 2008, "Over the next 15 years, I think we will see a transition from the old world of socially responsible investing (SRI) to the new world of sustainable investing. By sustainable investing, I mean the full integration of environmental, social and governance (ESG) factors into financial analysis and decision-making. This transition is critical if our industry is to broaden its market and maximize its impact on corporate behavior, on financial markets, and on global society itself."[38]

Employee Relations and Performance   The impact of treating employees well is far from trivial. Jeffrey Pfeffer and John Veiga summarized a good deal of research on the relationship between firm economic performance and employee relations.[39] Quoting from two major studies, they note:

> According to an award-winning study of the high performance work practices of 968 firms representing all major industries, "a one standard deviation increase

in use of such practices is associated with a . . . 7.05 percent decrease in turnover and, on a per employee basis, $27,044 more in sales and $18,641 and $3,814 more in market value and profits, respectively." Yes, you read those results correctly. That's an $18,000 increase in stock market value *per employee*! A subsequent study conducted on 702 firms in 1996 found even larger economic benefits: "A one standard deviation improvement in the human resources system was associated with an increase in shareholder wealth of $41,000 per employee"—about a 14 percent market value premium.[40]

Another award-winning study, by Alex Edmans of the Wharton School at the University of Pennsylvania, found that companies listed on the *Fortune* Best Companies to Work for annual rating earned more than twice the market return of companies not so listed during the period 1998–2005. The author suggested that employee satisfaction might actually improve company performance, among other findings.[41]

Many studies confirm these ideas, and are consistent with the model that Jeanne Liedtka developed, discussed in the previous chapter. For example, a study found that the stock market seemed to value companies meeting basic standards around diversity and environment, but most rewarded those companies that had proactive employee relations policies and practices.[42] Another study found that companies that undertook repeated layoffs or workforce reductions actually experienced a deteriorating level of operational indebtedness and failed to improve productivity, suggesting that the common "wisdom" of using layoffs to improve financial gains or productivity levels may be specious.[43] Another study shows that one key to creating satisfied customers, which is understood to be a source of better corporate performance, is having satisfied employees—that is, employees who feel good about working for the company.[44]

Employee turnover costs companies billions of dollars each year. One estimate by the Society for Human Resource Management suggests that it costs about $3,500 to replace an employee who earns $8.00 per hour, and as much as 150–400 percent of annual salary to replace managerial and specialized employees.[45] The American Management Association reported that it can cost between 25 percent and 250 percent of an employee's yearly salary to recruit a new employee, with higher-cost executive and management employees at the higher end of that range.[46] Greater employee satisfaction can result in lower turnover, lower recruitment costs, and less absenteeism. Although such costs are not typically included in financial statements, they can be considerable, and progressive companies do what they can to ensure that their employees like their work. A study by the Work Foundation and the Future Foundation examined how corporate responsibility influenced employees' views of their companies. They found that younger employees (aged 18–24) and older employees (45+) were more likely than others to take corporate responsibility into account. Employee loyalty was significantly correlated with the company's corporate responsibility rating.[47]

Pfeffer also shows the value of "putting people first," in terms of both company profitability and other organizational performance measures.[48] After looking at the five-year survival rates of initial public offerings, studies of profitability and stock price in numerous industries, and research on specific industries, Pfeffer concluded that gains on the order of 40 percent can be achieved when high-performance management practices are implemented. The analysis showed that survival rates were associated with the real value placed on people, as well as the reward system in the company. For example, policies such as employee stock ownership plans and profit sharing significantly improved survival rates.

Pfeffer and Veiga, in their summary of research on employee policies and organizational performance, conclude that progressive employee practices help companies improve their performance because:

> Simply put, people work harder because of the increased involvement and commitment that comes from having more control and say in their work; people work smarter because they are encouraged to build skills and competence; and people work more responsibly because more responsibility is placed in hands of employees further down in the organization.[49]

Given this strong relationship between the ways employees are treated and organizational performance, it makes sense to ask, "What kinds of company practices produce such results?" In some respects, the policies are easily determined and might be identified by anyone using common sense about the way he or she would like to be treated. Developing such policies simply means operating with integrity and implementing practices that employees find constructive rather than debilitating.

Implementation is difficult in part because of the values that often drive the economic sector, for example, economizing (which emphasizes efficiency as a first priority) and power aggrandizing (the accumulation of power). Perhaps by recognizing that these driving values underlie some of the more negative practices of corporate life, leaders can overcome their short-term desire for power or cut costs in the near term and develop practices that help the company achieve long-term success. Doing so and implementing positive employee policies can result in significant performance improvement, as demonstrated by many companies with satisfied employees, including Starbucks, Southwest Airlines, and Patagonia.

Diversity Management, Work/Family Policies, and Performance   Another approach to assessing the relationship between the way that companies treat employees and financial performance is to look at their approach to diversity management and the work/family relationship. Many management scholars believe that greater diversity in the workplace leads to better performance because, when more and different points of view are represented in decisions, better decisions are made and performance should improve.[50]

The advocacy group Catalyst studied the relationship between women's representation in management and companies' financial excellence, and determined that when companies have more women in managerial positions, they outperform companies with fewer women in management, suggesting that there is a business case for gender diversity.[51] Further, as noted earlier, a more recent study found that the stock market seems to value companies that promote diversity.[52] Similarly, in a series of studies reported in *The Wall Street Journal*, the reporter concluded, "A growing number of employers suspect improving employee satisfaction will have an indirect but important effect on profit."[53]

A study in Spain also found that gender diversity on the board of directors had a positive effect on firm value.[54] Because intellectual and human capital are becoming increasingly important sources of competitive advantage, and because there are structural changes in the economy that have caused a scarcity of skilled and knowledgeable employees, many companies have begun to find new ways to treat their employees with respect and integrity. As must be obvious, companies' treatment of one group of primary stakeholders is critically related to the way it is perceived—and the way it treats—other stakeholders as well. We will continue to explore these important interrelationships in the next sections.

Customers and Responsibility   Many customers also value responsible practices by the companies from which they purchase goods and services. Customer loyalty, which companies earn by providing high-quality products and services, is increasingly important to gaining status as a responsible company. Also, the reputation of the firm with customers is critical. Customers' perception of a company's overall level of responsibility influences their propensity to purchase from that company.

Happy customers are likely to tell six others about their experience, while unhappy customers are likely to tell twenty-two. So, while satisfied customers are a tremendous source of long-term business, unhappy customers are even more likely to deter business from a company that has not satisfied them.[55] Companies that operate with integrity want to ensure that their customers are satisfied not only with the quality of products but also with their usefulness. Further, customer surveys consistently indicate that many customers intend to make purchasing decisions with the company's responsibility reputation in mind, although there is no clear evidence that these attitudes translate into purchasing behavior.[56] Indeed, one study found that by far the best predictor of growth for companies in most industries is the percentage of customers who can be classified as "promoters"—that is, customers who will tell others positive things about the company.[57] Another found that there is a relationship between positive customer beliefs about a company's corporate responsibility and customers' likelihood of purchasing from that company, as well as long-term loyalty and advocacy about the company, particularly when it integrates its corporate responsibility strategy into its core business.[58] Researchers also found in exploratory research that companies with institutionalized corporate responsibility programs were most effective at enhancing customer loyalty and positive customer attitudes, while decreasing skepticism.[59]

Such numbers, however, need to be treated with care. It is not clear yet how much social and environmental issues actually affect consumers' purchasing decisions. Pat Auger and Timothy Devinney, for instance, have argued that traditional survey-based research on ethical consumption suffers from a social desirability bias and hence significantly overvalues good intentions.[60] However, even accounting for such limitations, it is clear that consumers care about firms' social and environmental performance.

Supplier Relationships   Many companies, particularly those using suppliers in developing nations, have found that the practices of their suppliers can get them in trouble with consumers and activists. Buying from suppliers accused of using child labor, fostering abusive or sweatshop working conditions, or abrogating global labor standards can create significant reputational problems—and even consumer boycotts or overt anti-company campaigns. To deal with this issue, many companies that outsource manufacturing have developed a code of conduct for themselves—and many require their suppliers to adhere to it as well. Increasingly, companies in the clothing, footwear, toy, and sports equipment industries actively monitor the practices of their suppliers, often using outside monitors, to ensure compliance and to prevent the loss of customer loyalty.[61]

Supplier relationships need to be considered part of the essential social capital that improves the results or performance of the purchasing company. Long-term suppliers can sometimes develop new production methods that help a company meet its quality or productivity targets, but will do so only if they have a good relationship with the company. This form of social capital, which is built on stable and trusting relationships, can increase efficiency through greater information diffusion and may also decrease opportunism, which can reduce monitoring costs as well as improve efficiency.[62] In research that supports this perspective, scholars suggest that "purchasing social responsibility" (PSR)—the involvement of purchasing managers in responsibility activities—has a positive relationship to supplier performance and improves trust and cooperation.[63] Later research by Craig Carter finds that PSR improves organizational learning and supplier performance, while reducing costs.[64]

NIKE—MANAGING A GLOBAL SUPPLY CHAIN

Hammered by the media and public boycotts of its products in the 1990s and early 2000s for labor and human rights abuses and sweatshop problems in its global supply chain, Nike had to respond with an integrated management approach to dealing with its supply chain responsibilities.

With 2010 revenues of over $19 billion, the footwear company, which considers itself mainly a design and marketing company, employs over 34,000 people directly. The business model underlying Nike is based on outsourcing production to contract factories, while design, marketing, and product innovation remain in-house. As of 2009, Nike's products (largely footwear, apparel, and sports equipment) are made in approximately 600 supply factories employing more than 800,000 workers in forty-six countries.[65]

It is within Nike's extended supply chain of manufacturing suppliers, which employ hundreds of thousands of mostly low-wage workers, that Nike experienced reputational difficulties. Because of concerns about sweatshop conditions (including child labor) in supply factories in the late 1990s, the company has had to explicitly manage its relationships with suppliers and attempt to ensure that they are living up to Nike's own corporate standards. In 1992, *Harper's Magazine* published an article by Jeffrey Ballinger criticizing labor conditions in one of Nike's supply factories in Indonesia.[66] A series of other critical articles about sweatshop labor in its supply factories quickly made Nike the poster child for corporate irresponsibility. Nike's initial reaction to these accusations was denial; the company adopted a defensive strategy and pointed out that its competitors were using similar business models.[67] This tactic, however, only increased the pressure by activists. Next, Nike hired professional labor-auditing firms and tried to better enforce its code of conduct. However, these efforts did not pay off. Nike still had to cope with a variety of revelations about sweatshop labor at its supply factories.

When the company began investigating the root causes of factories' lack of compliance with its labor code, it learned that one part of the problem was how it managed procurement practices. Its practice of tight inventory management caused problems when demand was not correctly forecasted (or changed on short notice). Changes in demand could cause suppliers to require overtime in the factories—a practice that Nike's code of conduct tried to prevent.[68] One important part of the solution to Nike's problems was to rethink the value of supplier relationships. Indeed, Richard Locke and Monica Romis's comparative study of two Nike supply factories in Mexico suggests that improvements in labor conditions depend on the nature of the relationship between supplier and buyer:

> At Plant A, relations between factory management and Nike's local staff were collaborative and open. Nike managers visited Plant A about once a month, and the owners of Plant A also frequently visited Nike's Mexico City Office. Over time, these visits led to greater transparency and trust between Nike and Plant A management as well as joint problem solving. . . . The relationship between Nike's regional office and Plant B management is more formal and distant.[69]

This research shows that benefits for the supplier (in terms of secured long-term contracts) and the buyer (in terms of improved production efficiency and brand protection) depend on a trustful and long-term relationship between the parties. A relationship based solely on compliance with a predefined code of conduct that is enforced through audits is unlikely to produce mutually satisfactory results. Locke and Romis's study demonstrates that long-term collaboration and the resulting transfer of management know-how (e.g., regarding the empowerment of workers) helps to create value in global supply chains.

Overall Stakeholder Relations and Enterprise Performance   Throughout this book, we have defined responsible enterprise as being the way that a company treats its stakeholders through its day-to-day operating practices. Using this definition, some years ago Sam Graves and Sandra Waddock conducted another study that assessed the link between the overall quality of management in firms and their stakeholder relations (including their relationship to owners, measured in terms of financial performance).[70] They found that higher management quality was strongly associated with better treatment of owners through financial performance, employee relations, and customers (through the product variable), and significantly associated with the treatment of society through community relations. Treatment of the environment had no apparent relationship to improved perception of quality of management by outside observers, such as the CEOs and analysts who contribute to *Fortune*'s ratings of quality of management and reputation.

Overall, however, the findings indicate that quality of management and quality of stakeholder relationships are highly interrelated, providing further support for the idea that good management can be equated with good stakeholder relationships. Since positive financial and social performance are also related, it would appear that there is mounting evidence that treating stakeholders respectfully and with integrity can contribute to corporate success.

The argument that a business case is always needed is problematic, according to social auditor Simon Zadek, who says "it often is not right in practice in the short run, and the short run (as John Maynard Keynes pointed out) can last a hell of a long time."[71] Indeed, at the 2010 meeting of the UN Global Compact Leaders' Summit in New York, Klaus Leisinger, former special advisor to the UN Secretary-General for the UN Global Compact, and president and CEO of the Novartis Foundation, noted that to think that there always is—or needs to be—a business case for responsible enterprise is (to use a less colorful term than he used) not realistic. Instead, as Zadek argues, this relationship really matters when stakeholders gain sufficient voice over corporate affairs that they are heard by management and can influence practice. As the studies cited above found, such stakeholder voice is an increasingly important part of the corporate landscape.

Social Capital and Performance

Responsible companies know that relationships with primary and secondary stakeholders matter now more than ever. Research on social capital enhances our understanding of why these relationships matter. Social capital can be viewed as the trust and alliances generated by the relationships that people in a system have developed over time. The emergence of strategic alliances and networked or virtual organizations, the connectedness imposed by electronic technology, and global awareness of company performance are only a few of the many factors that made relationships more valuable in recent years.

We have argued that integrity is critical to responsible enterprise. Integrity is also essential to building trusting and trustful relationships with stakeholders, with whom companies are increasingly interdependent. It is this interdependence, a characteristic of social capital, that companies are recognizing as critical to their long-term success. Companies that build positive and lasting relationships with their stakeholders, in every sphere of activity, can cope better with the connectedness and transparency imposed by globalism and technology. Such companies may also better understand the dynamics and forces operating in the political and civil society spheres of activity than companies with less well developed relationships.

Further, companies that operate with integrity and develop trusting relationships with their stakeholders are likely to boost their social and intellectual capital, potentially creating a new source of competitive advantage.[72] An emerging theory of the firm argues, as we have argued here, that a company needs to be understood not as a "nexus of contracts," but rather as a set of complex relationships—a web of relationships—with primary stakeholders.[73]

In this definition of the firm, social capital plays an important role in fostering interaction and efficiency or economizing. Scholars Janine Nahapiet and Sumantra Ghoshal have argued that social capital provides two distinct benefits to companies, both related to efficiency. First, social capital increases the diffusion of information and may also diminish opportunism, thereby decreasing monitoring costs. Second, because social capital is based on trust and relationship, it encourages cooperation and therefore innovation, thus improving efficiency.[74]

These same scholars say that a link between social and intellectual capital is increasingly important in the knowledge-based economy facing corporations in the 21st century. Defining intellectual capital as "the knowledge and knowing capability of a social collectivity," they argue that it is a valuable organizational resource created by the presence of an abundance of social capital. The combination of social and intellectual capital contributes to organizational advantage, in part because, based on relationships as it is, social and intellectual capital represents a resource or core competency that is difficult for competitors to imitate.

There is a system of relationships among the elements we have been addressing as we developed the concept of the stakeholder-relationship-based responsible enterprise. Starting with operational integrity—wholeness and honesty—we see that companies build trusting relationships and therefore social capital both internally and externally by creating constructive and positive operating practices that impact stakeholders. Because they are in-extricably embedded in a web of relationships inside and outside the com-pany, companies need to pay attention to the quality of those relationships—to their social capital. They need to do this because building social capital and its associated intellectual capital results in a system that works for all stakeholders.

Even when there are short-term trade-offs, the company that understands the inherent value of its relationships will act respectfully toward its stake-holders, continuing to build social and intellectual capital. As we shall see in the next two chapters, the future is likely to bring more connectedness and a greater need for transparency in all actions. Transparency is demanded be-cause of the increased public capacity to know what is happening within and to companies through the connections made available by the Internet.

Part III

MANAGING RESPONSIBLE ENTERPRISE

6 STAKEHOLDERS

The Relationship Key

I think the hardest thing about my job is the way Whole Foods
Market views itself philosophically— we are a business dedicated
to meeting all the various stakeholders of the company's best
interests. And by stakeholders we mean customers, team
members, stockholders, community, and the environment.
Sometimes what is in the best interest of one stakeholder may not
be in the best interest of another stakeholder, and as the CEO, I
have to balance the various interests of the different constituencies
and stakeholders to create win, win, win scenarios, and that can
sometimes be very difficult to do. Everybody wants something
from the CEO.

John Mackey, CEO, Whole Foods

A STAKEHOLDER PERSPECTIVE ON RESPONSIBLE ENTERPRISE

A stakeholder, broadly speaking, is any individual or group who is affected
by or can affect an organization.[1] Companies exist in relationship to and
because of their stakeholders. Simply stated, despite the prevailing idea that
the purpose of the firm is to maximize shareholder wealth (and although
companies must produce wealth to survive), because of their numerous
impacts, corporations are considerably more than profit-maximizing machines. Corporations are inherently and inextricably embedded in a web of
relationships with stakeholders that create the very context in which they
do business and that enable the enterprise to succeed. They also create purpose and meaning for many of their stakeholders, particularly employees,
and produce goods and services that customers are willing to buy. Without
its core stakeholders and a healthy natural environment to support it, the
company cannot survive over the long term, nor can it begin to make a profit, never mind maximize profits. Indeed, in many ways, any enterprise consists of nothing more and nothing less than its primary relationships. Legal
scholarship suggests that there is, in fact, no legally mandated requirement

in the United States for firms to "maximize" shareholder wealth, despite the common understanding that has spread widely around the world.[2]

Therefore, we offer this premise: Profits are essential to company success, and indeed to company survival. Profits are critical to sustaining democratic capitalism. But profits are a by-product of the many relationships on which a corporation—or any other organization—depends for its legitimacy, power, resources, and various kinds of capital investments. This perspective differs from the traditional neoclassical economics' perspective on the firm, which says that the sole purpose of the firm is to maximize profits or shareholder wealth. This view is called the stakeholder capitalism concept of the firm.

In this stakeholder view, stakeholder relationships and the operating practices (policies, processes, and procedures) that support those relationships are the basis of responsible enterprise.[3] The neoclassical economics model, which still dominates much business thinking, suggests that the corporation should maximize wealth for one set of stakeholders: the owners or shareholders. Conformance to existing law and meeting ethical responsibilities come next, especially in the view of the economist Milton Friedman, who espoused the neoclassical economics perspective. In his classic article arguing against the concept of social responsibility, entitled "The Social Responsibility of Business Is to Increase Its Profits," Friedman famously stated:

> But the doctrine of "social responsibility" taken seriously would extend the scope of the political mechanism to every human activity. It does not differ in philosophy from the most explicitly collectivist doctrine. It differs only in professing to believe that collectivist ends can be attained without collectivist means. That is why in my book *Capitalism and Freedom*, I have called it a "fundamentally subversive doctrine" in a free society, and have said that in such a society, there is one and only one social responsibility of business—to use its resources and engage in activities designed to increase its profits so long as it stays within the rules of the game, which is to say, engages in open and free competition without deception or fraud.[4]

But this view is too constricted to be useful in a world where it is increasingly recognized that other stakeholders are equally important to the survival and success of the firm and that they too make significant investments in the welfare of the firm. These relationships and investments are epitomized in an initiative of Boston's Tellus Institute, which argues for the development of a global corporate charter and associated chartering organization by 2020.[5] Propelled by issues of sustainable development, equity, a growing gap between rich and poor, and the increasing power of corporations, the Tellus Institute notes that "We need new mechanisms for harmonizing TNC [transnational corporation] conduct with the overarching aims of environmental resilience, poverty alleviation and economic stability."[6]

Still incipient, the global corporate charter movement would, initially at least, be voluntary on the part of companies, global in scope, and governed by a diverse multistakeholder board. The premise of a global corporate charter, if one is developed following Tellus's guidelines, would be that corporations have to define and pursue a social mission that is aligned with principles of sustainable development as articulated in documents like the Earth Charter, the United Nations Global Compact, the International Labour Organization, and the Global Reporting Initiative.[7] Such a charter, in one sense, brings corporations back to their roots, which originally demanded that any chartered company serve the public interest. It would consist of a mission statement and a statement of its compatibility with principles of sustainable development. It would also include a description of how the company aligns its practices and strategies with international norms, an ownership section that shows how corporate structure and mission are aligned, a governance section that specifies the role of the board in advancing the company's mission, and an accountability statement that outlines the company's transparency and stakeholder engagement policies and practices.

STAKES AND STAKEHOLDERS

In the business context, the word *stake* has three different meanings, each representing a different type of relationship between the stakeholder and the entity in which a stake exists (see Table 6.1). First, a stake is a claim of some sort, for example, a claim of ownership based on a set of expectations related to principles of ethics, such as legal or moral rights, justice or fairness, the greatest good for the greatest number, or the principle of care.

Second, a stake is an investment made by a stakeholder that puts some sort of capital at risk.[8] In this usage, a stake is an interest or a share in some

TABLE 6.1   *Three Types of Stakes*

Stake as:	Stake is based on:
• Claim	• Legal or moral right
	• Consideration of justice/fairness
	• Utility (greatest good for the greatest number)
	• Care
• Risk	• Investment of capital, including:
1. Owner	1. Financial capital
2. Community	2. Social/infrastructure capital
3. Employee	3. Knowledge/intellectual/human capital
4. Customer	4. Franchise (trust) capital
5. Supplier	5. Technological, infrastructure capital
• Bond (tether, tie)	• Identification (process)

Each type of stake creates a relationship that, when constructive and positive, is: mutual, interactive, consistent over time, and interdependent.

enterprise or activity, a prize (as in a horse race or other gamble) or perhaps a grubstake (for which the provider expects a return for the risk taken). Typically, the type of risk under consideration relates specifically to the type of capital invested. Thus, for example, owners invest financial capital in the firm, while communities may invest social capital—or relationships built on trust and association—in the firm's local presence or create infrastructure to support the firm's activities. Employees invest their human capital, their knowledge, and their intellectual energies—all forms of capital—in the firm. Customers invest their trust as part of the firm's franchise and hence their willingness to continue to purchase the goods and services produced by the firm. Suppliers may invest in specific technology, equipment, or infrastructure so that they can enhance their relationship to the firm over time and make it stronger.

The third meaning of stake is a bond, a tie or tether, something that creates links between entities, including tangible links that bind the entities together (e.g., contracts or long-term relationships for purchasing supplies) as well as intangible relational links. Intangible bonds can exist when a stake-holder identifies with the organization in a way that potentially creates one of the other types of stakes, a claim or a risk.[9]

STAKEHOLDER RELATIONSHIPS AND THE PUBLIC
RESPONSIBILITIES OF MANAGEMENT

Notice that each type of stake identified in Table 6.1 creates a relationship between the stakeholder and the organization.[10] For example, owners are clearly stakeholders. By making an investment, the stakeholder owner es-tablishes a relationship with the organization, though as management scholar Charles Handy points out, most shareholders today do exactly that—hold shares—without much real semblance of ownership.[11] Similarly, the stakeholder who puts something at risk for possible benefit through an enterprise creates a relationship with that enterprise, as communities do when they invest in local infrastructure that supports a firm's activities or employees do when they invest their own human or intellectual capital in their work. Bonds of identity also create ongoing relationships. The impor-tant point, then, is that for each type of stake, being a stakeholder creates an ongoing and interactive relationship between the stakeholder and the enterprise or activity.[12]

Stakeholder relationships also create a boundary around managerial re-sponsibilities so that enterprises are responsible not for all of the problems of society but only for those that the company affects or those issues that affect the company. Thus, the public responsibility of managers in a responsible enterprise is limited to the areas of primary and secondary involvement of their enterprises. The principle of public responsibility, which was developed by scholars Lee Preston and James Post, exists in part because companies are granted charters (literally, incorporation papers, or permission to exist by the states in which they are established). Those charters hold the companies re-sponsible for the impacts they have on their stakeholders and on the natural environment.[13]

The scope of managers' public responsibilities is quite wide given the resources that companies, particularly multinationals, command, the geographic and product/service scope of many large companies, and the resulting power they hold. According to Preston and Post, management's responsibilities are limited by the organization's primary and secondary involvements. Arenas of primary involvement are related to the main business mission and purpose of the firm as it attempts to live out its vision in society. Thus, "Primary involvement relationships, tested and mediated through the market mechanism, are essential to the existence of the organization over time."[14]

Primary involvement arenas are those that affect primary stakeholders—that is, those stakeholders without whom the company cannot stay in business.[15] Stakeholders interact with—or in the case of primary stakeholders actually constitute—organizations; that is, they are in relationship to an organization or company. Primary stakeholders typically consist of four groups: investors, employees, customers, and suppliers/allies. Companies are typically started and financed by owners, who in the current thinking of many business leaders are considered to be the dominant (and sometimes only important) stakeholder. But it is clear that other stakeholders are also critical to the success of companies because they too have placed various forms of their capital at risk, and are invested in or tied to companies. For example, employees are essential stakeholders because they develop, produce, and deliver the company's products and services. A company's existence is also contingent on the goodwill and continued purchases of customers. Companies also depend on the earth for raw materials (ultimately) and on suppliers and allies or partners, who produce the raw materials necessary for the company to generate its own goods and services. Relationships with these stakeholder groups constitute any company's primary stakeholder relationships.

Although some people believe that the environment is a stakeholder because it supplies the raw materials necessary to the company's existence,[16] we take the perspective that the environment is not a stakeholder but rather an essential underpinning to all human civilization. This underpinning needs to be supportive, diverse, and healthy for human civilization to survive;[17] thus the natural environment is in many instances treated as if it were a stakeholder.[18] Indeed, we are all, in a sense, stakeholders *of* the environment.

The public responsibilities of managers do not end with primary involvement arenas; they extend to arenas of secondary involvement, which include those arenas and relationships that affect or are affected by the firm's activities or by-products of those activities.[19] Among the critical secondary stakeholder relationships are community, government, nongovernmental organizations (NGOs), activists, and pressure groups. Firms rely on their local communities for an educated workforce and for the infrastructure that makes production of goods and services possible (e.g., roads, local services, and zoning regulations). Similarly, towns and cities located on a river downstream from a company that pollutes the river feel its impact and thus are secondary stakeholders. Firms ignore these impacts at their peril, because secondary stakeholders can be demanding or dangerous when their needs are urgent, when they have power or, if they have been inactive, when they are awakened into action.[20] Further, companies rely on governments—local, state/provincial, national, and increasingly international—to create societal rules that make trading, economic, and political relationships feasible over time. Stakeholders themselves bear responsibility for their actions and impacts on companies, so the interaction is never a one-sided one. Just as companies need to recognize their responsibilities, so too do stakeholders who pressure companies to make changes. NGOs, employees and labor unions, activists and pressure groups, customers, and investors, among others, need to behave responsibly and thoughtfully in their engagements with companies, just as they expect companies to do with them. Ethical practices apply to individuals and all organizations, not just businesses. Thus, just as companies need to understand the social, human rights, ecological, and related concerns of civil society stakeholders, so too do stakeholders from those spheres need to understand these issues as well as the economic imperatives under which businesses are operating.

By defining responsible enterprise through the lens of a company's strategies and operating practices, we take a practice-based stakeholder view of the corporation, which significantly broadens understanding of the stakeholders to whom a firm is accountable. This view incorporates the quality and nature of the relationships that companies develop with stakeholders and an assessment of the impacts of corporate activities on those stakeholders and on the natural environment. The interests of the environment are frequently represented by environmental activists, though the environment is not itself a stakeholder.[21]

Such a perspective on stakeholder relationships is a normative model—that is, it is a model of how, in the best of worlds, stakeholder relationships and company practices ought to be.[22]

WHOLE FOODS—CREATING
A STAKEHOLDER-FOCUSED CULTURE

Whole Foods Market is a supermarket chain with approximately 300 stores in the United States, Canada, and the UK, selling natural and organic food that is produced based on sustainable agriculture. Founded in 1980, the company employed roughly 58,000 people (called "team members") and reported revenues of more than $9 billion for the 2010 fiscal year.[23] The company grew substantially in the 1990s, acquiring other natural food chains, such as Bread & Circus of New England and Bread of Life of North Carolina.

What is different about Whole Foods Markets and its success is not the fact that the company sells natural and organic food, but its explicit social and environment commitment. As an article in the *Boston Globe* noted: "Lettuce you can get anywhere. Customers want self-affirmation, and Whole Foods slips it in every bag headed out the door."[24] Whole Foods is about more than shopping for natural and organic products; it is about understanding stakeholder needs and establishing long-term relationships with them. Early on, Whole Foods established a list of core values highlighting the company's stakeholder-focused culture:

- Selling the highest quality natural and organic products available,
- Satisfying and delighting our customers,
- Supporting team member happiness and excellence,
- Creating wealth through profits and growth,
- Caring about our communities and our environment,
- Creating ongoing win-win partnerships with our suppliers,
- Promoting the health of our stakeholders through healthy eating education.[25]

As early as 1985 the company created its "Declaration of Interdependence." This declaration spelled out the need to *integrate* and *balance* stakeholder interests, needs, and desires:

Satisfying all of our stakeholders and achieving our standards is our goal. One of the most important responsibilities of Whole Foods Market's leadership is to make sure the interests, desires and needs of our various stakeholders are kept in balance. We recognize that this is a dynamic process. It requires participation and communication by all of our stakeholders. It requires listening compassionately, thinking carefully and acting with integrity. Any conflicts must be mediated and win-win solutions found. Creating and nurturing this community of stakeholders is critical to the long-term success of our company.[26]

At the heart of Whole Foods' stakeholder philosophy is the idea of balancing different stakeholders' interests by creating a sense of interdependence among them. For instance, the company donates 5 percent of after-tax profits to not-for profit organizations operating in local communities. Further, employees enjoy a variety of benefits that make the company one of the top places to work according to *Fortune* magazine.[27] And the employee turnover rate is very low. The balancing of stakeholder interests does not just happen. As stated in the "Declaration," it requires continuous communication and participation by all stakeholder groups to achieve integration. According to CEO and co-founder John Mackey, thinking about stakeholders in an integrated way helps to establish a business based on passion and purpose.

An integrative perspective on stakeholders stands in contrast to the traditional assumption that there are trade-offs in satisfying the interests of different stakeholders. For example, when a company raises wages and provides benefits to its employees, it is usually assumed that somebody has to pay for this (most often customers through higher prices). However, John Mackey sees the issue in a different way: "You can also make the point that if you raise compensation, you will get better quality people which will benefit customers and shareholders."[28] Acknowledging the interdependence of stakeholder relationships implies an understanding of the inter-related nature of the different systems that stakeholders belong to. One way to reflect this philosophy in practice is the company's belief in "shared fate." Compensation of nonmanagement employees is just as coupled with the fate of the company as the compensation of management, and the company limits the compensation of top management (wages plus bonuses) to no more than nineteen times the average compensation of full-time employees.

However, Whole Foods' perspective on the interdependent nature of stakeholders also has its downside. The "Declaration" reads: "We strive to build positive and healthy relationships among Team Members. 'Us versus them' thinking has no place in our company." In other words, the company does not support unions and collective bargaining agreements. In fact, Whole Foods' anti-union stance has given rise to much criticism, not least because the right to collective bargaining is among the fundamental labor rights acknowledged by the international community.[29]

STAKEHOLDER RELATIONSHIP MANAGEMENT

Respect for others is at the heart of good stakeholder relations. While it is frequently true that companies are powerful because they command significant resources, they need to recognize the importance of maintaining good relationships with their stakeholders in order to experience outstanding long-term performance. Scholarly research shows that companies that score highly in *Fortune*'s reputational ratings are also consistently high performers with respect to their primary stakeholders.[30]

Companies' stakeholder relationships can evolve in one of three ways: reactively, proactively, or interactively.[31] The best stakeholder relationships are sustained by companies with an interactive stance.

Reactive Stance

When companies' managers merely react to their stakeholders' concerns and activities, they are likely not paying much attention to what is going on outside the firm. They may even deny that they have a responsibility to establish and maintain positive policies toward stakeholders, engage in legal battles to avoid responsibility, or do the bare minimum to meet the letter but not the spirit of the law.[32] Reaction is a defensive mode, not a positive one. Managers who fail to anticipate problems from stakeholders may find themselves wondering how things evolved in such a negative fashion.

Proactive Stance

Better, but probably still insufficient to establish truly positive stakeholder relationships, is the stance that companies sometimes take when they try to anticipate issues raised by external stakeholders. They may do this by establishing "boundary-spanning functions" for managing their external relations. Boundary-spanning functions are those that cross organizational boundaries, either internally or externally, in an attempt to develop and maintain relationships with one or more stakeholder groups. In modern multinational corporations these typically include: public affairs, community relations, public relations, media relations, investor relations, employee relations, government relations, lobbyists, union relations, sustainability officers, issues management, and, increasingly, for responsible enterprise, corporate social responsibility, and corporate citizenship functions. Even a proactive stance falls short of the ideal unless the company's boundary-spanning functions are managed interactively and with respect for the claims, risks, and bonds of stakeholders.

Interactive Stance

Because stakeholders exist in relationship to the firm, they are embedded in a network that makes them interdependent for their mutual success in activities where their interests overlap. Thus, arguably the best stance for showing ongoing respect for the firm's stakeholders is an engaged one—that is, a mutual and interactive one that is consistent over time and acknowledges both the mutuality of the relationship and the interdependence of the entities.

Such constructive and positive relationships between organizations and their stakeholders are built on a framework of interaction, mutual respect, and dialogue, rather than management or dominance. That is, progressive and responsible companies do not attempt to manage or dominate their stakeholders. Instead, they have recognized the importance of engaging with them in a relationship based on respect and dialogue or talking with each other rather than talking at each other. Building this relationship is not a one-time thing but an evolving, long-term process that requires commitment, energy, a willingness to admit mistakes, and a capacity for both parties to change when necessary. Implicitly, this approach recognizes that there is power on both sides of the conversation—and demands a willingness to acknowledge that mutuality.

BOUNDARY-SPANNING FOR PRIMARY
STAKEHOLDER RELATIONSHIPS

Boundary-spanning happens when companies set up formal units to reach across functions within the company to specific stakeholder groups, whether primary or secondary, and particularly when companies reach outside their own boundaries to external stakeholders. Managing boundary-spanning relationships is complex, but a firm's long-term success is intimately related to the way it treats its stakeholders in these essential relationships over time; thus, every manager ultimately is involved in some or most of these relationships. The next sections of this chapter detail the current state of the art in the boundary-spanning functions that deal with specific stakeholder groups.

Owners as Stakeholders

Although management thinker Charles Handy argued that today's investors are simply that—investors—and not owners in any real sense,[33] shareholders are important stakeholders because of the financial risks they take and because the financial bottom line is their yardstick. Investor relations functions manage communication and feedback from companies' shareholders through activities that include governance and annual meetings.

Investor Relations   Most large companies have a boundary-spanning function called investor relations that helps financial analysts value companies for the benefit of potential investors and that communicates with existing investors. The investor relations department is also typically responsible for producing a company's annual report, as well as online and more interactive information related to share prices and ownership. It provides both financial and strategic information to existing investors or shareholders. Sometimes the investor relations function falls under the broader umbrella of communications, public relations or public affairs, functions that are also responsible for managing external perceptions of the firm.

Many investors today are trying to evaluate whether companies and the boards of directors that oversee them are actually performing well for them, as a critical component of corporate governance. Particularly since the global financial crisis of 2008, some investors, particularly institutional investors, which can hold large numbers of shares, now put a premium on better corporate governance, greater transparency, and better information for investors in financial and other types of companies. The consulting firm McKinsey undertook a study that suggested a new era in corporate governance may be emerging, one that will shift shareholder expectations of boards of directors well beyond the tougher auditing standards and greater executive accountability demanded by the United States' Sarbanes-Oxley Act of 2002.[34] This study indicates that directors themselves expect investor relations to shift in important ways. Separating the roles of CEO and chair of the board, for example, would ensure that directors are more independent and accountable for their decisions, and perhaps reduce excessive levels of CEO compensation, which in 2000 peaked at 531 times the average pay of production workers.[35]

Globally, in country comparisons of CEO compensation with average wages, U.S. firms pay their executives disproportionally high amounts. Interestingly, CEO compensation throughout the world is only weakly influenced by firm profitability and size. There are, however, strong associations between the level of CEO compensation and the level of compensation of outside members of the board of directors. In other words, if outside board members are highly paid, there seem to be spillover effects to internal CEO compensation (e.g., because such outside members often also serve on the compensation committee).[36]

According to the U.S. labor union AFL-CIO, the average total compensation of U.S. CEOs in the S&P 500 in 2010 was US$11.3 million.[37] For some observers, this level of compensation raises concerns about social equity and the growing gap between rich and poor, particularly when firm performance does not seem to justify such compensation. In the United States, CEOs whose companies received "exceptional" government assistance from the Troubled Asset Relief Program (TARP) after the economic collapse of 2008 were required to take much of their salary in stock, and their other perks were limited. Financial institutions that were "bailed out" were prohibited by the American Recovery and Reinvestment Act of 2009 from receiving cash bonuses, retention awards, or incentive compensation, and their compensation in stock was also limited.[38] Generally, however, CEO compensation declined very slightly in the wake of the 2008 market crash, and it had begun rapidly rising again by 2010. Although the Dodd-Frank Wall Street Reform and Consumer Protection Act, passed in 2010, requires disclosure of the gap between the CEO's compensation and that of the average worker, the gap seems not to have narrowed.

Fiduciary Responsibilities   In addition to financial returns, appropriate and proper treatment of owners also has to do with respecting shareholders' right to have input into the governance of the company. Most important, treatment of shareholders includes their right to a fair return for the financial capital they risk when investing in the firm in the first place. The company's directors, who oversee the hiring of top management and the broad strategic direction of the firm, have a fiduciary responsibility to the shareholders. The top management team is responsible for developing and implementing the company's vision, values, and strategy. The fiduciary responsibility of corporate directors and their agents requires that the management team operates with due care, loyalty, and honesty with respect to the stockholders' financial investment or interest in the firm.[39] When companies don't do this, they are vulnerable to accusations of fraud, accounting irregularities, and other violations related to their financial performance.

One important role of the board is to try to reduce what is called the principal-agent problem. When the board hires a management team to implement corporate strategy that team thereby becomes an agent of the board. A problem can arise if the management team attempts to serve its own interests rather than those of the company. Many compensation schemes are designed to align the interests of management with those of the board or company in an attempt to avoid this problem. Financial theorist Michael Jensen was long an advocate of such alignment, which meant that top executives received incentives (such as stock options) if the company's share prices rose by a specified amount. So, for example, the financial interests of executives, particularly CEOs, were closely aligned with those of the company. Some critics claim that CEO compensation has gotten way out of line as a result of these practices, and that they have not done much to improve performance either.[40]

To be profitable, companies need to be as productive and efficient as possible, though profit can be considered a by-product of doing something that benefits someone—a customer or many customers—rather than an end in and of itself.[41] If profit becomes the sole goal of a company, it is an empty goal indeed. Still, how companies treat their shareholders financially is a legitimate concern to investors of all sorts, who have put their financial capital at risk on behalf of the firm with the expectation of reasonable financial returns. The fiduciary responsibility of corporate directors is generally seen by U.S. courts as giving corporate directors authority to prevent self-dealing, opportunistic behavior, and power-aggrandizing behavior on the part of managers.[42]

The primary responsibility of the company to its shareholders is therefore to safeguard their investments and ensure that the investor owners receive a fair return for the risk they have taken. The relationship is not one of agency, nor is it necessarily a contractual obligation between individuals. Rather, the fiduciary responsibility is intended to "protect legal owners who were not in a position to manage their own affairs from the unscrupulous self-dealing of those administrators the incompetent were forced to rely upon."[43] Thus, in some respects shareholders should be considered on a par with other stakeholders rather than elevated to a unique status as the most important stakeholders.

A UN study on the legal dimensions of integrating ESG issues into investment policies concluded that in both the common and civil legal traditions the nature of investment decisions is not exhaustively prescribed. The single-minded pursuit of profit maximization and hence the neglect of broader stakeholder responsibilities (when in conflict) is not prescribed by law,[44] neither in countries with a more rigid civil law tradition nor in countries, like the UK and the United States, where the more flexible common-law tradition allows for responding to changing societal conditions. Even in those countries where a duty to seek profitability is written into the law (as it is in Germany), the law does not prescribe a certain level of profitability, but instead indicates that profits must be earned in a sustainable way.[45]

The key to success is balance. The interests of the primary stakeholders and some critical secondary stakeholders have to be assessed and balanced with each other to achieve the desired outcome: a company that operates with integrity and adds value for owners and other stakeholders. To see how this can be done, in the sections that follow we address how other stakeholders can be treated well.

Employees as Stakeholders

The primary interests of employees are earning a good wage for their efforts and making personal contributions to the organization's achievement of its vision and values. Both of these interests are represented by the employee relations or human resources boundary-spanning function. Firms used to hire employees primarily to provide physical labor. Modern enterprises, particularly Web-based, e-commerce, and technologically sophisticated companies, tend to hire employees more for their knowledge, known as intellectual capital, than for their physical attributes. Intangible assets like intellectual and human capital, along with corporate reputation, now represent as much as 70 percent of the value of many companies,[46] so employee assets are more valuable than ever. In making a commitment to an enterprise, employees put at risk their work lives, their capacity to contribute, and their earning power. In return, they have a right to expect to contribute to a worthwhile enterprise and to be known and valued for their contributions.

Employees and the contributions they make are central to an organization's success. Many companies, recognizing the importance of good relationships with employees, claim to put people first. Despite the rhetoric, the modern corporate landscape is fraught with corporate restructurings, mergers, acquisitions, layoffs, outsourcing of work to low-wage countries with low workplace standards, contingent or part-time workforces (who receive no benefits), and other cost-cutting (or "efficiency") measures that affect employees negatively. Such measures leave many workers feeling devalued and erode their loyalty. Recent research shows that the more severe the extent of downsizing in a corporation, the lower employees' commitment.[47] In addition, it is widely acknowledged that the so-called Millennial Generation (born between, roughly, the mid-1970s and before 2000) value work that is meaningful to society. As Tip Fallon argues, "Millennials care about improving the world. . . . A paycheck is not always going to put a smile on their face at the end of the day."[48]

People—and their loyalty, commitment, and productive energy—do matter to the success and health of the firm. Treating employees well is essential for generating high levels of productivity and performance over time.[49] Treating employees well fosters commitment to the organization's purpose, particularly if that purpose is shared with employees and they understand their role in fulfilling it.

Despite claiming to value employees, many companies still maintain employee relationships based on failed assumptions; that is, their practice differs from their rhetoric. Employers' failed assumptions include viewing employees as costs rather than investments, focusing on the short term, dehumanizing employees (or infantilizing them), and failing to delegate responsibility to them.[50] Leaders tend also to adhere to two perverse norms about management: that good managers are tough or mean, and that good analysis is the same as good management[51] (a problem sometimes called "the paralysis of analysis").[52] Further, because of embedded cultures and long-term policies that devalue people and their contributions, many companies need to transform their employee policies to bring the rhetoric and the reality of their cultures and operating practices more into line with their vision and values statements.

Successful Employee Practices   Highly successful organizations engage in practices that provide employees with the sense of meaning that is important to productivity (see Table 6.2). These practices produce outcomes that are the opposite of management practices that erode employee loyalty and capacity (and, correspondingly, community health).[53]

High-performing companies provide security for employees who are carefully selected for the vision and values they share with the company. They establish compensation plans that tie rewards not only to individual performance but also to group and company performance. They demonstrate their employees' value to the company by providing training; reducing status differences between levels; and sharing information about the company's performance, and its policies. Employees, as stakeholders, are treated fairly and know that they are valued; they are not subjected to power-aggrandizing management whims or the shifting winds of profitability.

Employee Commitment/Company Commitment   Sustaining employee commitment and building loyalty are not easy in an era when loyalty, both from and to employees, seems a thing of the past. Many of today's employees have been "taught" by corporate downsizings, restructurings, and rightsizings (in plain language, layoffs) that their first objective is to be an individual contributor, almost an entrepreneur within the company, looking out for self rather than others or for the welfare of the firm. Others lack loyalty to companies because they are employed as contingent workers, hired temporarily or part-time so that employers can avoid the cost of benefits.

Gaining commitment and loyalty from employee stakeholders requires creating an almost cult-like culture within the organization.[54] Employees need and want to feel a part of something bigger than they are; that is, they seek meaning in their work and work setting.[55] Commitment derives from a set of internally developed practices that inspire people to believe in the work of the enterprise. These practices are based on well-articulated underlying values that reflect a clear organizational vision that allows employees to recognize that they are contributing to something bigger than themselves. The company also demonstrates commitment by operating with integrity and for the well-being of employees over the long term.

Companies that use the employee practices detailed in Table 6.2 know that there are significant benefits to be gained by treating employees well. Employment security, for example, benefits both companies and employees; cult-like cultures built on selective hiring practices screen out unsuitable job applicants (although, of course, there are dangers associated with "groupthink" in cultures that become "inbred" or lack sufficient diversity). Employees value working in decentralized systems where they can be part of self-managed teams and be compensated based on their contributions and performance. Highly successful companies provide extensive employee training, reduce status inequalities, and share relevant information with employees that allows them to perform their jobs well.[56]

Organizations that want to build employee loyalty can stress their values in orientation and training programs; they can reflect those values by building an organizational tradition through symbols and culture; and they can guarantee fairness and justice throughout the system, particularly through comprehensive grievance procedures. They should also make two-way communication possible at all levels, create a sense of community through common purpose, and hire people sympathetic with the company's vision and values. Such companies will distribute rewards equitably and emphasize teamwork but also celebrate individual achievement and employee development.[57]

TABLE 6.2 *Employment Practices of Successful Organizations*

Employment security	Provides job security even when productivity improves; retains knowledgeable, productive workers; builds commitment and retention; and decreases costs associated with layoffs (including training and recruitment).
Selective hiring	Creates cult-like cultures built on common values. Requires large applicant pool, clarity about necessary skills and attributes, clear sense of job requirements, and screening attributes difficult to change through training.
Self-managed teams and decentralization	Teams substitute peer-based control for hierarchical control; ideas are shared and creative solutions found. Decentralization increases shared responsibility for outcomes, stimulates initiative and effort, and removes levels of management (cost).
Comparatively high compensation	Produces organizational success; retains expertise and experience; rewards and reinforces high performance.
Compensation contingent on organization performance	Rewards the whole as well as individual effort. Requires employee training to understand links between ownership and rewards.
Extensive training	Values knowledge and skills (generalist, not specialist). Relies on frontline employees' skill and initiative in problem solving, innovation, responsibility for quality. Can be a source of competitive advantage.
Reduction of status differences	Premised on the belief that high performance is achieved when all employees' ideas, skills, efforts are fully tapped. To do this requires reducing differences between levels, both symbolically (language and labels, physical space, dress) and substantively (wage inequality).
Sharing information	Creates a high-trust organization; helps everyone know where contributions come from and where they stand.

SOURCE: Jeffrey Pfeffer and John F. Veiga, "Putting People First for Organizational Success," *Academy of Management Executive* 13, no. 2 (May 1999): 37–48.

Intellectual Capital   Building positive relationships with employees is fundamentally about treating all people with the same dignity and respect with which one would treat family, peers, or organizational superiors. It is not extremely difficult, but it does require sustained effort to overcome the tendency, inherent in business's dominant value of economizing, to view people as means rather than ends in themselves. Similarly, the premises of fairness and respect need to be constantly held up in light of the tendency to value power aggrandizement. In the end, however, the performance results from respecting the employee stakeholder make the effort well worthwhile.

The rationale for building respectful relationships with employees, especially for the modern enterprise, is that both the intellectual capital housed in the minds of employees and the social capital that can be developed by winning their hearts are great aids to productivity. Intellectual capital is a key, though not the only, source of competitive advantage in many organizations today. Companies that recognize this reality and develop practices that treat their employees with dignity and respect, rather than exploitation, and that develop cultures in which employees can fulfill personal needs and dreams while also working on the corporate vision, will succeed where others fail.

Customers as Stakeholders

Customer relationships have come to the fore in recent years with the emergence of relationship marketing. Marketers and business leaders have recognized that customers choose to purchase goods and services from one company as opposed to another because they have reason to trust that the company's products will meet their expectations. Thus, trust is a type of capital. Another type of capital is the loyalty that customers have to a company; some claim that long-term customer commitment is the most valuable resource companies have for growing the top line: revenue.[58] Further, one study suggests that the combination of satisfied customers and satisfied employees improves company performance. It is just one more of the relationships among primary stakeholders that affect outcomes for the company.[59]

Relationship marketing theory operates alongside the traditional marketing mix of product, price, place, and promotion. Relationship marketing is especially important in service and knowledge industries, where the relationship itself may be what matters most to customers. Relationships are, however, increasingly important for all types of companies because of technological connectivity, which allows many products (services) to be delivered electronically.[60] Terms such as relational contracting, relational marketing, working partnerships, symbiotic marketing, strategic alliances, co-marketing alliances, and internal marketing all have been used to describe aspects of relationship marketing: a network of sustained exchange relationships between customers and companies.[61]

Like other relationships among Web-connected companies and stakeholders, customer and supply chain relationships are gaining importance because of the recognition that companies are embedded in networks where cooperative relationships matter at least as much as competitive ones.[62] Equally deeply embedded in this emerging relational perspective on customers is recognition of the need for high-quality products and services, as well as high-quality relationships that will sustain the trust and commitment on which relationship marketing relies.[63] For example, the word *quality* is associated with, among other factors, customer satisfaction; business effectiveness and cost leadership; and cooperative relationships, even partnerships, with customers throughout the company's value chain. Higher quality, as assessed by Baldrige Quality Award winners, has been found to be linked to better financial performance.[64] Further, research has demonstrated that customer relationship management has positive impacts on how well new products do.[65]

Mutual trust in customer relationships (and other relationships as well) exists when each party has confidence in the other's reliability and integrity. Commitment exists when both parties value the relationship over time; that is, the relationship is enduring. Among the factors that result in trust and commitment between companies and their customers are shared values, timely communication, and the potential costs of ending the relationship. Opportunistic and self-serving behavior on one partner's part will very likely reduce trust and commitment.[66]

Customer Loyalty   The goal of improving customer relationships is to build loyalty among customers, who then make a long-term commitment to the company to continue purchasing goods and services and who tell others about the company's products and services.[67] Companies that produce shoddy or harmful products will find it increasingly difficult to maintain customer trust and commitment in an era in which sustained relationships and alliances of all sorts are increasingly central to producing sales. Information about problems spreads at the speed of electrons on the Internet, through blogs, social media, and other Web 2.0–based technologies. One study showed that it costs five times as much to acquire new customers as it does to retain existing customers—and that the average company loses nearly 10 percent of its customers every year. This study suggests that simply retaining 2 percent more customers a year is equivalent to cutting costs by 10 percent.[68] Another study found that in service organizations, good service and outcomes increase customer loyalty and reduce any perceived sacrifice on the part of customers.[69]

There are many benefits of establishing ongoing relationships with customers. As customer needs change over time, companies that are in communication with their customers can shift accordingly. The costs of maintaining the relationship and selling, distributing, and delivering goods and services (called transaction costs) also decrease as trust and commitment increase. Long-standing customers can provide feedback that helps a company improve its product and service quality. Maintaining customer relationships entails interacting regularly with customers to ensure that value is being added, which can create additional ties through technology, shared knowledge or expertise, or social capital.[70]

Quality and Customers   For most companies today, particularly those competing in the global arena, maintaining a high level of product and service quality is a given. Along with the quality revolution, which occurred in the United States during the last twenty years of the 20th century and in the prior thirty years in Japan, came customer demands for nearly complete satisfaction with the quality and nature of products and services.

Quality programs within companies, following the advice of the late quality guru W. Edwards Deming, typically focus on continual quality improvement through an emphasis on statistical process controls and quality management. The quality process, whether for product- or service-oriented companies, seeks to ensure that customer expectations are met and that trust is built. Table 6.3 lists the characteristics of service and manufacturing companies considered to be world class and designed to develop excellent relationships with customers (and suppliers), along with employees.[71]

Many of these characteristics are similar to those needed to generate excellence in employee relationships; both goals require that a company operates with integrity and a sound set of core values, and ultimately with principled leadership. In addition, the practices associated with world-class companies

TABLE 6.3   *Characteristics of World-Class Quality Operations*

Characteristics of World-Class Plants	*Characteristics of World-Class Service Organizations*
1. Safety	1. Accessibility and follow-up by employees
2. Involved and committed workforce	2. Competence (required skills and knowledge, proactive)
3. Just-in-time manufacturing and deliveries to customers	
4. Focus on product flow	3. Attitude (positive, flexible, continuous improvement)
5. Preventive/predictive maintenance	4. Communication
6. Bottlenecks managed	5. Credibility
7. Total quality management program	6. Features/innovation in services
8. Fast setups	7. Responsiveness
9. Extremely low inventories	8. Tangible results
10. Supportive policies/procedures	

SOURCE: Charles C. Poirier and William F. Houser, "Business Partnering for Continuous Improvement" (San Francisco, CA: Berrett-Koehler Publishers Inc,, 1993). Reprinted with permission of the publisher. www.bkconnection.com.

require integrity in all of the company's practices, including developing the goods and services that will be delivered to customers with whom the company hopes to establish a long-term relationship for repeat purchases and all-important word-of-mouth marketing.

Some scholars link product and service quality with business effectiveness, making connections among customers, and partnering with suppliers as sources of competitive advantage. One study of the relationship between quality programs and customer satisfaction and company productivity showed that when multiple quality management approaches are implemented together, both customer satisfaction and productivity rise.[72] The quality movement has pushed many companies to benchmark their own operations and product/service quality against those of leading competitors to ensure that they stay abreast of new developments and meet changing customer needs.[73] Among the services that companies can use to enhance actual and perceived quality as well as customer relationships are: providing technical service and user advice; installing just-in-time logistics systems in customer facilities; adapting invoicing to specific customer needs; and providing technical expertise, information, and social contact with customers.[74]

Suppliers, Distributors, Allies, and Partners as Stakeholders

Supply chain management has become a hot topic in the current era of anti-corporate activism, outsourcing, and network-structured enterprises, in part because outsourcing can take jobs away from home communities, and in part because the working and environmental conditions in many of the companies to which work is outsourced may be substandard. Alliances, joint ventures, partnerships, and outsourcing are all ways of reducing nonessential activities and controlling costs. The bottom line of supplier and ally relationships, as with employee relationships, can be found in the intellectual or knowledge capital inherent in the expertise for which the relationship is developed in the first place. Companies need to manage these relationships proactively to maximize their performance, and many of these relationships today have important impacts on companies' reputations.[75]

Traditional Supplier Relationships   Traditionally, companies formed relationships with suppliers to gain access to the raw materials and services necessary to the company's business. Typical contracts between suppliers and customers spell out the services or products to be delivered, the conditions under which they are to be delivered, and the relevant prices. The contract can stipulate an arm's-length relationship, meaning that the two businesses have little interaction other than that necessary to exchange goods and services and transfer payment.

Some companies—particularly in Asian countries where the ideology is communitarian and where long-term relationships are considered essential to doing business—develop networks of long-standing intercompany relationships to ensure access to necessary goods and services. There are families of companies—called kereitsu in Japan and chaebol in Korea—in similar and sometimes vastly different businesses whose links are sustained over long periods of time. These companies establish a form of social capital or a family-like relationship.

Traditional suppliers and customers are interdependent in that each company in the relationship relies on the other to deliver what has been promised. In contrast, when such relationships are solely contractual rather than based on trust and mutual interests, they can be dropped as prices or interests change without significant consequences to the purchasing company. Indeed, many companies, using a contractual mindset, attempt to keep multiple suppliers "on the line" so that they are not dependent on any single supplier.

Alliances and Supplier–Distributor Relationships   When companies form long-term customer–supplier relationships, joint ventures, or partnerships, they increase their interdependence and therefore their mutual responsibility for the success of their joint endeavors. They view supply and distribution chain management as a critical strategic resource that can improve performance.[76] Of course, not all joint ventures involve a supplier–customer relationship, but all of them do demand collaboration, integrity of intent, and trust if the relationship is to succeed.[77]

The popularity of strategic alliances over the past two decades arose in part from a recognition that cooperative alliances, such as Japanese kereitsu, could provide strategic advantages that pure competition could not. Such interlinked networks can, of course, lead to insufficient diversity and an inability to change, so links need to be balanced with innovation and the capacity to engage new people and ideas when they are needed. In general, when companies accept responsibility for their mutual success, they are more willing to invest in equipment, employee development, and market development than they would be if they thought that the relationship could end with the next price increase. Such relationships help companies focus on the long-term effects of their decisions. Companies in supplier–customer–distributor or allied relationships rely on each other for business. Because of this interdependence, they frequently make investments that align one company's resources with the other's needs, for example, by developing customer-specific equipment, standards, or products and services based on expectations that the relationship will continue.

Outsourcing   Many companies now outsource formerly internal functions such as production, human resource management, accounting, data management, customer service, and even information technology to experts. Thus a company like Nike has become largely a marketing company, holding within its structure the marketing and distribution functions, while outsourcing all of its production activity. Many clothing, footwear, sporting goods, and toy companies use outsourcing strategies for most of what they sell. Companies can be positively or negatively affected by their supplier (and distributor) relationships, because so much weight today is placed on corporate reputation, particularly for brand-name companies. One study shows that these relationships are helped by the implementation of a code of conduct governing suppliers. In addition, open and candid relationships between the supplier and customer company are necessary if the customer company's reputation and responsibility are to be upheld.[78]

As a means of economizing, some large companies outsource their production, customer support, or even programming operations to smaller suppliers in less-developed countries, where wages and working standards are lower. Most companies outsource in the expectation of reducing costs, improving asset efficiency, and increasing profitability, in the hopes that specialists in a function will be able to achieve greater efficiency and quality.[79] The practice of outsourcing supply relationships creates risks. Boundaries between the firm and its suppliers, customers, or competitors tend to blur when the links are tight. Even when the boundaries are quite clear in the eyes of both firms, they may be much less obvious to external observers, who view what happens in the supplying firm as integral to the integrity and responsibility of the supplied firm.

Codes of Conduct   To cope with supplier relationships and ensure that workers are treated fairly, many responsible companies adopt codes of conduct and require their suppliers to adhere to them as well. Companies also develop internal codes of conduct that detail their relationships with their suppliers and overtly recognize their interdependence. With supply relationships so strategically critical to many companies, it is essential that the conditions of work in those suppliers be carefully monitored if large companies hope to treat all of their stakeholders with respect and dignity. Operating with integrity demands nothing less. If integrity alone is insufficient, the growing numbers of activists with access to company-specific information can readily disseminate it through worldwide electronic connections and ensure that companies pay attention to working conditions.

A 2008 KMPG survey found that some 86 percent of the world's largest 200 corporations had adopted a code of conduct, that the number of new company codes had doubled in the previous ten years, and that companies that had older codes were updating and revising them.[80] The survey found that the most common drivers for adopting a corporate code of conduct were compliance with the law, creating shared company cultures, and improving or protecting the company's reputation. Among the most commonly cited values were integrity, teamwork, respect, innovation, and client focus. Implementation (or what the survey calls embedding) happens through e-learning, ethics hotlines, and whistleblower mechanisms that help employees detect and report ethical lapses.

CRITICAL AND PARTICULAR SECONDARY STAKEHOLDERS

Governments and communities are critical secondary stakeholders for all companies and sometimes become primary stakeholders—for example, when companies are highly regulated or are community-based, as utilities are. Governments establish the rules of society by which companies must live, and communities provide essential infrastructure to support company operations. The public affairs function and the community relations function have evolved to provide ongoing company interactions with these important stakeholder groups.

Public Affairs: Government and "Public" Relationships

Governments at all levels and in all branches wherever a company operates are critical secondary stakeholders for businesses. Business–government relationships are usually handled through the public affairs function, which can also serve as an umbrella for issues management, media relations, community relations (discussed below), public relations, and other external affairs activities. The goal of the public affairs office is to manage the legitimacy of the organization in its societies[81] and attempt to influence or modify issues, legislation, regulations, and rulings so that they are favorable to corporate interests.[82]

To the extent that public affairs encompasses the other external relations functions noted, its goal is also to present the company in a favorable light to its many publics, or external stakeholders. Thus, the public affairs function also manages external relations, including those involving public issues and associated activists, the media, and occasionally agencies in civil society to whom the contributions function is linked. The business–government relations function of the public affairs office helps companies understand, anticipate, manage, and ultimately cope with laws, regulations, and rulings generated by government agencies.[83]

Public affairs developed originally as a fairly minor responsibility of the CEO. It was not until the 1950s and 1960s that the function began to become more formalized and sophisticated during the 1980s and 1990s.[84] By 1980 more than 80 percent of large corporations had a public affairs office,[85] and today virtually all large companies have this function in some form. Among the activities that come under the public affairs umbrella are political action committees, grassroots organizing, government relations, lobbying, issues management, and international public affairs. In addition, sometimes companies place their ethics function, social responsibility activities, social media engagement, and public relations function under the public affairs umbrella. Because it encompasses so many of a typical corporation's boundary-spanning activities from inside to the outside environment, it is important to look a bit more deeply into managing public affairs.

Managing Public Affairs   The underlying goal of the public affairs function is to develop and maintain a positive relationship between the company and the various branches and levels of government whose activities influence—or are influenced by—the firm's activities. On one level, the function helps present the company to key public officials and opinion leaders in a positive light. The public affairs office also serves the reverse purpose of helping to explain the political environment to people within the corporation.[86] The public affairs function is particularly concerned with the political environment and political change as it is likely to affect the firm; its general charge is to establish and maintain relationships with public officials, whose bottom line is political capital and power. It accomplishes these objectives through effective communications campaigns, by collaborating with important partners, and by engaging in activities that help build relationships at the local level.[87]

In the global village, U.S. corporations undertake these activities both domestically and in other parts of the world when they need to work cooperatively with local governments. For example, many U.S. companies have divisions operating in the European Union that view themselves as European companies of American parentage (ECAPs) because they want to stress their European presence.[88]

Activities of public affairs officers involve lobbying public officials to ensure that they are well informed about the company's perspective pending legislative or regulatory action.[89] Political strategy for corporations can mean hiring lobbyists, whose job it is to inform public officials about the company's position on issues and pending legislation and regulation. It might also entail having corporate officers testify on the company's or industry's behalf before a public body. Many companies develop political strategies and support specific candidates for office, frequently through political action committees (PACs).[90] In the United States today, it increasingly involves engagement in political campaigns, particularly since the 2010 U.S. Supreme Court ruled in the Citizens United case that companies, including foreign companies, are allowed to contribute as much as they want anonymously to political campaigns.[91]

In the United States, political action can mean using corporate resources, often gathered through a PAC, to support political campaigns or to generate a grassroots letter-writing, phone, or e-mail campaign against or in favor of a proposed legislative or regulatory action. Lobbying also includes providing information to public officials and their staff or simply hiring lobbyists to represent the company's point of view to local, state, or national public bodies.

Companies need to develop their political strategies carefully because their resources give them great power, and they are sometimes accused of using their power to influence political decision makers in their favor. For this reason, there is a great deal of criticism of business involvement in political and public policy affairs, with critics arguing that the large donations made by corporate PACs to political candidates can sway their decision-making in favor of corporate over public interests.[92] This criticism has intensified since the Citizens United decision; many observers believe that it gives too much unaccountable power to corporations to try to influence legislation in their favor at the expense of democracy. The decision also raised the issue of "corporate personhood" as a public issue and has sparked a number of initiatives that are attempting to find ways to restrict that power.

Responsible companies will use their political power wisely, not merely to serve the short-term and exclusively financial interests of the firm, but more broadly, to think about the public responsibilities they bear simply because of the resources they command. Recognizing these responsibilities, they will work collaboratively and cooperatively with public officials in the public interest, not purely in their private interest. Working collaboratively involves a give-and-take that allows governments and their officials to do their appropriate work of representing the public interest and the common good even, occasionally, when it would be in the short-term interest of the firm to do otherwise.

Issues Management   In efforts to improve their reputation, communicate with stakeholders, and manage business–government or public relations, companies sometimes establish issues management units.[93] These units are sometimes independent of and sometimes within the public affairs function. Issues managers attempt to frame public issues in ways that are helpful to the company. Such framings frequently conflict with those articulated by different activist groups interested in the same issue. Working productively with activists to frame an issue means establishing an ongoing conversation about its nature, scope, and implications. Research indicates that proactive issues management can improve companies' competitiveness and standing among their peers.[94]

Issues managers must identify emerging issues relevant to corporate concerns, analyze the potential or actual impact of issues on the company, determine what kinds of responses the company should make, and in some cases implement the response or ensure that others do so.[95] Issues managers are charged with identifying where gaps exist between stakeholder expectations and reality. In the international setting, the scanning process is more complex, in part because so many different cultures and contexts exist in each country, differing levels of development generate different types of issues, and stakeholders may have very different expectations of companies than they do domestically.

Issues can cross national borders or affect only one country. Experience with an issue in one nation, such as dealing with human rights abuses, can help a company cope with it the next time the issue arises. Experience can help companies avoid mistakes in developing relationships with appropriate stakeholders and managing issues locally, but only to the extent that cultural differences and political realities are taken into account in the next country.

When companies operate in numerous countries or transnationally, they face considerable complexity in working with local governments and other stakeholders on relevant issues. Some countries, like the United States, readily permit pluralistic interest groups, including corporations, to contest public issues and provide varying opinions and information from different sources to policymakers. In other countries, however, where the ideology, public policy standards, and cultural norms are different, open lobbying on issues may be far less acceptable, particularly for foreign firms. In such circumstances, working through host country trade or industry associations, which represent the general interest of the companies in an industry, may be the only feasible way to try to influence public policy.[96]

Crisis Management   Organizational crises are highly ambiguous, low-probability situations that have no clear cause or effect but pose a major threat to the organization's survival and at least some organizational stakeholders. Crises frequently surprise the organization and present dilemmas whose resolution will either help or hurt the enterprise.[97] Although not everyone agrees that crises can be prevented, many organizations, particularly those where crisis is likely, have created crisis management units. Examples of crises are the kidnapping of an executive, a plane crash that kills members of the top management team, or a major fire or chemical spill. The 2008 global financial crisis was partly the result of a major problem in the subprime lending market, where banks and mortgage companies had made loans to borrowers who would not otherwise have met loan criteria, in some instances using what have been termed predatory lending practices. These riskier borrowers found it hard to meet their loan terms when, for example, interest rates rose on variable-rate mortgages or when "balloon" payments became due. Because of links to mortgage-backed securities, large financial institutions faced enormous losses; Citigroup, for example, reported nearly $10 billion in losses for only the last quarter of 2007.[98] Product problems can also create crises, as toymaker Mattel found out in 2007 when it had to recall nearly 19 million toys made in China that were tainted by lead paint or had loose magnets that could be swallowed by young children.[99]

Companies may not be able to predict crises, but they need to know what to do—and how to do it quickly—when one occurs. Although not all contingencies can or should be researched and planned for, rehearsal of an implementation plan is a crucial component of good crisis management.[100] That includes mobilizing public relations and a crisis team or crisis management unit, which is typically organized by existing employees rather than existing as a separate unit. In other types of organizations, such as hospitals, disasters are simulated to ensure that all parties understand what to do in the event of a real crisis. Crisis management efforts can be considered effective when the organization survives and can resume relatively normal operations, when losses to the organization and its stakeholders are minimized, and when enough is learned that it can be applied to the next crisis.[101] One study of Australian companies found that more than one-fourth of the companies failed following a crisis.[102] Crisis management can also be considered effective when a company's reputation as a good citizen is left undamaged by the actions taken during and following the crisis.

Sociologist Charles Perrow has studied high-risk technologies, such as those found in chemical plants, nuclear facilities, and aircraft. Such technologies have what Perrow calls "interactive complexity," which means they interact in complex ways, and "tight coupling," which means the functioning of each element is closely tied to related parts of the technology. Time may be of the essence should the technology begin to fail; slack may not be available, resulting in the quick escalation of the problem through a cascade of interdependent and largely unexpected effects. Perrow says that systems that are characterized by interactive complexity and tight coupling are prone to "normal accidents" because of the multiple unexpected interactions of failure.[103] One such "normal accident," Union Carbide's 1984 chemical spill in Bhopal, India, killed more than 2,000 people and injured many others. That accident is widely regarded as having been a pivotal responsibility crisis for the company, which is now part of Dow Chemical, because the company was ill-prepared to handle it at the time. Similar issues arose with BP's handling of the Deepwater Horizon explosion and subsequent massive oil spill in the Gulf of Mexico in 2010.

Community Relations

Healthy communities are those in which citizens are connected with each other, share a common vision of the community's identity and culture, and are willing to work together for the common good. Corporations that are rooted in and responsible to a community can play an important role in building and sustaining community health. Healthy communities support local companies through infrastructure planning and development and by providing an educated workforce and a stable working environment that enhances competitiveness. Most companies work directly with their communities to develop social capital (connections and relatedness) and to attract new employees through community relations functions.[104]

Community relations programs in the United States, where they are most common, typically have encompassed a number of areas, including charitable contributions or philanthropy, volunteer programs, and community-based (public–private or social) partnerships, and related social initiatives. The relationships with communities embodied in these programs are handled through a number of functions that are frequently consolidated into a single office called community relations (CR). Generally speaking, the community relations function deals with community members and groups active in the civil society (and sometimes the political) sphere of influence.

The major investment by the community in a company comes in the forms of social capital generated by strong and healthy communities and the infrastructure generated by communities from taxes paid by individual and corporate citizens. Social capital provides for healthy community-based relationships and positive civic and political action that helps balance both economic and governmental sources of power. The infrastructure provided by communities includes the local education system, which can supply the company with an educated workforce. Infrastructure also includes roads and highways, communications networks, local community-based services (e.g., garbage removal and sewage systems), and the local regulatory system, without which it would be impossible for firms to operate successfully.

Social capital is the key measure of success in healthy and well-functioning communities. Companies have a choice: They can destroy social capital by economizing at all costs, laying off employees and devastating their communities when lower-cost options arise, or they can develop lasting, trust-filled relationships with local communities and help strengthen those communities; in short, they can become rooted in communities rather than rootless. The result will enable companies to gain access to qualified, well-educated, loyal workers; communities with adequate infrastructure to support company needs; and civil relationships with local leaders who believe that the presence of the company is a benefit to the community.

CEMEX—STRENGTHENING LOCAL COMMUNITIES

Cemex is a global leader in the building materials and cement industry based in Mexico. With a strong orientation toward customers, as well as its own employees, Cemex grew rapidly from its founding as a small cement manufacturer in Mexico in 1906 to become one of the world's leading building materials manufacturers. By 2010, the company had operations in more than fifty countries on five continents, producing more than 96 million metric tons of cement annually, 51 million cubic meters of ready-mix concrete, and 158 million metric tons of aggregates. Cemex owned sixty-two cement plants and had close to 2,000 ready-mix concrete facilities.

Cemex identifies three main core values that support its business model: collaboration with others in a collective pursuit of excellence; integrity (act honestly, responsibly, and respectfully toward others at all times); and leadership (envision the future and focus on service, excellence, and competitiveness).[105] These values have served the company in good stead, particularly during the mid-1990s currency devaluation in Mexico, when the company, according to Ricardo Sandoval writing in the *Stanford Innovation Review*, issued a "declaration of ignorance," admitting that it had no idea how to help "the millions of poor Mexicans who spend as much as 10 years building the average four-room home on their own and in fits and starts dependent on irregular cash flows and lulls in spike-prone prices for building materials."[106]

Following this admission, the company focused on the do-it-yourself segment of the construction business and in 2000 Cemex established a new initiative called Patrimonio Hoy, focused on economic development and helping Mexico improve the housing situation of poorer people. The Patrimonio Hoy program is part of the company's community engagement efforts and operates as a separate social enterprise with more than 100 local offices in Mexico, Nicaragua, Costa Rica, Colombia, and the Dominican Republic. Similar to what the Grameen Bank does with microfinance, Cemex's Patrimonio Hoy works with family groups that commit to save enough over about ten weeks to pay for the materials they need to construct their homes. Cemex provides the building materials in the second week—with credit for the next weeks so that there is time for the families to finish the building. In the meantime, Cemex offers technical assistance, such as architectural advice.

By 2010, the Patrimonio Hoy program had helped more than 300,000 low-income families improve their housing situation through self-improvement initiatives sponsored by the company. By focusing on a market segment that has been traditionally underserved, Cemex's microfinance initiative has been able to grow its own cement business. Not simply a charity, Patrimonio Hoy is a self-sustaining social enterprise promoting local economic development. The program gives people who are usually cut off from the credit market access to money for building homes and creates a variety of local jobs (e.g., 29 percent of the new homeowners use their new home to start businesses).[107] Cemex states that the program helps to build long-term relationships and trust with low-income communities and also increases the company's competitiveness within the low-income market.

Media, Public Relations, and Web 2.0   The job of the media in a democracy is to report on newsworthy events and information so that the citizenry can be publicly engaged and politically active, vote knowledgeably, and actively influence policymakers on issues of importance to them. In general, the press reports on public issues because a reporter or an editor, or an opinion leader, has seen a gap between expectation and reality. Although the media are influential in shaping and framing public perceptions, their real job is to direct public attention to the issues rather than create the issues themselves.[108] In the modern world, this principle is sometimes violated.

Public relations includes efforts by companies to enhance their image and their reputation in public opinion through positive representation in the media, typically through reports for which the company does not pay (directly). The founder of the field, Edward Bernays, defined public relations as "the engineering of consent," or the ability to get diverse individuals with varying perceptions and values to "consent to a program or goal."[109] Public relations initiatives are efforts by companies to improve their reputations as credible, trusted, accountable, and responsible entities.[110] Reputations are built on perceptions, primarily those of external stakeholders. The Internet has generated increased transparency about corporate activities and made it more important than ever that companies keep their stakeholders informed.

Social media such as Twitter, Facebook, blogs, and similar technologies have dramatically changed the landscape between companies and the media, including all of their stakeholders, internal and external. Media relations thus takes on an entirely new context and set of meanings in what some call the Web 2.0 world of interconnected and engaged observers. These new social media give power to influence to anyone paying attention to a company's activities and, in some cases, provide a platform for activism around company issues. Companies are still in the early stages of learning to cope with these democratically oriented social media platforms, and how to engage responsibly with the new stakeholders with access to information about the company.[111]

Managing in a Web 2.0 environment means being aware of the changing interface between business and society. On the one hand, Web 2.0 allows firms to better communicate with stakeholders and gain real-time feedback on potential concerns and responsibility activities; on the other hand, it can make them vulnerable to stakeholders who are critical of company practices. The boot, shoe, and clothing company Timberland, for instance, has moved toward quarterly reporting of its key social and environmental metrics via a social media site called JustMeans.com. The idea is to initiate a sustained dialogue with key stakeholders on the company's responsibility activities. Web 2.0 technologies are also used by activists to better coordinate and speed up campaigning. Greenpeace, for instance, launched three major online campaigns against companies in 2010 alone. Web 2.0 technologies allow not only for viral marketing (i.e., marketing that relies on self-replicating effects through social media), but also for viral campaigning. The catchword here is viral.

The 2010 Greenpeace campaign against Nestlé's Kit Kat chocolate brand, criticizing the company's purchase of palm oil from suppliers whose practices destroy the rainforest, was based on a YouTube video that spread rapidly across the Internet and induced discussions on Facebook and Twitter. Nestlé requested that users refrain from using an altered Kit Kat logo (which had changed "Kit Kat" to "Killer") in posts on its own Facebook "fan" page, and even threatened users that posts would be removed. A Facebook user responded by saying, "Not sure you're going to win friends in the social media space with this sort of dogmatic approach. I understand that you're on your back-foot due to various issues not excluding Palm Oil but Social Media is about embracing your market, engaging and having a conversation rather than preaching!"[112] This story shows the perils of inexperience with or inattention to these emerging forms of stakeholder engagement, and highlights the growing importance of learning to use social media effectively as an engagement tool.

Some public relations practitioners see themselves as advocates for their companies (or, when they are in public relations firms, for their clients). Others see their role as building consensus among stakeholders on issues relevant to the firm by creating carefully crafted messages that put the company's point of view in the public's eyes and ears.[113] Thus, modern public relations officers are responsible in part for helping to build local communities and in part for sustaining positive relationships with a company's many stakeholders.[114] Highlighting the importance of integrity, one group of public relations scholars offers three important guidelines regarding public relations and reputation: always tell the truth because even small deceptions can negatively influence reputation; be loyal and adhere to the company's integrity and values; and always check sources for reliability, particularly in a world where Facebook, Twitter, and other Web 2.0 technologies allow for instant communication of problems.[115]

Public relations officers use many means of communicating the public image of the firm, including issuing press releases announcing the company's position on issues or positive developments within the firm (e.g., promotions, new product releases, special events, contributions made by the firm). Other mechanisms include blogs, electronic and paper newsletters, and Facebook postings, as well as the company's website. Publications like the annual report provide an opportunity for the company to put forward its own point of view; however, these documents can be viewed with skepticism by critical observers.

Increasingly companies use their websites to provide information to the computer-using public. The website not only offers product information and interactive services but can be a rich source of official information about a company. The company can make available on its website everything from its vision, values, and mission statements to its annual report, new product developments and releases, financial information, positive press coverage, and information about how to obtain its products and services. Many companies today use their websites to convey information about their stakeholder responsibilities as well, often putting their multiple-bottom-line or sustainability reports, which will be discussed in Chapter 8, online for the public to access.

The Web 2.0 world creates a whole new set of challenges for companies because the array of people able to report on a company's activities is virtually unlimited. Just about any interested and reasonably technologically sophisticated person can create a blog, post on a website, send a message to their own network, or put comments on public websites these days. Thus, it is difficult to generate a manageable list of media contacts beyond those in traditional media. A company's best defense under these circumstances is to be authentic in its responsible enterprise efforts—not just its "do-good" or pro-social activities, but its treatment of everyone with whom it interacts: all of its stakeholders. It is not enough in the Web 2.0 world to look responsible—a company actually needs to be responsible.

7 MANAGING FOR RESPONSIBILITY

> Learning is not compulsory . . . neither is survival.
> Quality guru Dr. W. Edwards Deming

Can responsible enterprise be managed? What does it mean to practice responsible enterprise—and to have one's practices assessed? Here we argue that responsibility to stakeholders and nature can be managed exactly as every other activity within a firm is managed. Further, we argue that responsibility needs to be managed explicitly, particularly in light of today's stakeholder pressures and risks. Companies' stakeholder and environmental relationships and practices form the core of responsible management—and that means that the whole business model is subject to responsibility management![1]

Companies achieve value added through their stakeholder practices and the associated processes, and they need to be explicit about managing those processes and practices—including quality improvement as well as customer, employee, community, investor, and government relations. There are always improvements that can be made, especially in the turbulence and dynamism of the modern economic and social landscapes; thus the model for responsibility management, as with quality management, is one of constant learning and improvement. This chapter focuses on establishing processes and practices aimed at continuous improvement in responsibility practices—total responsibility management (TRM) or simply responsibility management (RM). We introduce a system of RM that is inspired by the philosophy underlying total quality management (TQM). This is not to say that RM and TQM are the same, but that the practices underlying TQM can help us to understand how RM can be successfully integrated into the responsible corporation.[2]

FROM TQM TO TRM

In 1980, most American companies were paying little attention to quality management despite increasing public attentiveness to the quality of

products. Yet for thirty years Japanese firms had been implementing quality improvement processes based on the ideas of W. Edwards Deming and
Edward Juran, who had introduced quality control methods to the Japanese
after World War II, when U.S. managers had been uninterested.[3] As the public's perception of the quality of Japanese goods shifted from poor to excellent
during the 1960s and 1970s, managers in companies that had not yet "discovered" quality began to feel significant competitive heat.

Competition came especially from Japanese companies, which were by the
1970s producing goods of high quality at relatively low cost. A turning point
came in 1980 when NBC aired its white-paper documentary on the work of
Deming, "If Japan Can . . . Why Can't We?" Shortly afterward, the quality
revolution began in earnest in the United States (resulting in, among other
things, the Baldrige Award, recognizing U.S. organizations for performance
excellence) and in Europe (with the implementation of ISO quality standards
and the European Quality Award). As one book on managing quality puts it,
"[Deming's] name was soon a household word among corporate executives."[4]
Over time, numerous corporations began implementing quality management and improvement systems as a means of regaining global competitiveness in the face of the intense competition posed by the quality of products
produced by overseas competitors.

Most large businesses today operate in a global competitive environment,
both in producing and selling their wares, frequently using long supply chains
to produce goods. Attention by labor, human rights, environmental, and
social activists to working conditions and practices, pay scales, use of child
labor, hiring and firing policies, and environmental problems, particularly
in developing nations, has grown enormously in recent years, particularly
as the Internet has fueled global connectivity and transparency. Significant
negative publicity follows on the discovery by labor activists, for example, of
sweatshop conditions or child labor in footwear, toy, and apparel industries,
causing consumer boycotts and reputational damage that can cost companies customers and revenue. The attention to working conditions and environmental issues has raised the consciousness not only of activists but also of
consumers, investors, and multinational companies themselves to the greater
social expectations that are being placed on them—and on their suppliers.

Competitive pressures and widespread consumer attention to product and service quality mean that companies cannot compete successfully without paying close attention to those things as well. Although managers' acceptance of quality as a business imperative has not been easy to achieve, failure to pay attention to quality now can quickly contribute to business failure. We posit that a similar evolution is occurring with respect to managing a company's responsibility for its practices regarding labor, human rights, suppliers, customers, and the environment.

Companies are responding with systemic management approaches comparable in many ways to quality management systems. Following the language of TQM, Sandra Waddock and Charles Bodwell have labeled these approaches total responsibility management (TRM), in part to highlight the similarity of responsibility management systems to quality management approaches. Here we simplify the language to avoid the confusion that the word *total* implies by simply calling them responsibility management (RM). RM means that a company undertakes systemic efforts to manage its relationships with key stakeholders and the natural environment. These efforts tend to be built on common foundational values and have three main elements: (1) inspiration, the vision-setting, commitment, and leadership systems; (2) integration of responsibility into employee and other stakeholder relationships and into strategies and practices; and (3) innovation, which includes assessment, improvement, and learning systems and their associated indicators (see Figure 7.1).

In much the same way that TQM practices have done for quality management, RM practices constitute integrated systems for addressing the full range of companies' responsibilities. They can help companies maximize competitive success by continually monitoring and improving performance. RM works through engaged and mutually responsive relationships with employees and other key stakeholders: companies measure performance on multiple bottom lines (i.e., the triple bottom line of economic, societal, and ecological criteria, or as the current framing has it, the environmental, social, and governance [ESG] issues); and companies transparently accept responsibility and accountability for the impacts of corporate decisions, actions, and results. The following sections discuss the three main elements of the RM framework.

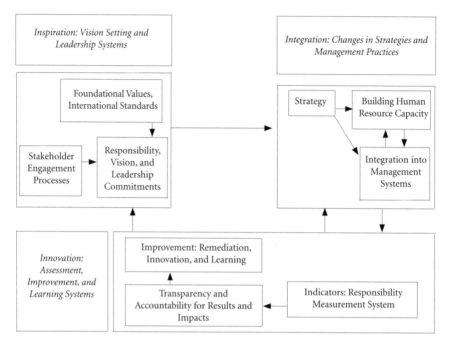

Figure 7.1: Sandra Waddock and Charles Bodwell, *Total Responsibility Management: The Manual* (Sheffield, UK: Greenleaf, 2007).

INSPIRATION: VISION SETTING
AND LEADERSHIP COMMITMENT

Inspiration involves the vision-setting and leadership commitment processes found in RM approaches, as well as stakeholder engagement and the establishment of foundational values. A key step in developing an RM approach is for the firm to establish and implement its responsibility objectives or the type of inspirational vision discussed earlier in this book.[5] The vision needs to be based on the company's unique competitive situation, stakeholders, and corporate history in much the same way that quality management goals are geared to a company's unique situation. Further, RM approaches can be implemented in a single corporate unit or systemically throughout a corporation, for those serving a global market or a single market. The inspiration process, or vision-setting and leadership commitment system, creates the organizational context for RM, involving stakeholder engagement processes, recognition of foundational values, and explicit development of the responsibility vision and leadership commitment.

Stakeholder Engagement Processes

TQM is centered on the roles of two sets of stakeholders (customers and employees) in a process of continuous improvement; RM approaches focus on multiple stakeholders. TQM emphasizes understanding and meeting customer expectations. In Japanese, the same word, okyakusama, is used to mean both "customer" and "honorable guest."[6] The successful TQM-based company seeks to treat the first like the second, maintaining an open dialogue with customers that allows them not only to meet current needs but also to anticipate future needs. TQM also relies on employee involvement, taking advantage of employees' knowledge, creativity, and enthusiasm for their job, while treating them honorably, honestly, and fairly. RM approaches similarly are centered on employees, recognizing that an investment in a workforce is an investment in the capacity of an organization and its suppliers to meet the social objectives it has established. At the same time, RM includes other stakeholders whose interests and concerns can affect the company, such as suppliers, activists, communities, governments, and of course, customers, and also deals with the natural environment.

As with TQM, many leading firms have established processes in consultation with their stakeholders. These stakeholder engagement processes, also called multisectoral collaboration or dialogue,[7] are mechanisms for gaining input from all key external and internal stakeholders.[8] This input tells companies what their critics are saying and where new pressure points are likely to emerge; it can also sometimes lead to the discovery of new competitive opportunities for the firm. Leading firms harness their employees' capacities to improve their responsibility, particularly in labor and human resource practices, because employees are directly affected and most aware of where improvement is needed; also, they are responsible for implementing the organization's vision. In the words of one union representative, "Empowered employees are your best source of monitoring; they know where the problems are."

RM approaches provide interaction with external stakeholders as well, including customers, investors, communities, and nongovernmental organizations (NGOs). Recognizing that companies are accountable not only to owners but also to other stakeholders, leading-edge companies develop engagement processes before they hit trouble spots or make significant changes.

These include interactive forums, dialogue, and online communications such as surveys, blogs, and use of social media.[9] Through dialogue, companies can work with stakeholders to develop trusting relationships in which differing points of view are expressed and shared.

Owners, customers, communities, and sometimes even governments can be brought into the stakeholder engagement process. Customers are increasingly aware of the conditions under which products are produced, and they make purchasing decisions on that basis. Because customers have many resources for finding out about product quality and defects, companies' marketing practices need to be monitored and aboveboard.[10] The same is true for other major stakeholders. While RM approaches are inherently more complex than TQM approaches because of the multiple stakeholders involved, they can provide significantly more information to management that can help the business improve its relationships with key constituents.

TALKING TO STAKEHOLDERS: MATTEL'S SAD HOLIDAY

As Christmas 2007 approached, toymaker Mattel, Inc., was not nearly as excited as the millions of children in the United States who were expecting gifts from Santa Claus. The previous August, the toymaker had been forced to make three major product recalls involving tens of millions of toys manufactured in China because of product safety concerns. The problems related to lead paint and product design problems that included loose magnets that could cause intestinal perforation or blockages in children who swallowed more than one.[11]

By December 1, 2007, Mattel was announcing its eleventh recall of the year with a total of some 21 million toys affected. In addition to recalling the defective toys, the company chose to recall all toys made without benefit of a newer manufacturing process that made it possible to secure the magnets permanently in place.[12]

Mattel's situation highlights the interconnectedness of today's economy and how a major company can be linked to suppliers in developing countries, where standards differ from domestic standards and control is difficult. Stakeholders in different spheres may have viewed Mattel's actions quite differently, as the company struggled to repair the damage of the sequence of recalls to its reputation. Clearly, investors and other stakeholders worried about the long-term viability of a company under such stress.

Mattel's CEO Robert Eckert expressed particular concern about the impact of the recalls on employees, who were not always aware of problems before they appeared in the media: "Clearly one of my frustrations was an inability to talk to one of the most important constituencies, our employees, in advance of the recall announcements. In general, I've always tried to communicate with employees first. You always want to hear what's happening at the company from management as opposed to reading about it in the newspaper."[13]

Eckert was also sensitive to customers outside the United States and to the Chinese reaction to the crisis. He commented, "All around the world, we apologized to parents. Because parents don't just live in the United States. These were global recalls and whenever we had the opportunity, we wanted to apologize to parents, and that included parents in China. There was a second issue, where Chinese vendor plants, not Mattel plants, were being criticized for quality. Certainly where it pertains to lead paint, that came out of Chinese plants. But really the magnets had nothing to do with the manufacturing process. So to the extent that Chinese manufacturers were being criticized for the magnet issue, we apologized for that. That wasn't their issue. That was science evolving and our requirement to use the best technology we could."[14]

Eckert told *Fortune*, "It's reinforced my belief that if you can consistently try to do the right thing, life is so much easier. If you live by your basic values, a) you'll get through it, and b) you'll feel satisfied that you did the best you could." The Mattel case shows that corporate responsibility is a continuous learning process that requires communicating with stakeholders and actually living the company's vision and values, particularly in times of crisis.

Foundational Values

The inspiration process also involves the recognition of foundational values. Foundational values are the baseline set of values below which the company (including members of its supply chain) knows it cannot go and still be accepted as a responsible corporation. Not just any values will do, however. RM approaches rely on employees, which means they need to be built on a foundation of constructive values that support human and worker rights and dignity—also called "hypernorms." Foundational values provide what some scholars refer to as a "moral minimum" of acceptable practice: respect for human dignity, avoidance of child labor, freedom of association, and adequate working conditions.[15]

A clearly articulated set of foundational values can be found in numerous international standards, perhaps most prominently in the International Labour Organization's (ILO's) Declaration on Fundamental Principles and Rights at Work (FPRW). The Declaration on FPRW targets standards to be set by national legislatures. The corresponding standard applicable at the corporate level, referencing the Declaration on FPRW, is the International Labour Organization's Tripartite Declaration of Principles concerning Multinational Enterprises and Social Policy. They are also promulgated in the United Nations (UN) Secretary-General's Global Compact, which includes the four labor principles present in the Declaration on FPRW as well as two human rights principles, three environmental principles, and one anti-corruption principle also derived from other UN conventions (see Chapter 10 for the principles themselves and a longer discussion).

Many firms have used these fundamental values to set standards within their own operations and supply chains, often in the form of codes of conduct. RM approaches in leading firms go beyond establishing foundational values to develop visions that are internalized in the culture of the organization. They set "stretch" goals for the organization in the areas of profitability or market segment dominance and social performance.

The core values embedded in the quality movement, as exemplified by the Baldrige Quality Award, inspire and can readily be matched to the values inherent in RM approaches. Table 7.1 illustrates this comparison.

Responsibility, Vision, and Leadership Commitments

Top management commitment to the company's vision and values with respect to responsibility is needed consistently over time. Two key questions stand out as vital in implementing an RM system (see also Chapter 4). One is the traditional strategy question: "What business are we in?" The second, and a more critical question for the RM approach, is the enterprise strategy question: "What do we stand for?"[16] These questions help shape vision and values, as well as related strategies and operating practices.

TABLE 7.1 *Core Values and Concepts of Responsibility Management (RM), as Inspired by the Baldrige Award and TQM*

Baldrige Award Core Values and Concepts	RM Core Values and Concepts
Visionary Leadership Leaders set direction and create customer focus, clear and visible values, and high expectations.	*Visionary and Committed Leadership* Leaders set direction of vision, clearly articulated and constructive values, and high expectations about responsible practices with respect to all stakeholders, but particularly employees, and for the consequences of corporate impacts on the natural environment.
Customer-Driven Excellence Customers judge quality and performance.	*Stakeholder-Driven Excellence and Responsible Practices* Stakeholders, especially employees, customers, suppliers/allies, and owners, judge responsibility and performance.
Organizational and Personal Learning Continuous improvement of existing approaches and adaptation to change lead to new goals and approaches, embedded in daily operations organizationally and individually.	*Organizational and Personal Learning through Dialogue and Mutual Engagement with Relevant Stakeholders* Stakeholder engagement processes provide a forum for continual learning and improvement of corporate practice.
Valuing Employees and Partners Success depends on knowledge, skills, creativity, and motivation of employees and partners.	*Valuing Employees, Partners, Other Stakeholders* Success depends on knowledge, skills, creativity, motivation, and engagement of employees, partners, and other relevant stakeholders on issues related to corporate practices and impacts.
Agility Success demands a capacity for rapid change and flexibility.	*Agility and Responsiveness* Success demands a capacity for rapid change, flexibility, and responsiveness when stakeholder-related issues or problems arise.

Focus on the Future (Short- and Long-Term)

Pursuit of sustainable growth and market leadership requires a strong future orientation and willingness to make long-term commitments to key stakeholders, customers, employees, suppliers and partners, stockholders, the public, and the community.

Managing for Innovation

Leaders make meaningful change to improve products, services, and processes, and to create new value for stakeholders.

Management by Fact

Measurement and analysis of performance, derived from business needs and strategy, provide data about key processes, outputs, and results.

Public Responsibility and Citizenship

Leaders should stress public and citizenship responsibilities, including meeting basic expectations related to ethics and protection of public health, safety, and environment.

Focus on the Future (Short- and Long-Term)

Pursuit of sustainable growth and market leadership requires a strong future orientation and willingness to respect and make long-term commitments to key stakeholders, customers, employees, suppliers and partners, stockholders, the public, the community, and the natural environment.

Managing for Responsibility

Leaders make meaningful change to ensure that practices that produce products and services are responsible, respectful, and value creating for key stakeholders.

Management by Fact, Transparency, Accountability

Measurement, evaluation, and transparency of the responsibility of corporate stakeholder and ecological practices provide data about the responsibility that is integral to corporate practices, outputs, and impacts.

Public Responsibility and Citizenship

Leaders should assure that corporate practices related to economic, societal, and ecological bottom lines are responsible, ethical, and transparent to relevant stakeholders and hold themselves accountable for their positive and negative impacts.

TABLE 7.1   *Core Values and Concepts of Responsibility Management (RM),
as Inspired by the Baldrige Award and TQM (continued)*

Focus on Results and Creating Value

Performance measures should focus on key results, and be used to create and balance value for key stakeholders—customers, employees, stockholders, suppliers and partners, the public, and the community.

Systems Perspective

The core values and seven Baldrige criteria provide a systems perspective for managing an enterprise, forming the building blocks, and integrating mechanism for the system, which, however, requires organization-specific synthesis and alignment.

- *Synthesis* means looking at the organization as a whole and building on key business requirements, strategic objectives, and action plans.
- *Alignment* means using key links among categories to provide key measures and indicators of success.

Focus on Positive Results, Impacts, and Value Added for Stakeholders with Responsible Ecological Practices

Performance measures should focus on key results and be used to create and balance value for key stakeholders—customers, employees, stockholders, suppliers and partners, the public, the community, and the natural environment.

Systems Perspective on Responsible Management Practices

RM's core values and criteria provide a framework for developing responsible management practices that can help a company integrate responsibility into all of its stakeholder and ecological practices, in alignment with the goals, objectives, values, and strategy of the organization.

- *Integration* means that responsibility is inherent or integral to corporate practices and cannot be dissociated from them. It also means that management recognizes the responsibility that is inherent to practices and actions that affect stakeholders or nature and works to reduce negative impacts.
- *Alignment* means using key links and indicators to determine how stakeholders and nature are affected by corporate practices and actions.

SOURCE: U.S. Department of Commerce, National Institute of Standards and Technology (NIST), "Baldrige Performance Excellence Program" (www.quality.nist.gov/2001_Criteriapdf.htm); and Baldrige National Quality Program 2001, Criteria for Performance Excellence.

Top management must be involved in establishing and implementing a responsibility vision in order for it to succeed. On the one hand, if management does not believe in the vision being articulated or sees it as merely a public relations exercise, then there is little hope for its becoming part of operating practices. On the other hand, if top management is involved in the development of a vision and communicates its commitment on a regular basis, and if the vision is supported through reward systems, allocations of resources, and changes in procedures, then the vision is more likely to move forward. Even better, however, is creating a shared vision co-developed by relevant stakeholders.

In organizations, there are, of course, different levels of management. Management commitment at each level and employee commitment throughout the enterprise is crucial; a senior manager in charge of country-level operations, quality control, or purchasing who does not believe in the company's specified principles can cause a breakdown of support for responsibility objectives within his or her functional area. Support needs to be generated at all levels in a cascading fashion from the top of the organization all the way down and through supply chain operations to supervisors and workers on the production lines.

INTEGRATION: CHANGES IN STRATEGIES AND MANAGEMENT PRACTICES

RM approaches integrate a company's vision, values, and leadership commitments into its corporate and business level strategies, then operationalize the vision through the operating practices that affect employees, other stakeholders, and the environment. Attention to workers' rights, human rights, and working conditions is increasingly a part of companies' overall strategies and corporate visions. And many apply similar standards to their supplier and distributor operations.

Strategy

Once established by the processes of inspiration, the company's responsibility goals and values must be integrated into corporate and functional strategies. In companies that adopt RM approaches, the corporate and business strategies must communicate the responsibility vision to all stakeholders. The vision can help firms deal with crises, as Johnson & Johnson was guided by its "Credo" during the Tylenol poisonings of the early 1980s: "Our Credo challenges us to put the needs and well-being of the people we serve first."[17] That credo, or pledge, guided management's decision to pull Tylenol from the market despite the $100 million cost of doing so. The need for continuously sustaining a responsibility vision and the difficulties of doing so were highlighted by a series of minor scandals for J&J in 2010. The company voluntarily recalled a number of its liquid infant and children's drug products because of manufacturing problems associated with their quality, purity, and potency.

Strategies, the broad operationalization of the visions held by the organization, need to clearly reflect the ultimate vision and also be linked to rewards. In integrating the vision and values into the strategies of the company, a key question must be asked: "How do we do business here?"

Building Human Resource Capacity

Integration of a company's vision and values should be the top priority in human resources practices as part of the process of building human resource capacity. There are two interrelated elements. First, human relations issues are typically behind the responsibility visions of organizations, in the best cases becoming part of their strategic plans for the treatment and development of employees. Second, employees are core members of the systems required to make the vision a reality. Reaching a firm's responsibility vision requires the commitment and involvement of managers and the participation of employees throughout supply chains, from the top of the hierarchy to the bottom.

The first step is building understanding about the reasons for and benefits of carrying forward the responsibility vision among employees and among managers who allocate resources. This aspect of integration entails the development of supporting materials, training, and regular, consistent communication about the responsibility vision and, if it exists, the code of conduct. Reward structures, evaluation procedures, training programs, and requirement systems must all support the strategic objectives and the responsibility objectives.

Employees are core elements in the implementation of RM approaches. Most codes of conduct incorporate responsible treatment of employees, even (or especially) within extended supply chains, as well as expectations that employees will perform with integrity. Integrating a corporate vision into human resources practices means ensuring that high standards (such as those specified in many codes of conduct and the ILO conventions) are met. Thus, the codes of conduct that have evolved into RM approaches typically include policies on working conditions; hiring, retention, and dismissal; remuneration (wages and benefits); hours of work; forced and child labor; discrimination; promotion; freedom of association; and collective bargaining; among others.

RM approaches emphasize that these policies need to be upheld within the confines of the firm and by its partners and suppliers. The emphasis on standards within a company's supply chain is particularly critical to RM because the boundaries between a (multinational) company and its suppliers are increasingly blurred, especially in the eyes of activists, consumers, and other stakeholders.

Integration into Management Systems

RM approaches incorporate the responsibility vision into other operating practices and management systems. Initially, the task of managing the corporate codes of conduct and RM issues rested with compliance departments or other groups specifically dedicated to responsibility management. Similarly, before the quality revolution, responsibility for quality rested with the quality control officers at the end of the line. Eventually, everyone became responsible for quality—and we expect that everyone in the system will become responsible for responsibility as well. As indicated in Chapter 1, we understand responsible enterprise as being an integral part of a company's day-to-day operations and routines; isolating responsible enterprise issues from core business activities and functions can easily lead to an old-fashioned philanthropic and discretionary understanding of RM.

Carrying out all of the elements required by the responsibility vision has broad implications. Moving responsible practices into supplier operations, for example, means that the role of purchasing is crucial. Yet expanding the focus of the purchasing vision from quality, delivery, and cost to include labor practices can be challenging, given the bottom-line financial concerns of the firms in a supply chain. Further, a company implementing RM approaches needs to be aware of the implications of its products and process for customers, suppliers, and other stakeholders.

Integration goes further than modifying purchasing procedures, in particular since buyers for firms are only infrequently present in supplier factories. The compliance or responsibility group is typically limited in size, and hence able to visit and monitor suppliers only sporadically. As a result, many managers in firms with heavily disaggregated supply chains highlight the important role of quality and manufacturing personnel in supporting responsibility objectives. The addition of RM to responsibilities already held by the quality control group can be a point of contention, but the benefits of broader RM can make it possible for companies to engage productively with numerous stakeholders, and help them avoid some of the reputational risks inherent in long supply chains. Ultimately, managers throughout the organization need to take responsibility for RM in order for it to have the impact that quality management does.

Integration also raises the question of whether firms are responsible for the practices of second-tier or maybe even third-tier suppliers. This is a tricky issue, as iconic brands will be held accountable for misconduct anywhere in their entire supply chain, regardless of whether they have any direct business contact with suppliers. Certification standards, such as Social Accountability 8000, which some brand-name companies use to monitor their first-tier suppliers, often require that the standard be applied to sub-suppliers.[18] An integration of RM practices into the entire supply chain also seems necessary and timely, because suppliers often outsource their own work to sub-suppliers. To determine the scope of RM integration many companies have started to assess supplier risk according to criteria such as country of operation, industry sector, and the nature of the underlying transaction.[19]

INNOVATION: ASSESSMENT, IMPROVEMENT, AND LEARNING SYSTEMS

One of the great benefits of TQM approaches is that the companies using them do not expect perfection. Rather, the goal of TQM is to continually improve not just the products or outputs but also the processes associated with developing them. Much the same can be said of RM approaches. No company is—or is ever likely to be—perfect. Companies can, however, put in place processes to determine where problems exist and provide for remediation, innovation, and learning that help to solve them. Defining where needs exist is the role of the innovation and improvement systems associated with RM approaches, with the help of an RM measurement system that provides relevant indicators.

Indicators: The RM Measurement System

RM necessitates new approaches to measurement and information dissemination—for example, measuring operating practices, stakeholder relationships, and results in new ways and on multiple bottom lines rather than strictly in traditional productivity and financial terms. Taking an RM approach involves creating accounting and reporting systems that satisfy the needs of internal stakeholders and managers for information that improves company performance and simultaneously satisfies the demands of external stakeholders, including unions, NGOs, investors, governments, and local communities. Internal feedback is essential, along with external accountability and transparency.

RM approaches deal with multiple objectives, frequently the triple bottom line of economics, society, and environment,[20] or ESG performance indicators, many of which are already available but need to be reassembled for use in RM. Measurement and performance systems need to reflect the added complexity of multiple objectives. Single-bottom-line performance assessment systems are increasingly outdated, with the advent of multiple-bottom-line auditing systems, strategic system audit models,[21] holistic performance assessment models,[22] and blended value[23] or balanced scorecard[24] approaches.

Appropriate measurements can improve performance because, as the accounting axiom goes, what gets measured and rewarded is what gets done and is also where management attention goes. Thus, RM approaches need to cover far more than simple productivity and financial performance, because responsible practice is integral to all of a company's operations. Human resource practices need to be evaluated to ensure that they are in line with the core values and codes of conduct the company has established. Customer and marketing practices are directly related to product quality, customer satisfaction, and corporate reputation, among other factors. Similarly, quality can be addressed through a wide range of quality standards, such as criteria for the Baldrige Award, the European Quality Award, and the Deming Prize (Japan).[25] Social auditing methods (e.g., internal responsibility audits of employee, community, quality, and environmental processes)[26] or more stakeholder-oriented auditing techniques (e.g., those of AccountAbility in England)[27] can provide useful information, although similar methods can also be developed and applied in-house.

Transparency and Accountability

Indicators found in the responsibility measurement system provide organizational decision makers with necessary information for improving the system, and doing so cost-effectively, but they are merely a first step. The Global Reporting Initiative (GRI), which has become the global standard for external ESG reporting and will be discussed more later, provides a framework for external reporting that can also provide helpful measures for dealing with ESG issues internally. Companies find that the data they gather for their GRI reports also provide management information that helps them identify problems and issues, creating a common basis for thinking through them.

Transparency holds the company accountable for its impacts, and, as noted, the GRI has become the accepted global standard for external reporting or transparency on ESG and related issues. Transparency typically means that companies produce a sustainability, triple-bottom-line, or similar report that details their internal activities related to ESG and, increasingly, indicates where improvement is needed. Access to information and data gathered by employees and managers alike can provide a dynamic tension that moves a company forward, supporting its continuous improvement of practices. Visibility or transparency helps ensure that information enhances performance, by putting pressure on those who can influence the process of achieving responsibility goals to make choices based on responsibility considerations.

Through transparency, companies can develop better relationships with employees and other key stakeholders, such as activists, customers, and communities, as well as owners. In addition, multiple-bottom-line reporting can lead to the development of more trusting relationships with key stakeholders because data are perceived as both valid and reliable. Accountability, of course, means living up to one's stated vision and values, or being authentic. Transparency and accountability thus create incentives and expectations of authenticity for companies, because when transparency exists stakeholders expect companies to be true to their stated vision and values—and with data can hold them accountable when they are not.

Innovation, Improvement, and Learning Systems

Implementing a responsibility vision is an ongoing and cyclical process of innovation and improvement, remediation, and organizational learning. Innovation and learning systems guide managers by encouraging responsible practices and emphasize ongoing organizational learning and development that push the company toward ever more responsible practice. Remediation focuses on meeting basic standards and then improving on them. Further, remediation provides a mechanism for immediately eliminating practices that do not conform to the foundational values.

RM approaches to learning and innovation are systemic and multidimensional. Learning is multidimensional in the sense that information systems provide inputs at the corporate level about organization-wide efforts and at the top level when crises occur. Innovation is multidimensional in that inputs are required at the country level and within factories or operations dispersed around the globe to flag local issues that need attention. Inspection, measurement, and analysis are expected to take place where the work occurs and to provide feedback that improves performance. Such systems can extend responsibility measurement throughout firms, guiding individual managers and employees alike in problem solving. Like other holistic approaches to organizational learning,[28] RM is an iterative process of improvement over time rather than a single initiative that is implemented and then ends.

RM is an integrated approach to implementing responsibility objectives, with elements that work together rather than independently or in isolation. Thus, RM is a set of processes and goals, but not a strict set of guidelines for performance. The RM approach represents a framework within which a company can plan and organize how to take responsibility for its practices and impacts.

Self-assessment is a critical component of RM. While external evaluation, monitoring, and certification are important, RM approaches are fundamentally internal and voluntary management systems that help companies improve performance with respect to all of their stakeholders. Through the identification of stakeholders and the impacts that company practices have on them, and by engaging in a dialogic process to improve its stakeholder relationships, a company will be better prepared for problems when they arise—and more likely be able to avert some of them. RM approaches can also provide a means for integrating external demands and pressures for responsible practice, calls for accountability and transparency, the proliferation of codes of conduct, managing supply chains responsibly and in a sustainable manner, and stakeholder engagement into a single approach to responsibility practices within the firm. We discuss those factors in the next chapters.

8 ASSESSING RESPONSIBLE ENTERPRISE

> Measures have always had the power to shape a corporation's
> destiny, but the focus on financial figures alone limited their
> utility. Management accounting of the past forced managers
> to build world-class organizations with a truncated set of
> chromosomes. Today, though, with the help of revitalized cost
> accounting and nonfinancial measurement, managers can develop
> a full set of instructions—financial, operational, and social—for
> the enterprise. These instructions give them the capability to
> create accountability they never had before.
>
> Marc J. Epstein and Bill Birchard, *Counting What Counts: Turning
> Corporate Accountability to Competitive Advantage*

Companies today, particularly large ones but also small and medium-sized enterprises (SMEs), are increasingly being evaluated on ESG criteria as well as on financial performance, whether they want to be or not. Sometimes these ESG factors create risks that are significant enough to be material to investors or other stakeholders. So much information is available about company practices, in fact, that its very availability may sometimes cause managers to do the right thing. As activists, nongovernmental organizations (NGOs), and the general public have begun to demand greater accountability, responsibility, and transparency from companies, new ways of thinking about measurement have begun to evolve.

External assessments were pioneered by the social investment community using measures to screen out or approve certain types of practices and products. Social investment also includes direct investment in social projects and ventures by investors willing to accept a lower-than-market rate of return, loans to microenterprises (as pioneered by the Grameen Bank, discussed later in this chapter), social venture capital, and corporate social investment and philanthropy. Companies are increasingly being evaluated externally through the numerous "best of" ratings and other rankings.

Since the mid-1990s, a responsibility assurance system has emerged whose aim is to check whether companies' actions match their rhetoric. Responsibility assurance includes four core elements: (1) the voluntary responsibility management (RM) approaches discussed in the last chapter; (2) principles that represent foundational values; (3) credible certification systems; and (4) generally accepted reporting procedures like the Global Reporting Initiative (GRI) mentioned in the previous chapter.[1] Numerous other sources of pressure for more responsible enterprise have evolved in recent years as well.

ASSESSING RESPONSIBLE ENTERPRISE: PRINCIPLES, CERTIFICATION, AND REPORTING

Anti-globalization and anti-corporate rhetoric combined with corruption, accounting restatements, outright frauds, and ecological scandals have created a context in which public trust in companies is quite low. In 2010, the global public relations firm Edelman released its eleventh annual "trust barometer," which found that after the global economic slowdown there was a modest, but slow, global rise in trust in businesses, with trust in CEOs' credibility rising again and continuing to rise in 2011.[2] Notably, this picture of trust represented an improvement over the same survey one year earlier. Still, there were significant trust issues in business related to CEO compensation, outsourcing, and corruption, to name only a few. Outsourcing of many manufacturing activities from companies in industrialized nations to smaller companies in countries where labor is inexpensive and standards are not rigorously enforced has resulted in numerous charges of sweatshop working conditions, child labor, abuse of workers, environmental problems, and complicity in violence and human rights abuses by transnational corporations.

As the public has become aware of these problems, it has demanded both transparency and accountability, particularly that companies prove they are living up to their claims about responsibility and ethical behavior. As a result, new standards for monitoring and certifying company performance, both in extended supply chains and within established companies themselves, have emerged in a growing responsibility assurance framework that complements the responsibility management framework discussed in the last chapter.

Initiatives for assessing firms' responsibility efforts fall into three major categories:

- Overarching *principles* that companies agree to live by (e.g., the UN Global Compact). While these principles do not directly assess corporate social/environmental performance, they are foundational values upon which firms can base their responsibility efforts.

- *Certification* initiatives offering monitoring and verification systems. Leading examples are AA 1000 and SA 8000 (and, although not a certification standard, the ISO 26000 released in 2011) that attempt to hold companies accountable for their impacts.

- Standardized *reporting* systems to ensure transparency, of which the Global Reporting Initiative (GRI) is the global standard.

FOUNDATION PRINCIPLES: FOUNDATION VALUES OF RESPONSIBLE ENTERPRISE

Corporate critics might ask whether a company that employed 180 forced laborers yesterday and only 160 today could really be considered to be more responsible—or still irresponsible. Although the company shows "improvement," its practice of using forced labor—akin to slavery—is reprehensible. It is violating a fundamental value inherent in responsible practice. Such baseline-level behaviors, practices, and values are foundation principles, and they are often operationalized in sets of principles or codes of conduct.

Foundation values or principles are generally agreed-on standards that provide a floor of acceptable practice below which it is ethically and managerially problematic to go. They are called hypernorms by business ethicists Donaldson and Dunfee, who define them as "principles so fundamental to human existence that they serve as a guide in evaluating lower level moral norms."[3] Most enterprise responsibility standards are explicitly based on a set of selected foundation principles or hypernorms.

The adoption by businesses of a common set of foundation principles—a baseline or a moral minimum for operating practice—would provide a level playing field for companies. One author argues that a set of universal moral standards would include trustworthiness, respect, responsibility, fairness, caring, and citizenship; such principles could underpin the development of standards themselves.[4] Agreement on foundation principles could help companies avoid the information overload and "code mania" associated with different sets of principles as the number and types of standards initiatives grow, as well as disparities between developed and developing nations.[5]

To the extent that foundation principles or hypernorms exist, they can be found in broad-based consensus agreements among the nations of the world, such as those promulgated by the United Nations, the world's longest-existing multilateral organization. Although a few nations may disagree with some of the principles articulated in those documents (e.g., China on human rights), they nonetheless represent the world's best efforts to date to find agreed-on values.

The development of the UN's Global Compact, formulated in 1999 by former Secretary-General Kofi Annan and formally launched in 2000, provides insight into the difficulty of reaching global agreement on hypernorms.

The UN Global Compact

At the World Economic Forum, held in Davos, Switzerland, in January 1999, former UN Secretary-General Kofi Annan challenged world business leaders to "embrace and enact" a Global Compact, both in their individual corporate practices and by supporting appropriate public policies. The principles he articulated included human rights, labor standards, the natural environment, and anti-corruption (see Table 8.1). The tenth principle, on anti-corruption, was added in 2004 at a summit of leaders engaged in Global Compact activities. The Global Compact's ten principles are derived from the following UN declarations and conventions: the Universal Declaration of Human Rights, the International Labour Organization's Declaration on Fundamental Principles and Rights at Work, the Rio Declaration on Environment and Development, and the United Nations Convention against Corruption. Whereas these declarations and conventions are mostly applicable to nation-states (and not corporations directly), the Global Compact "translates" these intergovernmental agreements into principles that are directly relevant for businesses.

The Global Compact, with some 8,700 participants, including 6,200 businesses from 130 nations by 2011, has established a multistakeholder network—consisting of businesses, local and global NGOs, business associations, workers' or labor organizations, national governments, academic institutions, and other types of organizations. The Global Compact promotes core values of responsibility by getting (global) companies to voluntarily agree to operate in accordance with a core set of principles that establish standards with respect to labor, human rights, environmental practices, and anti-corruption.

Not everyone greeted Annan's attempt with cheers. Indeed, many NGO and union leaders believe that the Global Compact puts the UN's credibility at risk because it too closely aligns the UN with corporate forces. The fifty or so companies that signed on to the Global Compact by the end of 2000 did so voluntarily. And there is no external monitoring of their activities on the four main areas covered by the principles and little power to enforce the standards. Corporations hoping to live up to the principles embedded in the Global Compact, as well as some of the other standards noted below, have a long way to go before their activities are fully transparent to NGOs and activists and before they can be held fully accountable.

However, the Global Compact should not be judged on the basis of something it never intended or pretended to be. The initiative was not set up with the intention to monitor companies. As a UN-driven initiative, the Global Compact has neither a mandate nor the financial and logistical resources to monitor compliance. This, however, is not to say that the initiative completely lacks teeth. Signatory businesses need to report annually on their implementation of the ten principles (see Table 8.1). Nonreporting companies are expelled from the initiative. More than 2,400 firms have been delisted from the Global Compact for failure to submit a so-called Communication-on-Progress (COP) report (as of July 2011). The main value of the initiative lies in creating a platform for businesses and civil society to share and develop knowledge about responsibility practices. In this sense, the Global Compact should be understood as a complement to monitoring-based initiatives (e.g., SA 8000) and government regulations.[6]

Sets of principles, codes of conduct, and values statements abound in addition to the Global Compact's ten principles. Most large companies today have codes of conduct that are company-specific and that frequently apply

TABLE 8.1   *The Ten Principles of the Global Compact*

Human Rights:

Principle 1:   Businesses should support and respect the protection of internationally proclaimed human rights; and

Principle 2:   make sure that they are not complicit in human rights abuses.

Labour Standards:

Principle 3:   Businesses should uphold the freedom of association and the effective recognition of the right to collective bargaining;

Principle 4:   the elimination of all forms of forced and compulsory labour;

Principle 5:   the effective abolition of child labour; and

Principle 6:   the elimination of discrimination in respect of employment and occupation.

Environment:

Principle 7:   Businesses should support a precautionary approach to environmental challenges;

Principle 8:   undertake initiatives to promote greater environmental responsibility; and

Principle 9:   encourage the development and diffusion of environmentally friendly technologies.

Anti-Corruption:

Principle 10: Businesses should work against corruption in all its forms, including extortion and bribery.

SOURCE: UN Global Compact, "The Ten Principles" (http://www.unglobalcompact.org/AboutTheGC/TheTenPrinciples/index.html).

not only to the company itself, but also to its supply chain partners. Some companies have developed specific codes of conduct for their supply chains. Other business associations and multistakeholder coalitions have developed their own codes, among them the Principles for Responsible Investment; the Equator Principles; the Principles for Responsible Management Education; the OECD Guidelines for Multi-National Enterprises; and the Caux Round-table Principles for Business.

The proliferation of principles has caused some observers to suggest the need for some rationalization of principles to prevent businesses from becoming overwhelmed or confused about what is really important.[7] Still, principles, codes of conduct, and values statements do provide some clarity about how businesses can be expected to treat their stakeholders and the natural environment. But because there is lack of trust of many companies, there is need for certification and reporting approaches, which are discussed next.

IMPLEMENTING THE UN GLOBAL COMPACT AT NOVARTIS

Novartis is a multinational pharmaceutical company that in 2010 had over $50 billion in revenues and close to 120,000 employees.[8] The company was among the first signatories to the UN Global Compact in 2000 and continues to support the Compact's ten principles. According to Klaus Leisinger, the president and executive director of the Novartis Foundation for Sustainable Development, it was the CEO of Novartis (Daniel Vasella) who initiated Novartis's participation.[9] Commitment to the UN Global Compact by a firm's top management is a prerequisite to formally joining the initiative, because management support tells employees that it is serious about the ten principles. As Leisinger writes:

> In retrospect, this early and unequivocal commitment at the highest level was the decisive factor that endowed the GC [Global Compact] at Novartis with the weight and importance it enjoys today. Coherent and consistent signals from management are of major importance in all institutions, including companies, because employees are on the lookout for such signals.[10]

Because the Global Compact requires signatories to reflect on what issues need to be addressed to align strategies and operations with the ten principles, continued top-management support is essential so as not to isolate implementation within single divisions or units, but rather distribute it across the entire organization.

Leisinger said that companywide communication of the firm's commitment to the initiative was the most important factor in implementing the Global Compact at Novartis. Employees were informed about the principles, and the company put an internal organizational structure in place to oversee and manage commitment to the Global Compact. A steering committee helped to embed the ten principles into existing business practices. According to Leisinger, companywide support for the Global Compact can only be expected when employees perceive it as important internally:

> New or changed guidelines on how to proceed can only be sustainable and effectively implemented in large institutions—whether they be companies, unions, churches, multilateral organisations or others—when they are not perceived by their members as "foreign" or "imposed from the outside." Wherever there is a lack of personal identification with the objective ("not invented here"), the chances of it becoming a natural and integral part of corporate reality are not high.[11]

Embedding the Global Compact into a company's day-to-day activities requires "translating" the ten principles into specific objectives. The ten principles can direct a company toward relevant issues (e.g., human rights or anti-corruption); however, they do not provide specific guidance or identify the business activities that need to be changed. Turning commitment into implementation requires defining measurable objectives, which are based on a firm's interpretation of the ten principles. For instance, as a pharmaceutical company, Novartis identified human rights principles related to health issues: patent and pricing policies for life-saving drugs, research priorities (e.g., research on neglected diseases), and patient assistance programs for uninsured people.[12] Novartis has developed measurements for benchmarking progress in these areas. Access to medicine throughout the world is measured by the number of patients who can be reached through such programs (85.5 million in 2010) and the monetary value of the program itself ($1.5 billion in 2010). Specific measures like these and a deliberate management of the underlying issues are necessary to root the Global Compact in a multinational corporation like Novartis.

Commitment to the Global Compact is not a "free lunch," to use Leisinger's words.[13] Operationalizing the ten principles requires discussing the meaning behind the words to develop measurable objectives and making adherence to the objectives part of employees' performance appraisal. Further, implementation needs to be backed up with sufficient budgets. In many cases, the actual change of day-to-day business practices (such as working conditions) is in the hands of line managers, who require sufficient resources (monetary and nonmonetary) to carry out the work. In the end, aligning the operations and strategies of a multinational corporation like Novartis with the Global Compact's ten principles is not an easy task. But no one claims that corporate responsibility is easy.

Certification Initiatives: Credible Verification and Monitoring

Certification programs for companies attempting to demonstrate their responsibility are important because, without them, external observers have no way of knowing whether the company is doing what it says it is doing. There are numerous such programs in the world today, but we will focus on three of the most notable below.

AA 1000: Stakeholder Engagement   The AA 1000 framework was launched in 1999 by the UK organization AccountAbility to provide a way for companies to systematize their stakeholder engagement practices and to provide some assurance about the quality of those engagements. It provides organizations with an internationally accepted, freely available set of standards to frame and structure the way in which they understand, govern, administer, implement, evaluate, and communicate their accountability. Developed through a multistakeholder engagement process, the AA 1000 standards have three main components. The AA 1000 AccountAbility Principles Standard is a framework to help organizations understand the process of achieving greater accountability to its stakeholders, for example by focusing on the inclusivity of stakeholder engagement. The AA 1000 Assurance Standard provides an approach that assurance practitioners can use to evaluate an enterprise's adherence to the principles. The third element is the AA 1000 Stakeholder Engagement Standard, which is a framework that can help companies develop rigorous and useful stakeholder engagement processes.

The AA 1000 Assurance Standard is of particular interest, as it reflects a robust and widely used comprehensive framework to hold firms accountable for their social and environmental performance. The Assurance Standard defines a variety of best practices that should be used by assurance providers offering auditing services in the context of responsible enterprise. Since social and environmental auditing and reporting remain largely unregulated, such a standard is welcome and useful. The overall aim of the AA 1000 Stakeholder Engagement Standard is to create an inclusive, transparent, and long-lasting dialogue between the corporations and its stakeholders.[14]

SA 8000 Workplace Standards   The SA 8000 labor standards are designed to provide accountability for companies with extended supply chains operating in global networks. SA 8000 is the first social accountability standard for retailers, brand companies, suppliers, and other organizations to use in monitoring decent working conditions throughout their supply chain. The standard sets minimum requirements for workplace conditions that need to be met by corporations and their suppliers. SA 8000 is a voluntary initiative and is applicable to a wide range of industry sectors and to any size organization in all countries (except Myanmar). SA 8000 represents an important breakthrough in social accounting because it was the first auditable standard for promoting labor rights for workers around the world. The initiative requires an independent, third-party auditing process of production facilities. Once an organization has implemented any necessary corrective actions identified in the audit, it earns a certificate attesting to its compliance with SA 8000.[15]

The New York–based NGO Social Accountability International (SAI) is the responsible body for the standard. The number of certified facilities grew to more than 1,000 in 2006, and in 2007 the so-called Social Accountability Accreditation Services (SAAS) was formally established as an independent, not-for-profit organization. SAAS accredits qualified organizations known as "certification bodies" (CBs), which are then granted the right to perform certifications of facilities in accordance with SA 8000. SAAS ensures that the certification process of SA 8000 is functioning by undertaking regular and impartial assessments of the CBs. In 2010 there were nineteen accredited CBs and 2,151 certified facilities.[16]

SAI believes that the SA 8000 certification will benefit workers, trade unions, and NGOs by giving them greater capacity to educate workers about labor rights and work directly with businesses on labor issues, as well as increasing public awareness about working conditions. Certified businesses will ensure the viability and credibility of their brand and reputation, improve their ability to recruit and retain employees, and develop overall better supply chain management. Customers and investors will benefit from knowing that products are made responsibly.[17]

LABOR AUDITING: DOES IT REALLY WORK?

Although SA 8000 is a widely used standard for labor auditing, there are other similar certification initiatives for monitoring working conditions at supply factories. They include, but are not limited to: the Fair Labor Association (FLA), the Ethical Trading Initiative (ETI), the Worker Rights Consortium (WRC), and Worldwide Responsible Accredited Production (WRAP). Although these initiatives differ in detail (mostly because they are driven by different stakeholder groups), they all face the challenge of making auditing practices reliable.

Several studies have shown that labor monitoring often, though not always, suffers from weak auditor training (one of the reasons why SA 8000 accredits its CBs) and sloppy auditing practices. Although this criticism does not apply equally to all initiatives and also applies to the direct monitoring of firms' codes of conduct (without the involvement of separate initiatives), it is important to realize that labor auditing is a contested practice. Dara O'Rourke's research "raises serious questions about the legitimacy and competence of accounting firms as independent monitors of labor and environmental issues."[18] O'Rourke criticizes the auditing methodology (e.g., for using primarily factory managers as a source of data, rather than engaging directly with workers) and finds that auditors frequently overlook some key issues (such as the verbal abuse of workers). It is also known that corruption and cheating by suppliers (e.g., running model factories while subcontracting the majority of work to noncertified factories) are common practices that undercut the credibility of labor monitoring.[19]

Putting labor regulation in the hands of nongovernmental actors (instead of governments) creates several additional challenges. Because brand-name companies typically require their suppliers to comply with certification initiatives and/or their own (internal) codes of conduct, suppliers may be asked to comply with the labor standards of different initiatives at the same time. Moreover, outsourcing labor regulation to nongovernmental actors means that legal sanctions are replaced by "market" sanctions (e.g., cutting contracts with noncompliant suppliers). Richard Locke and colleagues argue that power relations in global supply chains are not necessarily asymmetric (buyer-driven), but that "Asian-based suppliers have grown tremendously both in size and sophistication and thus wield a tremendous amount of influence over the global brands they serve."[20]

In other words, the traditional assumption that brand-name companies "dictate" the rules of the game in labor auditing does not always hold. In some cases, the orders of multinational brand-name companies reflects only a rather small share of suppliers' total business. In this context, the ability of brand-name companies to effectively pressure suppliers to improve labor conditions is limited.

The question of whether labor auditing really works always depends on empirical observations in specific factories, but it is possible to identify some broad conditions under which auditing practices can be improved. One important step is to enhance their transparency. SAI, for instance, does not publish auditing reports, which makes it impossible for stakeholders (such as consumers) to assess the level of compliance by a particular factory. Further, professional auditing firms often conduct certification visits on their own, while local stakeholders (such as NGOs and unions), who often have good knowledge about labor violations in local factories, are not much involved. Empowering local actors to participate in certification visits can improve the level of compliance and also help to uncover cheating by suppliers.

ISO 26000 Social Responsibility   One initiative, ISO 26000, has gained significant public attention. Launched in 2010, ISO 26000 is a voluntary "guidance document" offering a framework for dealing with social responsibility issues in companies. Promulgated by the International Standards Organization (ISO), the framework was developed by a multistakeholder working group consisting of representatives from industry, government, labor, consumers, NGOs, and other interested parties. The group began its work in 2005, creating what ISO calls harmonized, globally relevant guidelines on social responsibility for all kinds of private and public sector organizations. Its goal is to "encourage the implementation of best practice in social responsibility worldwide."[21] Among ISO 26000's goals are to create an international consensus on what social responsibility is, help organizations translate principles into effective action, and refine and enhance best practices.[22]

ISO 26000 educates corporations about responsible enterprise and how it can be implemented. ISO 26000 "provides guidance on the underlying principles of social responsibility, the core subjects and issues pertaining to social responsibility . . . and on ways to integrate socially responsible behavior into existing organizational strategies, systems, practices and processes."[23] Its main purpose is to distinguish important terms (e.g., responsibility, accountability, transparency) related to social responsibility. In addition, the standard also discusses possible implementation mechanisms for social responsibility and highlights issues that need to be addressed by any organization interested in this field. The designation "social responsibility" is meant to apply to many types of organizations, not just corporations, and the guidelines are meant to help companies and other organizations by providing a common framework, basic definitions, and methods of evaluation.

The adoption of ISO 26000 is intended to influence both the perception and the reality of an organization's responsibility performance. The standard can improve a company's competitive advantage and reputation and its ability to attract and retain qualified workers or members, customers, clients, and users. Its use can also help improve employee morale, commitment, and productivity, and enhance the ways in which investors, owners, donors, sponsors, and the financial community view an organization. Finally, it is meant to improve an organization's relationships, particularly with governments, the media, suppliers, peers, customers, and local communities. The ISO guidance document provides background, trends, and characteristics of social responsibility, articulates principles and practices, and specifies the areas that organizations need to pay attention to in becoming more responsible. It emphasizes the integration, implementation, and promotion of responsible practices, and helps enterprises engage with stakeholders by communicating their responsibility commitments and performance outcomes.[24]

Even though ISO 26000 was not designed to certify organizations' social responsibility efforts, there are two ways in which the standard nevertheless influences certification practices. First, because of ISO's global reach and the popularity of other standards such as the ISO 14000 series, key definitions provided by ISO 26000 will likely be adopted by other standards in the responsible enterprise field. Second, although not intended by ISO, local initiatives could use their "interpretations" of the standard to establish their own certification regimes. For instance, a certification firm in Hong Kong, Accredited Certification International, started to certify organizations that were in compliance with ISO 26000.[25] Although ISO claims that any effort to turn ISO 26000 into a certifiable standard contradicts its original purpose, it has not prohibited efforts by others to do so.

Reporting Initiatives

As transparency has become more important and common, standardized reporting on social and environmental issues enables companies to be compared across their responsibility performance. In the financial arena, standardized accounting principles—also known as generally accepted accounting principles (GAAP)—are available for providing common guidelines and comparable reports. The Global Reporting Initiative today is the accepted global standard for ESG or what is sometimes called "nonfinancial" reporting. On the horizon, however, is a move to integrate ESG and financial reporting.

The Global Reporting Initiative   A company's monitoring of its responsibility performance using approaches like ISO 26000, AA 1000, or SA 8000 is an important way for it to demonstrate responsibility. Because these approaches are voluntary, however, each company can decide for itself what to monitor and how or even whether to report the results publicly. Many corporate critics and stakeholders are unsatisfied with nonstandardized and voluntary assurance programs, particularly since there is currently little comparability across the different reports being issued by companies. Today's economic reporting alone is unsatisfactory to many stakeholders, unless it is done in an integrative way and focuses on ESG issues as well as financial matters. Designed through a multistakeholder collaborative process involving representatives of businesses; accounting and investment firms; and environmental, human rights, labor, and research organizations, the Global Reporting Initiative (GRI) seeks to provide common reporting standards for ESG factors for organizations in all industries, sectors, and parts of the world.

The G3 (or third version) of the GRI Reporting Framework was released in 2006 to help companies benchmark their own performance against "laws, norms, codes, performance standards, and voluntary initiatives; demonstrate organizational commitment to sustainable development; and compare organizational performance overtime" along ESG measures.[26] A fourth wave or G4 is under way at this writing, with the expectation that new reporting guidelines will be released by 2013. The G3 framework consists of three main elements: (1) the guidelines, which include principles and guidance around standard disclosures and indicators, (2) the protocols, which are the "recipe" behind indicators including key terms and methodologies, and (3) sector-specific supplements, which focus on industry segments with their specific reporting requirements.[27]

The core reporting principles of GRI (see Table 8.2) attempt to create a common set of reporting guidelines similar to generally accepted accounting principles (GAAP) in the financial realm, but expanded to encompass social, ecological, and economic impacts and outcomes. The principles of materiality and stakeholder inclusiveness provide an overall framework for defining

TABLE 8.2   *Reporting Guidance for Defining Content*

Materiality: The information in a report should cover topics and indicators that reflect the organization's significant economic, environmental, and social impacts, or that would substantively influence the assessments and decisions of stakeholders.

Stakeholder Inclusiveness: The reporting organization should identify its stakeholders and explain in the report how it has responded to their reasonable expectations and interests.

Sustainability Context: The report should present the organization's performance in the wider context of sustainability.

Completeness: Coverage of the material topics and indicators and definition of the report boundary should be sufficient to reflect significant economic, environmental, and social impacts and enable stakeholders to assess the reporting organization's performance in the reporting period.

Reliability: Information and processes used in the preparation of a report should be gathered, recorded, compiled, analyzed, and disclosed in a way that could be subject to examination and that establishes the quality and materiality of the information.

Clarity: Information should be made available in a manner that is understandable and accessible to stakeholders using the report.

Balance: The report should reflect positive and negative aspects of the organization's performance to enable a reasoned assessment of overall performance.

Comparability: Issues and information should be selected, compiled, and reported consistently.

Accuracy: The reported information should be sufficiently accurate and detailed for stakeholders to assess the reporting organization's performance.

Timeliness: Reporting occurs on a regular schedule and information is available in time for stakeholders to make informed decisions.

SOURCE: Global Reporting Initiative, G3 Reporting Framework "Defining Report Content" (http://www.globalreporting.org/ReportingFramework/G3Online /DefiningReportContent/.

report content. The principles of completeness and sustainability context are meant to help companies determine what they should be reporting on. The principles of accuracy, reliability, neutrality (balance), and comparability are used to ensure that what is reported is truthful and that data can be compared from company to company. Finally, the principles of clarity and timeliness attempt to ensure that what is reported is understandable and reported on a regular schedule.

The GRI has assembled several thousand stakeholders from different sectors to help in the development of the GRI framework. At this writing, about 2,000 companies have formally adopted the GRI framework for reporting, with several thousand more using it informally or partially, making it the de facto global standard for ESG reporting. The credibility of GRI is enhanced by its multistakeholder development process as well as links with the United Nations Environment Programme and the UN Global Compact, which now urges its signatories to use the GRI framework in their annual Communications on Progress (CoPs). Reporting companies operate in a wide array of industries, including automobiles, utilities, consumer products, pharmaceuticals, financial services, telecommunications, energy, and chemicals. Some NGOs, government agencies, universities, and nonprofits also use the guidelines in their reporting. GRI's organizers believe that there are numerous benefits of using the common standards, including better internal management processes, comparability across units and companies, better reputation, and possible strategic differentiation.

Integrated Reporting   Integrated reporting may well be the next wave of reporting for companies. Integrated reporting means that companies produce one report that provides both financial and ESG information, demonstrating the connection between the company's strategy, governance, and financial performance and its ESG activities and impacts. The core idea behind integrated reporting is that it can help companies make more sustainable decisions and provide information to investors and other stakeholders that enable them to evaluate how well the company is actually performing.

Some progressive companies already issue integrated reports (e.g., Southwest Airlines). Most companies that produce ESG reports, however, still do so using the GRI framework or by putting whatever they like into the report and issuing it separately from the required annual financial report, which makes comparison across companies difficult at best. In 2010 an International Integrated Reporting Committee (IIRC) was created by the Prince's Accounting for Sustainability Project in England and the GRI to develop a globally accepted integrated reporting framework. Supported by all the major accounting firms, the GRI, and numerous other stakeholders, the IIRC's goal is to build on the work already done by GRI around ESG reporting and find ways to integrate that information in comparable ways in different companies operating in countries and regions around the world.

The IIRC has several goals with respect to an integrated reporting model:

1. Support the information needs of long-term investors, by showing the broader and longer-term consequences of decision making;

2. Reflect the interconnections between environmental, social, governance and financial factors in decisions that affect long-term performance and condition, making clear the link between sustainability and economic value;

3. Provide the necessary framework for environmental and social factors to be taken into account systematically in reporting and decision making;

4. Rebalance performance metrics away from an undue emphasis on short-term financial performance; and

5. Bring reporting closer to the information used by management to run the business on a day-to-day basis.[28]

The reason to develop an integrated reporting framework is clear, as the IIRC notes on its website: "Integrated Reporting is a vital building block to enable the global economy to meet the challenges of the 21st century: to help the development of an economy which can maintain standards of living for people who already enjoy a good quality of life, and create them for the hundreds of millions who do not, without the present unsustainable over-consumption of the world's finite natural resources."[29] The IIRC sees its role as raising awareness of the need for integrated reporting among numerous constituencies, developing an overarching integrated reporting framework, identifying priority areas for more work, and considering where the framework should be voluntary or mandatory, while simultaneously facilitating collaboration among standard-setters—and emphasizing the need for convergence in standards that underpin the future of integrated reporting (for more on standards, see the next chapter).[30]

In a 2010 report, the international accounting firm KPMG said that integrated reporting is virtually inevitable because of shifts in how companies are already reporting to their stakeholders. KPMG's own research found that ESG or corporate responsibility reporting had become the "de facto law for business" by 2011,[31] and noted that a combination of ESG and financial reporting leads to integrated reporting. In the 2011 survey KPMG found that 95 percent of the world's 250 largest corporations now report on corporate responsibility, with two-thirds of non-reporters being U.S.-based. While only about 3 percent of companies were reporting using an integrated reporting framework in 2010, the number is rapidly increasing as companies move toward greater integration of responsible enterprise issues into their business models, so that it "starts to be at the heart of the business."[32]

The other rationale for moving in the direction of integrated reporting is that many nations' regulatory bodies are beginning to look seriously at requiring it. In KPMG's view, an integrated report should link a company's strategic goals and performance measures to the actual performance of the firm so that any relevant stakeholder can both understand and evaluate the company's performance. Thus integrated reporting does more than simply combine existing reports; it focuses on strategy and its outcomes for the enterprise as a whole.[33] According to Ernst Ligteringen, chief of the GRI, the development of integrated reporting is really about "rewiring homo economicus" and creating "a fundamental change . . . in the way we deal with our world."[34]

Beyond the enterprise responsibility assessment framework that has just been described, there are numerous other ways in which companies today are feeling pressured to improve their ESG performance. Below we briefly explore some of them.

EXTERNAL ASSESSMENT BY SOCIAL INVESTORS

One of the earliest sources of social and environmental pressure on companies came from the investment community itself through what is often called socially responsible (or ethical) investing. To some extent, external assessment of responsible enterprise in the stakeholder and environmental arenas described above developed out of the interests of social investors—that is, individuals and fund managers for whom social and environmental criteria are part of their investment strategies. Most social investment has some emphasis or purpose related either to (1) improving society or community or (2) putting pressure on companies to change various corporate practices so that specific stakeholders and the natural environment are better treated.

Many social investors use screening techniques to assess how well companies perform in specific stakeholder, environmental, and issue arenas. Some seek to pass resolutions about certain corporate practices they would like to see changed. Some invest in companies that are engaged in socially desirable activities such as building affordable housing or economic development of disadvantaged areas, including microlending.[35] And some investors provide venture capital to small capitalization firms, microenterprises or social entrepreneurs, particularly in disadvantaged areas or to disadvantaged groups, to help them build their own economic base. Below we discuss these different approaches.

Social Screens/Social Investing

In recent years, the movement variously called social, ethical, or values-based investing has come of age. Social investing was started decades ago by religious investors, who wanted to be sure that they were investing according to the values espoused by their faith. By the mid-1980s investor activists had focused attention on companies operating in South Africa under the now-disbanded apartheid system.[36] Investor protests caused some companies to divest their South African holdings, and investors interested in this and other important political and social issues called on large pension funds, universities, and other major institutional investors to pay attention to the ways in which they were investing their money.

By the late 1980s, some investors were using social screening, or "issue screens," to monitor companies' investments or market presence in South Africa (and later Myanmar [formerly Burma], the Sudan, and other countries with authoritarian regimes known for human rights abuses). Among the issues "screened" by certain investors are corporate involvement with specific products or services, such as tobacco, alcohol, gaming, pornography, and military contracting, as well as involvement in nuclear power, child labor, and animal testing. Negative or exclusionary screens tend to focus on issues that some investors consider unacceptable because they pose incalculable risks to stakeholder groups or to society in general.[37] Fund managers and investors use these exclusionary screens to eliminate from their portfolios companies that are involved in those issues or practices.

By the early 1990s, investor interest in a range of corporate practices had grown, and so had social screening for investment purposes. Several investment houses, led by Trillium, Calvert Funds, and Domini Social Funds, developed and expanded rating systems to encompass specific stakeholder concerns in addition to the issue screens. In the United States, KLD Research and Analytics, now MSCI ESG, was established in 1990 to rate all of the Standard & Poor's (S&P) 500 largest companies (now the Russell 3000) annually. MSCI ESG now sells social and ecological information to interested investors and Wall Street financial houses and operates a variety of ESG indexes.[38] Such indexes, which can include global, climate, best of class, and similarly constructed funds, help investors to incorporate ESG issues into their investment decisions by screening companies according to a variety of social and environmental factors.

In 1999, the Dow Jones Sustainability Index was launched in the United States as the first global index of leading companies focused on sustainability. The Morningstar rating firm launched the first Japanese socially responsible investment (SRI) index in 2003, and in 2003 Kempen Capital Management and SNS Asset Management launched Europe's first SRI index for smaller companies. In 2004, the Johannesburg Stock Exchange launched the first South African SRI index, containing fifty-one companies that met specific social criteria. Also in 2004 a nonprofit organization, an accounting firm, and two newspapers introduced the Corporate Responsibility Index (CRI) in Australia, which targets the 150 Australian companies with the largest capitalization.

In Europe, FTSE4Good was launched in 2001 and includes companies that meet a range of constantly evolving criteria in five areas. In 2011, the areas were: (a) working toward environmental sustainability, (b) developing positive relationships with stakeholders, (c) upholding and supporting universal human rights, (d) ensuring good supply chain labor standards, and (e) countering bribery.[39] The FTSE4Good index excludes tobacco producers, companies manufacturing either whole, strategic parts, or platforms for nuclear weapon systems, companies manufacturing whole weapons systems, owners or operators of nuclear power stations, and companies involved in the extraction or processing of uranium.[40] In 2004, FTSE4Good launched a related index focusing on responsible Japanese companies and an exclusive stand-alone index highlighting firms' environmental performance.

In the United States many socially responsible investment (SRI) activities are reported by the U.S. Forum for Sustainable and Responsible Investment

(US SIF), whose mission is to promote the concept, practice, and growth of SRI. In the United Kingdom, there is a similar organization promoting SRI called the UK Social Investment Forum,[41] and the European Social Investment Forum addresses broad SRI issues across the European Union (EU), where the EU Commission has taken a highly proactive stance on social investment.[42]

US SIF notes the substantial growth in socially and environmentally screened funds over the past ten years, and that mainstream money managers are increasingly incorporating ESG information into their own analyses. Social investing by professional asset managers grew by more than 380 percent between 1995 and 2010. Further, the number of investment funds considering ESG factors in decision-making also rose sharply, from 260 (in 2007) to 493 (in 2010).[43] In Europe, the European Social Investment Forum (Eurosif) brings together institutional investors, financial services providers, academic institutes, trade unions, and NGOs for lobbying, research, communications, and networking on social investment in the European Union. Collectively, its members represent more than €1 trillion in assets.[44]

Social investment, like other forms of responsible enterprise, puts companies' stakeholder and environmental practices under considerable scrutiny. In addition to investors, activists, customers, and NGOs can readily communicate their dissatisfaction with a company's practices globally, through their networks, in blogs, and via videos posted on the Internet, among other ways. Anti-corporate and anti-globalization demonstrations around the world by labor, human rights, and environmental activists, which first erupted notably at the 1999 World Trade Organization meeting in Seattle (dubbed by journalists "the battle of Seattle") to protest continuing globalization, demonstrate the speed with which information circulates, and the power of unsatisfied stakeholders to take concerted action. Many screens permit companies to be assessed for negative or problematic behaviors that pose concerns for different groups of investors. They also allow companies to be rewarded for proactive and progressive behaviors. Managers of social choice funds, which tend to be for the sole use of investors in those funds, use their own screens built around similar ideas.

Social Investing in Projects and Ventures

Some social investors want to invest their assets in projects that are explicitly designed to benefit society or help disadvantaged groups. There are several emerging types of social investment projects: projects to economically, academically, or socially develop otherwise disadvantaged communities or groups; philanthropy strategically given to nonprofit and public agencies to meet the dual bottom line of social benefit and business gain; and venture capital to fund small businesses or even microbusinesses in disadvantaged areas or by disadvantaged groups and individuals.

Social Investment Projects   Sometimes social investors wish to invest their assets in socially beneficial projects, such as hotels or businesses that can help rebuild an economic base in disadvantaged communities. Some investors expect market returns from these investments, while others are more concerned with making a difference in society and are therefore willing to accept less than market rates of return. The Calvert Social Investment Foundation, for example, has developed funds that invest in affordable housing, the development of microenterprises, and community development. In these funds, investors can sometimes choose the rate of return they desire (which in some cases is less than the market rate). Their investment is then used to fund, for example, economic development activities in inner cities, such as a new hotel complex that has been constructed in Harlem in New York City.

In the United States, lending institutions, particularly banks, are subject to the requirements of the Community Reinvestment Act (CRA) of 1977.[45] The CRA requires banks that benefit from and are subject to the regulatory oversight of the Federal Deposit Insurance Corporation (FDIC) to prove that they are acting to meet the credit needs of the entire community within their service areas. A bank's entire service area includes low- and moderate-income neighborhoods, particularly those in the inner city and rural areas that have been historically underserved by financial institutions. Many of these areas have been subject to redlining by banks in the past, the practice of drawing (figurative or literal) red lines on municipal maps to indicate where loans are discouraged or not made. The CRA was intended to stop this practice, opening up those neighborhoods to loans, credit, and other banking services that are readily accessible in more advantaged areas.

To ensure that banks meet their CRA obligations and invest in their communities appropriately, the FDIC rates banks' CRA performance on a scale from "outstanding" to "substantial noncompliance." Like other data assessing corporate performance on significant stakeholder dimensions, CRA ratings are published by the government.[46] This information then becomes available to activists, community members, and other parties interested in institutional performance.

Advantages of Disadvantaged Areas   Some investors believe that there can be competitive advantage to investments in disadvantaged areas when an asset- and resource-based approach, rather than a deficit-based approach, is used. One creative initiative (among many) was established in 1994 through the Initiative for a Competitive Inner City (ICIC). Taking an asset-based perspective on economic development of disadvantaged areas, ICIC is based on Harvard professor Michael Porter's ideas about how cities can gain competitive advantage.[47] Porter recognized that a systemic approach to rebuilding deteriorated inner cities was necessary and that social and community health depends on access to jobs that pay a living wage. Using an asset-based approach to understanding the inner city, Porter identified four main competitive advantages of the inner city: (1) strategic location in the downtown area (and, as it turns out, access to highways); (2) local market demand; (3) integration with regional clusters within and surrounding the city; and (4) human resources. Competitive clusters, according to Porter, create advantages for new business formation, particularly for business-to-business opportunities, and access to downstream products and services in local markets.

The ICIC focuses on U.S. inner cities; however, the asset-based perspective is applicable to any disadvantaged or less-developed area, according to Porter's framework. These and similar projects illustrate the "both/and" logic of operating with an asset-based approach to community and economic development. They also suggest new approaches that businesses and investors interested in making a positive difference in their communities can take. One approach to recognize excellence in economic development of inner cities is the Inner City 100 rating, which documents the 100 fastest-growing companies in inner cities.

In 2011, ICIC claimed that its research had "awakened" major retails to a billion-dollar opportunity in U.S. inner cities, and that Inner City 100 companies had created more than 71,000 new jobs between 1999 and 2010.[48] An ICIC report in 2011 noted that local business clusters in inner cities together employed 85 million people, accounting for some 70 percent of national employment, a proportion that is likely to continue to grow. Local clusters include opportunities in health and commercial services, hospitality, real estate and construction, retail, financial services, and food and beverage processing and distribution, among others. Pointing out that only 23 percent of local cluster jobs demand a college education and the jobs are reasonably well paying, the report argued for strengthening such local clusters so that employment opportunities would be available to inner-city residents who may not have had opportunities for college or university education.[49]

SHAREHOLDER ACTIVISM AND CORPORATE GOVERNANCE

Many people in the social investment community view shareholder activism as another form of social investment; companies need to be aware that such activism can affect their decisions—and that activists are watching their responsibility practices. Managers cannot make decisions in a vacuum when shareholders are affected—or when they wish to exert influence. Shareholders have found new ways of making their voices heard, including shareholder resolutions, engagement with management on specific issues, and letter-writing campaigns.

Shareholders are supposed to be the stakeholders to whom corporate managers pay the most attention, according to the logic of the neoclassical economic model, which dominates the financial community globally. Yet the many scandals related to the global financial crisis in 2008 were at least partially generated by managers' efforts to maximize shareholder wealth; instead, they ended up hurting shareholders when the companies collapsed. In many scandal-ridden companies and financial institutions, managers put self-interest well ahead of shareholders' interest, and boards of directors either were not paying sufficient attention or did not have enough information to make good decisions. Thus, some shareholders have found it difficult to have a voice in corporate affairs, even in situations where shareholders theoretically do come first. Most large companies have issued millions of shares that are held by investors who are largely unfamiliar with the company's activities. As a result, management dominates corporate decision-making, leaving some shareholders wanting more influence. The issue of corporate governance—how well companies' boards of directors represent stockholder and other stakeholder interests, especially around financial performance—is therefore a major concern of activist shareholders.

Shareholder activists tend to express their views through the votes accorded to them via their ownership interest in the firm, typically by submitting shareholder resolutions to a vote during the annual meeting. Shareholder resolutions can draw attention to concerns about corporate abuse of power, weak governance structures, and poor managerial decision-making, among other factors. Some resolutions attempt to counter corporate tendencies to economize (e.g., through excessive layoffs) or improve efficiency (e.g., by stopping companies from paying top managers inflated salaries and benefits, particularly when performance does not meet expectations). Activist shareholders may argue against a company's tendency to make acquisitions simply for the sake of growth (to accumulate power) when there is little strategic reason to do so. Investors can influence corporate practice directly by calling for discussion of shareholder resolutions at their companies' annual meetings. This is also a way to gain publicity for issues that worry them.

Although corporate governance principles are influenced by national legislation, some organizations have also proposed the establishment of universal global principles. For example, the California Public Employees' Retirement System (CalPERS), a trust fund committed to improving corporate governance practices, has articulated eight principles of good corporate governance for shareowners—the "Global Principles of Accountable Corporate Governance":

1. Corporate governance practices should focus broad attention on optimizing the company's operating performance and returns to shareowners.

2. Directors should be accountable to shareowners, and management accountable to directors. To ensure this accountability, directors must be accessible to shareowner inquiry concerning their key decisions affecting the company's strategic direction.

3. Information about companies must be readily transparent to permit accurate market comparisons; this includes disclosure and transparency of objective globally accepted minimum accounting standards.

4. All investors must be treated equitably and upon the principle of one-share/ one-vote.

5. Proxy materials should be written in a manner designed to provide share-owners with the information necessary to make informed voting decisions. Similarly, proxy materials should be distributed in a manner designed to encourage shareowner participation. All shareowner votes, whether cast in person or by proxy, should be formally counted with vote outcomes formally announced.

6. Each capital market in which shares are issued and traded should adopt its own Code of Best Practices; and, where such a code is adopted, companies should disclose to their shareowners whether they are in compliance.

7. Corporate directors and management should have a long-term strategic vision that, at its core, emphasizes sustained shareowner value. In turn, despite differing investment strategies and tactics, shareowners should encourage corporate management to resist short-term behavior by supporting and rewarding long-term superior returns.

8. Shareholders should have effective access to the director nomination process.[50]

Other groups that have attempted to build guiding principles for corporate governance in the United States are the Council of Institutional Investors and the National Association of Corporate Directors; major business associations, such as the Business Roundtable; large institutional investors like the Teachers Insurance and Annuity Association/College Retirement Equities Fund (TIAA-CREF); and religious activists such as the Interfaith Center on Corporate Responsibility.

Internationally, a great deal of work has been done to develop similar codes and principles for governing multinational corporations and making them accountable to their important stakeholders. Australia, Belgium, Canada, Germany, Hong Kong, India, Italy, Japan, the Netherlands, South Africa, Spain, Sweden, the United Kingdom, and the United States have undertaken efforts to reform or improve governance practices within corporations. In 2004, the thirty countries of the Organization for Economic Cooperation and Development (OECD) approved a revision of the OECD's Principles of Corporate Governance.[51]

It is noteworthy that institutional investors hold a significant proportion of listed stocks. Because institutional owners own shares of most of the companies whose shares are publicly traded, they have become what Simon Zadek, former CEO of AccountAbility, has called "universal owners."[52] Universal ownership, according to James Hawley and Andrew Williams, who have studied the phenomenon, means that corporate ownership is concentrated in the hands of institutional owners—that is, professional money managers such as those who run pension and mutual funds who own "a small but representative fraction of most companies in the economy."[53] Hawley and Williams theorize that the concentration of ownership in institutions means that to meet their fiduciary responsibilities, such owners are more dependent on general economic conditions than on any individual firm's performance—and thus have a keen interest in ensuring sustainable economic development (in all senses of the word sustainable) since the fate of the market is aligned with the fate of their portfolio.[54]

One study of directors concluded that "independent, intrepid, informed, diverse (in background and expertise) directors willing to speak up when concerned or in doubt and to challenge management and each other are crucial to healthy and constructive boardroom dynamics and to effective corporate governance."[55] Meeting growing obligations to govern corporations properly means living up to the types of standards found in the principles discussed above. The principles usually call for clear and fair election rules for directors, director independence from management, disclosure of sufficient information to allow shareholders and directors to make effective strategic decisions (transparency), and board committee structures that are independent of undue management influence. The reason shareholder activists should pay attention to governance is perhaps best stated by Supreme Court Justice Louis Brandeis:

> There is no such thing to my mind . . . as an innocent stockholder. He may be innocent in fact, but socially he cannot be held innocent. He accepts the benefits of the system. It is his business and his obligation to see that those who represent him carry out a policy which is consistent with the public welfare.[56]

SOCIAL VENTURING THROUGH MICROENTERPRISE

Globally, about 3 billion people live on less than US$2.50 a day. Some 22,000 children die daily as a consequence of living in poverty. The UN estimates that some 27–28 percent of children in developing nations are underweight or malnourished, and more than 72 million children are thought not to be in school (57 percent of them girls) in 2005. Of the world's nearly 7 billion people, about a billion are illiterate.[57] Despite these numbers, overall rates of poverty have improved in recent decades, consistent with new initiatives to reduce poverty. Efforts by the United Nations, through its Millennium Development Goals (MDGs) to reduce poverty, along with those of NGOs and even some businesses, have had some effect. For example, the world is generally on track to meet the goal of reducing poverty by half by 2015, and a higher percentage of children in sub-Saharan Africa are now attending school than ever before. Disease-related deaths have been reduced from 12.4 million in 1990 to 8.8 million in 2008, and the rate of deforestation has been reduced, though overall deforestation remains unacceptably high.[58] Attempts to improve the lives of people living in dire poverty historically have come through grants, technical assistance, and other forms of philanthropy. Poor people were typically viewed as having deficits that needed to be overcome through the help and assets that could be provided by wealthier people. Traditional approaches to poverty, including much corporate philanthropy and foundation giving, assumed that poor people needed money because they could not help themselves. One of the problems with this approach is that only a tiny fraction of people who need help can be reached through charitable donations.

In recent years, both in the United States and around the world, a different model—an asset-based model—has begun to take shape. It operates on the assumption not that poor people have deficits and are in need of fixing, but rather that they have many assets, possess many strengths, and, given the right opportunities, will find a way to become more advantaged through their own resources. It is a philosophy similar to that now being used by social venture capitalists investing in U.S. inner cities, such as the ICIC: positive deviance.

Positive deviants are individuals (or groups) who use intentional behaviors to depart from social norms in honorable or positive ways and thereby help improve their circumstances.[59] By tapping into local resources and ideas, social entrepreneurs have used the amplification of positive deviance to help struggling local residents find acceptable ways of improving their living conditions, health, and other aspects of their lives. In one Vietnamese village in the late 1990s, Save the Children's Jerry Sternin and his wife, Monique, found that some families in a very poor community had well-nourished children. By determining which culturally acceptable, but not widely used, ways of feeding children were being used by a few families—positive deviants—and making it possible for villagers to spread the word themselves, the Sternins were able to help improve the well-being of those who were undernourished.[60] The amplification of positive deviance has been used in a wide variety of projects, including improving nutrition and child care in Bengal, India, and nutrition in Boston; preventing girl trafficking in Indonesia; and promoting family planning in Guatemala, to name just a few.[61]

Such asset-based views of poor people also argue that, given some resources, many poor people will be able to start, manage, and grow small businesses that will enable them to build better lives for themselves and their families, although they are unlikely to get rich. One way of putting this perspective to work has evolved in the growing field of microenterprise development. This form of social investment has paid enormous social dividends through organizations like the Grameen Bank, founded in Bangladesh in 1976 by Mohammad Yunus, 2006 winner of the Nobel Peace Prize for his work. Grameen Bank was formalized as a bank in 1983.[62] Recognizing that individuals, particularly women, living in dire poverty could not accumulate even the minimal amount of capital needed to begin small businesses that could support them and their families, Yunus created a system for granting very small loans to would-be entrepreneurs. Each borrower is accountable for repaying the loan to a peer group of microentrepreneur lenders living in the same village. A bank employee meets with each group once a week to ensure that the entrepreneurs' businesses are operating and that the loans are on track to being repaid.

Grameen Bank's system (like other microenterprise systems) uses peer pressure and the social capital generated through weekly meetings to create a system in which not repaying the loan breaks trust with others. By creating a trust-based system, Grameen reverses traditional banking practices—and costs. By tapping the individual strengths and creative energies of borrowers, this grassroots initiative generates both social and financial capital in very poor villages. The main form of collateral is each borrower's reputation within the village's local lending unit.

Today, Grameen Bank has more than 8.34 million borrowers, of whom 97 percent are women, because Yunus believes that women are more likely than men to use the fruits of their entrepreneurship to feed, clothe, and shelter their families. The bank had 2,565 branches covering 81,376 villages in Bangladesh by 2010, and the loan recovery rate was 97.37 percent, a figure that would be the envy of any traditional bank. The bank has been profitable in all but three years of its existence. By 2010, Grameen had loaned more than $10.12 billion in total and had become a model for microlending, a concept central to the United Nations' strategy for economic development around the world.[63]

To complement its microlending, Grameen has started numerous other types of businesses as a means of building not only healthy communities but also bigger enterprises that might in the future operate in the world economy. For example, Grameen Shakti is a nonprofit enterprise supplying renewable energy to unelectrified villages in Bangladesh; and Grameen Shikkha/Education combines the efforts of a number of companies to promote education in rural areas, financially supports loans and grants for education, and uses information technology to help alleviate illiteracy. Grameen also has founded a telecommunications company, Grameen Telecom, to ensure that the information revolution reaches Bangladesh's rural population, and a knitwear company, Grameen Knitwear Limited, that produces high-quality garments for sale mostly in European markets.[64]

In the United States and Latin America, an organization called Acción International also has done pioneering work in microlending.[65] With some loans as small as $500 in the United States and $100 in Latin America, the Caribbean, Asia, and sub-Saharan Africa, Acción International helps entrepreneurs get off of welfare, rebuild their communities through business activities, and create new jobs in places that large corporations have abandoned. Like Grameen, Acción uses a peer network system that draws on local social capital to ensure repayments and site visits to replace traditional bank paperwork (and reduce costs to make the loans feasible). By 2009, Acción was serving as an umbrella organization for lending activities in more than thirty-one countries on four continents. In the United States, Acción is active in more than forty-six states. It has loaned money to more than 8.6 million people, disbursed some $31.8 billion, and like Grameen, has a 97 percent repayment rate.

The high payback rates associated with Grameen's and Acción's microloans, as well as other microloans using similar techniques, create revolving funds that can be used to make additional loans and foster additional entrepreneurship among disadvantaged people.[66] Such lenders assume that their clients possess assets on which they will build their enterprises. For example, Grameen bases its loans on the three Cs of credit: character (integrity and past history of the borrower); capacity (debt capacity, income stream, and repayment history); and capital (current assets of the borrower as a form of collateral). Microenterprise activities have been so successful globally that in 1997 the United Nations issued a resolution promoting the use of microlending on a global scale. Indeed, the activities of both Grameen and Acción have helped to spawn an industry of microlenders who believe that helping people to help themselves is a far better way for countries and individuals to pursue economic development than simply giving handouts. And it can be a profitable way to socially invest as well.

SOCIAL VENTURE CAPITAL

Another type of social investment is providing venture capital to firms or individuals working to improve the lot of the disadvantaged through community and economic development enterprises. Businesses that can use social venture capital are significantly larger than microenterprises, often requiring amounts over (sometimes significantly over) $100,000. Sometimes social venture capital loans money for working capital, equipment purchases, debt refinancing, business acquisition, expansion, or credit lines. One prominent social venture capitalist is Calvert's Social Venture Capital Fund, which invests in market-based solutions to seemingly intractable social, environmental, and health problems,[67] and Britain's New Economics Foundation Social

Venture Capital Fund, which invests in community enterprises as a means of building healthy, sustainable communities.[68]

Social venture capitalists tend to focus on underserved populations, otherwise unmet social needs, and ventures designed to improve the natural environment. They use the same criteria as traditional venture capitalists: due diligence regarding management strength, product or service concept, market opportunity, and expected financial return (though some are willing to accept less than market rates of return). Social venture capitalists may ask additional questions of the entrepreneur, such as whether the project meets an unmet social or ecological need, what the impact of the project on future generations is likely to be, and whether the project's results are likely to have a positive impact on society. One example of a Calvert social venture investment is Powerspan, which works on decreasing emissions from power plants at low cost.[69]

CORPORATE RANKINGS AND REPUTATION

Responsible enterprise can also be assessed through corporate rankings. Having a good reputation is essential to responsible enterprise and is another of the many factors under public scrutiny today. Regular rankings identify the best corporations for a whole range of behaviors, including *Fortune*'s "most admired" corporations,[70] the Global 100 Most Sustainable Corporations in the World (by Corporate Knights and partners),[71] and an annual Harris Poll–Reputation Institute survey of corporate reputation published by the *Wall Street Journal*. Many observers believe that a corporation's reputation for accepting its responsibilities will be a determining factor in gaining competitive advantage in the future. Rankings that measure one or another aspect of firms' responsibility are increasingly common.

The business press and many interest groups regularly investigate corporate practices and behaviors with respect to particular stakeholders. Following the lead of *Fortune*, which has issued its "most admired corporations" list since 1983, numerous other publications now issue lists and rankings of companies that are the best or worst in various categories. These best-companies lists rank or name companies that are, for example, the "best to work for," "best for Blacks and Hispanics," "most family friendly," "best and worst governed," "best corporate citizens," "best corporate reputation," "best companies for gay men and lesbians," and "best for working women," to name only a few. One observer noted that in 2009 there were over "700 primetime corporate rankings that companies can compete on and receive recognition."[72]

Reputation is the external assessment of a company or any other organization held by external stakeholders. Reputation includes several dimensions, including an organization's perceived capacity to meet those stakeholders' expectations, the rational attachments that a stakeholder forms with an organization, and the overall image that stakeholders have of the organization. Corporate reputation tends to be associated with a company's brand identity and image, according to Gary Davies of the University of Manchester in England. A company's identity has to do with how it views itself, while its image is what is projected to stakeholders. Employee satisfaction and retention are linked to corporate identity, and customer loyalty and satisfaction are linked to image.[73]

Fortune magazine issues an annual "reputation index," a list that many companies aspire to be on because of its prestige in the business world. Annual company ratings are beginning to appear in other countries as well, including *Asian Business*'s "Asia's Most Admired Companies," the *Far Eastern Economic Review*'s "Review 200," *Management Today*'s "Britain's Most Admired Companies," and the *Financial Times*'s "Europe's Most Respected Companies." As more such rating systems emerge and put companies under additional external scrutiny, companies will have to pay greater attention to their stakeholder-related practices.

Charles Fombrun and the New Economics Foundation in the UK assess corporate reputation and performance from the perspective of stakeholders themselves. Using this methodology, Fombrun has been able to attach a dollar amount to the value of reputation in relationship to a company's stock price. Such measures will likely gain increasing public attention in the future, further enhancing the critical importance of reputation to companies, not only for sustaining customer goodwill and continued purchases but also for being granted a license to operate by communities and governments.[74]

THE MEASUREMENT OF RESPONSIBLE BUSINESS PRACTICE

This chapter has discussed three different criteria for assessing responsible enterprise: (1) principles, certification initiatives, and reporting standards, (2) social investment and shareholder activism, and (3) corporate rankings.

You get what you measure. That slogan is at the core of accounting practice, and it is also at the heart of responsible enterprise. Leaders of companies that hope to meet the highest standards of responsible enterprise need to take the time to identify what those standards are and the best ways to measure whether they are actually meeting them. Having a clear corporate vision with its attendant values is only the first step in an iterative process that involves next determining what kinds of measurements are appropriate internally, as well as the ways in which the company will be—and is already being—evaluated externally.

Assessment and reporting of responsible enterprise is an ongoing proposition—and it goes on whether the company itself is involved or not. Increasingly, progressive companies are taking charge of that reporting by issuing social and environmental statements—and the most progressive are already anticipating the future and issuing integrated reports that demonstrate the relationship between their strategic goals and their stakeholder-related performance—that is, their enterprise responsibility.

9   SUSTAINABILITY
AND THE GLOBAL VILLAGE

Partnership is an essential characteristic of sustainable
communities. . . .

In human communities partnership means democracy and
personal empowerment, because each member of the community
plays an important role. Combining the principle of partnership
with the dynamic of change and development, we may also use
the term "coevolution" metaphorically in human communities.
As a partnership proceeds, each partner better understands the
needs of the other. In a true, committed partnership both partners
learn and change—they co-evolve. Here again we notice the basic
tension between the challenge of ecological sustainability and
the way in which our present societies are structured, between
economics and ecology. Economics emphasizes competition,
expansion, and domination; ecology emphasizes cooperation,
conservation, and partnership.

Fritjof Capra, *The Web of Life*[1]

SUSTAINING A HEALTHY NATURAL ECOLOGY

During the last third of the 20th century it became clear that the health of the
natural environment that surrounds and underpins societies and the economies they produce is increasingly in peril. This danger was dramatically highlighted by the two influential documentaries, *An Inconvenient Truth* (2006),
which awakened many people to the issues associated with global warming,
species extinction, and sustainability in general, and *2011 Carbon Nation*
(2011), which offers a more action-oriented assessment of what can be done
about sustainability. Because ecological systems are so interdependent, many
environmental problems are global rather than local in scope, necessitating
that companies, governments, and communities alike develop comprehensive new approaches to the use and disposal of natural resources. Corporate
programs of environmental management, especially those aimed at sustainability of both the natural and community environments, have also begun to
gain traction toward more responsible use of environmental resources.

Climate change, ozone depletion, water and air pollution, pesticide use, toxic waste disposal and run-off, desertification, water shortages, and waste disposal are only a few of the environmental problems facing the planet. Add in the burning of tropical rain forests to clear land for short-term farming, other processes that lead to deforestation and even desertification, the resulting decimation of wildlife and plant species, and coastal and wetlands erosion resulting from development; further consider the scarcity of fresh water in some regions of the world, acid rain, and severe climate patterns that are increasingly attributed to changes in the ecology. Then recognize the continuing pressures that population growth places on ecological resources, especially water—and it quickly becomes clear that human civilization faces ecological crises the likes of which have never before been seen.

Many ecological problems are boundary-less in that they cannot be contained readily, or at all, within community, regional, or even national borders. The impacts of many of these problems affect communities far beyond their sources and require wholly new approaches to sustainable development and governance.

PRESSURES ON THE ECOLOGY

A series of innovative studies pioneered by Mathis Wackernagel and his colleagues at the Global Footprint Network estimate that humanity is now in ecological "overshoot" by some 50 percent; that is, humans are placing 50 percent more annual demand on the planet than the earth's renewable resources can regenerate. According to the "Living Planet Index," this overshoot means that it now takes the earth about one year and six months to regenerate the resources humanity uses in a single year, which is akin to deficit spending in a budget. In other words, we currently use 1.5 planets to absorb the waste created on earth. According to the report, virtually no country in the world today is sustainable from an ecological perspective (see Figure 9.1).[2]

One interesting insight is that people in the developed world leave significantly larger ecological footprints than do people in the less-developed world, in part because they have fewer resources and therefore consume less. From this viewpoint, Africa is the most sustainable region of the world in part because many of its people live in abject poverty and hence place few

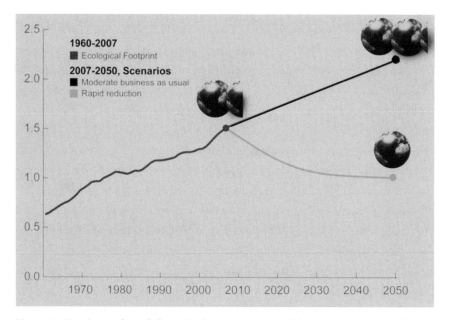

Figure 9.1: Y-axis: number of Planet Earths, X-axis, years. Global Footprint Network, http://www.footprintnetwork.org/gfn_sub.php?content=global_footprint.

demands on the natural environment, while the ecological footprint of the United States is among the biggest, with 8.0 planets needed to sustain its residents' lifestyles.

Table 9.1 indicates that the United Arab Emirates is the biggest consumer of environmental resources per capita, with an average ecological footprint of 10.7, far greater than those of less-developed countries like Afghanistan and Bangladesh, which are well under the 1.8 hectares per capita defined as the world's sustainable biocapacity rate. By these calculations, the earth reached its carrying capacity in the mid-1970s. Though there is a tremendous burgeoning of population in less-developed countries, people's individual ecological footprints are much smaller, in part because the poor require far fewer environmental resources to maintain their lifestyles. Lacking well-developed industrialization, developing nations do not consume or waste nearly as much as developed nations.

The 2010 edition of the *Living Planet Report* sends a clear message: "Under a 'business as usual' scenario, the outlook is serious: even with modest UN projections for population growth, consumption and climate change, by 2030 humanity will need the capacity of two Earths to absorb CO_2 waste and keep

TABLE 9.1   *Ecological Footprints of Selected Nations*

Country	Footprint (global hectares per capita)
United Arab Emirates	10.7
Qatar	10.5
Denmark	8.3
Belgium	8.0
United States of America	8.0
Estonia	7.9
Canada	7.0
Australia	6.8
Congo, Democratic Republic of	1.0
Pakistan	0.8
Occupied Palestinian Territory	0.7
Malawi	0.7
Haiti	0.7
Afghanistan	0.6
Bangladesh	0.6
Timor-Leste	0.4

SOURCE: Global Footprint Network, *National Footprint Accounts* (2010 edition), selected countries, (http://www.footprintnetwork.org/gfn_sub.php?content=global_footprint).

up with natural resource consumption."[3] What this means is that current approaches to economic and societal development are draining the earth's resources faster than nature can replace them even without the explosive growth in population that is expected over the next several decades. Clearly, the current approach to development and lifestyles is unsustainable in the long term.

ORGANIZING FOR SUSTAINABILITY

Sustainability of ecological resources and what is sometimes called the greening of business are fast becoming norms in responsible companies with visions supported by values that respect both nature and human civilization, particularly when companies openly recognize their ecological impacts.

Responsible corporations recognize that their own survival and well-being—as well as those of their customers, employees, and other stakeholders—depend on a shift of perspective related to business's impacts on the natural environment and the necessary changes in corporate practices to move toward sustainability. The following sections of this chapter focus on ways in which companies manage their relationship with the earth.

Change of Perspective

Truly greening a company involves generating a new awareness among its leaders of the importance of the natural environment. This shift of consciousness moves thinking away from the dualism, fragmentation, and mechanistic view of nature found in traditional Western ways of viewing the world toward the more holistic, organic, and integrated perspective, what Peter Senge called a metanoia, or shift of consciousness.[4] The shift of consciousness and awareness depends in part on having leaders and their associates at the post-conventional levels of cognitive and moral (and emotional) development discussed earlier. Making this shift can help better align the interests of all stakeholders with those of the ecological sphere that underpins human civilization. Where this shift of perspective takes hold, it becomes clear to observers that balance among economic, political, and social activities is essential to long-term sustainability and that corporations, which are responsible for much of the consumption of earth's resources, have a significant role to play in the movement toward sustainability.[5]

Throughout the world, corporations are adopting environmental management and sustainability practices under pressure from stakeholders who want them to create more sustainable products.[6] Some researchers believe that this shift and the accompanying changes in awareness may even represent a new industrial revolution, although any such revolution is clearly in its early stages.[7] To manage this change of perspective, many companies are adopting proactive practices of environmental management, focused on waste reduction and cost cutting, which have the by-product of satisfying customer demands for greener businesses and social investors' interest in environmental sustainability. In addition, many companies are finding, to their surprise, that there is a "both/and" of enhanced profits and greening.[8]

Indeed, one study found that multinational corporations, rather than suffering from environmental regulations, are actually rewarded with higher stock market performance when they adopt strict global environmental standards.[9]

A study of executives in 2010 by MIT's Sloan Management Review and the Boston Consulting Group (BCG) on Sustainability & Innovation found that companies are either "embracing" sustainability-driven management or undertaking it as "cautious adopters." Noting that the embracers are likely to be models for future strategies around sustainability, the study also found that most companies maintained—and expected to increase—spending on sustainability after the global financial crisis that began in 2007-2008, but again the commitment to sustainability varies from cautious adoption to fully embracing a sustainability orientation. The embracers focus on widespread implementation of sustainability throughout the enterprise, but both approaches have some benefits in efficiency and waste management. Though exact cost models remain elusive, companies are beginning to find ways to measure and account for some of the intangibles associated with sustainability, and embracers believe that their sustainability efforts give them a degree of competitive advantage.[10]

The MIT-BCG study provides guidance on how companies that are lagging behind the embracers can begin to catch up on the sustainability front, suggesting seven specific steps that can be taken. The first of these is to "move early even if information is incomplete," in part because action on sustainability cannot be undertaken formulaically and some risks will have to be taken. The second piece of advice is to "balance broad, long-term [sustainability] vision with projects offering concrete, near-term 'wins,'" and to do so, as a third recommendation, both from the top down and bottom up. In undertaking this approach, the report recommends (fourth) that companies "aggressively de-silo sustainability—integrating it throughout company operations," and fifth, "measure everything (and if ways of measuring something don't exist, start inventing them)." The sixth and seventh recommendations are to "value intangible benefits seriously" and "try to be authentic and transparent—internally and externally."[11] Sound familiar?

Note the similarity of this process to the responsibility management processes outlined earlier in this book. There is nothing necessarily "new" about managing for sustainability or responsibility. But businesses need to recognize that the successful approaches will be whole systems approaches that are driven systemically throughout the enterprise, not piecemeal or patchwork approaches (as Liedtka noted in the study cited earlier).[12]

Stages of Environmental Awareness

Just as there are stages of corporate citizenship, there are also stages of environmental or sustainability awareness in companies. Ecologist and management theorist Stuart Hart proposed a developmental framework along which firms and their leaders progress as they begin to shift their thinking toward environmentally sustainable strategies.[13] Later, he and Mark Milstein created a "sustainable value framework" that tracked how companies move from an internal-today-oriented mindset focused on pollution prevention to an external-today-oriented strategy aimed at product stewardship.[14] Hart pointed out that pollution prevention strategies resemble the quality movement in that they emphasize continual improvement in reducing energy use and waste. Pollution prevention is also aligned with the emerging global environmental standards embodied in ISO 14001. Importantly, Hart noted that "the emerging economies [and the environment itself] cannot afford to repeat all the mistakes of Western development."[15]

At the first stage in Hart's framework companies operating in a product stewardship mode attempt to minimize not only pollution related to manufacturing processes but also all other sources of environmental impacts. Full-cost or life-cycle accounting for products can be used to reduce materials usage and begin a process of fundamental change in product and process design, which is necessary in the shift toward sustainability. Fully costing production of both goods and services raises leaders' awareness of all of the company's ecological impacts.

For developing nations, it makes sense to emulate not the plunder-and-pillage environmental strategies of earlier stages of development, but rather the best modern practices associated with sustainable development. Of course, this way of thinking represents a long-term view in which costs are internalized; thus, the next stage shifts the focus to tomorrow rather than today, and costs are internalized rather than externalized.[16] Some developing nations find it difficult to think about ecological sustainability when they need to help their citizens put food on the table and shelter overhead. Hart's point, however, is that this long-term thinking is critical for world health, as well as for the ultimate health of developing nations.[17]

The third stage in Hart's framework is called clean technology. In this stage, companies shift production and products toward altogether new technologies that use many fewer resources and that last a long time. This shift, which is still rare, happens when leaders recognize that no matter how much they reduce waste or conserve resources, many of today's technologies are simply not sustainable. The payoff for companies engaging in clean technology comes in repositioning the company in an attempt to reduce its ecological footprint.[18]

A final stage, driven by population growth, poverty, and inequity in the world, is called the sustainability vision. In Hart and Milstein's view, this vision taps into the huge unmet need in the world, providing a growth trajectory for companies, while simultaneously focusing on the long-term vision of sustainability oriented toward meeting external demands and needs.[19] According to Hart and Clayton Christensen, companies can both generate internal growth and satisfy the social and ecological needs of stakeholders through "a 'great leap' to the base of the economic pyramid, where 4 billion people aspire to join the market economy for the first time."[20]

This thinking is similar to the economic development strategies for the bottom of the pyramid that the late C. K. Prahalad and Stuart Hart developed except applied to environmental issues.[21] To effectively implement environmental strategies, however, companies have to develop technologies, manufacturing processes, and resource uses that are sustainable for the entire population over the long term. Although few companies have yet reached this stage of development, many ecologists, such as Hart, believe this is the necessary next step for the planet's ecological health.

Environmental Management Practices

In recent years, significant gains have been made in environmental sensitivity and performance in developed nations, mostly resulting from the so-called greening of business, tough environmental regulations, and outsourcing practices that have removed heavily polluting industries to less industrialized nations.[22] Of course, outsourcing pollution creates potential problems in that, as developing countries industrialize, they generate additional pollution and extract more natural resources, shifting the ecological balance in a negative direction. Hart claims that developing nations must follow a different and more enlightened path today. Already, there are quite a number of management practices that can help move companies toward ecological sustainability.

According to researchers Michael Berry and Dennis Rondinelli, comprehensive environmental management systems include five major elements: "waste minimization and prevention, demand-side management, design for environment, product stewardship, and full-cost accounting."[23] Each element of this comprehensive system is explained in Table 9.2. Berry and Rondinelli note that demand-side management can actually improve profitability. For example, International Truck and Engine Corporation, which manufactures buses, trucks, and parts, reduced its lead component by 98 percent, saving, time, money, and energy.[24]

Demand-side management allows better relationships with customers because customers are being sold only and exactly what they need, rather than having salespeople sell them more simply to fill their quotas. Stewardship involves taking care of the resources and products that are developed by paying close attention to all aspects of their development and use—that is, by assuming full responsibility for the products or services and their impacts, whether those impacts are direct or indirect. Full-cost accounting (or life-cycle accounting) is necessary to take into account all of the costs of production, sales, distribution, and use, rather than externalizing them to society.

Environmental Cost Accounting and Life-Cycle Accounting

One managerial tool being used increasingly to assess the overall ecological costs of producing goods and services is called environmental cost accounting. Traditional cost accounting is a tool used by managers to assess the full costs of producing something within the firm (indirect as well as direct costs of production). Similarly, environmental cost accounting attempts to take into account all of the ecological costs of production, such as energy consumed, waste produced, cleanup costs, and possible liabilities associated with production, and as such is an essential part of an environmental management system.[25]

To fully account for environmental impacts, some companies are using full-cost or life-cycle accounting, which attempts to holistically assess the impacts of a product or service throughout its life cycle.[26] Based on the principle of ecological stewardship—or care taking—life-cycle accounting encompasses multiple disciplines in a holistic assessment of the planning for a product, its management during its useful life, industrial design associated with it (including engineering and design specification), and costs associated with environmental and health protection.[27]

The Society of Environmental Toxicology and Chemistry has defined a complete life-cycle assessment as having three interrelated parts, which are listed in Table 9.3. These three elements—life-cycle inventory, impact analysis, and improvement analysis—combine to create a system through which costs can be calculated for all of the impacts of designing, developing, producing, delivering, and finally disposing of a product or service.

One study finds that for plant-level managers these sophisticated approaches to full costing may be too complex and that a simpler framework might be useful for what the authors call total quality environmental management or TQEM.[28] This approach applies the principles of TQM (total quality management) to environmental management, in part because TQM is a system with which most managers are already familiar. This approach helps managers to identify the costs associated with environmental issues. Some of these costs include, for example, external failures, contingent liability costs associated with future corrective action, and less tangible costs associated with lower consumer acceptance of products. Internal failures can also be costly, including the costs of waste management, the need to label hazardous waste, related recordkeeping costs, and notification costs in the event of a crisis. Employee costs can include strained relationships in the event of problems and added training costs to handle hazardous waste or emergencies.[29] Because such costs are frequently buried in overhead or not considered to be direct expenses, sometimes it is hard to see them, but they are invariably somewhere in the system.

TABLE 9.2 *Elements of Comprehensive Environmental Management Systems*

Element	Explanation
Waste minimization and prevention	Prevent rather than control pollution by reducing, minimizing, or eliminating pollutants and wastes at their source. Includes materials substitution, process modification, materials reuse, recycling, and reuse within different processes.
Demand-side management	Understand customers' needs and preferences so (1) product is not wasted; (2) what is sold is exactly what is needed; (3) the customer becomes more efficient in using the product.
Design for environment	Produce for disassembly, modular upgradability, and recyclability initially (rather than face product disposal), thereby reducing reprocessing costs and returning products to the market more quickly.
Product stewardship	Stewardship implies taking care in design, manufacturing, distribution, use, and disposal of products to reduce environmental risks and problems. Life-cycle analysis determines waste reduction at all stages. Seek less polluting or wasteful alternatives; reduce conformance and liability costs.
Full-cost accounting	Identify, quantify, and allocate direct and indirect environmental costs of operations. Four levels of costs: (1) direct costs, like labor, capital, and raw materials; (2) hidden costs, such as monitoring and reporting; (3) contingent liability costs, such as fines and remedial action; and (4) less tangible costs, such as public relations and goodwill.

SOURCE: Michael A. Berry and Dennis A. Rondinelli, "Proactive Corporate Environment Management: A New Industrial Revolution," *Academy of Management Executive 12*, no. 2 (May 1998): 38–50.

Environmental Audits

Because responsible corporations take responsibility for their ecological impacts, they frequently undertake and publish environmental audits, along with audits associated with other stakeholder impacts. Environmental audits cover ecological areas of concern to stakeholders, including regulatory agencies and employees, whose training should include environmental stewardship. An environmental audit uses life-cycle, full-cost,

TABLE 9.3   *Measuring the Full Cost of Production: Components of a Complete Life-Cycle Assessment*

Phase	Corporate Activity
Scope of Life-Cycle Analysis	Reflect on the reasons for carrying out the life-cycle assessment and define the scope of the analysis within the company (i.e., which products/services are to be assessed in relation to which part of the company). Decide on the methods to be used to carry out the assessment.
Life-Cycle Inventory (LCI)	Collect data on how a product/service interacts with the environment. Look at which inputs from nature are used (e.g., energy, water, raw materials) and then assess the outputs to nature (e.g., pollution, waste) that the product/service creates. The analysis should be carried out in reference to the defined scope of the assessment (i.e., the part of the company under study).
Life-Cycle Impact Analysis (LCIA)	Assess the impact of the input and output flows identified during the inventory assessment. The flows are grouped into impact categories that are backed up with impact indicators. The different categories are weighted according to their importance in the overall environmental impact of the product/service.
Life-Cycle Interpretation	Interpret the results of the impact analysis against the background of the identified scope of the overall assessment. Identify specific actions to reduce the environmental impact of the product/service under study.

SOURCE: Based on information provided by UNEP's Life-Cycle Initiative (http://lcinitiative. unep.fr/) and in particular the *Guidelines for Social Life-Cycle Assessment of Products* (http:// www.unep.fr/shared/publications/pdf/DTIx1164xPA-guidelines_sLCA.pdf).

or environmental-cost accounting techniques to assess the real and fully internalized costs of company production and distribution practices to the company and the customer (and, as a by-product, to society). Like other audits, environmental audits are published, frequently as part of triple-bottom-line or ESG reports.

The completed audit points out problems and identifies opportunities for waste or pollution reduction, as well as potential cost savings. The audit can help the company establish a cost basis for operations and set priorities for future initiatives.[30] Indeed, one scholar argues that investments in environmental sustainability make sense simply because they help companies gain a competitive advantage, achieve positive financial returns, reduce risks, and outpace competitors, who may be using less progressive practices.[31]

Sustainable Business Practices and Competitive Advantage

In the United States, efforts to move corporate thinking toward sustainable practice have tended to focus on ways companies can build new businesses, save money, or gain a competitive advantage through more environmentally responsible practices. One approach, as articulated by Forest Reinhardt, is to try to use the problems of the environment strategically to gain advantage.[32] Reinhardt identified five approaches that companies can use to integrate an environmental perspective into business operations:

- *Differentiate* by using products or processes with great environmental benefits or that use fewer natural resources in their production, for which ecologically sensitive consumers will pay higher prices (e.g., as Wal-Mart has done in identifying its green products for consumers).

- *Manage competitors* by working with industry groups to change society's rules or the rules of competition so that competitors need to incur higher costs to respond to environmental regulation maintaining a first-mover advantage because the company has been able to anticipate what will be needed (e.g., as the chemical industry has done in establishing its Responsible Care initiative).

- *Save costs* by improving environmental performance internally (e.g., as hotels have done in asking customers to reuse towels and linens).

- *Manage environmental risk* by avoiding costs associated with accidents, spills, consumer boycotts, and environmentally related lawsuits.

- *Redefine markets* by using several of these approaches simultaneously and convincing customers of their benefits ecologically and competitively (e.g., as BMW has done with cars that can be disassembled for recycling and are now in compliance with strict German "take-back" laws).[33]

Management systems are also keys to responsible environmental practice. Companies using proactive environmental management and full-cost accounting systems also emphasize pollution prevention and recycling, responsible purchasing policies, and new manufacturing strategies that reduce waste. In addition, because communities are frequently affected by environmental problems, community involvement is a critical aspect of a good environmental management system.[34] It is likely that in the future traditional and environmentally oriented accounting methods will be integrated as more and more companies are expected to account for all of their costs rather than externalizing them to society.

Future Sustainability Practices

Simply using the environment as a source of competitive advantage, as many companies are currently doing, overlooks the fundamental problem of sustainability. Ultimately, balance demands a far broader perspective from companies and their leaders. Indeed Daniel Esty and Andrew Winston argue in their book *Green to Gold: How Smart Companies Use Environmental Strategy to Innovate, Create Value, and Build Competitive Advantage* that there is a need to go beyond what another author, James Collins, characterized as "good to great" to succeed today. The phrase, "green to gold," suggests that companies that will flourish in the world we now face will be both "great and good" environmentally; and they will have to take into account economic, societal, and political considerations in determining what the public good is.[35]

A number of emerging corporate practices can help move a company along the path toward sustainability. One is product accountability, which applies the stewardship principle to all of the negative impacts of a product or service, as does life-cycle accounting. Another is life-cycle management, discussed above with reference to life-cycle accounting, but here applied to the managerial practices along the entire value chain associated with developing, selling, using, and ultimately disposing of a product. A third practice involves spreading the costs among all emitting parties, thereby eliminating both free ridership and prisoner's dilemma situations.[36] Some companies concerned with carbon dioxide emissions are also using benchmarking to compare their own performance with that of best-practice firms in a fourth practice likely to become more popular as ecology continues to gain corporations' interest and attention.[37]

UNILEVER'S SUSTAINABILITY LIVING PLAN

Unilever is a multinational company that owns a variety of well-known brands in the foods and beverages, cleaning, and personal care segments. In 2010, the company employed around 167,000 people and created revenues of more than €44 billion.[38] Although Unilever has been addressing sustainability issues for a long time, it raised its engagement to the next level with its "Sustainability Living Plan" (hereafter the Plan).

Unlike other companies, which often still understand sustainability as prevention and compliance with regulations, Unilever seeks systemic change and thus recognizes that the problems it needs to address are interrelated (with each other and also with its economic success).[39] Many of the firm's sustainability challenges are located in developing countries (e.g., dealing with poor sanitation and water scarcity). Since more than half of Unilever's sales are in these countries, it makes economic and ecological sense to strengthen consumer trust by developing business processes and products that help people to address these challenges in their daily lives.[40] The Plan consolidates the company's efforts in the sustainability context and sets specific targets for the future.

The Plan was developed in collaboration with a variety of key external stakeholder groups. Based on Unilever's existing stakeholder infrastructure (such as the Unilever Sustainability Development Group, an external advisory group), the company developed goals and related metrics for benchmarking success. Senior brand leaders and other managers throughout the company were also involved in the development of the Plan.[41] This collaborative approach was important because the Plan encourages management to consider a longer time horizon for the strategic and operational dimensions of Unilever's business.

The Plan consists of goals in four issue areas broadly reflecting Unilever's potential impacts: health and hygiene, nutrition, environmental impacts, and sustainable sourcing. For each area the Plan identifies sub-areas (e.g., environmental impact relates to greenhouse gas emissions, water use, and waste management), specific approaches for addressing the underlying problems, and metrics for measuring success (e.g., water use is measured by the water in the product and the water needed to use the product). The Plan then outlines targets and a time horizon for meeting them (e.g., reaching more than 200 million consumers with products that use less water by 2015).[42]

The Plan also outlines how the company will integrate sustainability into its business processes (which, of course, is a precondition for meeting the ambitious targets). Decisions about product launches and innovation projects have an explicit sustainability dimension and need to meet sustainability-related criteria to be operationalized. Unilever has allocated parts of its R&D budget to develop products that will help meet the Plan's targets. Implementing the Plan has become part of the personal work objectives of the senior management team.[43]

The Unilever Sustainable Living Plan reflects an integrated understanding of sustainability-related problems. One key advantage of the Plan is that it goes to the heart of the company's business and also addresses problems that might not be perceived as sustainability issues. For instance, a systems perspective suggests that sustainable communities not only depend on a healthy natural environment, but also on living in a healthy way. Unilever's Plan integrates health-related objectives into the company's overall sustainability objectives (e.g., by educating people about how using soap can help prevent diarrhea).

CEO Paul Polman realizes that "Delivering these commitments won't be easy."[44] In the end, implementing the Plan will depend not only on what Unilever does but also on the actions of governments, NGOs, suppliers, and, most of all, the people who use the company's products every day.

ECOLOGY AND DEVELOPMENT

Between 1980 and 2000, according to the World Bank, the world's population grew from 4.4 billion to 6 billion people, with most of that growth in developing nations, and in 2011 it surpassed 7 billion. The World Bank expects that another billion will be added by 2015, and that by 2015 six of every seven people will live in developing nations.[45] One concern is that in some parts of the developed world population is actually declining, while in the developing world it is still growing rapidly. However, even as population growth rates have fallen in some countries, the overall population in these nations continues to grow. In low-income countries, according to the World Bank, more than a third of the population is under the age of 15, while that percentage is less than 20 percent in the developed world.[46] Combined with government policies, economic development, distribution of technological and land resources, and consumption patterns, this growth puts significant strains on ecological resources. Population growth, which some believe is at the level of crisis, illuminates the need to bring balance among the three spheres of human activity and the natural environment as an imperative no human being or enterprise can any longer afford to ignore.[47]

Surveys undertaken by the Worldwatch Institute found that in 2004 (the latest available data) private consumption expenditures of over $20 trillion in 2000 were dominated by the United States (with 5.2 percent of the population and 31.5 percent of the spending) and Western Europe (with 6.4 percent of the population and 28.7 percent of the spending). The same report identified other interesting tidbits, such as that three-fourths of the world's population has at least one television set and consumers now spend $35 billion annually on bottled water. Still, Worldwatch estimated that 2.8 billion people live on less than $2 per day and that as many as one-fifth of the world's population does not have adequate access to safe drinking water. Worldwatch claims that providing adequate food, clean water, and basic education for the world's poorest could all be achieved for less than people spend annually on unnecessary consumer goods. For example, consumers spend $18 billion on makeup annually versus the $12 billion estimated for reproductive health care for all women, $11 billion on ice cream in Europe versus $1.3 billion for immunizing every child, and $14 billion on ocean cruises versus $10 billion estimated to bring clean drinking water to all who need it.[48]

Economic development in the current economizing mode, where externalities are shifted to society, clearly has many deleterious impacts on the natural environment, in part because as nations develop economically, people tend to leave larger ecological footprints, consuming more resources in their daily lives and generating more waste and pollution. Factors that appear to result in this greater ecological impact include increasing urbanization and associated patterns of migration from more rural to more urban (as well as resource-rich coastal) areas.[49] Consumption of goods and services, as well as energy, tends to be higher on a per capita basis in urban than in rural areas. Others, like ecologist Bill McKibben, claim that it is too late to try to avert climate change because it is already here. The best we can do is to learn to live with it on the planet he now calls Eaarth, to signify that the earth has already become a different place.[50]

According to futurist Hazel Henderson, population growth poses two critical issues for balancing the ecological impacts of human civilization. The first is that industrialized societies' levels of consumption and ecological footprints are significantly greater than those of less-developed nations, which as we have seen above is an inherently unsustainable situation. Second, there is a growing global consensus that one way to stabilize population growth is to educate and empower poor women, who serve as family educators, food producers, and family providers. The empowerment of women is ideologically problematic for some fundamentalists in patriarchal societies and religious traditions; nonetheless, educating women appears to be a socially stabilizing force. Further, ecologist James Lovelock argues in a frightening book that human-caused climate and sustainability crises may result in a reduction of the population to about 500 million people scattered in remote regions of the world.[51]

Water wars may be the next big global ecological concern, as scarcity of water is predicted for many nations in the not-too-distant future. A study undertaken in 2002 by the World Resources Institute, a nonprofit environmental think tank, suggests that it is becoming harder to ensure adequate supplies of water for both human consumption and nature. Humans withdraw as much as 20 percent of the flow of the world's rivers annually, and about 41 percent of the world's population (or about 2.3 billion people) live in conditions of "water stress" and are subject to frequent water shortages. It is estimated that 3.5 billion people, or about 48 percent of the projected population, will live in "highly stressed" conditions by 2025.[52]

Energy consumption increased 100-fold in the years between 1850 and 2000, with consequent increases in carbon dioxide emissions, creating the so-called greenhouse effect and possibly global warming. Over the past 100 years, the earth's mean temperature rose by 0.74 degrees Celsius.[53] The two largest-emitting economies—China and the United States—account for about 42 percent of total emissions worldwide. Corporations from these economies thus bear a special responsibility to adopt and promote low-carbon technologies (e.g., carbon capture and hybrid automobiles). Economist Jeffrey Sachs points out that such technologies are comparatively cheap (when considering the negative financial effects of even modest predictions of the impact of global warming). Collective and sustained action by the world's biggest emitters could avoid the doubling of carbon dioxide emissions at a cost of less than 1 percent of annual global income.[54]

The list of environmentally degraded and endangered resources is virtually endless.[55] However, one vital point to consider is that problems like climate change and water scarcity do not exist in isolation. For instance, climate change is likely to adversely affect those regions in the world that depend on snowmelt or glacier melt for their water.[56] Responsible enterprise has to acknowledge the interdependent and systemic nature of these problems. Looking for isolated solutions and ignoring the wider context of problems is unlikely to produce any lasting effects.

INTEGRATING SUSTAINABILITY HOLISTICALLY

Sustainability is being used more often to refer to practices in businesses, communities, and, indeed, whole societies. The rest of this chapter discusses society as an ecological system and attempts to form an integrated systems perspective on the links needed to build effective societies, communities, and businesses that sustain themselves ecologically and whose members share meaningful relationships. Business has an essential role to play in this mix, a role in which its power needs to be balanced with that of actors in the political and civil society spheres.

Ironically, despite the forces of globalization and the intense competition that characterize much of the modern economic sphere, local connections and a sense of the ecology of the whole of society connected with nature still appear to be vitally important to long-term economic success. Important work by the economist Michael Porter has highlighted this ecological perspective.[57] In studying successful firms all over the world, Porter discovered that businesses are most successful when they operate in clusters representing critical masses of related businesses, not when they attempt to operate independently of such networks.[58] In what he terms the "paradox of location in a global economy," Porter finds that long-term competitive advantage lies in creating localized advantages that rivals find hard to duplicate. The sources of these advantages, far from being low-cost outsourcing that has the potential of mistreating employees, turns out to be the soft stuff of knowledge, relationships, and motivation.

Porter defines clusters as "geographic concentrations of interconnected companies and institutions in a particular field."[59] Clusters include an array of stakeholders: suppliers of inputs specialized to the industry or creators of industry-specific infrastructure, customers (particularly for business-to-business relationships and purchases), and manufacturers of complementary products and services. Further, as Porter notes, clusters can also include government bodies and trade associations as well as key educational institutions (such as Harvard and MIT in Massachusetts and Berkeley and Stanford in California, which provide talent for their local high-technology clusters). All of these institutions can work collectively when they are in a cluster in ways that a company acting alone would find impossible. These enterprises are found in all three spheres of activity that we have been discussing.

Clusters have interesting characteristics. They represent, at one level, an ecological system comprising interdependent, symbiotic, collaborative and simultaneously competitive organizations. These are the same as the characteristics of a healthy ecosystem, as discussed above. The boundaries of a cluster can be determined by assessing the "linkages and complementarities across boundaries that are most important to competition."[60] Clusters are not necessarily bounded by standard industry classification schemes because they include so many types of institutions, just as the effects of burning down large sections of rain forest go well beyond the boundaries of the forest itself and, indeed, may affect the global climate.

Interestingly, Porter views clusters as a new way of creating a value chain and a new form of organizing without as much dependence on the hierarchical values associated with power aggrandizing. Clusters, in their ecological formation, are more emergent in that they are largely self-organizing, with new businesses and other institutions springing from entrepreneurial roots as the need for them is recognized.

Clusters create "glocal" companies—that is, companies that are simultaneously rooted in local communities and able to compete globally.[61] Because they are local as well as global, glocal companies operating within clusters—arguably all companies—need to be aware of their multiple-bottom-line responsibilities to their different primary and critical secondary stakeholders. In part, their interdependence arises because glocal companies are deeply rooted in the local culture, community, and cluster. Such rootedness, based on the social capital that emerges out of economic clusters, seems to be an important indicator of the potential for economic sustainability and even competitive advantage.

Long-Term Competitive Success and Social Capital

Porter's work on clusters highlights a frequently overlooked reality: one of the most important factors in successful economic development is the existence of trusting relationships and long-term connectedness among the entities that comprise economically successful clusters. Ironically, this form of social capital, a cooperative and collaborative posture of interdependence, is more important than individual action and cutthroat competition. Research on the relationship between economic and political development supports the idea that tight links between economic institutions provide a basis for success. Examples include Asia's "network capitalism" and the industrial districts that develop when there is collaboration among workers and small entrepreneurs.[62]

Other research supports the link between plentiful social capital and economic success. As reported in *BusinessWeek*, researchers at the American University found that high levels of trust were associated with strong economic performance.[63] They found that businesses operating where there are many positive social ties and a lot of trust have incentives for innovation and capital accumulation, because they are confident about the future.

Further, work in fields as diverse as education, urban poverty, unemployment, crime and drug abuse, and health care has shown that communities—civil society—too are more successful when there are strong social bonds.[64] Finally Putnam's research on Italy's political districts suggests that governments are also more successful when there are rich norms of connectedness and civic engagement.[65] World Bank research corroborates these findings, suggesting that whole villages are better off if social capital is plentiful.[66] Economic prosperity appears to complement a sense of community and place. Community and place need to be sustained as ecologies themselves and in balance with the natural environment on which we all depend.

10 RESPONSIBILITY INITIATIVES AND GUIDANCE DOCUMENTS

> An array of codes, standards, guidelines and frameworks
> are available to guide companies in integrating corporate
> responsibility into their business strategies and management
> processes. Their purpose is to drive the performance of companies
> in line with the goals of sustainable development. Executives
> no longer wonder whether to use such tools; they wonder about
> which ones to use, and in what combination.
> Ernst Ligteringen and Simon Zadek[1]

THE CHANGING CONTEXT OF RESPONSIBLE ENTERPRISE

Earlier we discussed the emerging responsibility assessment system and other pressures that companies are facing to improve their responsibility practices. In this chapter we explore the broader context and emerging standards and principles with which business operates today. While the initiatives introduced in Chapter 8 are designed to assess the responsible enterprise performance of companies, the standards and reference documents discussed in this chapter provide more general guidance.

The processes of globalization and the explosion of connectivity engendered by the Internet have made it obvious that some standards and principles of action need to be global and have fostered numerous related business initiatives. Global standards and principles are typically established through consensus-building processes set up by international bodies, sometimes industry organizations, and frequently coalitions of interested stakeholders, and then translated into responsibility management practices within companies. Despite the vast diversity and pluralism of societies, the emergence of these statements of principles is testimony to the fact that, after all is said and done, we live in one world. Why, then, do companies turn to responsibility standards?

As public attention shifts from topic to topic, global brands are often targets of exposés and activist pressures.[2] Religious groups, for example, spearheaded a consumer boycott of the Nestlé Corporation for its sales of infant formula in developing nations in the late 1970s: the infant formula was too expensive for poor people to afford, and could not safely be used in unsanitary conditions that were also without refrigeration. The boycott culminated in Nestlé's appointment of an internal infant formula audit commission. Combined with a global boycott of products from companies operating in South Africa, these and similar forms of consumer activism vividly demonstrate the usefulness of consumer movements in attempting to change corporate behavior and hold companies accountable. Enterprise responsibility allows corporations to "signal" their responsibility to relevant stakeholders, although the strength and credibility of such signaling depends on the accountability of the respective practices and standards used.

Outsourcing, strategic and other alliances, and just-in-time inventory management systems began to blur the boundaries between companies and their suppliers and customers during the 1980s and 1990s, a trend that continues apace. Outsourcing has created new global supply chains, often in developing nations, and human rights, labor, and environmental activists became concerned about corporate practices in the increasingly long supply chains of consumer goods, clothing, and toy companies.[3] Boundaries between multinational companies and their suppliers, clear perhaps in the eyes of managers, have been much less clear to activists wanting to create corporate accountability.

Similarly, demands for greater corporate accountability, responsibility, and transparency, as well as anti-corruption measures coming from a wide range of stakeholders, are fostering new responsible enterprise initiatives among coalitions of business, labor, human rights, investor, and governmental bodies. The array of emerging initiatives suggests that there is a gap between growing public expectations and actual company performance. Pressures from stakeholders appear to be pushing companies toward a common set of guidelines for what ought to be.[4]

GUIDANCE ON SOCIAL ISSUES

In the following sections we briefly explore some of the most important initiatives as well as reference documents and the promulgating organizations that provide guidance on social issues. We begin this exploration in the sphere of civil society, with basic human rights.

Human Rights: Making Civilizing Real

Foundation principles related to human rights are best known from their promulgation in the UN Declaration on Human Rights, first written in 1948 and more recently updated to include basic environmental concerns. Based on this declaration and other sources, Thomas Donaldson and Thomas Dunfee suggest that there is significant cross-cultural agreement on the following principles of respect for the dignity and humanity of individuals:

- The right to freedom of physical movement.
- The right to ownership of property.
- The right to freedom from torture.
- The right to a fair trial.
- The right to nondiscriminatory treatment.
- The right to physical security.
- The right to freedom of speech and association.
- The right to minimal education.
- The right to political participation.
- The right to subsistence.[5]

Some of these foundation principles are congruent with the core labor and human rights identified in the UN Global Compact. Like governmental foundation principles, foundational human rights protect democratic values (i.e., the right to political participation and the freedoms of speech and association) rather than more authoritarian values. These rights allow for individual, national, and cultural differences (i.e., nondiscriminatory treatment and the freedom of speech and association), in what Donaldson and Dunfee term the "moral free space" in which individual differences of opinions about right and wrong exist.

Human Rights: The "Protect, Respect and Remedy" Framework   In 2011, the Special Representative of the UN Secretary-General on Business and Human Rights, John Ruggie, forged an important framework on business and human rights. The "Protect, Respect and Remedy" Framework, which was unanimously approved by the Human Rights Council of the UN, rests on three pillars. First, the state has a duty to protect its citizens against human rights abuses, including businesses. Second, the corporation has a responsibility to respect human rights. Third, victims should have greater access to effective remedy for abuses, both judicial and nonjudicial.[6] The UN also proposed a set of guiding principles to help with the framework's implementation.[7]

This document outlines the responsibilities of the state and businesses in upholding human rights. It also specifies their role in areas of conflict and when interacting with multilateral institutions like the UN. It points out that respect for human rights applies to all businesses, regardless of size, ownership structure, or organizational structure. According to the guidelines, companies should develop policies appropriate to their size and situation that are approved by top management, informed by consultation with internal and external stakeholders, clear about expectations of employees and partners, and communicated widely throughout the company and to relevant stakeholders, and reflected in policies and procedures. The implementation guidelines also outline the due diligence procedures for respecting human rights and providing remedies when problems are discovered. Internally accepted human rights apply in all contexts, even where local governments may be weaker with respect to human rights, and it is businesses' duty to respect those rights whatever the context.[8]

INTEGRATING HUMAN RIGHTS IN BUSINESS PRACTICE: THE "PROTECT, RESPECT AND REMEDY" FRAMEWORK IN ACTION

The "Protect, Respect and Remedy" framework, which was proposed by the Special Representative of the UN Secretary-General on Business and Human Rights, John Ruggie, has received wide recognition by governments, businesses, and civil society organizations. The framework clearly defines the roles of different actors: states have a duty to protect human rights, while corporations have the responsibility to respect human rights. What are the implications of this distinction? How can corporations make sure that they respect human rights?

For Ruggie, the responsibility to respect human rights requires the corporation to conduct human rights due diligence on a regular basis. Due diligence is "the steps a company must take to become aware of, prevent and address adverse human rights impacts."[9] According to Ruggie's report to the UN Human Rights Council, human rights due diligence should include: (1) a human rights policy that is both general and specific in its support of human rights; (2) a human rights impact assessment to analyze how existing and future business activities affect human rights; (3) integration of human rights policies into the day-to-day business activities; and (4) performance tracking and reporting.[10]

It seems clear that integrating human rights policies throughout the business is by far the biggest challenge to a large corporation. How can firms make sure that the commitment to human rights is not isolated in single departments? How can companies ensure consistent action throughout the company? The Global Compact Network in the Netherlands specified Ruggie's framework for implementing human rights based on the experiences of ten companies.[11] According to these companies, it is important that the responsibility for human rights be clearly assigned within the corporation. While each business function (e.g., procurement and production) must accept responsibility for implementing human rights (usually based on a prior impact assessment), one person in the organization should oversee and integrate the individual efforts.

Because human rights due diligence is not yet a widely used technique, top management must foster a culture of respect for human rights in the company. Making human rights a leadership task sends a strong signal to employees that such discussions are taken seriously and that the firm wants to move beyond developing and communicating policies. Integrating respect for human rights into a company's culture is not an overnight task. Human rights concerns should be incorporated in performance reviews, recruitment policies, and employee training. Nonfinancial targets for performance appraisal can demonstrate that addressing human rights in the company means more than "ticking a box." Understood in this way, integrating human rights into business practices is as much about making "technical" changes to operational processes as it is about changing corporate culture.

Ruggie's framework acknowledges that often people do not even recognize that they are dealing with a human rights issue. Product safety, for example, is a human rights concern (as it affects the health of customers); human resource management practices can adversely affect human rights (e.g., when people are discriminated against); marketing and sales can infringe on human rights (e.g., when the company stores customer data without permission). The Ruggie framework does not deliver clear-cut answers to all these problems, but it gives companies ideas for how to approach the business and human rights debate.

The Sweatshop Quandary

Companies that have spent the time and energy to develop their vision and values need to ensure that their suppliers are working up to the same set of standards and share the same values. Otherwise, they can find themselves in the midst of controversies, as happened to Wal-Mart when the International Labour Organization (ILO) found dreadful working conditions in Wal-Mart's supplier firms in less-developed countries.[12]

In addition to the ILO, watchdog activists like the Clean Clothes Campaign,[13] the National Labor Committee,[14] United Students against Sweatshops,[15] and the Not for Sale Campaign[16] pay close attention to suppliers' working conditions. When the customer firm purchases goods without sufficient attention to the conditions under which workers labor, and when those conditions are significantly worse than would be allowed under domestic law, companies can become the target of activists.

Companies accused of permitting substandard conditions to exist in their suppliers' factories sometimes rightly claim that it is difficult to monitor these long-distance relationships. But to be considered responsible, such companies need to recognize that sourcing from suppliers where such conditions prevail not only goes against the vision and values they have themselves articulated and applied to domestic operations, and the codes of conduct that most multinational corporations have implemented today, but also denigrates the value of human life in other parts of the world. Treating workers as if they were mere cogs in a machine implies a lack of respect for human worth and dignity and for the communities these people come from. Further, negative publicity hurts corporate reputations when companies are caught sourcing from substandard suppliers. U.S. firms have been subject to scrutiny by activists for many years, and the scrutiny is now spreading to European firms as well.[17]

Nike, Reebok, Liz Claiborne, Phillips–Van Heusen, and many other companies that have faced controversy about their sourcing practices have banded together to form a self-regulating association called the Fair Labor Association (FLA).[18] Also, the American Apparel Manufacturers Association (AAMA), an industry trade group, has created a less stringent set of standards for monitoring factories.[19]

The Union of Needletrades, Industrial and Textile Employees (UNITE), the Retail, Wholesale and Department Store Union, and the Interfaith Center on Corporate Responsibility (ICCR) are among the activist groups that believe that corporate-based regulation of suppliers' working conditions is mainly a public relations, rather than a substantive, move. The companies that formed the FLA hope that by regulating themselves they will be able to avoid some of the negative publicity and associated diminishment of their reputational capital and customer loyalty associated with activists uncovering human rights and worker abuses in supplier companies. Companies in industrialized nations sourcing from developing nations naturally argue that if they were to pay prevailing domestic wage rates to workers in developing nations, they would lose the very competitive advantage and economizing benefits they had sought to gain in outsourcing production in the first place.

Human rights and labor activists, on the other hand, argue that working conditions and pay scales need to be monitored not just by industry groups like the FLA and the AAMA, which are likely to be biased in favor of the companies, but by more objective external bodies, which is in part why the responsibility assurance system has evolved. In fact, activist groups have strongly criticized the formation of industry-based monitoring organizations. Governments of developing nations, of course, argue that transnational companies bring much-needed jobs and economic development to their nations; they are therefore sometimes willing to overlook transgressions of basic human rights and dignity in the interest of economic development.

What Is a Sweatshop?   There is no single definition of a sweatshop; however, the U.S. Department of Labor defines one as "any factory that violates two or more labor laws, such as those pertaining to wages and benefits, working hours, and child labor." Activists claim that companies need to go beyond the mere letter of the law to avoid sweatshops, and the watchdog group Green America notes that factories need to "pay a living wage in safe working conditions, enforce reasonable work hours, provide for sick leave and maternity leave, and allow workers to organize to avoid being labeled a sweatshop."[20] The following is an excerpt from Global Exchange, graphically describing conditions in sweatshops both in the United States and in developing nations:

> Around the world, garment workers spend dozens upon dozens of hours a week at their sewing machines to make the clothes and shoes that eventually end up on retailers' shelves. Verbal, physical and sexual abuse are common. Workplace injuries occur regularly. The wages are low. And when workers try to organize to defend their interests and assert their dignity, their efforts are invariably repressed. In country after country, the stories are hauntingly the same.
>
> Workers at a plant in El Salvador, for example, say they are frequently required to work mandatory overtime. . . . That means they often put in 11–hour shifts, six days a week. If the workers at that factory refuse to work overtime, they lose a day's pay. Workers making jeans in Mexico say that sometimes they are forced to work all night shifts, and are prevented from leaving the factory by armed security guards. . . .
>
> In the grueling atmosphere of desperate cost-cutting by corporations, work is accorded little value and, by extension, workers are afforded little dignity. Viewed more as production units than as people, sweatshop workers regularly suffer abuse and intimidation from factory supervisors. "They don't respect us as human beings," a Nicaraguan worker has told anti-sweatshop groups.
>
> Verbal abuse is particularly common, and workers regularly report being harassed and bullied by shop managers. Workers who managers think are not working fast enough are usually the target of shouting and yelling. Physical abuse is also not unusual. Workers at a factory in Mexico making collegiate apparel . . . have said managers there regularly hit them and slap them, according to the Workers' Rights Consortium.
>
> Sexual abuse is endemic. Most garment workers are women, the vast majority of them young women in their teens or twenties who have left their homes for the first time so that they can earn money to send back to their families.[21]

Sweatshop conditions clearly fail to respect the basic human dignity of the workers who labor there. Companies that operate with integrity and hope to implement their vision and values through their stakeholder relationships, particularly with suppliers, need to be well aware of the conditions of work in those suppliers' operations. Integrity demands closely monitoring working conditions and ensuring that employees are treated with respect and dignity, including providing a living wage even when economizing pressures push a company toward exploitive practices as they pursue a better financial bottom line.

The Living Wage Debate   The Ethical Trading Initiative (ETI) calls raising global wages an "urgent imperative," stating that such higher wages would allow workers to provide for themselves and their families, buy essential medicines, send children to school, and have something left over to save for the future. According to ETI, signs of poverty-level wages include workers skipping meals to be able to feed their children, indebtedness, eliminating "nonessential" spending on medicines or clothes, and taking on extra work.[22] ETI notes that there is no agreed way to calculate a living wage, but that typical approaches include the cost of feeding, clothing, and housing a family, and that such estimates need to be localized.

Generally a "living wage" pegs the wage scale in any nation to the standard of living in that nation. Exactly how to calculate this living wage is a matter for debate, but all approaches attempt to ensure that wages allow people to meet their basic human needs for shelter, food, and clothing. A coalition of activists, academics, and representatives of developing countries defined living wages in the global garment and shoe industries as a take-home wage earned by working within the country's legal maximum hours per week (but not more than 48 hours) that provides nutrition, water, housing, energy, transportation, clothing, health care, child care, and education for the average family, plus some savings or discretionary income.[23]

GUIDANCE ON ANTI-CORRUPTION: ENSURING INTEGRITY

Companies in the global arena know that they need to understand how local governments operate in all of the countries where they locate facilities, market products and services, or procure materials. They need to be aware of local rules and regulations, as well as the ways companies are expected to operate in different cultures and with respect to governments. Different ideologies make for very different contexts, which must be analyzed individually and discussed by corporate leaders to ensure that integrity is maintained.

One serious issue facing companies when they operate outside their homelands is differing standards of integrity in different cultures. In some countries, business leaders must deal with corrupt officials (and business-people) when they attempt to operate locally. In such circumstances, many have discovered that adhering to their own internally developed values and standards of integrity is, in the long run, the best practice. Sustaining the integrity of the business and economic system demands trust in the system, particularly at the intersection between government (with its power to regulate and create the rules by which businesses operate) and business. Governments have the capacity to use coercive power (or power-aggrandizing tendencies) to create the system under which other types of entities exist. System integrity and accountability are fundamentally undermined by corruption and bribery, which make both the economic and political systems untrustworthy.

"Corruption is found, to some degree, in every society. As a sign that something has gone wrong in the relationship between society and the state, corruption is becoming a pervasive phenomenon."[24] So begins Transparency International's source book on national integrity systems. Transparency International (TI) is a Berlin-based international nongovernmental organization (INGO) that has as its mission increasing government accountability and curbing national and international corruption. Founded in 1993 by Peter Eigen, TI works by creating coalitions of people with integrity from all three spheres of activity.

Because corruption undermines the integrity of not only the business system but also the political and civil society systems, TI has multiple concerns:

- Humanitarian, as corruption undermines and distorts development and leads to increasing levels of human rights abuse;
- Democratic, as corruption undermines democracies and in particular the achievements of many developing countries and countries in transition;
- Ethical, as corruption undermines a society's integrity; and
- Practical, as corruption distorts the operations of markets and deprives ordinary people of the benefits which should flow from them.[25]

Using a systems perspective on each country in which it operates, TI attempts to understand the causes, loopholes, and incentives feeding corrupt practices locally. It then attempts to determine the main types of corruption within the public domain and the leverage points for change within that system. According to TI, "Policy response to combating corruption has several elements common to every society: the reform of substantive programs; changes in the structure of government and its methods of assuring accountability; changes in moral and ethical attitudes; and, perhaps most importantly, the involvement and support of government, the private business sector, and civil society."[26] Some of these needed changes can be made quickly, while others take longer.

According to the United Nations Economic and Social Commission for Asia and the Pacific (UN ESCAP), there are eight characteristics of good governance. Governance is the "process of decision-making and the process by which decisions are implemented or not implemented," according to ESCAP.[27] The characteristics of good governance include participation by both genders either directly or through legitimate intermediaries, and an orientation toward the rule of law, that is a fair and just legal framework impartially enforced, which protects human rights. Also part of good governance is transparency in decision-making, including following the rule of law and ensuring that information about decisions and the decision-making process is freely available. Another important contributor to good governance is responsiveness to stakeholders in a timely way, along with a consensus orientation. Good governance also includes equity and inclusiveness, and accountability, not just for government institutions, but also for private sector and civil society enterprises.[28]

According to TI, five areas of reform are particularly helpful in reducing corrupt governmental practices: public programs, government reorganization, law enforcement, public awareness, and the creation of institutions to prevent corruption. Each country's situation must be analyzed to determine what specifically can be done, in part because action in any one area will have ripple effects to the others because they are part of a whole system where change needs to be leveraged to have the greatest effect. TI also annually produces a Corruption Perceptions Index that ranks countries on a scale from 10 (highly clean) to 0 (highly corrupt). To create the index, TI consolidates the results of sixteen different surveys, requiring a minimum of three surveys for each country included, so as to ensure the validity of the results.

Combating corruption globally requires enforceable and consistent laws on an international scale. There are positive signs that corruption is becoming less accepted globally. TI has made tremendous inroads into dealing openly with corrupt systems, and in 1997 some thirty-four nations signed the OECD Convention on Combating Bribery of Foreign Public Officials designed to outlaw bribery on a global scale.[29] Of these, twenty-nine nations are members of the OECD; that is, they are among the largest economies in the world. Before this treaty, only the U.S. government had outlawed bribery, through the Foreign Corrupt Practices Act, which business leaders sometimes felt put their companies at a competitive disadvantage. With passage of this treaty, bribery became a criminal act in virtually every important economy in the world. In 2003 more than 140 nations signed the UN Convention Against Corruption requiring signatories to implement a variety of measures (e.g., on asset recovery and international information exchange) to prevent corruption.

TI points out that company directors and leaders need to understand and accept responsibility for adhering to both the letter and the spirit of the law in countries where they operate. Voluntary codes of conduct, accompanied by internal enforcement procedures, can help companies maintain their integrity in the face of potential lost business when they refuse to pay a bribe. And, as TI points out, "grand corruption is the enemy of high standards and efficiency"[30] and thus goes against business's core value of economizing in the long run.

GUIDANCE ON SUSTAINABILITY

In the face of climate change and a global sustainability crisis, ecological sustainability is critical to the long-term well-being of humanity on the planet. Below we explore the major initiatives associated with the natural environment and business.

The UN and Agenda 21

The United Nations recognized the importance of environmental sustainability through development of its Agenda 21 initiative, which was adopted at the global environmental conference held in Rio de Janeiro on June 14, 1992.[31] Agenda 21 is based in part on the principles of environment and development adopted at the Rio conference, which was the first-ever global conference on the environment.[32] Among the most important principles for responsible companies to be aware of is the sovereign right of nations to use their own natural resources to meet the needs of future and present generations. The principles emphasize the need for sustainable development and its link to environmental protection by focusing on eradicating poverty, meeting the needs of developing countries as a priority, and ensuring that the voices of vulnerable groups—such as women, youth, indigenous, and oppressed peoples—are heard.

The Rio Principles also emphasize the need for global partnership in conserving and protecting the earth's ecosystem. In an open and global economic system countries should establish fair trade policies, discourage the transfer of environmentally harmful activities to more vulnerable or weaker nations, and internalize costs. Nation-states are encouraged to promote country-wide initiatives to improve sustainability, scientifically and technologically, through citizen participation and effective environmental legislation.

Agenda 21 is a comprehensive document that sets forth an ambitious set of goals linking economic and social development with ecological sustainability: (1) promoting sustainable development through trade liberalization; (2) making trade and environmental goals mutually supportive; (3) providing adequate financial resources to developing countries and dealing with international debt; and (4) encouraging macroeconomic policies conducive to environmental protection and development.[33]

Agenda 21 focuses on combating poverty, changing consumption patterns, encouraging sustainability, and responding to population or demographic shifts. It also focuses on protecting and promoting human health, while simultaneously promoting the integration of environment and development in decision-making processes. Arenas of environmental concern include the atmosphere, the forests, and fragile ecosystems (such as the desertification of some areas of the world resulting from overpopulation and overuse of the land and creating sustainable mountain, agricultural, and rural areas). Companies and nations need to learn to manage and protect biological diversity and to manage biotechnology safely. Pollution and waste management systems can protect the oceans and other bodies of water and the atmosphere by reducing hazardous wastes and toxic chemicals, solid wastes and sewage, and radioactive wastes.

Business-Led Sustainability Initiatives

One of the leading business-oriented organizations in fostering collaborative relationships among parties interested in sustainable ecology is the Coalition for Environmentally Responsible Economies (CERES). Composed of more than fifty investor, environmental, religious, labor, and social justice organizations, CERES has drafted a set of principles that some seventy companies and organizations have endorsed. Two other groups that promote sustainable ecology are the World Business Council for Sustainable Development (WBC-SD) and the chemical industry's Responsible Care initiative. The ISO organization's ISO 14000 series provides ways for businesses to actually implement sustainability and environmental management practices.

CERES Principles

The CERES Principles came into existence following the 1989 Exxon Valdez oil spill in Prince William Sound in Alaska. The spill brought renewed activist and indeed global public attention to the need for ecologically sustainable business practices. Initiated in 1989, the CERES Principles (see Table 10.1) were first called the Valdez Principles and were then broadened in scope and tactics in an effort to influence corporate environmental strategies through conversations between shareholders and corporate directors about company practices.[34]

The CERES coalition views itself as successfully modeling cooperation and dialogue among investors, environmentalists, and companies; as a leader in standardizing corporate reporting on the environment; and as a catalyst for measurable improvements in companies' environmental practices. CERES has accomplished much of this through its ten principles, which point to specific ways that companies can change their behaviors and practices to achieve the ecological sustainability demanded by the four core principles of The Natural Step process discussed earlier (see Table 2.2). By signing the CERES Principles, companies agree to meet rigorous environmental standards, although the signatories do not yet actually operate in fully sustainable ways.

World Business Council for Sustainable Development

The World Business Council for Sustainable Development (WBCSD) is a CEO-led coalition of about 200 transnational companies from more than thirty countries and twenty industry sectors with a network of about sixty national and regional business councils and regional partners. They share a commitment to sustainable development through a triple-bottom-line orientation—economic, ecological, and social—through business leadership in the area of sustainability, innovation, and corporate social responsibility. The coalition has five main objectives:

- Be a leading business advocate on sustainable development;
- Participate in policy development to create the right framework conditions for business to make an effective contribution to sustainable human progress;
- Develop and promote the business case for sustainable development;
- Demonstrate the business contribution to sustainable development solutions and share leading-edge practices among members;
- Contribute to a sustainable future for developing nations and nations in transition.[35]

WBCSD came about as a way to get businesses involved in the UN's Earth Summit in Rio in 1992, where Agenda 21 was developed. Since that time, in addition to providing information and bringing together the nearly 1,000 business leaders involved around issues of environment, the WBCSD has undertaken projects involving accountability, advocacy, capacity building, energy and climate, the role of the financial sector, sustainable livelihoods, and water.[36]

Responsible Care   Another industry-led environmental initiative involving multiple companies is Responsible Care, an initiative of the Chemical

Manufacturers Association, which has received considerable public attention for its leadership. The chemical industry is, for obvious reasons, under pressure to improve its environmental performance. Responsible Care is a voluntary effort by chemical companies to commit to continual environmental, health, and safety improvements in a manner that is responsive to the public interest.[37] Companies signing on commit themselves to continually improving their own performance and collaborating with others to improve theirs, measuring progress, and seeking public input on their efforts. Responsible care follows a set of guiding principles and detailed guidelines for management practice in six operating arenas important to chemical companies.

ISO 14000 Series   Another set of important environmental standards that many companies, particularly those operating in the European Union, use are the ISO 14000 standards. Modeled in part on the International Organization for Standardization (ISO) 9000 quality standards, the ISO 14000 standards deal with avoiding or minimizing the harmful effects of corporate activities on the environment. ISO 14000 and the related ISO 14001 auditing standards are largely industry-driven and generally represent internal guidelines (developed by firms based on the ISO 14000 framework), rather than a more globally defined set of absolute standards and principles to which a company agrees to adhere.[38]

ISO 14000 emphasizes the operating policies and practices within the company, rather than the nature or use of products or services generated.[39] The goal of the ISO standards is to reduce harmful environmental effects of the production process itself caused by pollution and waste or the depletion of natural resources. ISO 14000 is actually a family of related standards designed to align businesses, industries, governments, and consumers around common ecological interests. Generally, ISO expects that companies will develop their own standards and environmental management systems, in compliance with relevant legislation and regulations, and then audit their practices to ensure that they conform to internal standards. Companies operating under the ISO 14000 standards are also expected to make continual improvements in their environmental practices.

TABLE 10.1 *The Ceres Principles*

Protection of the Biosphere

We will reduce and make continual progress toward eliminating the release of any substance that may cause environmental damage to the air, water, or the earth or its inhabitants. We will safeguard all habitats affected by our operations and will protect open spaces and wilderness, while preserving biodiversity.

Sustainable Use of Natural Resources

We will make sustainable use of renewable natural resources, such as water, soils and forests. We will conserve non-renewable natural resources through efficient use and careful planning.

Reduction and Disposal of Wastes

We will reduce and where possible eliminate waste through source reduction and recycling. All waste will be handled and disposed of through safe and responsible methods.

Energy Conservation

We will conserve energy and improve the energy efficiency of our internal operations and of the goods and services we sell. We will make every effort to use environmentally safe and sustainable energy sources.

Risk Reduction

We will strive to minimize the environmental, health and safety risks to our employees and the communities in which we operate through safe technologies, facilities and operating procedures, and by being prepared for emergencies.

Safe Products and Services

We will reduce and where possible eliminate the use, manufacture or sale of products and services that cause environmental damage or health or safety hazards. We will inform our customers of the environmental impacts of our products or services and try to correct unsafe use.

Environmental Restoration

We will promptly and responsibly correct conditions we have caused that endanger health, safety or the environment. To the extent feasible, we will redress injuries we have caused to persons or damage we have caused to the environment and will restore the environment.

Informing the Public

We will inform in a timely manner everyone who may be affected by conditions caused by our company that might endanger health, safety or the environment. We will regularly seek advice and counsel through dialogue with persons in communities near our facilities. We will not take any action against employees for reporting dangerous incidents or conditions to management or to appropriate authorities.

TABLE 10.1   *The Ceres Principles (continued)*

Management Commitment

We will implement these Principles and sustain a process that ensures that the Board of Directors and Chief Executive Officer are fully informed about pertinent environmental issues and are fully responsible for environmental policy. In selecting our Board of Directors, we will consider demonstrated environmental commitment as a factor.

Audits and Reports

We will conduct an annual self-evaluation of our progress in implementing these Principles. We will support the timely creation of generally accepted environmental audit procedures. We will annually complete the Ceres Report, which will be made available to the public.

SOURCE: Ceres, http://www.ceres.org/about-us/our-history/ceres-principles.

ISO 14000 standards tackle several different aspects of environmental management, including life-cycle assessment, which describes the environmental performance of products, the integration of environmental concerns into product or service design and development, and communication about environmental performance (e.g., through labels, declarations, and general corporate communications). Other aspects of this process, which is similar to the quality management process of plan, do, check, act, are ongoing monitoring of environmental performance and auditing performance.[40] Many companies now must use the ISO 9000 quality standards to compete successfully, simply because their partners, suppliers, customers, or allies demand it. A similar developmental cycle is likely for the ISO 14000 family of environmental standards and/or the CERES Principles. Hence, it makes sense for companies that wish to be responsible to begin moving toward meeting such standards.

Looking to the Future: Natural Capitalism

In a 1999 *Harvard Business Review* article, "A Road Map for Natural Capitalism," Amory Lovins, L. Hunter Lovins, and Paul Hawken argued that simple changes in corporate practices can provide benefits that will both protect the natural environment but also potentially be very profitable.[41] If the idea of natural capitalism—sustainability—took hold, then becoming sustainable would require businesses to:

- Dramatically increase the productivity of natural resources by reducing wasteful practices, changing production design and technology, and stretching ecological resources significantly further than they are being stretched today.

- Shift to biologically inspired closed-loop production models, in which all the by-products of one process become an input for another process so that nothing is wasted.

- Move to a solutions-based business model, in which value is delivered as a flow of services rather than products and well-being is measured by satisfying expectations for quality, utility, and performance of products and services.

- Reinvest in natural capital by restoring, sustaining, and expanding the planet's ecosystem.[42]

Also, toxic materials that are now regularly used in production processes would need to be eliminated from the supply chain, and products would need to be built to last rather than built for obsolescence. In part, natural capitalism is based not on the law of diminishing returns, which informs much current economic thinking, but rather on a radically different perspective: the concept of expanding returns. This concept, which underpins approaches like lean manufacturing and whole system design, implies that saving a lot of resources can be less costly than saving a smaller amount.[43]

Manufacturing and innovation giant 3M Corporation began a program called Pollution Prevention Pays in 1975. By 2007, 3M's program had prevented more than 2.6 billion pounds of pollutants and saved more than $1 billion (aggregated). Pollution Prevention Pays (3P) focuses on preventing pollution at the source, much as Lovins and his co-authors argue should be done. Source prevention means reducing waste in the manufacturing process and in product design rather than dealing with it after a product has already been made.[44] In 2010 3M Corporation developed its first set of sustainability goals, which went out to 2015; they include reducing volatile air emissions by 15 percent (from 2010 as the base), reducing waste by 10 percent, improving energy efficiency by 26 percent and greenhouse gas emissions by 5 percent, and conserving water when 3M is in a water-constrained area.[45] Lovins and his co-authors argue that companies can go further and rethink manufacturing processes entirely, creating new products and processes that prevent waste in the first place. This technique, looking at the whole system rather than just production, is biologically based in the concept of "waste equals food."[46]

The authors of these radical approaches to capitalism and production systems argue, and we agree, that by thinking about the whole system—the closed loop—leaders will find numerous small changes that result in big savings, a point that Peter Senge calls "finding leverage."[47] Any shift toward natural capitalism requires a major shift in mindset—away from growth and consumption as the goals of business activity and, increasingly, toward well-being—not just for humans but for all the living beings and ecosystems on the planet. The move would be toward thriving with minimal use of resources, a more localized economy for things like food and other goods, based in the types of natural systems that Hawken and his collaborators describe as natural capitalism. Sociologist Juliet Schor calls such a shift "plenitude" and suggests that in many (relatively nascent and still small) areas, it is already under way.[48]

OTHER INITIATIVES AND GUIDANCE DOCUMENTS

In the current context of enterprise responsibility there is no shortage of initiatives that offer firms guidance on improving their social and environmental behavior. Below we provide details about some other important initiatives that do not easily fit into the social, environmental, or anti-corruption domains discussed above.

OECD Guidelines for Multinational Enterprises

Thirty-eight nations agreed to a nonbinding set of guidelines for multinational corporations through the Organization for Economic Cooperation and Development (OECD), to which thirty member nations and eight affiliates belong. These guidelines, called the OECD Guidelines for Multinational Enterprises, provide guidance on all aspects of firm behavior in the global arena, including employment and industrial relations, human rights, environment, information disclosure, competition, taxation, and science and technology.[49] By following these guidelines, companies will meet most societal and government expectations. Because they are issued by the OECD, the guidelines have considerable credibility and are rapidly becoming one of the world's best sources of guidance for companies about their corporate responsibilities.

Caux Principles for Business

The Caux Round Table, working in collaboration with the Minnesota Center for Corporate Responsibility, bases its principles for business on two basic ethical ideals. One ethical ideal is the Japanese concept of kyosei, which means living and working together for the common good, to enable cooperation and mutual prosperity to coexist with health and fair competition. The second ethical ideal is human dignity, which in Caux's usage simply means the sacredness or intrinsic value of each person as an end, not as a means to the fulfillment of others' purposes.[50] The Caux Round Table was founded in 1986 by Frederick Philips, former president of Philips Electronics, and Olivier Giscard d'Estaing, vice chairman of the international business school INSEAD. Its purpose is to reduce trade tensions by enhancing economic and social relationships among participants' countries and to focus broadly on building a better world. The Caux principles build on an earlier effort by the Minnesota Center for Corporate Responsibility.[51] These principles are designed to help businesses and their leaders move toward looking first to their own actions and behaviors as they determine the right thing to do.

Equator Principles

Demonstrating that the financial community also recognizes the importance of social and environmental principles, the Equator Principles were first adopted by ten banks in 2003 and had accumulated twenty-five signatories in fourteen countries within a year, and seventy signatories by 2011.[52] The principles are formulated to help financial institutions manage the social and environmental risks in financing projects around the world, particularly in emerging markets.

The Equator Principles website quotes Herman Mulder, a banking executive who helped establish the principles, as saying: "It is our fundamental belief that the Equator Principles are appropriately becoming the reference standard for financial institutions to ensure that the principles of responsible environmental stewardship and socially responsible development are embedded within our project finance activities. Moreover, the Equator Principles are an excellent example how our financial sector is able to self-regulate on high value issues."[53]

Principles for Responsible Investment

In 2005 then Secretary-General of the United Nations Kofi Annan brought together a group of the world's largest institutional investors to consider how investment professionals should respond to ESG issues. Like the UN Global Compact, the Principles for Responsible Investment (PRI) are aspirational and voluntary and intended to help larger investors incorporate ESG issues into their investment decisions and avoid the risks that these issues might otherwise pose. Signatories to the PRI agree that:

1. We will incorporate ESG issues into investment analysis and decision-making processes.
2. We will be active owners and incorporate ESG issues into our ownership policies and practices.
3. We will seek appropriate disclosures on ESG issues by the entities in which we invest.
4. We will promote acceptance and implementation of the Principles within the investment industry.
5. We will work together to enhance our effectiveness in implementing the Principles.
6. We will each report on our activities and progress towards implementing the Principles.[54]

Within the first year of the PRI's launch in 2006, more than 200 institutional investors with assets totaling over US$9 trillion had become signatories and were actively integrating ESG issues into their investment policies. By late 2011 there were more than 915 signatories from 45 different nations, and these investors collectively controlled the equivalent of US$30 trillion.[55]

ACCOUNTABILITY AND DISCLOSURE: PUBLIC POLICY MANDATE

Although responsibility management and assurance represent improvements in performance, they are in many respects incomplete without a system of accountability. The principles described in this chapter and the initiatives discussed in Chapter 8 are still voluntary and have been adopted by a small fraction of the estimated 80,000-plus transnational corporations in the world (with their hundreds of thousands of subsidiaries and partners), and an even smaller proportion of the many millions of small and medium-sized enterprises. Indeed, it appears that the largest, most visible brand-name companies are the ones adopting these standards of performance, while business-to-business companies and those with less visibility operate largely under the radar screen of accountability.

In the U.S. legal system and increasingly around the world, corporations believe that they are accountable only to their shareholders and only for profit maximization, without regard to the impacts that they might have on other stakeholders, though increasingly legal scholars suggest otherwise and argue for taking other stakeholders into consideration.[56] While numerous U.S. states now permit companies to take other stakeholders' interest into consideration, current law is interpreted to embed only a narrow shareholder orientation into corporate goals in the United States. Critical observers of corporations recognize that voluntary responsibility management approaches may not be enough to curb corporate power or forestall future abuses. Corporate critics argue for some significant countervailing power to the increasingly global power commanded by corporations.[57] This power could come from governments or from civil society and NGO interests protesting the acts of organizations like the World Trade Organization around the world during the late 1990s and early 2000s. It could involve political action by citizens to dismantle some of the privileges that have allowed corporations to gain the power they currently have.

Further, there is an emerging set of laws and regulation involving disclosure and accountability in nations around the world. More proactive governments are beginning to establish new expectations of corporations and fund managers regarding triple-bottom-line issues. In the United Kingdom, for example, the 2000 Socially Responsible Investment Regulation requires pension fund managers to disclose policies on SRI, including shareholder activism. While pension fund managers do not actually have to do anything differently—or even take triple-bottom-line issues into account—the regulation puts significant peer pressure on pension fund managers to think about such matters and, by implication, companies as well. In 2001, France became the first nation in the world to require social and environmental impact assessment in corporate reports for all companies listed on the French stock exchange. In the wake of this law, French retirement funds need to rely on both financial and social criteria in making investment decisions. While implementation is not yet fully achieved, some progress is being made.

Germany, since 2001, has required companies to indicate how social and environmental policies are being integrated, and to declare whether or not they are adhering to codes of conduct. The Netherlands has required mandatory compliance with the OECD's Guidelines for Multinational Enterprises if companies are to obtain export credits since 2002. Sweden and Norway have required environmental reports since 1999. The European Commission has signaled its support of enterprise responsibility and SRI generally through a white paper issued in 2002 and has communicated to the European Union's Parliament that corporate social responsibility criteria will be introduced in legislation of member states. Denmark, for instance, has introduced a law requiring all large corporations and institutional investors to report on their responsibility policies and their implementation.

As of 2003, audits of listed companies in Japan are required to disclose material information on risk related to corporate viability. Included risks go beyond financial and business risks to encompass reputational and brand image. Finally, since 2003, Australia has required investment firms to disclose how they take SRI into account.

Such laws are only the very early steps of a framework for holding companies and investment managers accountable for social and ecological performance as well as financial performance. They do, however, signal a future that could conceivably be different from the present with respect to the art of responsible enterprise. In some ways, regulations like these play an important role in leveling the playing field for all companies, by establishing the same—and presumably fair—rules of the game for everyone. Accountability, responsibility, and transparency are the fundamental demands made of companies today in order to sustain their legitimacy in society—or maintain their so-called license to operate.

Over the next several decades, as sustainability issues become more prominent, we expect such laws to make more and broader demands on companies, including mandatory integrated financial and ESG reporting. While many companies find regulation and legislation problematic, one clear function of a mandate is to create a level playing field for all. As the interconnectedness of countries and corporations becomes ever clearer, the importance of that level playing field will only increase and perhaps some new forms of global governance will be necessary.

There are other interesting nonregulatory developments that will force corporate attention to social and environmental matters, in addition to financial ones. The California Public Employees Retirement System is paying more attention to good corporate governance and to measuring, monitoring, and managing risk, including the types of risk that come with environmental and social problems. Further, a coalition of socially responsible investment (SRI) firms petitioned the U.S. Securities and Exchange Commission (SEC) in 2002 to require that companies disclose financially significant environmental risk. While not mandated into law at this point, such moves put new pressures on companies for transparency about their impacts and seek to hold them accountable.

Part IV

REINVENTING CSR

CORPORATE SUSTAINABILITY
AND RESPONSIBILITY

11 SCANNING THE FUTURE

Finding Pattern in Chaos

Prediction is very difficult, especially if it's about the future.
Niels Bohr[1]

SEEKING THE FUTURE

Responsible and sustainable companies know that they need to understand very clearly the forces at play not only in the economic sphere but also in the political, civil society, and ecological spheres. Changes are swiftly appearing in all these spheres, and our ability to address them will depend significantly on our willingness to learn about the redefined role of business in global society. As previous chapters make clear, corporate leaders are already learning that they need to operate in sustainable ways with respect to the natural environment because of the limitations of the ecological system in supporting life as we know it on earth. To further this learning, we need to enhance awareness of what is likely to happen in the future.

We cannot predict the future, as the physicist Niels Bohr implied in the comment quoted at the start of this chapter, but we can understand patterns, potentials, and scenarios. Like many of the dynamics and relationships we have explored in this book, future trends are embedded in chaotic processes, the immediate outcomes of which cannot be known. Chaos and complexity theories do tell us that we can seek patterns that provide significant insights. These patterns become evident when we look carefully at dynamics and think creatively about what is happening now, what might happen, and the possible implications.

Using all of our leadership insights and our expanded awareness so that we can hold multiple perspectives (remember the higher stages of development discussed in Chapter 3), we can explore what might initially seem to be a chaos of information, trends, and interrelationships and try to identify large-scale patterns that can help us think through appropriate actions for coping with a changing world. We need to look at data and think creatively about possibilities for responding to trends and dynamics that might be sources of competitive advantage.

To do this "futures pattern seeking," responsible companies carefully monitor the shifting dynamics and concerns of their multiple stakeholders, as well as the broader (and, importantly, more subtle) technological, competitive, and social shifts that take place in societies. They do this monitoring not only because these forces and dynamics may present problems but also because they represent interesting and potentially profitable new opportunities for business development. If one company overlooks opportunities or challenges, other companies that pay closer attention can gain at least short-term competitive advantage.

Once a company uncovers current trends, data, and patterns, it can use a range of techniques to project these patterns out into the future and think about their potential implications for the enterprise. One such technique, called scenario analysis, has been used successfully by Royal Dutch Shell, among other prominent companies. Scenario analysis was particularly helpful to Shell in preparing for falling oil prices (which some observers had considered unrealistic) in the 1980s. There are many other techniques for scanning the future that are useful for bringing the perspectives of multiple stakeholders together.

For any responsible company, having a futures-scanning role is a critical element of the boundary-spanning discussed earlier. The company can use information gathered within functions to develop future scenarios to help prepare for any of multiple possible outcomes. It is important that leaders heed the advice of baseball great Yogi Berra, who once said, "If you don't know where you're going, you wind up somewhere else."[2]

Below we explore some of the current dynamics and trends that are shaping the future to provide a core framework for the future that enterprises can use to cope with the inevitable patterns of change and complexity. The values are added, as the section title of Part IV suggests, because we need to think in new ways not only about CSR—corporate sustainability and responsibility—but also about what is meaningful and important to stakeholders, and ultimately to ourselves as citizens of organizations, of particular societies, and of the world.

SHELL'S ENERGY SCENARIOS TO 2050: SCRAMBLE OR BLUEPRINT?

Royal Dutch Shell, the global energy giant, pioneered scenario planning in the 1970s. Scenarios do not forecast the future. They are, instead, alternative perspectives on the future. Scenarios describe possible futures based on an identification of likely events as well as actors and their motivations.[3] They are possible (and usually competing) images of the future that seem compelling and intuitively possible.[4] Often, developing scenarios involves systems thinking, because many of the factors that need to be considered interact with each other.

In 2008, Shell published two major scenarios, "Scramble" and "Blueprint," that outline the possible future of the global energy system until the year 2050.[5] Both scenarios are based on the belief that the conditions (supply, demand, and effects on the natural environment) underlying the current global energy system will change significantly throughout the next decades. On the demand side, tensions are likely to occur, because of increased energy use by emerging economies (e.g., China and India) and rising population levels. On the supply side, Shell realizes that traditional energy sources will be harder to access after 2015, while alternative energy sources and improvements in energy efficiency cannot completely offset rising demand.[6] Even with significantly lower carbon emissions, it will be hard to control global warming and the related carbon dioxide concentration in the atmosphere.

Given this basic information, Shell's energy scenarios ask not whether change will happen, but what kind of change will happen and how.

> Will national governments simply *Scramble* to secure their own energy supplies? Or will new *Blueprints* emerge from coalitions between various levels of societies and government, ranging from the local to the international, that begin to add up to a new energy framework?[7]

"Scramble" reflects a scenario in which the focus is on nation-states and their energy needs. Securing the energy needs of nations puts much emphasis on securing an adequate supply of energy, while the demand side and also reflections on the natural environment are unlikely to play a major role. We should note that nation-states (and hence politicians) are the major actors in this scenario. Because reducing energy demand via public policies is unlikely (because it would make politicians unpopular), the focus is not on international cooperation and coordination, but rather on securing a state's economic growth by providing a sufficient energy supply (e.g., through bilateral deals between governments). Energy will be largely supplied through coal, biofuels, and renewable sources (used in a sequential way to satisfy rising demand over time). Overall, "Scramble" is characterized by the existence of a variety of uncoordinated national energy policies.

The "Blueprint" scenario looks very different. It is based on the belief that "broader fears about life style and economic prospects forge new alliances that promote action in both developed and developing nations. This leads to the emergence of a critical mass of parallel responses to supply, demand, and climate stresses."[8] The movements that develop these new blueprints are not mandated from the top; they start at the grassroots level (e.g., as alliances between multiple stakeholders or multiple cities that want to secure their energy needs or simply have clean air). Over time, these movements become connected and aligned (nationally and internationally) and create a critical mass to address the underlying problems. For instance, carbon trading becomes mainstream (with reasonable prices attached early on), while improvements in energy efficiency create positive effects for developing and emerging economies (e.g., energy is more affordable when less is needed and when prices rise slowly). Energy supply is largely covered by non-fossil sources, while coal continues to play an important role.[9]

PREDICTING THE SHAPE OF THE FUTURE

What is it that shapes the future? Although as human beings we have little control over nature, we do in some sense control our own destiny. We make decisions that influence our future on a daily basis, whether in our leadership capacities or in the organizations that we manage. For example, to the extent that we take environmental stewardship responsibility for our own impacts on the ecological environment, nature will reward us bountifully. Arguably, however, because of rapid population growth, humanity now faces a dramatically uncertain future around issues of sustainability. As we illustrated in

Chapters 9 and 10, the world community has yet to deal seriously with sustainability issues in either the financial or the ecological realm. To the extent that civilization provides for appropriate balance among the three spheres of activity in human civilization, with respect to the natural environment and also with respect to each other, societies will be more equitable, productive, sustainable, and meaningful places in which to live, work, and play.

Also, it seems likely that beginning to understand future patterns and their implications demands the relatively higher levels of cognitive, emotional, and moral development of postconventional development. Otherwise, as developmental psychologist Robert Kegan put it, we will really be "in over our heads" amid the "mental demands of modern life."[10] Tomorrow's leaders, then, need to develop a sense of what is meaningful to others and to think through the systems implications of their decisions in order to move toward understanding the future. Such systems thinking—built as it is on understanding where the points of leverage and dynamics are and what the interactions among variables, issues, and relationships mean—also requires shifting perspectives to encompass data that might ordinarily be ignored or overlooked. It is what we have been trying to provide throughout this book. Understanding these dynamics is important, because as complexity theory tells us, small shifts in chaotic systems can result in large changes down the road.

GLOBAL TRENDS, ISSUES, AND OPPORTUNITIES

Certain trends, issues, and opportunities—some technological, some economic, others social and political—make understanding the complexities of global dynamics an imperative for those leading companies today. Some trends may also provide significant business opportunities for creative entrepreneurs. Futurists can help provide understanding by identifying significant shifts in the world around us. The next sections of this chapter briefly explore some of the major shifts several futurists expect to affect corporations in the 21st century.

A Knowledge Economy[11]

Many observers, beginning with sociologists Alvin and Heidi Toffler, have observed that the developed world has entered a knowledge economy—a post-industrial economy where knowledge resources are at least as important as material resources.[12] Today, we could argue that the post-industrial society is passing and we are entering an era of sustainability—or that we need to if human civilization is to survive in anything like the form we currently know. Equally some might claim that we are entering an age of biogenetics, nanotechnology, or scarcity. Below, we consider some of the implications of the knowledge and sustainability economy, and in the next section we focus on some of the fractures that exist in the world that create potential issues for companies.

Knowledge develops when people integrate or synthesize information and data in useful or meaningful ways. As a resource, knowledge differs considerably from physical resources. For example, knowledge is abundant, not scarce. Unlike physical assets, knowledge assets expand when they are shared. In some respects, knowledge acts as a public good once it is out there: it can be shared at no or very little cost.[13] As Google understands, knowledge works best through sharing, not hoarding. Once knowledge is out in the world, it becomes usable by anyone, and in that sense it is far more difficult to control than physical assets or equipment, or even labor. Further, one person's knowledge is usually built upon others' knowledge in a way that can create two-plus-two-equals-five synergies.[14] Knowledge resides in people, thereby making intellectual/human capital the most valuable asset—not physical, financial, or even technological resources, yet because it is intangible, mobile, and not fungible, possibly the most difficult to be generated and sustained. That means that knowledge derives from learning and experience. Thus, education plays a crucial role in a world based on knowledge.[15]

Given these characteristics of knowledge, a knowledge economy differs from an industrial economy in that it is knowledge intensive, depending on industries where human intellectual capital—the skills, knowledge, and information that people bring to work—is paramount, rather than other sorts of raw materials. The knowledge economy is also technologically and electronically connected, and it is connected globally, making almost instant communication possible and allowing some types of work to be conducted in different parts of the world on a 24/7 basis. In some instances individuals from many cultures contribute to the work, and in other instances, businesses are operating in numerous cultures and countries simultaneously, which means that people are bringing their insights, ideas, and capabilities to bear in wholly new ways. In those circumstances, the capacity to see multiple perspectives simultaneously is critically important. Such instantaneous global communications across boundaries and in diverse environments are rapidly becoming the norm.

The availability of information electronically and the reach of supply chains and distribution chains across national borders and among different firms means that many companies are now operating in a global context, even if they think of themselves as domestic firms. The globalization of the developed world and the instant availability of communications has created a context in which boundaries between companies—and many other types of institutions—are becoming more permeable, creating in some senses a boundary-less world. It is also a world in which transparency is the norm, whether or not it is desired by enterprises, simply because it is so easy for observers to find out information and transmit it to others.

All of these conditions make collaboration at least as important as competition for companies' and other institutions' survival, meaning that new skills of working together creatively, constructively, and collaboratively are increasingly demanded, particularly when issues facing companies, such as ecological concerns, inherently have no boundaries themselves. What is demanded of leaders today are skills for dealing with many cultures, ideologies, and worldviews, a capacity to understand and integrate multiple perspectives simultaneously, and an ability to work effectively in a dynamic and fast-paced environment, where intellectual capital is the premium resource.

THE STATE OF THE WORLD: A DEVELOPMENT PERSPECTIVE

One good way to assess the state of the world is to discuss which of the UN Millennium Development Goals (MDGs) have been achieved so far and what still remains to be done. These goals deal with the world's major problems of poverty, lack of education, and inequity. Officially established during the

UN Millennium Development Summit in 2000, the eight goals are supported by all 193 UN member states and a variety of international organizations. It is widely acknowledged that businesses play a significant role in helping to achieve the MDGs by 2015. Participants in the UN Global Compact, for example, are asked to support the MDGs by setting up public-private partnerships. The eight goals represent a partnership between the developed countries and the developing countries determined, as the Millennium Declaration states, "to create an environment—at the national and global levels alike—which is conducive to development and the elimination of poverty."

Some progress has been made toward achieving the MDGs, although much remains to be done, as follows:[16]

1. **Eradicate Extreme Poverty and Hunger:** *Target for 2015: Halve the proportion of people living on less than a dollar a day and those who suffer from hunger.* While in 1990 1.8 billion people lived on less than $1.25 a day, this number was down to 1.4 billion in 2005. Although the global financial crisis (2007–2008) negatively impacted poverty reduction, the UN stills expects to halve the number of people living in poverty by 2015. On the other hand, the consequences of the global economic crisis (e.g., higher food prices) have slowed down progress and make the full achievement of this part of the first MDG unlikely.

2. **Achieve Universal Primary Education:** *Target for 2015: Ensure that all boys and girls complete primary school.* Although enrollment in primary education has risen to 89 percent in the developing world, enrollment in sub-Saharan Africa remains low (76 percent). It is also noteworthy that more and more girls are attending primary education.

3. **Promote Gender Equality and Empower Women:** Targets for 2005 and 2015: Eliminate gender disparities in primary and secondary education preferably by 2005, and at all levels by 2015. In 2008, there were 95 girls for every 100 boys enrolled in secondary education (up from an 88:100 ratio in 1999). However, gender parity in primary and secondary education still remains out of reach for many developing nations. The 2010 MDG Report also points out that men still outnumber women in paid employment (except in the Commonwealth of Independent States [former Soviet countries]).

4. **Reduce Child Mortality:** *Target for 2015: Reduce by two-thirds the mortality rate among children under 5.* Even though the mortality rate of children under the age of 5 in developing countries has dropped by 28 percent since 1990, a variety of countries still have high child death rates, making the achievement of this target unlikely. In sub-Saharan Africa one in every seven children still dies before his or her fifth birthday.

5. **Improve Maternal Health:** *Target for 2015: Reduce by three-quarters the ratio of women dying in childbirth.* Data indicate that more women receive medical assistance during and after delivery (from 53 percent in 1990 to 63 percent in 2008). However, it is also clear that the vast majority of maternal deaths are avoidable if improved skilled medical assistance can be delivered on a broader scale.

6. **Combat HIV/AIDS, Malaria, and Other Diseases:** *Target for 2015: Halt and begin to reverse the spread of HIV/AIDS and the incidence of malaria and other major diseases.* The spread of HIV has stabilized in some regions but continues to rise in Eastern Europe, Central Asia, and parts of Africa. Sub-Saharan Africa is the most heavily affected region, accounting for 72 percent of all new infections in 2008. Lack of knowledge about protection against HIV is the key driver of the disease.

7. **Ensure Environmental Sustainability:** *Targets: Integrate the principles of sustainable development into country policies and programs and reverse the loss of environmental resources. By 2015, reduce by half the proportion of people without access to safe drinking water. By 2020 achieve significant improvement in the lives of at least 100 million slum dwellers.* Environmental sustainability remains a challenge as emissions from carbon dioxide keep rising. In addition, the rate of deforestation is alarmingly high in most parts of the world, while the number of species facing extinction is growing at a rapid pace. However, there are also success stories: The universal ratification of the Montreal Protocol for the protection of the ozone layer has led to a dramatic decrease in the consumption of ozone-depleting substances.

8. **Develop a Global Partnership for Development:** *Targets: Further develop an open trading and financial system that includes a commitment*

to good governance, development, and poverty reduction—nationally and internationally. Address the least developed countries' special needs, and the special needs of landlocked and small island developing states. Deal comprehensively with developing countries' debt problems. Develop decent and productive work for youth. In cooperation with pharmaceutical companies, provide access to affordable essential drugs in developing countries. In cooperation with the private sector, make available the benefits of new technologies—especially information and communications technologies. Further extending development assistance remains a challenge. Only five countries met the UN target for development assistance (0.7 percent of gross national income). Development is positively influenced by many developing countries gaining access to the markets of developed countries. It is also noteworthy that debt burdens eased for many countries, affecting their creditworthiness and vulnerability to external economic shocks.[17]

More than ten years after the launch of the MDGs it is clear that most of the goals will not be fully reached by 2015. This reality means that corporations need to (and should) play a much bigger role in accepting their responsibilities related to some of the MDGs. Corporations and their supply partners often have a direct impact on people's living standards (Goal 1), workers' education (Goal 2), and gender equality (Goal 3). Take the case of child labor: children, in many cases young girls, often do not receive primary education because they need to support their impoverished families. The problem is complex because removing these children from the workplace often means that they end up in even less desirable circumstances, such as prostitution or virtual slavery, rather than in school.

We have already recognized that economic development cannot continue apace without consideration of what is ecologically and socially sustainable. Sustainability in this case also includes the sustainability of democratic institutions, free-market economies, and healthy local communities in the face of enormous inequities in the distribution and use of resources. The wide availability of information and connectivity, lack of productive employment, and the rich-poor gap led to significant disturbances among peoples in the Middle East and even the US in 2011, and more uprisings can be expected if these fundamental problems are poorly handled. The gap between rich and poor exists in most if not all nations, as well as, generally speaking, between northern and southern countries or, alternatively, developed and developing nations, including in the United States.

New, more ecologically sensitive and responsible practices are needed to serve the needs of the billions of people in the world who now live in poverty. Businesses have an essential role to play in developing the goods and services needed to close these gaps. But facing up to these global realities means that some significant shifts in lifestyle and production processes may be needed, particularly for wealthier and more powerful citizens. For aware and innovative companies, significant opportunities may exist. Increasingly, new companies embed pro-social or pro-ecological goals in their missions and incorporate multiple-bottom-line orientations into what some call their company DNA. Such firms are called social entrepreneurships or for-benefit companies. In the United States, a movement toward "conscious capitalism" has begun, along with the establishment of so-called B Corporations, which deliberately and explicitly build in transparency, along with social and environmental standards.[18] We discuss these trends more in the final chapter.

TRENDS FACING BUSINESS AND THE WORLD

All businesses today face a constantly changing and incredibly dynamic world. Although it is not possible to predict the future precisely, following major trends can be helpful in framing actions and responsibilities going forward.

Millennium Project's Trends

The Center for Strategic and International Studies (CSIS) in Washington, D.C., has developed the Millennium Project to identify the major trends in the world today.[19] Michael Mazarr and the other futurists identify several foundations as part of the first trend: demography, natural resources, and the environment and culture.

Demography, Ecology, Culture   Although the population growth rate is slowing in some parts of the world, population itself continues to grow and will do so until it levels off somewhere between 8 and 12 billion people globally. Modernization, education, and expansion of women's rights reduce fertility and have tended to slow the rate of population growth. But because 95 percent of that growth will occur in less-developed countries, the gap between rich and poor can be expected to widen, and processes of urbanization, already under way, will likely continue.

Although sustainable development is gaining momentum, population growth and many current organizational practices will continue to strain the natural environment. Although knowledge businesses are less dependent on the ecology than industrial businesses are, higher agricultural yields, demand for crop lands, the intensity of modern farming methods (with resulting soil erosion, desertification, and over-farming), and fisheries will continue to cause ecological problems. Some eighty countries already face water shortages, a problem that will be exacerbated by continued population growth.[20]

Science, Technology, Modernization   An important factor in the dynamics facing corporations, according to the Millennium Project, is the push by science and technology to continuously modernize. Miniaturization, biogenetic engineering, and information and communications technology are among the fastest changing fields. The gap between rich and poor will intensify the gap between the information/technology rich and poor as well, as access to technological advances becomes essential to taking a role in the modern world.

Mazarr observes, "Richer countries tend to look the same—freer, more individualistic and less hierarchical, more concerned with the environment."[21] Not only does this "looking alike" foster greater homogeneity, but it also places considerable pressures for constructive—democratic—reform on repressive regimes. And, Mazarr notes, this process may well result in more peace and less war, unless of course fundamentalism and tribalism in their various guises lead to more local wars or terrorism.

Human Resources and Complexity   The third trend identified by the Millennium Project involves the move toward a knowledge-based economic system and the resulting expected increased attention to and valuing of human resources—employee stakeholders. Mazarr identifies four features of the "new economy" to which companies in the future will need to pay attention:[22]

- Human capital—because knowledge resides in human beings.
- Freedom and empowerment—because empowered people create and innovate.
- Disorganization—because companies using complexity and chaos theories as a base for organizing will outpace companies organized more hierarchically and traditionally.
- Networks and alliances—because partnerships will become critical to organizational effectiveness and efficiency.

Mazarr identifies the principles of the knowledge era as speed, flexibility, decentralization, and empowerment. Organizations that adhere to these principles imply that they trust their stakeholders, especially their employees, and give them responsibilities that go far beyond traditional responsibilities. Ultimately, as these principles become the norm, companies will have to redesign themselves with the values of integrity and responsibility embedded in all of their operations.

Global Tribalism   Much international trading occurs within, not among, the three major trading blocs of Europe, the Americas, and East Asia.[23] Mazarr points out that enhanced communications and the rise of the multinational corporation as a powerful social institution will require greater global awareness. But, when threatened, ideologies tend to erupt in the forms of tribalism that political scientist Benjamin Barber calls Jihads. Thus, we can expect continued attempts by ethnic, religious, political, and cultural groups to sustain their identities in the face of global pluralism.[24]

Transforming Authority   According to the Millennium Project, traditional institutions will face greater challenges to their authority in the knowledge era, in which communications are instantaneous and information is widely shared. This trend will be particularly strong in the political sphere, as democratization spreads throughout the world, and as information becomes more readily available and widely shared.

Authorities will tend to decentralize their organizations, creating virtual structures (as many companies already are doing), influencing through knowledge and allegiance rather than coercion, and acquiring power through competence and effectiveness rather than tradition.[25]

Trends Identified by Monitor Group's Eamonn Kelly[26]

Monitor Group's Global Business Network CEO Eamonn Kelly has identified a number of trends that he believes will affect the future significantly—and to which businesses are going to have to respond. Calling some changes disruptive surprises that are difficult to prepare for, Kelly argues that businesses can prepare for predictable trends that will transform our future.

One key force is demography. The world's population has quadrupled since 1900 and will continue to grow, albeit at a somewhat reduced rate until about 2050 (absent, of course, a major ecological or other catastrophe). Kelly notes that at the start of the 20th century, the gap between rich and poor countries was eight to one, but by 2000, it was 80 to one. Since more educated populations tend to have fewer children, in the industrialized nations of the global North, there will be fewer young people working to support the growing population of elders. The opposite will happen in the less industrialized and poorer countries of the South, where higher productivity and a burgeoning youth population will lead to fewer jobs and higher unemployment. The result may be the kind of disruption that occurred in the Middle East in 2011.

A second major trend Kelly identifies is urbanization: most people in the world now live in urban areas—or what he calls a "city planet." Migrants tend to move from rural to urban areas, and two-thirds of the world's population is likely to live in cities by 2030. A third force has to do with changing values and communication patterns among the millennial generation, particularly with respect to information and technology. These young people have articulated a greater desire for meaning, spirituality, and belonging than previous generations, a change that is likely to shape workplaces and communities in the future.

Brazil, Russia, India, and China—the so-called BRIC nations—are already reshaping the world's economic and political structures—bringing values, histories, economic ideas, and cultural traditions considerably different from the ones that have dominated the world in the past. As these countries gain economic clout and become stronger economic competitors, the world's businesses will need to adapt and accommodate them. Kelly believes that Africa, which has some 900 million people and abundant resources, and which has been marginalized in the past, may be an important partner and source of economic development in the future. Simultaneously, the world will move toward what Kelly calls a "post-Western globalization," in which the BRICs, Africa (BRICA nations?), and alliances and NGOs of various sorts will play important and new roles in governance, technology, and economic development. With this shift, Kelly believes, Western nations will likely become importers—not exporters—of ideas and technologies, and exporters of talent. Once again themes of collaboration and diversity will likely be paramount in this new world.

Another important force of the future will be BANG technologies: bits (digital technology), atoms (nanotechnology), neurons (cognitive science), and genes (biotechnology). Kelly says that these elements are "mutually catalytic" and will generate amazing new insights and ideas when combined. The technological convergence will create a potential explosion of creative new ideas that will rapidly accelerate progress. Tied to BANG is the idea of human enhancement, in which BANG technologies will be used to improve individuals and their lives in currently unforeseen ways, making humans smarter, better, and stronger. They will create ethical and other opportunities and dilemmas that change, in Kelly's view, what it means to be human.

Energy is another force for change, particularly since reliance on carbon sources like oil and coal is no longer tenable. What types of energy, whether based on wind, thermal, tidal, solar, or something else, will power the world is not yet clear, but what is clear is that change is on its way. Related to this is the reality of climate change, which is dramatically altering the world in unpredictable and still-unknown ways. Whether current estimates are too optimistic or too pessimistic, the implications of climate change for food and water, land events, extreme weather, and infrastructure will be part of the context that businesses operate in as they struggle not to mitigate, but to adapt.

The final element in Kelly's list is the inevitable social change that will result from all these other forces and shifts. In part because of the transparency, connectivity, information flows, and complexities that we have already discussed, social change is inevitable. NGOs, civil society organizations, and alliances of various sorts will be affected in ways that are entirely new, and that require significant organizational and institutional shifts to cope.

Institute for Global Futures Top 10 Trends of the Extreme Future[27]

Dr. James Canton, futurist and CEO of the Institute for Global Futures, also has created a list of "extreme futures" with which he believes businesses and other institutions (and humanity) will have to contend. Among the extreme trends he has identified will be the need for new fuels, for example hydrogen rather than carbon-based fuels. He also argues that the economy will be transformed by innovation as a result of the convergence of free trade, technology and democracy (which some observers believe are not compatible), a huge and growing need for new jobs to employ people productively and meaningfully, and the convergence of what Kelly called BANG technologies with growing needs for peace and security.

Couple changing workforce characteristics, medical and "weird science" technologies that could dramatically lengthen healthy lives, with new types of threats from hackers and terrorists, and the world of tomorrow will be very different. Canton, too, warns of the impact of climate change, predicts an increasing role for China and India in the world, and expects positive trends related to human rights and individual freedom.

The Financial System, Strategy, and the World

The global financial crisis (GFC) of 2007–2008 highlighted an important facet of the world as it currently exists—and is likely to exist in the foreseeable future, unless significant changes are made in the financial world. That is, the role of financial markets has significantly shifted in recent years in ways that may not be favorable for the so-called "real" or productive economy. The GFC also highlighted the fact that global markets are now tightly and seemingly inextricably woven together. Perhaps there are some lessons to be taken from the GFC that might help in thinking about the future. In particular, the relationship between the financial and productive economies, which have long been largely separate, need to work cooperatively in a world that strives for integrity.

At one level the GFC can be understood as resulting from the dominance of an uncontrolled financial system that now represents about a third of economic "activity," much of which was (is?) characterized by what former U.S. Federal Reserve chairman Alan Greenspan once called "irrational exuberance." Although Greenspan has admitted to being wrong about the ability of "free" markets to correct themselves, the wave of deregulation that occurred in the United States and the rest of the world from the late 1970s until the GFC of 2008 allowed markets to reign, in some respects, over common sense. The GFC seems to have come about from a mix of excessive leverage, highly risky investments (e.g., many of the derivatives fostered by hedge fund managers) that were poorly understood by most people, short-termism in businesses and market strategies, and, of course, a massive housing bubble related to greed and deceptive and fraudulent practices in the mortgage and housing markets.

The thinking underlying the "free-market" ideology that dominated markets and society in the years before the GFC and to some extent still does, has been called a "religion" of market fundamentalism by economist Joseph Stiglitz.[28] Although Stiglitz believes that this market fundamentalism ended when the U.S. government let the global financial services firm Lehman Brothers collapse in September 2008, many signs indicate that financial markets (at this writing) continue business as usual. Earlier, in academic research, Stiglitz had shown that market fundamentalism was fundamentally flawed, demonstrating that small information imperfections (of which there are many in financial markets) created market inefficiencies and sometimes monopoly pricing. Stiglitz commented, "in other words, the standard neoclassical model on which so much of modern policy is based was not robust, and Adam Smith was dramatically wrong. . . . [W]henever information was imperfect, which is always, the reason that the invisible hand so often seemed invisible was that, in fact, it was not there."[29]

Paul Volcker, a former chairman of the U.S. Federal Reserve, agreed with Stiglitz about the problems of too much market fundamentalism holding sway, noting: "We need to break up our biggest banks and return to the basic split of activities that existed under the Glass-Steagall Act of 1933—one highly regulated (and somewhat boring) set of banks to run the payments system, and a completely separate set of financial entities to help raise capital (and to trade securities)."[30] Interestingly, Volcker also argued to a group of financial executives that "There is no benefit to running our financial system in its current fashion, with high risks (for society) and high returns (for top bankers). Most of financial innovation . . . is not just worthless to society—it is downright dangerous to our broader economic health."[31]

The Nobel Prize–winning economist Paul Krugman asked an important question in the wake of the GFC: "How Did Economists Get it So Wrong?"[32] He pointed out that many economists were quite self-congratulatory about the "success" of economics, but few actually anticipated the GFC because of what he termed the "profession's blindness to the very possibility of catastrophic failures in a market economy." Krugman's colorful diagnosis is that "economists, as a group, mistook beauty, clad in impressive-looking mathematics, for truth." With this orientation, economists tended to ignore the very real potential for market bubbles (they have been endemic to markets since the great tulip craze in Holland in the 1600s) to collapse.

In considering the future, Krugman argues for more Keynesian than Friedman-esque (free-market or neoliberal) economic approaches. Krugman commented that Keynes "challenge[d] the notion that free-market economies can function without a minder, [and expressed] particular contempt for financial markets, which he viewed as being dominated by short-term speculation with little regard for fundamentals." Thus, Keynes was a proponent of active government regulation and intervention, rather than the "free-market" theories of Milton Friedman, who advocated as little government as possible.

One observer, Umair Haque of Edge Economy, similarly argues that yesterday's economic growth—the growth of the 20th century—was nothing less than "dumb." Haque points to the need for what he terms a "tectonic global shift" that means that tomorrow's enterprises, institutions and organizations will need to play by new rules.[33] Among the "new rules" that Haque suggests are "choosing good" over evil as not only a moral but also a strategic imperative that relates an enterprise to its stakeholders. Haque also says that "purpose is self-interest." "Choosing good" is especially needed for a long-term, enlightened self-interest approach to the consequences of decisions—a capacity that management theorist Russell Ackoff called wisdom.[34] Haque also notes that in the future maximizing economic and environmental destructiveness, for example, by externalizing costs, will need to be eliminated, while being constructive and internalizing costs will take centerstage. Future growth will require co-creating, co-producing, and co-operating, recognizing that differentiation is passé, whereas recognizing and honoring "difference" (diversity of all sorts) will be the new imperative.

Because markets can succeed only when its participants have trust in the system—and because cycles of deregulation are inevitably followed by market failures that result in the need for new regulations (and vice versa over time), there is likely to be a wave of new regulations, particularly in the financial industry (but also affecting health care, telecommunications and broadcast media, the Internet, transportation, energy, and other sectors) to deal with changing technologies and emerging needs. Various approaches to restoring stability and trust—and in a sense, sanity—to financial markets, which some observers characterize as nothing less than a global gambling casino, are being offered. One approach has been developed by renowned futurist Hazel Henderson through the Network for Sustainable Financial Markets. This initiative offers a set of guiding principles for stabilizing financial markets in the future (see Table 11.1).

These principles are aimed at reducing mere speculation (what some call gambling) in financial markets and reemphasizing the necessary and helpful aspects of the financial system: providing needed capital to businesses and other enterprises, with an orientation toward long-term value. They are also aimed at incorporating currently externalized costs and risks that derive from "nonfinancial" sources such as ESG and ensuring that all such risks and costs are accounted for adequately (including the risks taken by "too big to fail" institutions that have previously been bailed out by governments). Note that these principles are consistent with the UN's Principles for Responsible Investment, discussed in the previous chapter.

Two years after the beginning of the global financial crisis, in 2010, the U.S. Congress passed the Dodd-Frank Wall Street Reform and Consumer Protection Act.[35] The legislation called for the creation of a watchdog agency to protect financial consumers from deceptive practices and prevent future bailouts of financial institutions deemed "too big to fail." It also calls for an advance warning system that identifies and addresses potential systemic risks before they become a major threat to the economy, and for transparency and accountability of "exotic" instruments (i.e., many of the derivatives and other

TABLE 11.1   *Guiding Principles for Sustainable Financial Markets*

---

1. The economic and social purpose of markets is to create long-term sustainable value, which requires the efficient allocation of capital toward that goal.
2. Sustainable value creation requires that hidden risks and rewards be identified and valued.
3. Balance between short-term and long-term views is needed.
4. Market participants must take responsibility for their actions.
5. Governance at all financial institutions should be improved.
6. Better alignment of financial interests is needed to reduce agency costs.
7. A coordinated global approach is needed to better protect the financial markets.

SOURCE: Network for Sustainable Financial Markets (NFSM), "Guiding Principles," 2011 (http://www.sustainablefinancialmarkets.net).

complicated financial transactions whose workings are mysterious to many, and that were at the core of the GFC). The bill requires companies to report executive compensation and is designed to improve corporate governance and protect investors by creating tough rules around transparency and accountability for rating agencies.

Global Governance: The Soft-Law Emergence of GANs (Global Action Networks)

In a world fraught with global issues related to sustainability, climate change, globalized finance, global energy supply, food security, personal security, clean water supplies, and supply chains, to name just a few, there is a clear need for global, not just local, regional, or even national standards and policies. The reach of government often stops at national borders. The United Nations' resources are stretched and its enforcement capabilities limited; the only other global entities with significant enforcement clout (power to mandate) are the so-called Bretton Woods organizations—the World Bank, the International Monetary Fund, and the World Trade Organization. But it is exactly these entities that have fostered the current system of international "free" trade, through a neoliberal agenda that, as we have just discussed, has been seen to be flawed, especially in light of societal needs and the sustainability crisis. Despite a growing need for global governance, beyond the entities already noted, there are few truly international bodies that deal explicitly with sustainability, human development, peace, and security with the enforcement clout necessary to effect change at the global level.

In a context of global problems without global governance, so-called Global Action Networks (GANs) have evolved to help fill the gap. These new types of governance mechanisms, fueled by the connectivity of digital technologies, are multistakeholder, global networks that come together typically around public policy issues of importance to an industry or sector, but where the scope of the problem goes beyond what any one actor can deal with.[36] The UN Global Compact, Transparency International, and the Global Reporting Initiative, discussed earlier, are examples of GANs. Others include the Marine Stewardship Council, the Forest Stewardship Council, Rugmark, the Business Alliance for Local Living Economies, the Slow Food movement, and the Healthy Cities Movement, to name only a few. GANs go beyond simple multistakeholder coalitions in their desire to effect change through collaborative action that engages numerous interested parties around important issues of public policy or the public good.[37]

Steve Waddell notes that GANs tend to operate in contexts where global challenges that are too big or complex for a single actor (e.g., government) or even an entire sector to resolve exist. The competencies needed to resolve the huge issues that GANs address need to be brought together from multiple sectors and types of entities in creative problem-solving approaches that allow various and often competing perspectives. GANs have characteristics that differentiate them from simple networks. They are global, multi-level, entrepreneurial, and action-oriented networks focused on making systemic changes. Governments may or may not be involved. Frequently, their joint work leads to new industry norms that no single entity could achieve alone (e.g., as the Forest Stewardship Council has done), or to mechanisms for global actions (GRI's ESG reporting framework). Because they are essentially stakeholder-engagement platforms, they tend to be structured as interorganizational networks based on democratic principles and forms, and their legitimacy derives from the direct engagement and involvement of numerous interested stakeholders rather than from governmental authority.

In a world where global problems too often overwhelm the capacity of local authorities—and where a global government is highly unlikely to develop anytime soon—GANs may well represent the world's best hope for dealing with systemic problems. But if GANs are to succeed, business and other leaders will need to foster the collaborative, visioning, and emotional skills necessary to support them.

WE CANNOT PREDICT THE FUTURE, BUT . . .

Although this chapter has presented but a small sampling of future possibilities, we hope that it provides a sense of the patterns, forces, and dynamics that are likely to influence the future—and the enterprises that have to operate in that future. Predicting the future is virtually impossible because change is an inherently chaotic process in which small changes can make large and fundamental differences. What people and companies can do, however, is prepare themselves to cope with whatever happens by paying attention to their stakeholders. They can seek their stakeholders' input on the company's future plans, problems and opportunities, and issues and trends, and they can continually scan the horizon for imminent developments, whether technological, ecological, social, or political. By establishing relationships with key stakeholders, companies can prepare themselves—systematically and thoughtfully—for what the future is likely to bring.

Getting the kind of information that can only be gained when people with different points of view are brought together will enhance a company's capacity to be a respected corporate citizen but also provide the basis for revealing new trends, competitive threats, and possible new opportunities. Traditional channels of market research and new product/service development are unlikely to reveal these possibilities. By putting in place interactive and dialogic engagement processes with stakeholders and scanning the environment systematically, as futurists do, and by incorporating new learning into stakeholder practices, responsible companies can operate with integrity and will be more likely to succeed.

12 VALUE ADDED FOR THE GLOBAL FUTURE

> Imagine a global economy that is healthy and self-governing.
> Imagine markets that are organized to empower people. Imagine
> an economy that is free, humane, competitive, profitable,
> decentralized, non-bureaucratic, and socially accountable.
> Imagine a global economy that operates for the common good,
> a market that develops local-to-global structures to build
> sustainable community.
>> Severyn Bruyn, *A Civil Economy: Transforming the Market*
>> *in the Twenty-First Century*

Severyn Bruyn's prescient statement synthesizes this book's message: companies and societies must prepare for the future in the context of an economy that is sustainable, responsible, equitable, and generative for all. Responsible corporations respect human dignity and the natural ecology that supports it, through a balanced approach to the three spheres of human activity that constitute civilization—economic, political, and civil society. Responsible companies pay attention to their stakeholders and ecological interests and needs, as well as to making money, and make decisions and evaluate their impacts wisely by implementing a consistent vision, values- and value-added approach. Responsible companies "live" responsible enterprise.

Throughout this book, we have presented what we hope is a realistic but forward-looking perspective on how responsible companies can be successful not alongside or separate from but rather within and as part of societies and the natural environment, by engaging in what we can call the New CSR: not just corporate social responsibility (the old framing), but corporate sustainability and responsibility. We have tried to develop this perspective through presentation of the systemic issues both within and external to the firm. Further, we have tried to show the connections between vision, values, and value added that lead to corporate accountability, responsibility, transparency, and sustainability—the ARTS of responsible enterprise.

By recognizing that responsibility and sustainability need to be integrated into all of the organizational strategies and practices that impact stakeholders and the natural environment, companies can discover the power of vision and values to create both value added and meaning for the organization and its stakeholders. In the previous chapter we looked at some of the trends in the macro-environments that will shape tomorrow's business context; these go well beyond the usual concerns about competition and industry dynamics. Indeed, it is in this broader context that businesses must address sustainable practice, resource scarcity, constant connection, and transparency. In this world of changed imperatives, tomorrow's company will not look a lot like today's company—at least if it hopes to be successful and part of a sustainable society. Yet there are still few blueprints to provide guidance, despite the fact that the signs of change are already here. In this final chapter we explore some of the ways in which businesses will need to operate differently if they hope to survive, never mind thrive, in the future.

A WORLD OF COMPLEXITY: COGNITIVE, EMOTIONAL, AND MORAL DEMANDS

One of the clear issues facing enterprise managers and leaders today is the expanding complexity of the world they have to deal with. In addition to the usual competitive and business issues, leaders need to take into account the vast amount of information that is available about the company and its practices to its stakeholders. They have to incorporate sustainability and ecological issues into their business practices. They have to communicate with diverse stakeholders with different interests and needs in a huge variety of outlets—ranging from traditional print and broadcast media to emerging social networking websites, blogs, and other forms of two-way interaction. To be effective, they have to consider the potential impacts of their decisions on employees, communities, investors, suppliers, and customers (at a minimum), and how these stakeholders are likely to react.

This complexity was illustrated strikingly in a 2010 study of CEOs by IBM Corporation entitled "Capitalizing on Complexity." In face-to-face interviews with more than 1,500 CEOs, general managers, and senior public sector leaders of different-sized organizations in sixty countries and thirty-three industries, IBM identified what IBM CEO Samuel J. Palmisano called the "escalation" of complexity facing these executives. The complexity is a direct result of the need for global integration around issues like climate change, energy and water supplies, vulnerabilities in food supply, medicine, and talent supply, and threats to global security. As Palmisano states in his foreword, "We occupy a world that is connected on multiple dimensions, and at a deep level—a global system of systems. That means, among other things, that it is subject to systems-level failures, which require systems-level thinking about the effectiveness of its physical and digital infrastructures."[1]

The IBM study found that there has been a rapid acceleration of such complexity in recent years and that it represents the biggest challenge to executives for the foreseeable future. The CEOs interviewed believe that their organizations are ill-equipped to cope with the level of complexity that already exists, never mind increases in the future. The solution to this problem is creativity as a key leadership competency.[2] The CEOs also believe that successful companies of the future will "co-create" products and services with their key stakeholders, and work to simplify operations and products, while simultaneously increasing dexterity or adaptability.[3] Dealing with the complexity that now exists will require creativity and new ways of thinking, as well as new types of relationships with stakeholders. As the physicist Albert Einstein is frequently quoted as saying, "You cannot solve a problem from the same consciousness that created it. You must learn to see the world anew."

It is, of course, exactly this need to see the world anew and a willingness to make necessary changes that true responsible enterprise and sustainability demand of tomorrow's leaders. They also require significant courage—because stepping out ahead of the pack is risky. Of course, as developmental psychologist Robert Kegan notes, the complexity the IBM study identified and the many demands on leaders today already strain most leaders' capacity to handle them, a situation he noted as being "in over our heads."[4] Michael Mazarr, writing for the Millennium Project discussed in the last chapter, also believes that the knowledge era stretches the limits of human understanding and cognitive capacity. These demands will push the need for many more people to develop higher-level cognitive, moral, and emotional skills. The pace of change, the multiplicity of stakeholders and their numerous demands, and the complexity of coping simultaneously with technology all create the potential for anxiety and alienation.[5]

LOOKING TOWARD A SUSTAINABLE FUTURE: THE CORPORATION 2020 FRAMEWORK

The need for systemic change has become increasingly apparent to many observers of the current system—and one of the entities that may well need to change is the corporation itself. Since responsible enterprise began gaining prominence in the mid-1990s, numerous attempts have been made to enhance corporations' impact on society, and corporations themselves have undertaken many helpful and hopeful initiatives as well. A growing institutional infrastructure for responsibility has focused companies' attention on responsible enterprise in new and evolving ways. Although still inadequate to hold companies accountable given its limited reach and voluntary nature, this emerging system represents a significant advance in corporate accountability and responsibility, although it leaves the current system—and design of the corporation—intact.

But responsible enterprise and sustainability measures alone are insufficient to meet the systemic challenge companies and the rest of us are facing, because the structure of the firm and its current imperatives to economize and maximize shareholder wealth are structurally inappropriate to the planet and humanity's current needs. The needs of the 21st century make it clear that future companies will need to be:

- Far more flexible and adaptive to meet significantly changing social and ecological conditions;
- Interdependent and collaborative with other institutions, stakeholders, societies, and nature;
- Effectively networked with other institutions and organizations in society;
- Relationally oriented to cope effectively with stakeholders, and equitable in their dealings with those stakeholders;
- Willing to actively engage, interact with, and (importantly) share power with other institutions and stakeholders;

- Leaderful—full of leaders throughout the company; and
- Wise and reflective about their own roles, decisions, actions, behaviors, and their consequences—and willing and able to make necessary changes.[6]

Company purposes, strategies, and practices, in other words, are very likely to be broader and more societally and ecologically oriented than is the assumed purpose of corporations today (i.e., to maximize shareholder wealth). Indeed, company purposes might be much more like what early corporate charters demanded—that companies contribute to the betterment of society in order to retain their charters.[7]

Leaving the system intact and current corporate charters unchanged, thus, according to observers Allen White and Marjorie Kelley of the Tellus Institute in Boston, founders of Corporation 2020, an initiative to redesign the corporation, will be insufficient to meet the changing needs of societies and nature in the 21st century. Organizations—particularly responsible companies—of the 21st century will need an explicit new social contract that matches changing public expectations for business's roles in society. Corporation 2020 has articulated the following set of principles on which the multistakeholder coalition that created them believes corporations should be structured—and repurposed:

1. The purpose of the corporation is to harness private interests to serve the public interest.
2. Corporations shall accrue fair returns for shareholders, but not at the expense of the legitimate interests of other stakeholders.
3. Corporations shall operate sustainably, meeting the needs of the present generation without compromising the ability of future generations to meet their needs.
4. Corporations shall distribute their wealth equitably among those who contribute to its creation.
5. Corporations shall be governed in a manner that is participatory, transparent, ethical, and accountable.

6. Corporations shall not infringe on the right of natural persons to govern themselves, nor infringe on other universal human rights.[8]

The conversation about the future purpose of the corporation has just begun; however, people from all around the world, many of them through global action networks (GANs, of which Corporation 2020 is another example), are engaged in such questioning, including business executives participating in initiatives like the World Business Council for Sustainable Development, the World Economic Forum, England's Tomorrow's Company, and the UN Global Compact.

A Different Future for Responsible Companies

One thing seems clear from the work on Corporation 2020, the sustainability and climate change crises, the connectivity that now exists globally, the GFC, and all of the other issues we have covered in earlier chapters: however much some companies and some people might want business-as-usual to continue, at some point the system will change—and probably fairly dramatically. Although we hope that it will not take a major catastrophe (e.g., an ecological meltdown or another global financial crisis) to bring about change, such a catastrophe is certainly possible. Better that companies and their leaders, working in concert with leaders from the other three spheres and organizations concerned about the natural environment, act collectively, interactively, and with foresight to bring this new world into existence. Below we explore briefly some of the implications for companies (and others) of the type of rethinking that has already begun.[9]

From Growth to Well-Being   There is a too often unspoken reality that underlies the need for systemic change, and it fuels the complexities facing business leaders today: the growth model that underlies most business (and other) decision-making today is fundamentally flawed in a resource-constrained world. For all the exponential growth in complexity discussed above, one of the very real risks that at least parts of the world face is what author Jared Diamond called "collapse" —a world in which complex eco- and other systems literally collapse because they are stripped of activity, diversity, and capacity to support living beings.[10]

Generally speaking, "systems" that evolve, such as human beings and the planet itself, become more, rather than less, complex. Yet the overuse of resources strips away the diversity that provides resilience in such systems, leading to the risk of collapse. By definition growth demands ever escalating use of resources that are becoming increasingly scarce, or the more efficient use of resources (which is not happening). The essential risk is that at least parts of the human or ecological system will be pushed beyond some point of no return—toward something less complex and dynamic that cannot sustain the way of life we currently know.

Fully incorporating the emerging paradigm of enterprise responsibility and sustainability into the dominant management paradigm will require radical shifts in the current business model, in power dynamics, and in balance among the three spheres of human activity, which themselves must be put into sustainable relationships with stakeholders and the natural environment. Part of the needed wisdom can derive from principles embedded in nature itself, using what author David Korten terms a "life-centered approach" that taps the wisdom of nature and ecological systems.

Others talk about drawing from nature in various ways, including thinking about the "waste equals food" model of McDonough and Baumgart's Cradle to Cradle approach to product, or Natural Capitalism's similar ecologically based dynamic.[11] Others talk about imitating the processes by which nature produces things to make production processes less resource-intensive and less toxic using an approach called biomimicry.[12] Considering business to be part of rather than separate from the social-ecological-political constellation is also a more ecologically oriented approach to thinking about business that will require significantly changing leaders' mindsets about the role of their companies in the world.[13] Growth in this model is not toward "more," or ever-increasing size, but rather toward greater complexity and mutual survival—toward well-being.

Indeed, because growth itself is the problem in a future where sustainability and mutual responsibility are essential to sheer survival, we humans and businesses may need to rethink our orientation toward competition. We know there is another path, because biologists tell us that nature thrives not with competition alone—but even more important, with the synergistic effects of symbiosis—or, in human terms, collaboration and cooperation. Working with each other, working with the other living beings on the planet to ensure our mutual survival, working collaboratively with stakeholders to co-create new ideas, products, services, and even whole businesses and industries, may well be the path of the future. That is, we need to adopt a significantly more biologically based and collaborative orientation toward developing our businesses, our industries, the products and services that we create in a model that is aimed not at growth, but at synergies, collaboration, and mutual respect.

Well-Being, Plenitude, and Thrivability   There is an alternative underlying premise that might help businesses and humanity deal with the issue of resource overuse, but for many it is not an appealing one because it involves drastically changing the goal of businesses from growth to some conception of well-being. In other words, businesses would move away from business-as-usual and toward a new set of goals and new emphases, away from materialism, consumption, and growth, toward well-being, plenitude, and thrivability.[14]

In a report by the Commission on the Measurement of Economic Performance and Social Progress, Nobel laureates Joseph Stiglitz and Amartya Sen, with Jean-Paul Fitoussi, document the wide intellectual schism that currently exists between measuring wealth and measuring well-being. Standard measures of wealth include variables like growth, inflation, and gross domestic product, none of which actually get at real measures of well-being or human progress.[15] This important study highlighted a number of key issues related to growth and how it is measured: the concepts that are used to measure growth are in question, the notion of per capita may not apply in situations where there are big inequities, and, crucially, commonly used indicators like gross domestic product (GDP) do not capture well-being—and indeed sometimes capture negative impacts and report them as if they were positive. Pointing out that ill-designed measures result in misguided action, they further note that although GDP is the most commonly reported measure, net national product (which includes depreciation) or real household income might be better measures.[16] Others have formulated indicators like the Genuine Progress Indicator or Gross Happiness Indicator to deal with this same issue.

Importantly, the Stiglitz report concludes that it is necessary to move from "measuring economic production to measuring people's well-being" and that it needs to be done in a context of sustainability.[17] The report offers several recommendations for making this critical transition: look at income and consumption, not production, to evaluate material well-being, do so at the household level, and consider income, consumption, and well-being together. The authors further recommend emphasizing income, consumption, and wealth distribution, not just raw numbers, and broadening the income measure to include nonmarket activities such as services that households provide for themselves.[18]

Defining well-being, of course, is important if it is to begin substituting for GDP or the financial wealth indicators currently in use. Well-being has both objective and subjective elements, and both are important. The Stiglitz report offers a multidimensional perspective on what well-being is. In the view of the economists and social scientists who contributed to the report, well-being comprises material living standards (income, consumption, and wealth), health, education, personal activities including work, political voice and governance, social connections and relationship, environment (present and future), and physical and economic security.[19]

For responsible companies, a transition away from growth at all costs—the current paradigm—toward a model of well-being in the future will mean doing business very differently and evaluating performance using very different criteria. Far from simply being measured on maximizing shareholder wealth, companies would be evaluated on the ways in which their products and services actually contribute to (and do not detract from) the quality of life for stakeholders and in the societies where they are doing business, as well as for issues of sustainability. Under such a regime, companies would be judged by how truly sustainable they are. Such questions would be raised as: Are companies replacing renewable resources, and what are they doing to avoid using nonrenewables? Is the waste that is being produced being used as raw material for some other system? Is there equity (not equality) of pay for employees in all types of positions within the firm? Do working conditions and pay scales meet international standards for all employees, no matter where they are? Many other questions dealing with the issues raised earlier would also be part of the consideration of the overall company performance, rather than growth measures.

Ultimately, however, businesses will find ways not just to survive and sustain but actually to thrive under conditions of stability, with well-being—including indicators of health, happiness, and social connections—as the focal goal rather than growth. Juliet Schor points out in her book *Plenitude* that there are already many organizations attempting to develop such ways of thriving without making growth the central goal.[20] Thus, rather than emphasizing growth and profit maximization, central goals for future businesses may well be oriented toward well-being, plenitude (or more-than-adequate sufficiency), and thrivability (going beyond sustainability to thriving while not using excess resources or constantly needing to consume).

An Integrated Stakeholder-Connected ARTS Orientation   As issues of society and ecology have grown more prominent, it has become increasingly clear that the traditional single bottom line of corporations is no longer an adequate assessment of company performance. Just as the growth orientation may have to give way to a more truly ecologically sustainability, even thrivability, model in which companies are judged on how well their activities support society, so too will the ways in which companies report their performance to various stakeholders shift. Indeed, as we have noted, it is already doing so as companies produce a variety of multiple-bottom-line (sustainability, social, ESG) reports.

With more attention to sustainability is also likely to come some form of mandate for integrated reporting, in which what we earlier alluded to as the ARTS of responsible enterprise—accountability, responsibility, transparency, and sustainability—are integrated into a single report with multiple bottom lines. It is not just the multiple-bottom-line reporting that will shift, however. It is also that companies, in paying attention to these multiple bottom lines, will need to shift their focus to the impacts that their activities have on the wide variety of stakeholders with whom they interact, ensuring that those impacts and relationships are solid, productive, and positive—or toward the types of goals discussed in the preceding section, which are related to well-being, plenitude, and thrivability. While such integrated reporting is inherently more complex, it also provides significantly more insight for companies into how the business is actually running, as well as, when coupled with stakeholder engagement processes, potentially better ways of managing the business, finding new opportunities, and ensuring stakeholder satisfaction.

Connected and Engaged   The world of transparency that has been foisted on companies (willingly or not) by digital technologies has also provided new opportunities for companies to engage with the wide variety of stakeholders that can affect or be affected by company activities. In the future, social media and other digital technologies are likely to provide entirely new and unexpected ways for companies to both find out what their stakeholders (customers, investors, employees) are thinking about—and possibly also to get themselves into trouble if they do not handle those relationships well.

The 1990s and early 2000s highlighted the reputational issues caused by supply chain problems, and in a globally connected world dominated by social media, blogs, and other forms of instant communication. Going forward in an even more digitally connected world will require companies to develop and use effectively wholly new forms of stakeholder engagement via social media, interactive blogs, and, of course, in person via multistakeholder engagement processes. For example, new business opportunities can be developed through creative assessment of the concerns of customers, and potential problems could be averted by creative engagement with activists, NGOs, and the media.

Collaborative by Design   Until quite recently, interactions among enterprises in the civil society sphere,[21] the political sphere, and the business/economic sphere have typically been given scant attention in management thought, though a good deal of attention has been paid to strategic alliances among and between businesses. Yet much of what we are discussing suggests that collaboration, perhaps even more than competition (which will still exist, of course), will be the norm of the future. Companies that hope to succeed in the future will be collaborative by design, as well as competitive, imitating their biological brethren in understanding the importance of synergistic interaction in dealing with the important problems they will be facing.

To their credit, many global business leaders have recognized the need to create strategic alliances, multistakeholder engagements, and more cooperative strategies not only with each other but also with governmental and nongovernmental organizations, as the burgeoning in social and tri-sector partnerships around the world attests.[22] Clearly this aspect of the pluralistic global economic and societal situation demands new skills of collaboration and mutual understanding of differences in perspective, culture, and ideology, among other factors, some of which shape the economic and political worlds as well as the relational world of civil society.

The kinds of problems identified in the previous two chapters suggest that old-fashioned single-sector solutions will no longer work. These problems by their nature cross boundaries and are what scholar Russell Ackoff once called "messes," that is, intractable and difficult problems that various organizations, groups, and individuals must work together to resolve. Such unstructured problems require innovation and creativity, placing significant demands on any one organization's knowledge, skills, and resource base, and thus elicit multisector approaches for their solutions.[23] Because they are now frequently the most powerful players on the planet, businesses, particularly large multinational corporations, will have to be engaged in dealing with these issues. For one thing, they depend on the health and well-being of societies in which they operate for much of their business in a globalized economic system. On the other hand, there are significant movements underway to regionalize or localize economies as ways of increasing sustainability, and such movements are also likely to affect the ways in which business is done in the future, also requiring collaborative albeit more local efforts.

Although establishing multisector collaborations is not easy, there is increasing information on some factors that make such collaboration successful. First, there has to be some overriding reason why the actors should work together—a compelling shared vision, a common problem, a crisis to overcome, or a leader everyone wants to work with. Then there need to be ways in which the relevant actors and organizations can be brought together, through networks and alliances, through a "brokering" or mediating enterprise of some sort (e.g., a grant or an organization that plays a mediating role). Finally, there needs to be sufficient mutual education about other stakeholders and their interests, and sufficient benefits to be gained by all to keep these parties, which typically may never interact, working together over time.[24] Companies, as dominant players in many societies, will increasingly be called upon to participate in such collaborative processes—and these types of engagements will place new demands on leaders.

New Types of Enterprise   We have become used to the corporate form of enterprise, especially for large companies, however, the rapid advancement of the BRIC nations, and what economist Joseph Schumpeter called the creative destruction processes[25] going on both inside and outside of companies suggest that there are likely to be many new company forms in the future. Perhaps, in some respects, the corporate form itself will become like dinosaurs—extinct, and be replaced by other forms with different DNA at their start.

We can already see this process of creative destruction beginning to happen in the form of enterprises like Google, which has what could in some respects be considered a public good at its core—access to the world's information! We can see it in the emergence of new forms of enterprise that have yet to gain the dominance of the corporation, but are beginning to grow rapidly. For example, in many of the emerging nations of the world, which are likely to be the dominant economic players in the future, as well as elsewhere, state- or foundation-owned enterprises are common. Because they are not beholden to financial markets for initial funding or share price, they have different imperatives than do traditional publicly owned companies. Many companies also have been taken private through private equity in recent times to avoid the short-termism foisted on them by the way that today's financial markets are structured.

Cooperatives and employee-owned companies represent still other (sometimes corporate) company forms that have different guiding principles. Similarly, a recent phenomenon in the United States has been the development of the for-benefit or B corporation, companies that establish themselves with charters directly oriented toward their stakeholders and multiple bottom lines—so that being responsible and sustainable is built right into their operating principles from the start.

One other development in company forms deserves mention and that is the numerous forms of social enterprise—entities that blend a financial and social (or sustainability) bottom-line orientation. These might be not-for-profit entities that develop a business model to help support their mission. Alternatively, they might be entities that are for-profit but that deeply embed some sort of social mission into their strategies. Micro-enterprises of all sorts might be put into some of these categories (some are for-profit and others nonprofit, but many aim to provide funds for poor people who might not otherwise have access), and in the financial services arena, new forms of financing of small and medium-sized enterprises (SMEs) through micro- and meso-lending are rapidly evolving as well. All of this development indicates that the traditional corporate form as we know it is likely to undergo significant change in the not so distant future.

Metanoia (Shift of Perspective) Needed   As we have seen throughout this book, responsible companies create meaningful visions and underpin those visions with operating practices that result in integrity in all senses of the word. Powerful and meaningful visions create a sense of higher purpose for the enterprise that brings everyone involved into a common vision and helps create a strong internal community and sense of belonging, where all know what they individually have to contribute and how that contribution helps move the vision along. Such visions need to be underscored by constructive values that help stakeholders, employees in particular, know their place in the organization's efforts to make significant contributions to building a better world and a sustainable future. The combination of vision and stakeholder-meaningful values results in the development of responsible day-to-day practices that allow the organization to add value in the by-product of profits and wealth generation. Combined, these ideas mean operating with integrity, sustainability, and responsibility firmly in mind.

We have argued that it is sustainable and responsible companies with these characteristics that will succeed in the complexities, dynamism, and connectedness likely to continue to evolve in the future. They will do so in conversation with their stakeholders and increasingly in accordance with the dictates of nature as sustainability continues to grow in importance. Such firms also incorporate not only objective data and information—that which can be observed—but also the subjective and inter-subjective or more interpretive elements of life, such as aesthetics, emotions, and meaningfulness, into their everyday activities. They understand the need for ecological and community sustainability and are prepared to operate with issues of sustainability fully in mind. Developing responsible corporations that have these attributes calls for nothing less than a shift of mind. Peter Senge calls this shift *metanoia*, which literally means a shift of mind, even transcendence toward a higher purpose.[26]

This metanoia will take responsible companies away from thinking that their actions—as individuals or as organizations—can be taken in isolation. It will move them toward more ecological or systems understanding of embeddedness, interconnectedness, and interdependence. It also will ask them to think about the decisions they make as managers/leaders in an integrated way, that is, not only with their heads but also with their hearts and spirits. It will ask leaders to think about the meaning their decisions and actions have and the meaning embedded in the work that they and others jointly do—and then to create and tell stories that help them to share the meanings with others. It will ask them, in short, to think about the system in which they are embedded and the consequences that their decisions have on others.

This perspective thus asks leaders of and within responsible and sustainable companies to think deeply about the meaning and implications of all of the decisions they are making and what their impact on the world around us is likely to be. Progressive corporations in the context of corporate sustainability and responsibility can do this because they explicitly recognize that there will be impacts and consequences of decisions. They know that all decisions are embedded with a set of values that either honors the relationships and stakeholders they impact or not. They are engaged in ongoing relationships with stakeholders and understand their perspectives, even when they are radically different from the company's internal perspective and even when they may disagree with each other. This metanoia asks firms to seek meaning and meaningfulness in decisions so that everyone can bring his or her whole self—mind, heart, body, spirit—to work (as opposed to checking their brains or heart at the door). It demands mindful rather than mindless action, thought, and decisions from managers who are connected to their hearts as well as their pocketbooks.

The changes in organizations and societies today also demand that leadership be distributed throughout the enterprise rather than held closely in a few top managers' hands. Distributed leadership means taking responsibility for the consequences of one's actions (and thinking through what those consequences are likely to be). It also asks many—most—individuals to assume qualities more like entrepreneurs, self-initiators, and leaders than ever before, to be responsible for their own productive engagement with others and for the results that the decisions they make achieve. Leadership, in this sense, falls to everyone who takes part in bringing to reality the vision embodied in the higher purposes shared by individuals within the enterprise.

Ultimately, this metanoia asks leaders everywhere in enterprise of any sort to seek wisdom and mindfulness in their work as leaders of and within responsible companies.[27] Mindful and wise leaders think through the consequences of their decisions to all of the stakeholders those decisions impact. Mindful leaders are aware that they do not and cannot know all that they need to know, but take seriously the responsibilities—all of them—attendant on their leadership. They continue to grow, learn, develop, and embed learning practices within their enterprises as part of the culture. They seek wisdom, knowing that, in the words of leading management thinker Russell Ackoff:

> *Wisdom is the ability to perceive and evaluate the long-run consequences of behavior.* It is normally associated with a willingness to make short-run sacrifices for the sake of long-run gains.[28]

RESPONSIBILITY AND SUSTAINABILITY

Throughout this book, we discussed a paradigm shift from enterprise responsibility and sustainability to wholly new ways of conceiving the role of business in society. We have taken an optimistic rather than a pessimistic view in suggesting that such a shift is already taking place and will continue to evolve in a constructive and positive direction. Clearly, power and resource inequities exist. Just as clearly, not all corporations behave responsibly or sustainably, pushed by intense competition and demands for shareholder value to economize in sometimes destructive ways.

Why do we believe that this optimistic scenario makes sense? After all, problems abound in the economic, political, and civil society spheres of activity that constitute human civilization—as well as in the natural environment. There is clearly uneven development in different nations of the world, and the world's ecological resources are ever-more strained by the population's demands on nature. Factions in many parts of the world create inequities and growing gaps between rich and poor, between fundamentalists and progressives, between material and more human or spiritual matters. Still, we have attempted to paint a picture of how companies can act if they hope to become responsible and sustainable. We can do this because there are signs that many progressive companies are already beginning to move in that direction.

Responsible enterprise requires wisdom and the leadership to take steps that others view as against the mainstream in a time of turbulence and pressure to perform. It requires courage to be accountable for the consequences of one's actions. Responsible enterprise demands mindfulness and respect for stakeholders, the confidence to engage with them rather than making assumptions about them and their needs.

Is taking this path always easy? No. Is it always more profitable in the short run? No. Will irresponsible competitors still act in aggressive and competitive dog-eat-dog ways to defeat the responsible? Yes. But are companies that act with respect for stakeholders, with consideration for the full impacts of their decisions, with integrity and wisdom, successful? The evidence strongly suggests that the answer is yes.

NOTES

CHAPTER 1

1. Kofi Annan, "Business and the U.N.: A Global Compact of Shared Values and Principles," World Economic Forum, Davos, Switzerland, January 31, 1999, reprinted in *Vital Speeches of the Day* 65, no. 9 (February 1999): 260–61. For further information on the Global Compact, see www.unglobalcompact.org.

2. The classic references are R. Edward Freeman, *Strategic Management: A Stakeholder Approach* (New York: Basic Books, 1984); and William M. Evan and R. Edward Freeman, "A Stakeholder Theory of the Modern Corporation: Kantian Capitalism," in *Ethical Theory and Business*, ed. Tom L. Beauchamp and Norman E. Bowie (Englewood Cliffs, NJ: Prentice Hall, 1998, pp. 75–84). Max Clarkson identifies stakeholders as primary and secondary, depending on the level of risk they have taken with respect to the organization. See Max B. E. Clarkson, "A Stakeholder Framework for Analyzing and Evaluating Corporate Social Performance," *Academy of Management Review* 20, no. 1 (1995): 92–117. Freeman has recently updated the original book. See R. Edward Freeman, Jeffrey Harrison, and Andrew Wicks, *Managing for Stakeholders: Business in the 21st Century* (New Haven, CT: Yale University Press, 2007).

3. Dirk Matten and Andrew Crane, "Corporate Citizenship: Towards an Extended Theoretical Conceptualization," *Academy of Management Review* 30, no.1 (2005): 166–79.

4. See, for example, Bill McKibben, *Eaarth: Making a Life on a Tough New Planet* (New York: Times Books, 2010); James Lovelock, *The Vanishing Face of Gaia: Earth's Climate Crisis and the Fate of Humanity* (New York: Basic Books, 2010); and James G. Speth, *The Bridge at the Edge of the World: Capitalism, the Environment, and Crossing from Crisis to Sustainability* (New Haven, CT: Yale University Press, 2009).

5. These ideas are fully developed in John Cavanagh et al., *Alternatives to Economic Globalization* (San Francisco: Berrett-Koehler, 2002).

6. Matten and Crane, "Corporate Citizenship," 166–79.

7. See the works of Ken Wilber, for example, *A Brief History of Everything* (Boston: Shambhala, 1996); *Eye of the Spirit: An Integral Vision for a World Gone Slightly Mad* (Boston: Shambhala, 1998); and *The Marriage of Sense and Soul: Integrating Science and Reason* (New York: Random House, 1998). For a discussion of the web that constitutes life and the ways in which all matter is interrelated, see Fritjof Capra, *The Web of Life: A New Scientific Understanding of Living Systems* (New York: Anchor Doubleday, 1995).

8. Michael Porter's views on corporate (social) responsibility are characteristic of this perspective. See Michael E. Porter and Mark R. Kramer, "The Competitive Advantage of Philanthropy," *Harvard Business Review* 80, no. 12 (December 2002): 56–69; see also Michael E. Porter and Mark R. Kramer, "Strategy and Society: The Link between Competitive Advantage and Corporate Social Responsibility," *Harvard Business Review* (December 2006): 78–92.

9. Sandra Waddock, "Companies, Academics, and the Progress of Corporate Citizenship," *Business and Society Review* 109 (March 2004): 5–42.

10. Marc Gunther, "Is It Time to Do Away with Corporate Social Responsibility?," July 11, 2011 (http://www.greenbiz.com/print/43391).

11. See "UN Global Compact Annual Review 2010," UN Global Compact, 2011 (http://www.unglobalcompact.org/docs/news_events/8.1/UN_Global_Compact_Annual_Review_2010.pdf).

12. For a discussion of these drivers see Andrew Crane et al., eds., *The Oxford Handbook of Corporate Social Responsibility* (Oxford, UK: Oxford University Press, 2008), particularly the chapters by Diane Swanson, Lloyd Kurtz, and N. Craig Smith, as well as Jeremy Moon and David Vogel.

13. Charles Handy, "What's a Business For?," *Harvard Business Review* (December 2002).

14. See Jeanne M. Logsdon and Donna J. Wood, "Business Citizenship: From Domestic to Global Level Analysis," *Business Ethics Quarterly* 12 (2002): 155–88.

15. See the discussions in Andreas G. Scherer and Guido Palazzo, eds., *Handbook of Research on Global Corporate Citizenship* (Cheltenham, UK: Edward Elgar, 2008).

16. For a discussion of the interrelated nature of corporate responsibility and globalization, see in particular: Andreas G. Scherer, Guido Palazzo, and Dirk Matten, "Introduction to the Special Issue: Globalization as a Challenge for Business Responsibilities," *Business Ethics Quarterly* 19 (2009): 327–47; and also Scherer and Palazzo, "Globalization and Corporate Social Responsibility," in *The Oxford Handbook of Corporate Social Responsibility*, ed. Crane et al., 413–31. Our discussion here is drawn from these analyses.

17. For a comprehensive discussion of the different dimension of globalization, see Jan A. Scholte, *Globalization: A Critical Introduction* (New York: Palgrave Macmillan, 2005).

18. Cavanagh et al., *Alternatives to Economic Globalization*.

19. Eddy Lee and Marco Viverelli, "The Social Impact of Globalization in the Developing Countries," *International Labour Review* 145, no. 3 (2006): 168–83, lay out both the pros and cons of this argument. Information in this paragraph is drawn from this article.

20. See Andreas Rasche and Daniel E. Esser, "From Stakeholder Management to Stakeholder Accountability: Applying Habermasian Discourse Ethics to Accountability Research," *Journal of Business Ethics* 65 (2006): 251–67.

21. Conservation International, "The World's 10 Most Threatened Forest Hotspots," 2011 (http://www.conservation.org/newsroom/pressreleases/Pages/The-Worlds-10-Most-Threatened-Forest-Hotspots.aspx).

22. Philipp H. Pattberg, "The Forest Stewardship Council: Risk and Potential of Private Forest Governance," *Journal of Environmental Development* 14 (2005): 356–74, here 362.

23. For some insight into these topics, start with James Gleick, *Chaos: Making a New Science* (New York: Viking, 1987); Stuart Kauffman, *At Home in the Universe: The Search for the Laws of Self-Organization and Complexity* (New York: Oxford University Press, 1995); Fritjof Capra, *The Web of Life: A New Scientific Understanding of Living Systems* (New York: Anchor Doubleday, 1995); Humberto R. Maturana and Francisco J. Varela, *The Tree of Knowledge: The Biological Roots of Human Understanding*, rev. ed. (Boston: Shambhala, 1998); and of course Peter M. Senge, *The Fifth Discipline: The Art and Practice of the Learning Organization*, rev. ed. (New York: Doubleday, 2006).

24. Senge, *The Fifth Discipline.*

25. The term *holon* is from Arthur Koestler and is extensively developed in Ken Wilber's work. Relevant works by Wilber include *Sex, Ecology, Spirituality: The Spirit of Evolution* (Boston: Shambhala, 1995), *Eye of the Spirit* (Boston: Shambhala, 1997); and *A Brief History of Everything* (Boston: Shambhala, 1996).

26. Thomas N. Gladwin, James J. Kennelly, and Tara-Shelomith Krause, "Shifting Paradigms for Sustainable Development: Implications for Management Theory and Research," *Academy of Management Review* 20, no. 4 (October 1995): 874–907; Fritjof Capra, *The Turning Point: Science, Society, and the Rising Culture* (New York: Bantam Books, 1983); and Margaret J. Wheatley, *Leadership and the New Science: Learning about Organization from an Orderly New Universe* (San Francisco: Berrett-Koehler, 1992).

CHAPTER 2

1. "Vision 2050: The New Agenda for Business, Geneva: WBSCD," World Business Council for Sustainable Development, 2010 (http://www.wbcsd.org/vision2050.aspx).

2. See Richard D'Aveni, *Hyper-Competition: Managing the Dynamics of Strategic Maneuvering* (New York: Free Press, 1994).

3. Gretchen C. Daily, Anne H. Ehrlich, and Paul R. Ehrlich, "Optimum Human Population Size," *Population and Environment* 15, no. 6 (1994): 469–75.

4. James Lovelock, *The Vanishing Face of Gaia: A Final Warning* (New York: Basic Books, 2010).

5. For a marvelous and accessible description of the interconnectedness of living and material entities, see Fritjof Capra, *The Web of Life: A New Scientific Understanding of Living Systems* (New York: Anchor Doubleday, 1995).

6. Andreas G. Scherer, Guido Palazzo, and Dorothée Baumann, "Global Rules and Private Actors: Towards a New Role of the TNC in Global Governance," *Business Ethics Quarterly* 16 (2006): 502–32.

7. William C. Frederick, *Values, Nature, and Culture in the American Corporation* (New York: Oxford University Press, 1995). Much of the discussion in this section is adapted from Frederick; however, the application to other spheres is that of the present authors.

8. Ibid., 92.

9. Ibid., 9.

10. See, for example, William McDonough and Michael Braungart, *Cradle to Cradle: Remaking the Way We Make Things* (New York: North Point Press, 2002); and Paul Hawken, Amory Lovens, and L. Hunter Lovens, *Natural Capitalism: Creating the Next Industrial Revolution* (Boston: Little, Brown, 1999).

11. Nel Noddings, *Caring: A Feminine Approach to Ethics and Moral Education* (Berkeley: University of California Press, 1984).

12. Frederick, *Values, Nature, and Culture*, 201–3.

13. These figures are updated from work in 2000 and 2004 by Sarah Anderson and John Cavanagh, *Top 200: The Rise of Corporate Global Power* (Washington, DC: Institute for Policy Studies, 2000).

14. Frederick, *Values, Nature, and Culture*, 28.

15. C. K. Prahalad and Allen Hammond, "Serving the World's Poor Profitably," *Harvard Business Review* 80, no. 9 (September 2002): 48–57.

16. See also C. K. Prahalad, *The Fortune at the Bottom of the Pyramid: Eradicating Poverty through Profits* (New Delhi: Pearson Education / Wharton School Publishing, 2005).

17. Ibid.

18. Aneel Karnani, "Mirage at the Bottom of the Pyramid: How the Private Sector Can Help Alleviate Poverty," *California Management Review* 49, no. 4 (Summer 2007): 90–111.

19. Ibid.

20. Ibrahim M. Badawi and Adrian P. Fitzsimons, "Sarbanes-Oxley Act and SEC Proposals Address Corporate Responsibility," *Bank Accounting and Finance* (October 2002): 30–35.

21. See Kent Greenfield, "A New Era for Corporate Law: Using Corporate Governance to Benefit All Stakeholders," *Paper Series on Corporate Design: Summit on the Future of the Corporation* (2007): 19–28 (http://www.corporation2020.org/SummitPaperSeries.pdf); and Kent Greenfield, "New Principles for Corporate Law," *Hastings Business Law Journal* 1 (May 2007): 87–118.

22. Charles Derber, *Corporation Nation: How Corporations Are Taking Over Our Lives and What We Can Do about It* (New York: St. Martin's Press, 1998), 122. Derber's ideas are used in this paragraph.

23. Supreme Court of the United States, *Citizens United v Federal Election Commission*, 2010 (http://www.supremecourt.gov/opinions/09pdf/08-205.pdf).

24. Cogent and articulate explanations of free-market capitalism and critiques of neoclassical assumptions can be found in a number of sources, including Derber, *Corporation Nation* (New York: St. Martin's Press, 1998); David C. Korten, *When Corporations Rule the World* (San Francisco: Berrett-Koehler, 1995); David Korten, *The Post-Corporate World: Life after Capitalism* (San Francisco: Berrett-Koehler, 1999); and Lee E. Preston and James E. Post, *Private Management and Public Policy* (New York: Prentice Hall, 1975). This section is consolidated from these texts and general understanding.

25. See Korten, *The Post-Corporate World*, 37–63; and Derber, *Corporation Nation*, 118–36.

26. Dominic Barton, "Capitalism for the Long Term," *Harvard Business Review* (March 2011) (http://hbr.org/2011/03/capitalism-for-the-long-term/ar/pr).

27. Charles Handy, "What's a Business For?," *Harvard Business Review* (December 2002): 49–55.

28. Korten, *The Post-Corporate World*, 51–59.

29. Robert B. Reich, *Supercapitalism: The Transformation of Business, Democracy, and Everyday Life* (New York: Knopf, 2007).

30. One interesting perspective on this can be found in James Moore, *The Death of Competition: Leadership and Strategy in the Age of Business Ecosystems* (New York: HarperBusiness, 1996).

31. Robert Reich, a secretary of labor in the Clinton administration and now professor of public policy at University of California, Berkeley, coined this term in a *New York Times* op-ed column on May 23, 1980; see http://robertreich.org/post/491676652/ the-paper-entrepreneurs-are-winning-over-the-product.

32. Robert Reich, "Lincoln to the Rescue," May 11, 2010 (http://robertreich.org/ post/591266284/lincoln-to-the-rescue).

33. See "Report of the Commission on the Measurement of Economic Performance and Social Progress" (the Stiglitz Commission), http://www.stiglitz-sen-fitoussi.fr/en /index.htm.

34. Joseph Stiglitz, "Moral Bankruptcy," *Mother Jones* (January–February 2010) (http://motherjones.com/politics/2010/01/joseph-stiglitz-wall-street-morals); see also Joseph Stiglitz, *Freefall: America, Free Markets, and the Sinking of the World Economy* (New York: Norton, 2010).

35. Matthew Goldstein, "JP Morgan Buys Bear on the Cheap," *BusinessWeek*, March 16, 2008 (http://www.businessweek.com/bwdaily/dnflash/content/mar2008 /db20080316_356646.htm).

36. Ibid.

37. "Subprime Mortgage Collapse: Why Bear Stearns Is Just the Start," *Money Week*, May 7, 2007, updated March 2008 (http://www.moneyweek.com/file/31699/subprime -mortgage-collapse-why-bear-stearns-is-just-the-start.html).

38. U.S. House of Representatives, "The Causes and Effects of the Lehman Brothers Bankruptcy," 2008 (https://house.resource.org/110/org.c-span.281618–1.raw.txt).

39. See "The Story of Stuff" (www.storyofstuff.org), a twenty-minute video that illustrates this linearity and its lack of sustainability.

40. Supreme Court, *Citizens United v Federal Election Commission*.

41. A summary of the Dodd-Frank bill can be found at http://banking.senate.gov/ public/_files/FinancialReformSummary231510FINAL.pdf.

42. Preston and Post, *Private Management and Public Policy*, 56.

43. Ibid.

44. See, for example, Dirk Matten and Andrew Crane, "Corporate Citizenship: Towards an Extended Theoretical Conceptualization," *Academy of Management Review* 30, no. 1 (2005): 166–79; Dirk Matten, Andrew Crane, and Wendy Chapple, "Behind the Mask: Revealing the True Face of Corporate Citizenship," *Journal of Business Ethics* 45, no. 1–2 (2003): 109–21; Andreas G. Scherer, Guido Palazzo, and Dorothée Baumann, "Global Rules and Private Actors—Towards a New Role of the TNC in the Global Governance," *Business Ethics Quarterly* 16, no. 4 (2006): 404–532; Andreas G. Scherer and Guido Palazzo, "Globalization and Corporate Social Responsibility," in *Oxford Handbook of Corporate Social Responsibility*, ed. Andrew Crane et al. (Oxford, UK: Oxford University Press, 2007).

45. See Steve Waddell, *Global Action Networks: Creating Our Future Together* (Hampshire, England: Palgrave-Macmillan, 2010). For more information about Global Action Networks, see http://www.networkingaction.net/.

46. Numerous other examples can be found at http://www.gan-net.net/, ibid.

47. SustainAbility, *Influencing Policy: Reviewing the Conduct and Content of Corporate Lobbying* (London: SustainAbility and World Wildlife Foundation, 2005) (http://www.csr-weltweit.de/uploads/tx_jpdownloads/SustainAbility-WWF_Influencing_power.pdf, 3).

48. Reich, *Supercapitalism*, 157–67.

49. Ibid., 161.

50. Ibid.

51. This definition is adapted from Steven L. Wartick and John F. Mahon, "Toward a Substantive Definition of the Corporate Issue Construct: A Review and Synthesis of the Literature," *Business and Society* 33, no. 3 (December 1994): 293–311. Wartick and Mahon discuss a corporate issue, while the discussion here focuses on public issues more generally and a broad range of stakeholder interests.

52. The public issue life cycle as outlined here is discussed in James E. Post, *Corporate Behavior and Social Change* (Reston, VA: Reston Publishing, 1978); and John F. Mahon and Sandra Waddock, "Strategic Issues Management: An Integration of Issue Life Cycle Perspectives," *Business & Society* 31, no. 1 (Spring 1992): 19–32. See also Henry A. Tombari, *Business and Society: Strategies for the Environment and Public Policy* (New York: Dryden Press, 1984), for an original discussion of the public issue life cycle used in Mahon and Waddock's article.

53. This example is used in Post, *Corporate Behavior*.

54. Ibid., 23.

55. For more information, see http://www.un.org/esa/sustdev/documents/agenda21/index.htm.

56. See Mahon and Waddock, "Strategic Issues Management."

57. See, for example, the entry "Non-Governmental Organizations" in Thomas M. Leonard, *Encyclopedia of the Developing World* (New York: Taylor & Francis, 2006).

58. Alan Wolfe, "Is Civil Society Obsolete? Revisiting Predictions of the Decline of Civil Society, in 'Whose Keeper?,'" *Brookings Review* 15, no. 4 (Fall 1997): 9–12.

59. Alan Wolfe, *Whose Keeper? Social Science and Moral Obligation* (Berkeley: University of California Press, 1989).

60. Frederick, *Values, Nature, and Culture*.

61. This paragraph is based in part on Karen Penner, "The Ties That Lead to Prosperity," *Business Week*, December 15, 1997, 153–55.

62. Jean B. Elshtain, "Not a Cure-All," *Brookings Review* 15, no. 4 (Fall 1997): 13–15.

63. See Global Footprint Network at http://www.footprintnetwork.org/en/index.php/GFN/page/footprint_basics_overview/.

64. "Intergovernmental Panel on Climate Change, Fourth Assessment Report, Climate Change 2007," (http://www.ipcc.ch/pdf/assessment-report/ar4/syr/ar4_syr_spm.pdf). Information in this paragraph is taken from this report.

65. The Natural Step's U.S. website is http://www.naturalstep.org/en/usa, and the organization's main website is http://www.naturalstep.org/en.

66. Brundtland Commission, "Our Common Future: Report of the World Commission on Environment and Development," 1987 (http://www.un.org/documents/ga/res/42/ares42–187.htm, 24).

67. Thomas N. Gladwin, James J. Kennelly, and Tara-Shelomith Krause, "Shifting Paradigms for Sustainable Development: Implications for Management Theory and Research," *Academy of Management Review* 20, no. 4 (1995): 874–907.

68. U.S. President's Council on Sustainable Development, quoted in Gladwin, Kennelly, and Krause, "Shifting Paradigms for Sustainable Development." Much of the discussion in these paragraphs is based on this article.

69. For a more in-depth discussion of the relationship between child labor and climate change, see Save the Children, *Feeling the Heat: Child Survival in a Changing Climate* (London: Save the Children, 2009).

70. These terms are developed in Gladwin, Kennelly, and Krause, "Shifting Paradigms."

71. Peter M. Senge, *The Fifth Discipline: The Art and Practice of the Learning Organization*, rev. ed. (New York: Doubleday, 2006).

72. Gregory Dees, "The Meaning of Social Entrepreneurship" working paper (Palo Alto, CA: Stanford University, 1998), here p. 4.

73. For background on the difference makers and the infrastructure that they build, see Sandra Waddock, *The Difference Makers: How Social and Institutional Entrepreneurs Built the Corporate Responsibility Movement* (Sheffield, UK: Greenleaf, 2008).

74. For detailed information on the Grameen-Danone social business joint venture, see Muhammed Yunus, *Creating a World without Poverty: Social Business and the Future of Capitalism* (New York: Public Affairs, 2008).

75. Data according to the World Bank Group (see http://data.worldbank.org/country/bangladesh for more information).

76. Paul Tracy and Nelson Phillips, "The Distinctive Challenge of Educating Social Entrepreneurs: A Postscript and Rejoinder to the Special Issue on Entrepreneurship Education," *Academy of Management Learning and Education* 6, no. 2 (2007): 264–71.

CHAPTER 3

1. Peter M. Senge, "Systems Citizenship: The Leadership Mandate for this Millennium," *Leader to Leader* 41 (Summer 2006) (http://www.leadertoleader.org/knowledgecenter/L2L/summer2006/senge.html/).

2. Peter M. Senge, *The Fifth Discipline: The Art and Practice of the Learning Organization*, rev. ed. (New York: Doubleday, 2006). Further definitions and multiple exercises to help develop a vision can be found in Peter M. Senge et al., *The Fifth Discipline Fieldbook: Strategies and Tools for Building a Learning Organization* (New York: Currency Doubleday, 1994).

3. See James C. Collins and Jerry I. Porras, *Built to Last: Successful Habits of Visionary Companies* (New York: HarperBusiness, 1994). See also James C. Collins and Jerry I. Porras, "Building Your Company's Vision," *Harvard Business Review* (September–October 1996): 65–77.

4. These outcomes of vision are derived from Senge, *The Fifth Discipline*, 207–11.

5. Joseph A. Raelin, *Creating Leaderful Organizations: How to Bring Out Leadership in Everyone* (San Francisco: Berrett-Koehler, 2003).

6. See Ken Wilber, *Sex, Ecology, Spirituality: The Spirit of Evolution* (Boston: Shambhala, 1995); Frans de Waal, *Good Natured: The Origins of Right and Wrong in Humans and Other Animals* (Cambridge, MA: Harvard University Press, 1996).

7. This said, de Waal, in *Good Natured*, does present evidence that some members of the primate group other than humans may have a degree of self-consciousness.

8. See, for example, Edward O. Wilson, *Consilience: The Unity of Knowledge* (New York: Alfred A. Knopf, 1998); and de Waal, *Good Natured*.

9. Humberto R. Maturana and Francisco J. Varela, *The Tree of Knowledge: The Biological Roots of Human Understanding*, rev. ed. (Boston: Shambhala, 1998).

10. de Waal, *Good Natured*, 67.

11. Ibid. See also William C. Frederick, *Values, Nature, and Culture in the American Corporation* (New York: Oxford University Press, 1995).

12. See Russell L. Ackoff, "On Learning and Systems That Facilitate It," *Center for Quality of Management Journal* 5, no. 2 (1996): 14.

13. Ibid.

14. We focus here mainly on three domains: cognitive (personality and social) development, moral development, and emotional development.

15. See, for example, Howard Gardner, *Frames of Mind* (New York: Basic Books, 1983); Howard Gardner, *Creating Minds* (New York: Basic Books, 1994); Jean Piaget, *The Psychology of the Child* (New York: Wiley, 1969); Lawrence Kohlberg, Charles Levine, and Alexandra Hewer, *Moral Stages: A Current Formulation and a Response to Critics*, (Basel: Karger, 1983); and Wilber, *Sex, Ecology, Spirituality*.

16. Some people criticize developmental theorists because their position that later stages are "better" than earlier stages seems elitist. In the sense that later stages supersede and encompass the earlier stages in the nesting fashion described in the text, this criticism has some foundation. We do not wish to engage in a debate here about developmental theory, but there is evidence that such nesting occurs. Each developmental stage incorporates a richer and more complex understanding than the previous stages, allowing the developing human being to consider more perspectives simultaneously. It is in this sense that human beings have a more developed sense of consciousness and are thus considered morally superior to animals. Wilber points out in *Sex, Ecology, Spirituality* that there is more "depth" of understanding (or complexity) at later stages of development, while there is more "span" or breadth at earlier stages.

17. Kohlberg, et al. "Moral Stages," 34.

18. Ibid., 33.

19. Ibid.

20. See, for example, Robert Kegan, *The Evolving Self: Problem and Process in Human Development* (Cambridge, MA: Harvard University Press, 1982); and particularly, for the argument about modern complexity, Robert Kegan, *In Over Our Heads: The Mental Demands of Modern Life* (Cambridge, MA: Harvard University Press, 1994).

21. William R. Torbert et al., *Action Inquiry: The Secret of Timely and Transforming Leadership* (San Francisco: Berrett-Koehler, 2004).

22. These ideas are elaborated in Sandra Waddock, "Leadership Integrity in a Fractured Knowledge World," *Academy of Management Learning and Education* 6, no. 4 (2007): 543–57. See also Joseph A. Raelin, *Creating Leaderful Organizations: How to Bring Out Leadership in Everyone* (San Francisco: Berrett-Koehler, 2003) and Torbert et al., *Action Inquiry*.

23. Torbert et al., *Action Inquiry*.

24. See ibid. See also William R. Torbert, *The Power of Balance: Transforming Self, Society, and Scientific Inquiry* (Newbury Park, CA: Sage, 1991).

25. William Isaacs, *Dialogue and the Art of Thinking Together* (New York: Doubleday Currency, 1999).

26. Kohlberg, et al. "Moral Stages." Much of this section draws from this book.

27. Thomas Donaldson and Thomas W. Dunfee, *Ties That Bind: A Social Contracts Approach to Business Ethics* (Boston: Harvard Business School Press, 1999).

28. Carol Gilligan, *In a Different Voice: Psychological Theory and Women's Development* (Cambridge, MA: Harvard University Press, 1982).

29. Kohlberg, et al. "Moral Stages," 48–50.

30. Daniel Goleman, *Emotional Intelligence* (New York: Bantam Books, 1995); Daniel Goleman, "The Emotional Intelligence of Leaders," *Leader to Leader* 10 (Fall 1998): 20–26.

31. Goleman, *Emotional Intelligence*. See also Daniel Goleman, *Working with Emotional Intelligence* (New York: Bantam Books, 1998). This section is drawn largely from Goleman's writings.

32. Kurt Matzler, Franz Bailom, and Todd A. Mooradian, "Intuitive Decision Making," *MIT Sloan Management Review* 49, no. 1 (Fall 2007): 13–15, p. 13.

33. Goleman, *Emotional Intelligence*, 56; Senge, *The Fifth Discipline*, 139ff.

34. Senge, *The Fifth Discipline*, 141.

35. Coca-Cola Company, "2009/2010 Sustainability Review" (http://www.thecoca-colacompany.com/citizenship/pdf/SR09/2009–2010_The_Coca-Cola_Company_Sustainability_Review.pdf).

36. Ratheesh Kaliyadan, "India: Coca-Cola Swallows Villagers Fresh Water," *GreenLeft*, May 22, 2002 (http://www.greenleft.org.au/back/2002/493/493p20.htm).

37. Amit Srivastava, "Coca Cola Misleading Public on Water Issues," *India Resource Center* (http://www.indiaresource.org/news/2006/1045.html).

38. Trevor Datson, "Coca Cola Admits That Dasani Is Nothing but Tap Water," *Common Dreams Newscenter*, March 4, 2004 (http://www.commondreams.org/cgi-bin/print.cgi?file=/headlines04/0304–04.htm).

39. Anthony France, "Coca Cola Recalls Water," *Sydney Morning Herald Online*, March 22, 2004 (http://www.smh.com.au/articles/2004/03/21/1079823239704.html?from=storyrhs&oneclick=true).

40. Coca-Cola Company, "Coca Cola Pledges to Replace the Water It Uses in Its Beverages and Their Production" (http://www.thecoca-colacompany.com/presscenter/nr_20070605_tccc_and_wwf_partnership.html).

41. Coca-Cola Company, "Mission, Vision & Values" (http://www.thecoca-colacompany.com/ourcompany/mission_vision_values.html).

42. "Our Water Conservation Goal," Coca-Cola Company (http://www.thecoca-colacompany.com/citizenship/water_pledge.html).

43. Jaepil Choi, "A Motivational Theory of Charismatic Leadership: Envisioning, Empathy, and Empowerment," *Journal of Leadership & Organizational Studies (Baker College)* 13, no. 1 (Summer 2006): 24–43.

44. Goleman, *Emotional Intelligence*, chap. 10.

45. Ibid., 194.

46. Senge, *The Fifth Discipline*; Stephen R. Covey, *The 7 Habits of Highly Effective People* (New York: Free Press, 1990).

47. Lawrence Kohlberg, "Moral Stages and Moralization: The Cognitive-Developmental Approach," in *Moral Development and Behavior: Theory, Research, and Social Issues*, ed. Thomas Lickona, Gilbert Geis, and Lawrence Kohlberg (New York: Holt, Rinehart and Winston, 1976).

48. Frame analysis is elaborated in Donald A. Schön and Martin Rein, *Frame Reflection: Toward the Resolution of Intractable Policy Controversies* (New York: Basic Books, 1994).

49. James C. Collins and Jerry I. Porras, *Built to Last: Successful Habits of Visionary Companies*, rev. ed. (New York: HarperBusiness, 2002).

50. Rajendra S. Sisodia, David B. Wolfe, and Jagdish N. Sheth, *Firms of Endearment: How World-Class Companies Profit from Passion and Purpose* (Upper Saddle River, NJ: Wharton School Publishing, 2007).

51. Ibid.

52. Procter & Gamble (http://www.pg.com/en_US/sustainability/environmental_sustainability/index.shtml).

53. Sara Harald, "The P&G Sustainability Vision: Reluctant Response or Strategic Shift" (http://www.triplepundit.com/2010/10/the-pg-sustainability-vision-reluctant-response-or-strategic-shift/).

54. Sisodia, Wolfe, and Sheth, *Firms of Endearment.*

55. See Philip Mirvis and Bradley Googins, "Stages of Corporate Citizenship." *California Management Review* 48, no. 2 (2006): 104–26. The framework suggested by Mirvis and Googins rests on the concept of "corporate citizenship," but we think that it applies equally in the context of corporate responsibility and responsible enterprise. Chapter 1 discusses the differences between the terms.

CHAPTER 4

1. See, for example, Ken Wilber, *A Brief History of Everything* (Boston: Shambhala, 1996).

2. James M. Burns, *Leadership* (New York: Harper Torchbooks, 1978), 74–76.

3. Ibid., 75.

4. James C. Collins and Jerry I. Porras, *Built to Last: Successful Habits of Visionary Companies* (New York: HarperBusiness, 1997).

5. Burns, *Leadership.*

6. See UN Global Compact's website at www.unglobalcompact.org.

7. The OECD Guidelines for Multinational Enterprises and other information can be found at www.oecd.org/daf/investment/guidelines.

8. See Business and Human Rights Resource Centre, at http://www.business-humanrights.org/SpecialRepPortal/Home.

9. Jerry Useem, "Should We Admire Wal-Mart?" *Fortune*, March 8, 2004, 118.

10. See CNN Money, "World's Most Admired Companies (http://money.cnn.com/magazines/fortune/mostadmired/2011/full_list/).

11. See Wal-Mart, "Three Basic Beliefs and Values" (http://walmartstores.com/AboutUs/321.aspx).

12. Jeffrey E. Garten, "Wal-Mart Gives Globalism a Bad Name," *Business Week,* March 8, 2004.

13. See NPR, "Supreme Court Limits Wal-Mart's Discrimination Case" (http://www.npr.org/2011/06/20/137296721/supreme-court-limits-wal-mart-discrimination-case); see also Newsmax.com, "Wal-Mart Faces Class-Action Lawsuit" (http://archive.newsmax.com/archives/articles/2007/2/6/130433.shtml).

14. Garten, "Wal-Mart."

15. See R. Edward Freeman and Daniel R. Gilbert Jr., *Corporate Strategy and the Search for Ethics* (Englewood Cliffs, NJ: Prentice Hall, 1988). Freeman rearticulated this concept of enterprise strategy in a 2007 revision of his class stakeholder book, R. Edward Freeman, Jeffrey Harrison, and Andrew Wicks, *Managing for Stakeholders: Business in the 21st Century* (New Haven, CT: Yale University Press, 2007).

16. See, for example, Robert C. Solomon, *A Better Way to Think about Business: How Personal Integrity Leads to Corporate Success* (New York: Oxford University Press, 1999).

17. This section draws in large part on an article by Jeanne Liedtka, "Constructing an Ethic for Business Practice: Competing Effectively and Doing Good," *Business and Society* 37, no. 3 (September 1998): 254–80.

18. Ibid.

19. See Collins and Porras, *Built to Last.*

20. Alisdair MacIntyre, *After Virtue* (Notre Dame, IN: University of Notre Dame Press, 1981).

21. Liedtka, "Constructing an Ethic," 260.

22. For an interesting analysis, see Jane W. Gibson and Dana V. Tesone, "Management Fads: Emergence, Evolution, and Implications for Managers," *Academy of Management Executive* 15, no. 4 (2001): 122–33.

23. The learning organization concept was popularized by Peter M. Senge, *The Fifth Discipline: The Art and Practice of the Learning Organization*, rev. ed. (New York: Currency Doubleday, 2006).

24. The seminal book is W. Edwards Deming, *Out of the Crisis* (Cambridge, MA: MIT Center for Advanced Engineering Study, 1982). Numerous books exist on total quality management.

25. The popular book on this topic is Michael Hammer and James Champy, *Re-Engineering the Corporation: A Manifesto for Business Revolution* (New York: HarperBusiness, 1993).

26. William C. Frederick, *Values, Nature, and Culture in the American Corporation* (New York: Oxford University Press, 1995).

27. See Michael Novak, *Business as a Calling: Work and the Examined Life* (New York: Free Press, 1996).

28. See Freeman and Gilbert, *Corporate Strategy.*

29. See Sandra Waddock, "Linking Community and Spirit: A Commentary and Some Propositions," *Journal of Organizational Change Management* 12, no. 4 (1999): 332–44.

30. See Henry Mintzberg, *The Rise and Fall of Strategic Planning* (New York: Free Press, 1994); or "The Fall and Rise of Strategic Planning," *Harvard Business Review* (January–February 1994): 107–14; and Senge, *The Fifth Discipline.*

31. For a discussion of continual, as opposed to continuous, improvement in the context of quality management and personal growth, see Dalmar Fisher and William R. Torbert, *Personal and Organizational Transformations: The True Challenge of Continual Quality Improvement* (London: McGraw-Hill, 1995).

32. See Waddock, "Linking Community and Spirit."

33. Stan Davis and Christopher Meyer discuss this at some length in *Blur: The Speed of Change in the Connected Economy* (Reading, MA: Addison-Wesley, 1998).

34. The term *good conversation* was developed by James A. Waters and published in Frederick R. Bird and James A. Waters, "The Moral Muteness of Managers," *California Management Review* (Fall 1989): 73–88.

35. Chris Argyris focuses on "undiscussability" in *Knowledge for Action: A Guide to Overcoming Barriers to Organizational Change* (San Francisco: Jossey-Bass, 1993). See also Bird and Waters, "Moral Muteness."

36. This section is based on the discussion in Sandra Waddock, "Creating Corporate Accountability: Foundational Principles to Make Corporate Citizenship Real," *Journal of Business Ethics* 50 (2004): 313–27.

37. Thomas Donaldson began developing these ideas in *The Ethics of International Business* (New York: Oxford University Press, 1992) and moved them forward in "Values in Tension: Ethics Away from Home," *Harvard Business Review* (September–October 1996): 1–12. He wrote about hypernorms with Thomas W. Dunfee in "Toward a Unified Conception of Social Contracts Theory," *Academy of Management Review* 19, no. 2 (1994): 252–84; and *Ties That Bind: A Social Contracts Approach to Business Ethics* (Boston: Harvard Business School Press, 1999).

38. Donaldson and Dunfee, "Toward a Unified Conception," 265.

39. S. Prakash Sethi, "Globalization and the Good Corporation: A Need for Proactive Co-existence," *Journal of Business Ethics* 43, no. 1/2 (2003), 21–31.

40. Donaldson, "Values in Tension," 6.

41. Ibid., 7–8.

42. Donaldson and Dunfee, *Ties That Bind*, 68.

43. Laura P. Hartman, Bill Shaw, and Rodney Stevenson, "Exploring the Ethics and Economics of Global Labor Standards: A Challenge to Integrated Social Contract Theory," *Business Ethics Quarterly* 13, no. 2 (April 2003), 193–225.

44. Frederick, *Values, Nature, and Culture.*

45. This case discussion relies on the following resources: Clay Chandler, "Inside the Great Firewall of China," *Fortune*, March 6, 2006; Gemme van Hesselt, "Google Losing Its Market Share in China," *Search Engine Journal*, September 21, 2006 (http://www.searchenginejournal.com/google-losing-market-share-in-china/3816/); Clive Thomp-

son, "Google's China Problem (and China's Google Problem)," *New York Times*, April 23, 2006.

46. Andrew McLaughlin, "Google in China." *The Official Google Blogspot*, posted January 27, 2006, http://googleblog.blogspot.com/2006/01/google-in-china.html.

47. Collins and Porras, *Built to Last*; Sisodia, Wolfe, and Sheth, *Firms of Endearment*.

48. Immanuel Kant, *Groundwork of the Metaphysics of Morals* (New York: H. J. Paton, 1964).

49. The decision-making framework is summarized in Gerald F. Cavanagh, *American Business Values: A Global Perspective* (Upper Saddle River, NJ: Prentice Hall, 2005). Much of the discussion in this section is adapted from either this book or one of the following articles: Manuel Velasquez, Dennis J. Moberg, and Gerald F. Cavanagh, "Organizational Statesmanship and Dirty Politics: Ethical Guidelines for the Organizational Politician," *Organizational Dynamics* (Autumn 1983): 65–80; Gerald F. Cavanagh, Dennis J. Moberg, and Manuel Velasquez, "The Ethics of Organizational Politics," *Academy of Management Review* 6, no. 3 (1981): 363–74; and Gerald F. Cavanagh, Dennis J. Moberg, and Manuel Velasquez, "Making Business Ethics Practical," *Business Ethics Quarterly* 5, no. 3 (July 1995): 399–418.

50. Cavanagh, *American Business Values*.

51. Ibid.

52. Ibid.; and John Rawls, *A Theory of Justice* (Cambridge, MA: Harvard University Press, 1971).

53. Rawls, *Theory of Justice*.

54. See Carol Gilligan, *In a Different Voice: Psychological Theory and Women's Development* (Cambridge, MA: Harvard University Press, 1982). For an extension of this work into cognitive domains, see also Mary F. Belenky et al., *Women's Ways of Knowing: The Development of Self, Voice, and Mind* (New York: Basic Books, 1986).

55. This difference became clear on a visit to the Boston College Center for Corporate Citizenship by a contingent of Japanese businessmen representing the Kaneiren, the Kansai Economic Federation of Japan in September 2000.

56. The five cultural differences discussed here are based on Mary O'Hara-Devereaux and Robert Johansen, *GlobalWork: Bridging Distance, Culture and Time* (San Francisco: Jossey-Bass, 1994). O'Hara-Devereaux and Johansen in turn draw from Edward T. Hall and Mildred Reed Hall, *Understanding Cultural Differences: Germans, French, and Americans* (Yarmouth, ME: Intercultural Press, 1990), and Geert Hofstede, *Cultures and Organizations: Software of the Mind* (London: McGraw-Hill, 1991).

57. See Robert B. Reich, *Supercapitalism: The Transformation of Business, Democracy, and Everyday Life* (New York: Knopf, 2007); and Corporation 2020 (www.corporation2020.org).

58. For an interesting perspective on the concept of presence, see Peter M. Senge et al., *Presence: Human Purpose and the Field of the Future* (Boston: Society for Organizational Learning, 2004).

CHAPTER 5

1. Jed Emerson, "The Blended Value Proposition: Integrating Social and Financial Returns," *California Management Review* 45, no. 4 (Summer 2003): 35–38.

2. John Elkington introduced the concept of the triple bottom line in *Cannibals with Forks: The Triple Bottom Line of Sustainability* (Gabriola Island, B.C., Canada: New Society Publishers, 1998).

3. Emerson, "The Blended Value Proposition."

4. William McDonough and Michael Braungart, *Cradle to Cradle: Remaking the Way We Make Things* (New York: North Point Press, 2002).

5. See, for example, Robert Costanza et al., "Beyond GDP: The Need for New Measures of Progress," *The Pardee Papers* no. 4 (January 2009): 7.

6. Quoted in ibid.

7. Happy Planet Index (http://www.happyplanetindex.org/learn/). 8. See ibid.; and Happy Planet Index (http://www.happyplanetindex.org/explore/global/index.html).

9. Redefining Progress, Genuine Progress Indicator (http://www.rprogress.org/sustainability_indicators/genuine_progress_indicator.htm). This website appears to have shut down, but information on the GPI is available at http://www.wordiq.com/definition/Genuine_Progress_Indicator.

10. Ibid.

11. Robert B. Reich, *Supercapitalism: The Transformation of Business, Democracy, and Everyday Life* (New York: Knopf, 2007).

12. Jordi Surroca, Josep A. Tribó, and Sandra Waddock, "Corporate Responsibility and Financial Performance: The Role of Intangible Resources," *Strategic Management Journal* 31, no. 5 (2010): 463–90.

13. Some studies have shown a slightly positive relationship generally between social and financial performance; see, for example, the metastudy by Marc Orlitzky, Frank L. Schmidt, and Sara L. Rynes, "Corporate Social and Financial Performance: A Meta-Analysis," *Organization Studies* 24 (2003): 403–41; and the analysis by Joshua D. Margolis and James P. Walsh, "Misery Loves Companies: Rethinking Social Initiatives by Business," *Administrative Science Quarterly* 48 (2003): 268–305, while a more recent meta-analysis of 167 studies, still unpublished, by these same authors and Hillary Elfenbein concludes that although there is a very slight positive association, it is not meaningful to go beyond thinking the relationship is neutral (see Joshua D. Margolis, Hilary A. Elfenbein, and James P. Walsh, "Does It Pay to Be Good . . . and Does It Matter? A Meta-Analysis of the Relationship between Corporate Social and Financial Performance" (working paper, Harvard Business School, Boston, MA, and University of Michigan, Ann Arbor, MI, 2009).

14. Quoted in William Blaue, "Moving from the Business Case for SRI and CSR to the Fiduciary Case" (sri-adviser.com; www.sri-adviser.com/article.mpl?sfArticleId=1346). Note that Innovest is at this writing part of RiskMetrics, itself a part of MSCI.

15. Russell L. Ackoff, "On Learning and the Systems That Facilitate It," *Reflections* 1, no. 1 (1999): 16, reprinted from the Center for Quality of Management, Cambridge, MA, 1996 (our italics).

16. Dirk Matten and Andrew Crane, "Corporate Citizenship: Towards an Extended Theoretical Conceptualization," *Academy of Management Review* 30, no.1 (2005): 166–79.

17. These two paragraphs are derived from Sandra Waddock and Neil Smith, "Corporate Responsibility Audits: Doing Well by Doing Good," *Sloan Management Review* 105, no. 1 (Spring 2000): 47–63.

18. James C. Collins and Jerry I. Porras, *Built to Last: Successful Habits of Visionary Companies* (New York: HarperBusiness, 1997).

19. Ibid., 4.

20. Ibid.

21. Ibid., 8.

22. Rajendra S. Sisodia, David B. Wolfe, and Jagdish N. Sheth, *Firms of Endearment: How World Class Companies Profit from Passion and Purpose* (Upper Saddle River, NJ: Wharton School Publishing, 2007).

23. John Helyer, "The Only Company Wal-Mart Fears," *Fortune*, November 24, 2003.

24. See Ann Zimmermann, "Costco's Dilemma: Be Kind to Its Workers, or Wall Street?," *Wall Street Journal*, March 26, 2004, B1–B3; Stanley Holmes and Wendy Zellner, "The Costco Way: Higher Wages Mean Higher Profits. But Try Telling Wall Street," *Business Week*, April 12, 2004, 76–77.

25. Holmes and Zellner, "The Costco Way," 76–77.

26. Ibid.

27. Quoted in Steven Greenhouse, "How Costco Became the Anti-Wal-Mart," *New York Times*, July 17, 2005 (http://www.nytimes.com/2005/07/17/business /yourmoney/17costco.html).

28. For a summary, see Joshua D. Margolis and Hillary A. Elfenbein, "Do Well by Doing Good? Don't Count on It," *Harvard Business Review* 86, no. 1 (January 2008): 19–20. The full study is Joshua D. Margolis et al., "Will Companies Cure What Ails Us? Don't Bank on It. Evidence from a Meta-Analysis of the Relationship between Corporate Social and Financial Performance" (working paper, Harvard Business School, Boston, MA, and University of Michigan, Ann Arbor, MI, 2008). See also Sandra Waddock and Samuel B. Graves, "The Corporate Social Performance—Financial Performance Link," *Strategic Management Journal* 18, no. 4 (1997): 303–19; and Sandra Waddock and Samuel B. Graves, "Quality of Management and Quality of Stakeholder Relations: Are They Synonymous?" *Business and Society* 36, no. 3 (September 1997): 250–79, both of which find positive associations.

29. Margolis and Elfenbein, "Do Well by Doing Good?," 19–20.

30. See Surroca, Tribó, and Waddock, "Corporate Responsibility and Financial Performance."

31. Stephen Brammer and Andrew Millington, "Does It Pay to Be Different? An Analysis of the Relationship between Corporate Social and Financial Performance," *Strategic Management Journal* 29, no. 12 (2008): 1325–43.

32. US SIF, Forum for Sustainable and Responsible Investment, "2010 Trends Report" (http://ussif.org/resources/pubs/trends/).

33. From US SIF, "Socially Responsible Investing Facts" (http://ussif.org/resources/ sriguide/srifacts.cfm).

34. Ibid.

35. US SIF, "Performance and Socially Responsible Investments" (http://ussif.org/resources/performance.cfm).

36. Stephen Barlas et al., "More Evidence of Better Financial Performance," *Strategic Finance* 85, no. 5 (November 2003): 2–3.

37. Darren D. Lee et al., "Socially Responsible Investment Fund Performance: The Impact of Screening Intensity," *Accounting and Finance* 50, no. 2 (2010): 352–70.

38. Joe Keefe, "From Socially Responsible Investing to Sustainable Investing," special anniversary issue, *GreenMoney Journal* (Winter 2007–2008) (http://www.greenmoneyjournal.com/article.mpl?newsletterid=41&articleid=544).

39. Jeffrey Pfeffer and John F. Veiga, "Putting People First for Organizational Success," *Academy of Management Executive* 13, no. 2 (May 1999): 37–48. See also Gary Dessler, "How to Earn Your Employees' Commitment," *Academy of Management Executive* 13, no. 2 (May 1999): 58–67, for a similar set of ideas.

40. Pfeffer and Veiga, "Putting People First," 37, 39. The first study cited is Bill Gates, "Compete, Don't Delete," *The Economist*, June 13, 1998, 19–21. The second study cited is Jeffrey Pfeffer, *Competitive Advantage through People: Unleashing the Power of the Workforce* (Boston: Harvard Business School Press, 1995), 9.

41. Alex Edmans, "Does the Stock Market Fully Value Intangibles? Employee Satisfaction and Equity Prices," December 13, 2007, available at SSRN (http://ssrn.com/abstract=985735). This paper won the 2007 Moskowitz Prize for research in socially responsible investing.

42. Ron Bird et al., "What Corporate Social Responsibility Activities Are Valued by the Market?" *Journal of Business Ethics* 75 (2007): 189–206.

43. Taoufik Saïd, Jeans-Yves Le Louarn, and Michel Tremblay, "The Performance Effects of Major Workforce Reductions: Longitudinal Evidence from North America," *International Journal of Human Resource Management* 18, no. 12 (December 2007): 2075–94.

44. Rebecca Wells, "Outstanding Customer Satisfaction: The Key to a Talented Workforce?" *Academy of Management Perspectives* 21, no. 3 (August 2007): 87–89.

45. Reporting in Ross Blake, "Employee Retention: What Employee Turnover Really Costs Your Company," *WebProNews*, July 24, 2005 (http://www.webpronews.com/expertarticles/2006/07/24/employee-retention-what-employee-turnover-really-costs-your-company).

46. Scott Allen, "The High Cost of Employee Turnover," *Money*, April 7, 2010 (http://www.openforum.com/idea-hub/topics/money/article/the-high-cost-of-employee-turnover-scott-allen).

47. Stephen Bevan et al., "Achieving High Performance: CSR at the Heart of Business," *The Work Foundation*, 2001. (http://www.newunionism.net/library/working%20life/Work%20Foundation%20-%20The%20Ethical%20Employee%20-%202006.pdf)

48. Jeffrey Pfeffer, *The Human Equation: Building Profits by Putting People First* (Boston: Harvard Business School Press, 1998).

49. Pfeffer and Veiga, "Putting People First," 39.

50. Jay Barney, *Gaining and Sustaining Competitive Advantage* (Reading, MA: Addison-Wesley, 1997). However, another study found no significant relationship between the number of women directors on boards and financial performance; see David A. Carter et al., "The Gender and Ethnic Diversity of U.S. Boards and Board Committees and Firm

Financial Performance," *Corporate Governance: An International Review* 18, no. 5 (2010): 396–414.

51. Catalyst, "The Bottom Line: Connecting Gender Diversity and Performance," 2004 (http://www.catalyst.org/publication/82/the-bottom-line-connecting-corporate -performance-and-gender-diversity).

52. Bird et al., "What Activities Are Valued by the Market?"

53. Sue Shellenbarger, "Companies Are Finding It Really Pays to Be Nice to Employees," *Wall Street Journal*, July 22, 1998.

54. Kevin Campbell and Antonio Minguez-Vera, "Gender Diversity in the Boardroom and Firm Financial Performance," *Journal of Business Ethics* 83, no. 3 (2008): 435–51.

55. Armand V. Feigenbaum, "Changing Concepts and Management of Quality Worldwide," *Quality Progress* 30, no. 12 (December 1997): 46.

56. C. Cone, "2002 Cone Corporate Citizenship Study" (http://www.coneinc.com /news/request.php?id=1085).

57. Frederick F. Reichheld, "The One Number You Need to Grow," *Harvard Business Review* (December 2003): 46–54.

58. Shuili Du, C. B. Battacharya, and Sankar Sen, "Reaping Relational Rewards from Corporate Social Responsibility: The Role of Competitive Positioning," *International Journal of Research in Marketing* 24, no. 3 (September, 2007): 224–41.

59. Julie Pirsch, Shruti Gupta, and Stacy Grau, "A Framework for Understanding Corporate Social Responsibility Programs as a Continuum: An Exploratory Study," *Journal of Business Ethics* 79, no. 2 (January 2007): 125–40.

60. Pat Auger and Timothy Devinney, "Do What Consumers Say Matter? The Misalignment of Preferences with Unconstrained Ethical Intentions," *Journal of Business Ethics* 76, no. 4 (2003): 361–83.

61. See, for example, Richard Locke, Fei Qin, and Alberto Brause, "Does Monitoring Improve Labor Standards? Lessons from Nike," *Industrial and Labor Relations Review* 61, no. 1 (2007): 3–31; and also Richard Locke and Monica Romis, "Improving Work Conditions in a Global Supply Chain," *MIT Sloan Management Review* 48, no. 2 (2007): 54–62.

62. See, for example, Janine Nahapiet and Sumantra Ghoshal, "Social Capital, Intellectual Capital, and the Organizational Advantage," *Academy of Management Review* 23, no. 2 (April 1998): 242–66.

63. Craig R. Carter and Marianne M. Jennings, "Social Responsibility and Supply Chain Relationships," *Logistics and Transportation Review* 38, no. 1 (January 2002): 37–52.

64. Craig R. Carter, "Purchasing Social Responsibility and Firm Performance," *International Journal of Physical Distribution & Logistics* 35, no. 3 (2005): 177–94.

65. "Corporate Responsibility Report FY 07, 08, 09," Nike, Inc., 2009 (http://www .nikebiz.com/crreport/content/pdf/documents/en-US/full-report.pdf).

66. Jeffrey Ballinger ,"The New Free Trade Heel," *Harper's Magazine*, August 1992, 64.

67. See Simon Zadek, "The Path to Corporate Responsibility," *Harvard Business Review* (December 2004): 125–32. Zadek discusses Nike's evolution of corporate responsibility practices in much detail.

68. Ibid.

69. Richard Locke and Monica Romis, "Improving Working Conditions in a Global Supply Chain," *MIT Sloan Management Review* (Winter 2007): 54–62, here 59–60.

70. See Waddock and Graves, "Quality of Management."

71. Simon Zadek, "Balancing, Performance, Ethics, and Accountability," *Journal of Business Ethics* 17, no. 3 (October 1998): 1421–41.

72. See Nahapiet and Ghoshal, "Social Capital."

73. Ibid.

74. Ibid.

CHAPTER 6

1. R. Edward Freeman, *Strategic Management: A Stakeholder Approach*, rev. ed. (Cambridge: Cambridge University Press, 2010); R. Edward Freeman, Jeffrey Harrison, and Andrew Wicks, *Managing for Stakeholders: Business in the 21st Century* (New Haven, CT: Yale University Press, 2007).

2. See, for example, Lynn A. Stout, "Why We Should Stop Teaching Dodge v. Ford," *Virginia Law & Business Review* 3, no. 1 (Spring 2008): 163–76; and Kent Greenfield, "A New Era for Corporate Law: Using Corporate Governance to Benefit All Stakeholders," *Paper Series on Corporate Design: Summit on the Future of the Corporation* (2007): 19–28 (http://www.corporation2020.org/SummitPaperSeries.pdf).

3. See, for example, James E. Post, Lee E. Preston, and Sybille Sachs, "Managing the Extended Enterprise: The New Stakeholder View," *California Management Review* 45, no. 1 (2002): 6–29; and James E. Post, Lee E. Preston, and Sybille Sachs, *Redefining the Corporation* (New York: Oxford University Press, 2002).

4. Milton Friedman, "The Social Responsibility of a Business Is to Increase Its Profits," *New York Times Magazine*, September 13, 1970.

5. Allen L. White, "When the World Rules Corporations: Pathway to a Global Corporate Charter," *Tellus Institute, Great Transition Initiative, Visions and Pathways for a Hopeful Future* (Boston, Tellus Institute, 2010) (http://www.gtinitiative.org/documents/IssuePerspectives/GTI-Perspectives-Global_Corporate_Charters.pdf).

6. White, "World Rules Corporation," 2.

7. In order, see www.earthcharterinaction.org/content/; www.unglobalcompact.org; www.ilo.org; and www.globalreporting.org.

8. See Max B. E. Clarkson, "A Stakeholder Framework for Analyzing and Evaluating Corporate Social Performance," *Academy of Management Review* 20, no. 1 (1995): 92–117, for an extended discussion of stakes. See also Ronald K. Mitchell, Bradley R. Agle, and Donna J. Wood, "Toward a Theory of Stakeholder Identification and Salience: Defining the Principle of Who and What Really Counts," *Academy of Management Review* 22, no. 4 (October 1997): 853–86.

9. For a perspective on this, see Tammy MacLean, "Creating Stakeholder Relationships: A Model of Organizational Social Identification—How the Southern Baptist Convention Became Stakeholders of Walt Disney,"(paper presented at the Annual Meeting of the Academy of Management, San Diego, CA, 1998).

10. Thanks are owed to Max B. E. Clarkson for providing a basis for thinking about corporate social performance in terms of stakeholder relationships. See Clarkson, "A Stakeholder Framework."

11. Charles Handy, "What's a Business For?" *Harvard Business Review* (December 2002): 49–55.

12. See, for example, Freeman, *Strategic Management*, and Evan and Freeman, "A Stakeholder Theory of the Modern Corporation." See also Clarkson, "A Stakeholder Framework," and Ronald K. Mitchell, Bradley R. Agle, and Donna J. Wood, "Toward a Theory of Stakeholder Identification and Salience: Defining the Principle of Who and What Really Counts," *Academy of Management Review* 22, no. 4 (1997): 853–86.

13. The concepts of primary and secondary involvement come from Lee E. Preston and James E. Post, *Private Management and Public Policy: The Principle of Public Responsibility* (Englewood Cliffs, NJ: Prentice Hall, 1975).

14. Ibid., 95.

15. This definition is from Clarkson, "A Stakeholder Framework," 106. However, the distinction goes back to Freeman, *Strategic Management*.

16. For example, Mark Starik, "Should Trees Have Managerial Standing? Toward Stakeholder Status for Non-Human Nature," *Journal of Business Ethics* 14 (1995): 204–17.

17. See, for example, Robert A. Phillips and Joel Reichart, "The Environment as a Stakeholder? A Fairness Based Approach," *Journal of Business Ethics* 23 (January 2000): 183–97.

18. For a theoretical explanation, see Duane Windsor, "Stakeholder Responsibilities: Lessons for Managers," in *Unfolding Stakeholder Thinking: Theory, Responsibility and Engagement*, ed. Jörg Andriof et al. (Sheffield, U.K.: Greenleaf, 2002): 137–54.

19. Clarkson, "A Stakeholder Framework," 107.

20. Ronald K. Mitchell, Bradley R. Agle, and Donna J. Wood, "Toward a Theory of Stakeholder Identification and Salience: Defining the Principle of Who and What Really Counts," *Academy of Management Review* 22, no. 4 (October 1997): 853–86. Mitchell, Agle, and Wood's model has been somewhat modified by Steven L. Wartick and Donna J. Wood, *International Business and Society* (Malden, MA: Blackwell Press, 1998), in the fashion incorporated into this discussion.

21. See Duane Windsor, "Stakeholder Responsibilities: Lessons for Managers," in *Unfolding Stakeholder Thinking: Theory, Responsibility and Engagement*, ed. Jörg Andriof et al. (Sheffield, UK: Greenleaf, 2002): 137–54.

22. For background on descriptive, instrumental, and normative branches of stakeholder theory, see Thomas Donaldson and Lee E. Preston, "The Stakeholder Theory of the Corporation: Concepts, Evidence, and Implications," *Academy of Management Review* 20 (January 1995): 1, 65–91.

23. Whole Foods Market, "2010 Stakeholder Report" (http://www.wholefoodsmarket.com/company/pdfs/ar10.pdf).

24. Patricia K. Hart, "Hitting the Organic Jackpot by Making Shopping a State of Mind: The Whole Foods Market Chain Has Become a Giant among Natural-Foods Retailers," *Boston Globe Magazine*, March 16, 2003.

25. Whole Foods Market, "2010 Stakeholder Report."

26. See Whole Foods Market, "Declaration of Interdependence" (http://www.wholefoodsmarket.com/company/declaration.php).

27. Hart, "Organic Jackpot."

28. Quoted in Elisabeth Fiock, "Whole Foods Is a Loose Cannon on Target," 2010 (http://business.in.com/printcontent/18072).

29. Hart, "Organic Jackpot."

30. Donaldson and Preston, "The Stakeholder Theory." This link is the basis for the instrumental argument for positive stakeholder relationships.

31. For a discussion of this framework, see Preston and Post, *Private Management.*

32. See also Clarkson, "A Stakeholder Framework," 109. Clarkson's "postures" are different from the stances outlined here.

33. Handy, "What's a Business For?" 49–55.

34. Robert F. Felton, Ken Berryman, and Tom Stephenson, "A New Era in Corporate Governance," *McKinsey Quarterly* 2 (2004): 28–44.

35. Jennifer Liberto, "CEOs Earn 343 Times More Than Typical Workers," *CNN Money,* April 20, 2011 (http://money.cnn.com/2011/04/19/news/economy/ceo_pay/index.htm).

36. Charles A. O'Reilly III, Brian G. Main, and Greaf S. Crystal, "CEO Compensation as Tournament and Social Comparison: A Tale of Two Theories," *Administrative Science Quarterly* 33 (1988): 257–74.

37. Executive PayWatch, "CEO Pay: Feeding the 1%" (http://www.aflcio.org/corporatewatch/paywatch/).

38. AFL-CIO, "Trends in CEO Pay" (http://www.aflcio.org/corporatewatch/paywatch/pay/index.cfm).

39. This argument is compellingly made by Richard Marens and Andrew Wicks, "Getting Real: Stakeholder Theory, Managerial Practice, and the General Irrelevance of Fiduciary Duties Owed to Shareholders," *Business Ethics Quarterly* 9, no. 2 (April 1999): 273–93.

40. See, for instance, Sydney Finkelstein's comment, "Rethinking CEO Stock Options," *Bloomberg Businessweek,* "Executive Compensation," April 17, 2009 (http://www.businessweek.com/managing/content/apr2009/ca20090417_941667.htm).

41. See James C. Collins and Jerry I. Porras, "Building Your Company's Vision," *Harvard Business Review* (September–October 1996): 65–77.

42. See Marens and Wicks, "Getting Real"; and Oliver E. Williamson, *Markets and Hierarchies: Analysis and Antitrust Implications* (New York: Free Press, 1975).

43. Marens and Wicks, "Getting Real," 277. The points in this paragraph are derived from this article.

44. See, for example, Kent Greenfield, "New Principles for Corporate Law," *Hastings Business Law Journal* 1 (May 2005): 87–118, and Kent Greenfield, "A New Era for Corporate Law: Using Corporate Governance to Benefit All Stakeholders," *Paper Series on Corporate Design: Summit on the Future of the Corporation* (2007): 19–28 (http://www.corporation2020.org/SummitPaperSeries.pdf); see also Lynn A. Stout, "Why We Should Stop Teaching Dodge v. Ford," *Virginia Law & Business Review* 3, no. 1 (Spring 2008): 163–76.

45. UNEP Finance Initiative, "A Legal Framework for the Integration of Environmental, Social and Governance Issues into Institutional Investment," (http://www.unepfi.org/fileadmin/documents/freshfields_legal_resp_20051123.pdf).

46. Robert B. Reich, *Supercapitalism: The Transformation of Business, Democracy, and Everyday Life* (New York: Knopf, 2007).

47. See Jaewon Lee and J. Martin Corbett, "The Impact of Downsizing on Employees' Affective Commitment," *Journal of Managerial Psychology* 21, no. 3 (2006): 176–99.

48. See Tip Fallon, "Retain and Motivate the Next Generation: 7 Ways to Get the Most Out of Your Millennial Workers," *Supervision* 70, no. 5 (May 2009): 5–7, here 6.

49. Two studies using *Fortune*'s 100 Best Companies to Work for in America rankings find a positive relationship between company performance and employee satisfaction and attitudes: Karn C. Chan, Michele V. Gee, and Thomas L. Steiner, "Employee Happiness and Corporate Financial Performance," *Financial Practice and Education* 10, no. 2 (Fall/Winter 2002): 47–52; and Ingrid S. Fulmer, Barry Gerhart, and Kimberly S. Scott, "Are the 100 Best Better? An Empirical Investigation of the Relationship between Being a 'Great Place to Work' and Firm Performance," *Personnel Psychology* 56, no. 4 (Winter 2003): 965–94.

50. Jeffrey Pfeffer and John F. Veiga, "Putting People First for Organizational Success," *Academy of Management Executive* 13, no. 2 (May 1999): 37–48. See also Gary Dessler, "How to Earn Your Employees' Commitment," *Academy of Management Executive* 13, no. 2 (May 1999): 58–67, for a similar set of ideas. The framework in this section is developed from these two review articles.

51. Pfeffer and Veiga, "Putting People First," 46.

52. Robert H. Hayes and William J. Abernathy, "Managing Our Way to Economic Decline," *Harvard Business Review* (July–August 1980): 66–77.

53. Rajendra S. Sisodia, David B. Wolfe, and Jagdish N. Sheth, *Firms of Endearment: How World Class Companies Profit from Passion and Purpose* (Upper Saddle River, NJ: Wharton School Publishing, 2007).

54. See Collins and Porras, "Building Your Company's Vision."

55. See Gary Dessler, "How to Earn Your Employees' Commitment," citing Rosabeth M. Kanter, *World Class: Thriving Locally in the Global Economy* (New York: Simon & Schuster, 1995), 59. Dessler's ideas are similar to those developed in Chapters 4 and 5 and are congruent with the practices of successful firms identified by Pfeffer and Veiga, "Putting People First."

56. Summarized from Pfeffer and Veiga, "Putting People First."

57. See Dessler, "Earn Your Employees' Commitment."

58. Frederick F. Reichheld, "The One Number You Need to Grow," *Harvard Business Review* 81, no. 12 (December 2003): 46–55.

59. Rebecca M. J. Wells, "Outstanding Customer Satisfaction: The Key to a Talented Workforce?" *Academy of Management Perspectives* 21, no. 3 (August 2007): 87–89.

60. See, for example, Christian Gronroos, "From Marketing Mix to Relationship Marketing: Towards a Paradigm Shift in Marketing," *Management Decision* 32, no. 2 (1994): 4–20; and Robert M. Morgan and Shelby D. Hunt, "The Commitment-Trust Theory of Relationship Marketing," *Journal of Marketing* 58, no. 3 (July 1994): 20–38.

61. Gronroos, "From Marketing Mix to Relationship Marketing."

62. Morgan and Hunt, "Commitment-Trust Theory"; see also M. Johnny Rungtusanatham et al., "Supply-Chain Linkages and Operational Performance," *International Journal of Operations & Production Management* 23, no. 9 (2003): 1084–1100.

63. See Kenneth M. York and Cynthia E. Miree, "Causation or Covariation: An Empirical Re-examination of the Link between TQM and Financial Performance," *Journal of Operations Management* 22, no. 3 (June 2004): 291–312; and Kaj Storbacka, Tore Strandvik, and Christian Gronroos, "Managing Customer Relationships for Profit: The Dynamics of Relationship Quality," *International Journal of Service Industry Management* 5, no. 5 (1994): 21–38.

64. See Armand V. Feigenbaum, "Changing Concepts and Management of Quality Worldwide," *Quality Progress* 30, no. 12 (December 1997): 45–48.

65. Holder Ernst et al., "Customer Relationship Management and Company Performance—The Mediating Role of New Product Performance," *Journal of the Academy of Marketing Science* 39, no. 2 (2011): 290–306.

66. Morgan and Hunt, "Commitment-Trust Theory." See also Christopher R. Moberg and Thomas W. Speh, "Evaluating the Relationship between Questionable Business Practices and the Strength of Supply Chain Relationships," *Supply Chain Management Review* 24, no. 2 (2003): 1–19.

67. Frederick F. Reichheld, "The One Number You Need to Grow," *Harvard Business Review* 81, no. 12 (2003): 46–54.

68. Emmet C. Murphy and Mark A. Murphy, *Leading on the Edge of Chaos: The 10 Critical Elements for Success in Volatile Times* (Upper Saddle River, NJ: Prentice Hall, 2002).

69. David Jingjun Xu, Izak Benbasat, and Ronald T. Cenfetelli, "The Effect of Perceived Service Quality, Perceived Sacrifice, and Perceived Service Outcome on Online Customer Loyalty," ICIS 2009 Proceedings, Paper 175 (htto://aisel.aisnet.org/icis2009/175/).

70. Gronoos, "Marketing Mix."

71. Charles C. Poirier and William F. Houser, *Business Partnering for Continuous Improvement* (San Francisco: Berrett-Koehler, 1993).

72. Milé Terziovski, "Quality Management Practices and Their Relationship with Customer Satisfaction and Productivity Improvement," *Management Research News* 29, no. 7 (2006): 414–24.

73. Feigenbaum, "Changing Concepts."

74. Gronroos, "From Marketing Mix to Relationship Marketing."

75. Michael Bendixen and Russell Abratt, "Corporate Identity, Ethics and Reputation in Supplier-Buyer Relationships," *Journal of Business Ethics* 75, no. 1 (December 2007): 69–82.

76. Rungtusanatham et al., "Supply Chain Linkages."

77. Kostas Dervitsiotis, "Beyond Stakeholder Satisfaction: Aiming for a New Frontier of Sustainable Stakeholder Trust," *Total Quality Management & Business Excellence* 14, no. 5 (July 2003): 515–28.

78. Bendixen and Abratt, "Corporate Identity."

79. Christopher B. Clott, "Perspectives on Global Outsourcing and the Changing Nature of Work," *Business & Society Review* 109, no. 20 (Summer 2004): 153–70.

80. Details in this paragraph are from KPMG, "Business Codes of the Global 200: Their Prevalence, Content and Embedding," KPMG Special Services, 2008 (http://www.kpmg.com/Global/en/IssuesAndInsights/ArticlesPublications/Documents/Business-Codes-of-the-Global-200.pdf).

81. Martin Meznar and Douglas Nigh, "Managing Corporate Legitimacy: Public Affairs Activities, Strategies, and Effectiveness," *Business and Society* 32, no. 1 (Spring 1993): 30–43.

82. Peter Hannaford, "What Is Public Affairs?," *Public Relations Quarterly* 33, no. 3 (Fall 1988): 11–14.

83. See, for example, James E. Post et al., "The Public Affairs Function in American Corporations: Development and Relations with Corporate Planning," *Long Range Planning* 15, no. 2 (April 1982): 12–21.

84. The history is given in Charles J. McMillan and Victor V. Murray, "Strategically Managing Public Affairs: Lessons from the Analysis of Business-Government Relations," *Business Quarterly* 48, no. 2 (Summer 1983): 94–100.

85. The current state of the art was detailed in James E. Post and Jennifer J. Griffin, *The State of Corporate Public Affairs: Final Report 1996 Survey* (Boston and Washington, DC: Boston University School of Management and Foundation for Public Affairs, 1996); and Alfred A. Marcus and Allen M. Kaufman, "The Continued Expansion of the Corporate Public-Affairs Function," *Business Horizons* 31, no. 2 (March/April 1988): 58–62.

86. See Keith MacMillan, "Managing Public Affairs in British Industry," *Journal of General Management* 9, no. 2 (1983/1984): 784–90.

87. Jennifer J. Griffin and Paul Dunn, "Corporate Public Affairs: Commitment, Resources, and Structure," *Business & Society* 43, no. 2 (June 2004): 196–220.

88. See D. Jeffrey Lenn et al., "Managing Corporate Public Affairs and Government Relations: US Multinational Corporations in Europe," in *Research in Corporate Social Performance and Policy*, vol. 15, ed. James E. Post (Greenwich, CT: JAI Press, 1993), 103–38.

89. A good review of the literature can be found in Amy J. Hillman, Gerald D. Keim, and Douglas Schuler, "Corporate Political Activity: A Review and Research Agenda," *Journal of Management* 30, no. 6 (2004): 837–57.

90. Post and Griffin, *Corporate Public Affairs.*

91. See, for example, Adam Liptak, "Justices, 5–4, Reject Corporate Spending Limit," *New York Times*, January 21, 2010 (http://www.nytimes.com/2010/01/22/us/politics/22scotus.html); "Who Is Helped, or Hurt, by the Citizens United Decision?" *Washington Post*, January 24, 2010 (http://www.washingtonpost.com/wp-dyn/content/article/2010/01/22/AR2010012203874.html); see also Wikipedia's entry at: http://en.wikipedia.org/wiki/Citizens_United_v._Federal_Election_Commission, for more background.

92. See William D. Oberman, "A Framework for the Ethical Analysis of Corporate Political Activity," *Business and Society Review* 109, no. 2 (2004): 245–62, for an elaboration of these ideas.

93. Steven L. Wartick and Pursey Heugens, "Future Directions for Issues Management," *Corporate Reputation Review* 6, no. 1 (Spring 2003): 7–18.

94. Pursey Heugens, "Strategic Issues Management," dissertation abstract, *Business & Society* 41, no. 4 (December 2002): 456–69.

95. See Douglas Nigh and Philip L. Cochran, "Issues Management and the Multinational Enterprise," special issue, *Management International Review* 34 (1994): 51–59.

96. Ibid.

97. Much of the information on crisis management in this section is derived from Christine M. Pearson and Judith A. Clair, "Reframing Crisis Management," *Academy of Management Review* 23, no. 1 (January 1998): 59–76. See also Ian I. Mitroff and Robert H. Kilman, *Corporate Tragedies: Product Tampering, Sabotage, and Other Catastrophes* (New York: Praeger, 1984); Ian I. Mitroff, Christine M. Pearson, and L. Kathleen Harrigan, *The Essential Guide to Managing Corporate Crises* (New York: Oxford University Press, 1996); Paul Shrivastava et al., "Understanding Industrial Crises," *Journal of Management Studies* 25 (1988): 285–303; and Norman R. Augustine, "Managing the Crisis You Tried to Prevent," *Harvard Business Review* (November–December 1995): 147–58.

98. "Citigroup's $9.8 bn Sub-prime Loss," *BBC News*, January 15, 2008 (http://news.bbc.co.uk/2/hi/business/7188909.stm).

99. David Ellis, "Mattel: 9M More Chinese Made Toys Recalled," *CNN Money*, August 15, 2007 (http://money.cnn.com/2007/08/14/news/companies/mattel/).

100. See Judith A. Clair and Sandra Waddock, "A 'Total' Responsibility Approach to Crisis Management and Signal Detection in Organizations," in *International Handbook of Organizational Crisis Management*, ed. Christine M. Pearson, Christophe Roux-Dufort, and Judith A. Clair (Thousand Oaks, CA: Sage, 2007), 299–314; and Jonathan Clark and Mark Harman, "On Crisis Management and Rehearsing," *Risk Management* 51, no. 5 (May 2004): 40–43.

101. Pearson and Clair, "Reframing Crisis Management."

102. Les Coleman, "The Frequency and Cost of Corporate Crises," *Journal of Contingencies & Crisis Management* 12, no. 10 (March 2004): 2–13.

103. Charles Perrow, *Normal Accidents: Living with High-Risk Technologies* (New York: Basic Books, 1984).

104. Kristin B. Backhaus, Brett A. Stone, and Karl Heiner, "Exploring the Relationship between Corporate Social Performance and Employer Attractiveness," *Business & Society* 41, no. 3 (September 2002): 292–318.

105. See Cemex, "About Us" (http://www.cemex.com/AboutUs/CompanyValues.aspx).

106. Ricardo Sandoval, "Block by Block: How One of the World's Largest Companies Builds Loyalty among Mexico's Poor," *Stanford Innovation Review* (Summer 2005): 35–36.

107. See Cemex, "Low Income Housing" (http://www.cemex.com/Sustainable Development/LowIncomeHousing.aspx).

108. Jennifer A. Kitto, "The Evolution of Public Issues Management," *Public Relations Quarterly* 43, no. 4 (Winter 1998/1999): 34–38.

109. Edward L. Bernays, *Public Relations* (Norman, OK: University of Oklahoma Press, 1952), quoted in Burton St. John III, "Public Relations as Community-Building Then and Now," *Public Relations Quarterly* 43, no. 1 (Spring 1998): 34–40.

110. Dirk Gibson, Jerra L. Gonzales, and Jaclynn Castanon, "The Importance of Reputation and the Role of Public Relations," *Public Relations Quarterly* 61, no. 3 (2006): 15–18.

111. See Brian Solis and Deirdre Breakenridge, *Putting the Public Back in Public Relations: How Social Media Is Reinventing the Aging Business of PR* (Upper Saddle River, NJ: FT Press, Pearson Education, 2009); and Sandra Waddock and Bradley K. Googins, "The Paradoxes of Communicating Corporate Citizenship: Sectors, Context, and

Stakeholders," in *Handbook of Communication and Corporate Social Responsibility*, ed. Øyvind Ihlen, Jennifer Bartlett, and Steve May (Malden, MA: Wiley Blackwell, 2011).

112. *Vesta Digital Blog*, "Nestle Cooks up Trouble with Their Social Media," April 7, 2010 (http://www.vestadigital.com/173/section.aspx/218/post/nestle-cooks-up-trouble-with-their-social-media).

113. Jodi B. Katzman, "What's the Role of Public Relations?" *Public Relations Journal* 49, no. 4 (April 1993): 11–16.

114. See St. John, "Public Relations"; and Augustine S. Ihator, "Effective Public Relations Techniques for the Small Business in a Competitive Market Environment," *Public Relations Quarterly* 43, no. 2 (Summer 1998): 28–32.

115. Gibson, Gonzales, and Castanon, "Importance of Reputation," 17; Waddock and Googins, "Communicating Corporate Citizenship."

CHAPTER 7

1. Much of this chapter is based on work co-authored with Charles Bodwell, and is drawn from Sandra Waddock and Charles Bodwell, "From TQM to TRM: Emerging Responsibility Management Approaches," *Journal of Corporate Citizenship* (Autumn 2002): 113–26 (used with permission); and Sandra Waddock and Charles Bodwell, *Total Responsibility Management: The Manual* (Sheffield, UK: Greenleaf, 2007).

2. For a discussion of the link between quality management and corporate social responsibility, see also Rodney McAdam and Denis Leonard, "Corporate Social Responsibility in a Total Quality Management Context: Opportunities for Sustainable Growth," *Corporate Governance* 3, no. 4 (Winter 2003): 36–45.

3. James R. Evans and William M. Lindsay, *The Management and Control of Quality*, 4th ed. (New York: West, 1999), here p. 9.

4. Ibid.

5. See Peter M. Senge, *The Fifth Discipline: The Art and Practice of the Learning Organization*, rev. ed. (New York: Currency Doubleday, 2006).

6. Evans and Lindsay, *Management and Control of Quality*.

7. Steve Waddell, "Six Societal Learning Concepts in an Era of Engagement," *Reflections: The SoL Journal* 3, no. 4 (Summer 2002).

8. Ann Svendsen, *The Stakeholder Strategy: Profiting from Collaborative Business Relationships* (San Francisco: Berrett-Koehler, 1998); Jerry M. Calton and Steven L. Payne, "Coping with Paradox: Multistakeholder Learning Dialogue as a Pluralist Sensemaking Process for Addressing Messy Problems," *Business & Society* 42, no. 1 (March 2003): 7–42.

9. Philip H. Mirvis, "Transformation at Shell: Commerce and Citizenship," *Business and Society Review* 105, no. 1 (Spring 2000): 63–85; see also Anne Lawrence, "The Drivers of Stakeholder Engagement: Reflections on the Case of Royal Dutch Shell," in *Unfolding Stakeholder Thinking*, eds. Jörg Andriof et al. (Sheffield, UK: Greenleaf, 2002), 201–16.

10. Roland T. Rust, Valerie A. Zeithaml, and Katherine N. Lemon, *Driving Customer Equity: How Customer Lifetime Value Is Reshaping Corporate Strategy* (New York: Free Press, 1999).

11. Judy Warner, "Mattel's Blues: Lessons from a Global Crisis Management Effort," *Directorship*, December 1, 2007 (http://www.directorship.com/mattels-blues-lessons-from-a-global-crisis-management-effort/).

12. Jia L. Yang, "Mattel's CEO Recalls a Rough Summer," *Fortune*, January 22, 2008 (http://money.cnn.com/2008/01/21/news/companies/mattel.fortune/index.htm).

13. Ibid.

14. Warner, "Mattel's Blues."

15. Thomas Donaldson and Thomas W. Dunfee, *Ties That Bind: A Social Contracts Approach to Business Ethics* (Boston: Harvard Business School Press, 1999).

16. R. Edward Freeman and Daniel R. Gilbert Jr., *Corporate Strategy and the Search for Ethics* (Englewood Cliffs, NJ: Prentice Hall, 1988).

17. For more details on the Johnson & Johnson Credo, see http://www.jnj.com /connect/about-jnj/jnj-credo/.

18. "Social Accountability 8000 Standard Document" (http://www.sa-intl.org /_data/n_0001/resources/live/2008StdEnglishFinal.pdf).

19. United Nations Global Compact and Business for Social Responsibility, *Supply Chain Sustainability: A Practical Guide for Continuous Improvement* (New York: UN Global Compact Office, 2010).

20. John Elkington, *Cannibals with Forks: The Triple Bottom Line of Sustainability* (Gabriola Island: New Society Publishers, 1998).

21. Timothy Bell et al., *Auditing Organizations through a Strategic-Systems Lens: The KPMG Business Measurement Process* (Zurich, KPMG International, 1997).

22. Patsy Lewellyn and Maria Sillanpää, "Holistic Performance Model," (paper presented at the International Association of Business in Society Annual Meeting, Sedona, AZ, March 2001).

23. Jed Emerson, "The Blended Value Proposition: Integrating Social and Financial Returns," *California Management Review* 45, no. 4 (Summer 2003): 35–51.

24. Robert S. Kaplan and David P. Norton, "The Balanced Scorecard—Measures That Drive Performance," *Harvard Business Review* (January–February 1992): 71–79.

25. Sime Curkovic et al., "Investigating the Linkage between Total Quality Management and Environmentally Responsible Manufacturing," *IEEE Transactions on Engineering Management* 47, no. 4 (November 2000): 444–64, provide a comparison of these different approaches.

26. Sandra Waddock and Neil Smith, "Corporate Responsibility Audits: Doing Well by Doing Good," *Sloan Management Review* 41, no. 2 (Winter 2000): 75–83.

27. Simon Zadek and Richard Evans, *Auditing the Market: A Practical Approach to Social Auditing* (Tyne and Wear, UK: Tradecraft Exchange, 1993).

28. Senge, *The Fifth Discipline*.

CHAPTER 8

1. Sandra Waddock, "What Will It Take to Create a Tipping Point for Corporate Responsibility?," in *The Accountable Corporation*, ed. Marc Epstein and Kirk O. Hanson (Greenfield, CT: Praeger, 2006), 75–96.

2. See "2010 Edelman Trust Barometer" (http://www.edelman.com/trust/2010 /docs/2010_Trust_Barometer_Executive_Summary.pdf), see also "2011 Edelman Trust Barometer" (http://edelman.com/trust/2011/uploads/Edelman%20Trust%20Barometer%20Global%20Deck.pdf).

3. Thomas Donaldson and Thomas W. Dunfee, "Toward a Unified Conception of Social Contracts Theory," *Academy of Management Review* 19, no. 2 (1994): 252–84; and Thomas Donaldson and Thomas W. Dunfee, *Ties That Bind: A Social Contracts Approach to Business Ethics* (Boston: Harvard Business School Press, 1999), 265. See also Thomas Donaldson, "Values in Tension: Ethics Away from Home," *Harvard Business Review* (September–October 1996): 1–12.

4. Mark S. Schwartz, "A Code of Ethics for Corporate Codes of Ethics," *Journal of Business Ethics* 41, no. 1/2 (November–December 2002): 27–42.

5. Jack N. Behrman, "Adequacy of International Codes of Behavior," *Journal of Business Ethics* 31, no. 1 (May 2001): 51–63.

6. Andreas Rasche, "A Necessary Supplement: What the United Nations Global Compact Is (Not)," *Business & Society* 48, no. 4 (2009): 511–37. See also Andreas Rasche and Georg Kell, eds., *The United Nations Global Compact: Achievements, Trends and Challenges* (Cambridge: Cambridge University Press, 2010).

7. Andreas Rasche, "Collaborative Governance 2.0," *Corporate Governance* 10 (2010): 500–11.

8. Novartis, "Annual Report 2010" (http://www.novartis.com/downloads/investors/reports/novartis-annual-report-2010–en.pdf).

9. Klaus Leisinger, "Opportunities and Risks of the United Nations Global Compact: The Novartis Case Study," *Journal of Corporate Citizenship* 11 (2003): 113–31.

10. Ibid., 115.

11. Ibid., 116–17.

12. Novartis, "2010 UN Global Compact Communication on Progress" (http://www.corporatecitizenship.novartis.com/downloads/managing-cc/10_principles.pdf).

13. Leisinger, "Opportunities and Risks," 127.

14. Further information on the different AA 1000 standards are available at http://www.accountability.org.

15. For a discussion, see Dirk U. Gilbert and Andreas Rasche, "Discourse Ethics and Social Accountability—The Ethics of SA 8000," *Business Ethics Quarterly* 17, no. 2 (2007): 187–216.

16. The reported data are taken from SAI's website: http://sa-intl.org.

17. Deborah Leipziger, *SA 8000: The Definitive Guide to the New Social Standard* (London: FT Prentice Hall, 2001).

18. Dara O'Rourke, "Smoke From a Hired Gun: A Critique of Nike's Labor and Environmental Auditing in Vietnam as Performed by Ernst & Young," 2004 (http://web.mit.edu/dorourke/www/PDF/smoke.pdf).

19. See, for example, Dara O'Rourke, "Outsourcing Regulation: Analyzing Nongovernmental Systems of Labor Standards and Monitoring," *Policy Studies Journal* 31, no. 1 (2003): 1–29.

20. Richard Locke, Matthew Amengual, and Akshay Mangla, "Virtue out of Necessity? Compliance, Commitment, and the Improvement of Labor Conditions in Global Supply Chains," *Politics & Society* 37, no. 3 (2009): 319–51, here 325.

21. International Organization for Standardization (ISO), "ISO 26000 — Social Responsibility" (http://www.iso.org/iso/iso_catalogue/management_and_leadership_standards/social_responsibility/sr_iso26000_overview.htm).

22. Ibid.

23. International Organization for Standardization (ISO), *Guidance on Social Responsibility: Draft International Standard ISO/DIS26000* (Geneva: ISO, 2010).

24. ISO 26000, Press Release, October 27, 2010 (http://www.iso.org/iso/pressrelease .htm?refid=Ref1366).

25. Rajesh Chhabara, "Analysis: ISO 26000—Certification Denied," 2001 (http://www .ethicalcorp.com/communications-reporting/analysis-iso-26000–certification-denied).

26. Global Reporting Initiative, "What We Do," (http://www.globalreporting.org/ AboutGRI/WhatWeDo/).

27. Information on all three components of the GRI framework and the specifics behind them can be found at: http://www.globalreporting.org/ReportingFramework /ReportingFrameworkOverview/.

28. International Integrated Reporting Committee, "Towards Integrated Reporting " (http://theiirc.org/wp-content/uploads/2011/09/IR-Discussion-Paper-2011_spreads.pdf).

29. International Integrated Reporting Committee (http://www.theiirc.org).

30. IIRC (http://www.integratedreporting.org/node/4).

31. "KPMG International Survey of Corporate Responsibility Reporting 2011" (Amsterdam: KPMG, 2011) (http://www.kpmg.com/PT/pt/IssuesAndInsights/Documents /corporate-responsibility2011.pdf, 2).

32. "KPMG, Integrated Reporting: Closing the Loop of Strategy" (Amsterdam: KPMG, 2010) (http://www.kpmg.com/Global/en/IssuesAndInsights/Articles Publications/Documents/Integrated-Reporting.pdf, 2).

33. Ibid.

34. Ernst Ligteringen, *Rewiring Homo Economicus, in KPMG Integrated Reporting Closing the Loop of Strategy, Advisory* (Amsterdam: KPMG, 2010) (http://www.kpmg .com/Global/en/IssuesAndInsights/ArticlesPublications/Documents/Integrated-Reporting.pdf, 7).

35. See the Social Investment Forum (SIF) website, www.socialinvest.org.

36. See, for example, Eric M. Weigand, Kenneth R. Brown, and Eileen M. Wilhem, "Socially Principled Investing: Caring about Ethics and Profitability," *Trusts & Estates* 135, no. 9 (August 1996): 36–42.

37. This view of incalculable risks was put forward by Steven R. Lydenberg and Karen Paul in "Stakeholder Theory and Socially Responsible Investing: Toward a Convergence of Theory and Practice," *Proceedings of the International Association for Business and Society,* ed. Jim Weber and Kathleen Rehbein (March 1997), 208–13.

38. For more information, see MSCI, Products and Services, "Environmental, Social & Governance" (http://www.msci.com/products/esg/); and "MSCI ESG Indices" (http:// www.msci.com/products/indices/thematic/esg/).

39. FTSE4Good, Inclusion Criteria (http://www.ftse.com/Indices/FTSE4Good _Index_Series/Downloads/FTSE4Good_Inclusion_Criteria.pdf).

40. Ibid.

41. See www.uksif.org.

42. See www.eurosif.org.

43. US SIF, cited above, accessed July 8, 2011.

44. Eurosif, "Mission" (http://www.eurosif.org/about-eurosif/mission).

45. For more information, see FFIEC, "Community Reinvestment Act" (http://www
.ffiec.gov/CRA/).

46. Ibid.

47. Michael E. Porter, "The Competitive Advantage of the Inner City," *Harvard Business Review* (May–June 1995). Ideas in this and the following paragraphs draw on Porter's article.

48. Initiative for a Competitive Inner City (ICIC) (http://www.icic.org/about).

49. ICIC, "The Promise of Local Clusters," *Inner City Insights* 1, no. 1 (2011) (http://www.icic.org/ee_uploads/publications/Local_Cluster_Paper.pdf).

50. CalPERS, "Global Principles of Accountable Corporate Governance" (http://www.calpers-governance.org/docs-sof/principles/2010–5–2–global-principles-of-accountable-corp-gov.pdf).

51. The OECD's principles can be found at http://www.oecd.org/dataoecd/32/18/31 557724.pdf.

52. In, for example, Simon Zadek, "The Path to Corporate Responsibility," *Harvard Business Review* (December 2004): 125–32, and elsewhere.

53. James P. Hawley and Andrew T. Williams, "The Universal Owner's Role in Sustainable Economic Development," *Corporate Environmental Strategy* 9, no. 3 (2002): 284–91, p. 284.

54. Ibid.

55. Lorin Letendre, "The Dynamics of the Boardroom," *Academy of Management Executive* 18, no. 1 (2004): 101–456. Quoted in Robert A. G. Monks and Nell Minnow, *Power and Accountability* (www.ragm.com/library/books/poweracc/contents.html, chap.1).

57. Anup Shah, "Poverty Facts and Stats," *Global Issues* (http://www.globalissues.org/article/26/poverty-facts-and-stats).

58. Data are from United Nations Department of Economic and Social Affairs, *United Nations, Millennium Development Goals Report 2010* (New York: 2010) (http://www.un.org/millenniumgoals/reports.shtml).

59. Gretchen M. Spreijtzer and Scott Sonenshein, "Toward the Construct Definition of Positive Deviance," *American Behavioral Scientist* 47, no. 6 (February 2004): 828–47.

60. Jerry Sternin and Robert Choo, "The Power of Positive Deviancy," *Harvard Business Review* (January–February 2000): 14–15. 61. For more examples, see the Positive Deviance website (www.positivedeviance.org), especially "Projects" (http://www.positivedeviance.org/projects/#IDAQBAS).

62. For the history, development, and achievements of Grameen Bank, see David Bornstein, *The Price of a Dream: The Story of the Grameen Bank* (Chicago: University of Chicago Press, 1996).

63. Data in this paragraph are from the Grameen Bank's website, http://www.grameen-info.org/index.php?option=com_content&task=view&id=26&Itemid=175.

64. See Bornstein, *Price of a Dream*; and see www.grameen-info.org for current data and information.

65. See Acción's website, www.accion.org. Data in this and the following paragraphs are from this website.

66. Not all microlenders operate ethically. Some microlenders, particularly for-profit ones, have come under fire for charging exorbitant interests rates and demanding payback schedules, and because those people who receive loans, while improving their lives, do not necessarily reach even the middle class.

67. Calvert Social Venture Capital Fund (http://www.calvert.com/sri_654.html).

68. New Economics Foundation Social Venture Fund (http://www.neweconomics .org/gen/access_socialventure.aspx).

69. See www.calvert.com/sri_654.html for details.

70. "Fortune's Most Admired Companies," (http://money.cnn.com/magazines/ fortune/mostadmired/2010/full_list/).

71. See Global Corporate 100 Sustainable Corporations in the World website, http:// www.global100.org.

72. Leslie Gaines-Ross, "Reputation Ranking Mania" (http://reputationxchange .com/2009/05/02/reputation-ranking-mania/).

73. Gary Davies et al., *Corporate Reputation and Competitiveness* (New York: Routledge, 2002).

74. For some background on Fombrun's work on reputation, as well as that of other scholars, see http://www.reputationinstitute.com/main/home.php. See also the New Economics Foundation's website at www.neweconomics.org/gen.

CHAPTER 9

1. Fritjof Capra, *The Web of Life: A New Scientific Understanding of Living Systems* (New York: Anchor Doubleday, 1995), 301.

2. World Wildlife Federation, *Living Planet Report 2006* (Gland, Switzerland, 2006) (http://www.footprintnetwork.org/newsletters/gfn_blast_0610.html).

3. WWF, Zoological Society of London, and Global Footprint Network, *Living Planet Report 2010* (http://www.footprintnetwork.org/press/LPR2010.pdf).

4. Peter M. Senge, *The Fifth Discipline: The Art and Practice of the Learning Organization*, rev. ed. (New York: Currency Doubleday, 2006).

5. Among the many articles and books that have raised this issue is a cover story in *Business Week*, "Beyond the Green Corporation," January 29, 2007. See also Daniel Esty and Andrew S. Winston, *Green to Gold: How Smart Companies Use Environmental Strategy to Innovate, Create Value, and Build Competitive Advantage* (New Haven, CT: Yale University Press, 2006). Important references are Paul Hawken, Amory Lovens, and L. Hunter Lovens, *Natural Capitalism: Creating the Next Industrial Revolution* (Boston: Little, Brown, 1999); and William McDonough and Michael Braungart, *Cradle to Cradle: Remaking the Way We Make Things* (New York: North Point Press, 2002).

6. Dorothy Maxwell and Rita van der Vorst, "Developing Sustainable Products and Services," *Journal of Cleaner Production* 11, no. 8 (December 2003): 883–95.

7. Michael A. Berry and Dennis A. Rondinelli lay out this argument in "Proactive Corporate Environment Management: A New Industrial Revolution," *Academy of Management Executive* 12, no. 2 (May 1998): 38–50.

8. See, for example, Stuart L. Hart, "Beyond Greening: Strategies for a Sustainable World," *Harvard Business Review* (January–February 1997): 66–76.

9. Glen Dowell, Stuart Hart, and Bernard Yeung, "Do Corporate Global Environmental Standards Create or Destroy Market Value?" *Management Science* 46, no. 8 (August 2000): 1059–74.

10. MIT Sloan Management Review and The Boston Consulting Group, "Sustainability: The 'Embracers' Seize Advantage" *MIT Sloan Management Review Research Report* (Winter 2011) (http://c0426007.cdn2.cloudfiles.rackspacecloud.com/MIT-SMR-BCG-sustainability-the-embracers-seize-advantage-2011.pdf).

11. Ibid., 19–21.

12. Jeanne Liedtka, "Constructing an Ethic for Business Practice: Competing Effectively and Doing Good," *Business and Society* 37, no. 3 (September 1998): 254–80.

13. Hart, "Beyond Greening"; and Stuart L. Hart and Mark B. Milstein, "Creating Sustainable Value," *Academy of Management Executive* 17, no. 2 (2003): 56–69.

14. Hart and Milstein, "Creating Sustainable Value."

15. Hart, "Beyond Greening," 71.

16. Hart and Milstein, "Creating Sustainable Value."

17. Hart, "Beyond Greening."

18. Hart and Milstein, "Creating Sustainable Value."

19. Ibid.

20. Stuart L. Hart and Clayton M. Christensen, "The Great Leap: Driving Innovation from the Base of the Pyramid," *Sloan Management Review* (Fall 2002): 51–56.

21. C. K. Prahalad, *The Fortune at the Bottom of the Pyramid: Eradicating Poverty through Profits* (New Delhi: Pearson Education / Wharton School Publishing, 2005); and Stuart L. Hart, *Capitalism at the Crossroads: The Unlimited Business Opportunities in Solving the World's Most Difficult Problems* (Philadelphia: Wharton School Publishing, 2005).

22. Hart, "Beyond Greening."

23. Michael A. Berry and Dennis A. Rondinelli lay out this argument in "Proactive Corporate Environment Management: A New Industrial Revolution," *Academy of Management Executive* 12, no. 2 (May 1998): 38–50.

24. See the Environmental Protection Agency's website at www.epa.gov/epaoswer/hazwaste/ minimize/intl_trk.htm.

25. Amy P. Lally, "ISO 14000 and Environmental Cost Accounting: The Gateway to the Global Market," *Law & Policy in International Business* 29, no. 4 (Summer 1998): 401–538.

26. William G. Russell, Steven L. Skalak, and Gail Miller, "Environmental Cost Accounting: The Bottom Line for Environmental Quality," *Environmental Quality Management* 3 (1994): 255–68.

27. Ibid.

28. Sime Curkovic, Robert Sroufe, and Robert Landeros, "Measuring TQEM Returns from the Application of Quality Frameworks," *Business Strategy and the Environment* 17 (2008): 93–106.

29. Ibid.

30. Berry and Rondinelli, "Proactive Corporate Environment Management."

31. Forest L. Reinhardt, "Bringing the Environment Down to Earth," *Harvard Business Review* (July–August 1999): 149–57.

32. Reinhardt, "Bringing the Environment Down to Earth," exemplifies this way of thinking, which comes from within the current set of management assumptions. The ideas in this and the next paragraph are drawn from Reinhardt's article. His ideas are more fully developed in *Down to Earth: Applying Business Principles to Environmental Management* (Boston: Harvard Business School Press, 2000).

33. Reinhardt, "Bringing the Environment Down to Earth."

34. Russell, Skalak, and Miller, "Environmental Cost Accounting."

35. Daniel C. Esty and Andrew S. Winston, *Green to Gold: How Smart Companies Use Environmental Strategy to Innovate, Create Value, and Build Competitive Advantage* (New Haven, CT: Yale University Press, 2006).

36. The idea of the prisoner's dilemma was first discussed in game theory and explains why two parties might not cooperate, even if it is in their interest to do so. If both parties decide to not cooperate (and hence behave in a rational way), the reward for each party is *lower* than if both had acted irrationally (i.e., cooperated). In other words, if actors behave strictly rationally and in their own self-interest, they will be worse off than if they were to act against their self-interest. For a discussion, see Robert Axelrod, *The Evolution of Cooperation* (New York: Basic Books, 1984).

37. Pieter Glasbergen, "Modern Environmental Agreements," *Journal of Environmental Planning and Management* 41 (1998): 693–709.

38. Unilever, "2010 Annual Report," 2010 (http://unilever.com/investorrelations/annual_reports/AnnualReportandAccounts2010/Downloadcentre.aspx).

39. MIT Sloan Management Review and The Boston Consulting Group, *Sustainability*, 14.

40. Ibid., 21

41. Unilever, "Developing the Plan," 2010 (http://www.sustainable-living.unilever.com/our-approach/developing-the-plan/).

42. Unilever, "Unilever Sustainable Living Plan: Small Actions, Big Difference," 2010 (http://www.uslp.unilever.com/wp-content/uploads/2010/10/UnileverSustainability-Plan2.pdf).

43. Unilever, "Integrating Sustainability into the Business," 2010 (http://www.sustainable-living.unilever.com/our-approach/integrating-sustainability-into-the-business/).

44. Unilever, "Unilever Sustainable Living Plan," 3.

45. See the World Bank website, www.worldbank.org/depweb/english/modules/social/pgr.

46. Ibid.

47. See also Jeffrey Sachs, *Common Wealth* (London: Penguin, 2008).

48. Worldwatch Institute, "State of the World 2004: Consumption by the Numbers" (www.worldwatch.org/press/news/2004/01/07).

49. Hazel Henderson, *Building a Win-Win World: Life Beyond Global Economic Warfare* (San Francisco: Berrett-Koehler, 1996).

50. Bill McKibben, *Eaarth: Making a Life on a Tough New Planet* (New York: Times Books, 2010).

51. James Lovelock, *The Vanishing Face of Gaia: A Final Warning* (New York: Basic Books, 2010).

52. Carmen Ravenga, "Will There Be Enough Water? Pilot Analysis of Global Eco-systems: Freshwater Systems," ed. Greg Mock (World Resources Institute, October 2000) (http://earthtrends.wri.org/features/view_feature.php?theme=2&fid=17).

53. Claude Fussler, "Caring for Climate," in *The United Nations Global Compact: Achievements, Trends and Challenges*, ed. Andreas Rasche and Georg Kell (Cambridge, UK: Cambridge University Press, 2010), 80–100.

54. Sachs, *Common Wealth*.

55. For some current statistics and information, see the World Resources Institute's Earth Trends website, http://earthtrends.wri.org/index.php.

56. Sachs, *Common Wealth*.

57. See Michael E. Porter, "Clusters and the New Economics of Competition," *Harvard Business Review* (November–December 1998): 77–90.

58. Ibid. See also Michael E. Porter, *The Competitive Advantage of Nations* (New York: Free Press, 1990); and Michael E. Porter, "The Competitive Advantage of Nations," *Harvard Business Review* (March–April 1990): 73–93.

59. Porter, "Clusters," 78.

60. Ibid., 79.

61. Thomas L. Friedman, *The Lexus and the Olive Tree* (New York: Anchor Books, 2000).

62. Robert D. Putnam, "Bowling Alone: America's Declining Social Capital," *Journal of Democracy* 6, no. 1 (January 1995): 65–78.

63. This work by Stephen Knanck of American University and Philip Keefer of the World Bank is cited in Karen Pennar, "The Ties That Lead to Prosperity," *Business Week*, December 15, 1997, 154–55.

64. Putnam, "Bowling Alone," 65.

65. Robert D. Putnam, *Making Democracy Work: Civic Traditions in Modern Italy* (Princeton, NJ: Princeton University Press, 1993).

66. Noted in Pennar, "The Ties That Lead to Prosperity."

CHAPTER 10

1. Ernst Ligteringen and Simon Zadek, "The Future of Corporate Responsibility Codes, Standards, and Frameworks," n.d. (http://www.greenbiz.com/sites/default/files/document/CustomO16C45F63376.pdf).

2. See, for example, Naomi Klein, *No Logo: No Space, No Choice, No Jobs* (New York: Picador, 2000); or Eric Schlosser, *Fast Food Nation: The Dark Side of the All-American Meal* (Boston: Houghton Mifflin, 2001).

3. See Pietra Rivoli, "Labor Standards in the Global Economy: Issues for Investors," *Journal of Business Ethics* 43 (March 2003): 223–32.

4. See, for example, Dara O'Rourke, "Monitoring the Monitors: A Critique of PricewaterhouseCoopers' Labor Monitoring," white paper, September 28, 2000; and Stephen J. Frenkel, "Globalization, Athletic Footwear Commodity Chains and Employment Relations in China," *Organization Studies* 22, no. 4 (2001): 531–62.

5. Thomas Donaldson and Thomas W. Dunfee, *Ties That Bind: A Social Contracts Approach to Business Ethics* (Boston: Harvard Business School Press, 1999), 68.

6. Complete information about the "Protect, Respect, and Remedy" Framework for Business and Human Rights can be found at http://www.business-humanrights.org /SpecialRepPortal/Home.

7. See http://www.business-humanrights.org/SpecialRepPortal/Home/Protect -Respect-Remedy-Framework/GuidingPrinciples.

8. Many more details can be found on the Protect, Respect, and Remedy website and in the guidance document itself, which was in draft form at this writing (http://www .business-humanrights.org/SpecialRepPortal/Home).

9. Human Rights Council, "Protect, Respect and Remedy: A Framework for Business and Human Rights"; Report of the Special Representative of the Secretary-General on the issue of human rights and transnational corporations and other business enterprises, John Ruggie. UN Human Rights Council, A/HRC/8/5, 2008.

10. Ibid., 18–19.

11. Business & Human Rights Initiative, "How to Do Business with Respect for Human Rights: A Guidance Tool for Companies" (The Hague: Global Compact Network Netherlands, 2010). Our discussion here is based on some of the points raised in this publication.

12. For a comprehensive study of the "sweatshop quandary," see Pamela Varley, ed., *The Sweatshop Quandary: Corporate Responsibility on the Global Frontier* (Washington, DC: Investor Responsibility Research Center, 1998).

13. See Clean Clothes Campaign, http://www.cleanclothes.org/.

14. See United Students Against Sweatshops, http://www.nlcnet.org/.

15. See the website of the United Students Against Sweatshops at http://usas.org/.

16. See Not for Sale, "End Human Trafficking and Slavery" (http://www.notforsale campaign.org/).

17. See William Echikson, "It's Europe's Turn to Sweat about Sweatshops," *Business Week*, July 19, 1999, 96.

18. Fair Labor Association, http://www.fairlabor.org/.

19. See, for example, Aaron Bernstein, "Sweatshop Reform: How to Solve the Stand-off," *Business Week*, May 3, 1999, 186–90.

20. Information in this paragraph is from Green America, "Sweatshops," (http:// www.greenamerica.org/programs/sweatshops/whattoknow.cfm).

21. Global Exchange, "Sweatshop FAQ" (http://www.globalexchange.org/campaigns /sweatshops/sweatshopsfaq.html).

22. Ethical Trading Initiative, "Living Wage" (http://www.ethicaltrade.org /in-action/issues/living%20wage).

23. See the Sweatshop Watch Web site, www.sweatshopwatch.org/swatch/newslet ter/4_2. html#living_wage; the link is now dead, but was accessed July 6, 2004.

24. Jeremy Pope, *TI Source Book 2000: Confronting Corruption: The Elements of a National Integrity System* (www.transparency.org/content/download/2458/14526).

25. Transparency International website, www.transparency.org.

26. Pope, *TI Source Book,* executive summary, 2.

27. "What Is Good Governance," UN Economic and Social Commission for Asia and the Pacific (http://www.unescap.org/pdd/prs/ProjectActivities/Ongoing/gg/governance .asp).

28. Ibid.

29. Skip Kaltenheuser, "Bribery Is Being Outlawed Virtually Worldwide," *Business Ethics* (May–June 1998): 11.

30. Pope, *TI Source Book*, Part B, 3.

31. The full text of Agenda 21 can be found at http://www.un.org/documents/ga /conf151/aconf15126–1annex1.htm.

32. The Rio Declaration can be found at http://www.un.org/esa/sustdev/documents /agenda21/index.htm.

33. Information on Agenda 21 can be found at http://www.un.org/esa/dsd/agenda21/.

34. Additional information about CERES and the CERES Principles can be found at www.ceres.org.

35. World Business Council for Sustainable Development, "About" (http://www .wbcsd.org/templates/TemplateWBCSD5/layout.asp?type=p&MenuId=NjA&doOpen= 1&ClickMenu=LeftMenu).

36. Ibid.

37. Information and the complete set of principles for Responsible Care can be found at www.responsiblecare.org.

38. For an extended discussion of ISO 14000 and 14001, see Amy Pesapane Lally, "ISO 14000 and Environmental Cost Accounting: The Gateway to the Global Market," *Law & Policy in International Business* 29, no. 4 (Summer 1998): 401–538.

39. Additional information on ISO and the various sets of standards can be found at http://www.iso.org/iso/home.htm.

40. Ibid.

41. Amory B. Lovins, L. Hunter Lovins, and Paul Hawken, "A Road Map for Natural Capitalism," *Harvard Business Review* (May–June 1999): 145–58.

42. Ibid., 146–48.

43. Ibid., 148.

44. 3M Corporation, "Pollution Prevention Pays, Sustainability at 3M" (http:// solutions.3m.com/wps/portal/3M/en_US/global/sustainability/management/ pollution-prevention-pays/).

45. 3M Corporation, "2015 Sustainability Goals" (http://solutions.3m.com/wps/ portal/3M/en_US/3M-Sustainability/Global/VisionHistory/Goals_2015/).

46. Lovins et al., "Road Map," 152.

47. Peter M. Senge, *The Fifth Discipline: The Art & Practice of The Learning Organiza- tion*, rev. ed. (New York: Currency Doubleday, 2006).

48. Juliet Schor, *Plenitude: The New Economics of Real Wealth* (New York: Penguin, 2010).

49. For more information, see the OECD website, http://www.oecd.org/document/2 8/0,3343,en_2649_34889_2397532_1_1_1_1,00.html.

50. Details about the Caux Round Table and this framing of the two ethical ideals can be found at www.cauxroundtable.org.

51. The Caux Roundtable principles can be found at http://www.cauxroundtable.org /index.cfm?&menuid=8.

52. Information on the Equator Principles can be found at www.equator-principles .com.

53. Quoted in ibid.

54. UN Principles for Responsible Investment, "Principles" (http://www.unpri.org /principles/).

55. UN Principles for Responsible Investment (http://www.unpri.org/about/); and Institutional Investor, "Principles of Responsible Investment Gets More Traction" (http://www.institutionalinvestor.com/green_investing/Articles/2754437/Principles-of-Responsible-Investment-Gets-More-Traction.html).

56. See for example, Lynn A. Stout, "Why We Should Stop Teaching Dodge v. Ford," UCLA School of Law, Law-Econ Research Paper No. 07–11, 2006 (http://ssrn.com/ abstract=1013744); Kent Greenfield, "A New Era for Corporate Law: Using Corporate Governance to Benefit All Stakeholders," *Paper Series on Corporate Design: Summit on the Future of the Corporation* (2007): 19–28 (http://www.corporation2020.org/Summit PaperSeries.pdf); and Kent Greenfield, "New Principles for Corporate Law," *Hastings Business Law Journal* 1 (May 2005): 87–118.

57. Ibid. See also John Cavanagh et al., *Alternatives to Economic Globalization* (San Francisco: Berrett-Koehler, 2002); Charles Derber, *Regime Change Begins at Home: Freeing America From Corporate Rule* (San Francisco: Berrett-Koehler, 2004).

CHAPTER 11

1. Robert Spiegel, "Yogi Berra's Business Wisdom, Growth and Leadership," *Business Know-How* (www.businessknowhow.com/growth/yogi.htm).

2. Robert Kegan, *In Over Our Heads: The Mental Demands of Modern Life* (Cambridge, MA: Harvard University Press, 1994).

3. Royal Dutch Shell, *Scenarios and Explorers Guide* (The Hague: Shell, 2008), 8.

4. Ibid.

5. Royal Dutch Shell, *Shell Energy Scenarios to 2050* (The Hague: Shell, 2008). Our discussion of both scenarios is based on the information given in this publication. More information on Shell scenarios is available at http://www.shell.com/scenarios.

6. Ibid., 8.

7. Ibid., 10.

8. Ibid., 25.

9. Ibid., 33.

10. Kegan, *In Over Our Heads*, 11. Much of this section and the next is from Sandra Waddock, "Leadership Integrity in a Fractured Knowledge World," *Academy of Management Learning and Education* 6, no. 4 (2007): 543–57.

12. Alvin Toffler, *The Third Wave* (New York: Bantam, 1984).

13. John S. Brown and Paul Duguid, *The Social Life of Information* (Boston: Harvard Business School Press, 2000).

14. Brown and Duguid, *Social Life*.

15. Waddock, "Leadership Integrity."

16. United Nations, "Millennium Development Goals" (http://www.un.org /millenniumgoals/).

17. Ibid.

18. These developments are reviewed in depth in Sandra Waddock and Malcolm McIntosh, *SEE Change: Making the Transition to a Sustainable Enterprise Economy* (Sheffield, UK: Greenleaf, 2011).

19. See, for example, the Center for Strategic and International Studies website, www.csis.org. Trends identified in this section are from Michael J. Mazarr, *Global Trends 2005: The Challenge of a New Millennium* (Washington, DC: Center for Strategic and International Studies, 1997). See www.csis.org/gt2005.

20. See Ibid.

21. Ibid., 13.

22. Ibid., 16–24.

23. Ibid., 25.

24. Benjamin Barber, *Jihad vs. McWorld* (New York: Times Books; Random House, 1995).

25. Mazarr, *Global Trends 2005*, 31.

26. All the trends identified in this section are explored in Eamonn Kelly's "Forces of the Future" (http://www.monitor.com/portals/0/monitormedia/videos/forces_of_the_future.html).

27. This section draws from James Canton, *The Extreme Future: The Top Trends That Will Reshape the World in the Next 20 Years* (New York: Plume, 2007).

28. Joseph E. Stiglitz, "Moving beyond Market Fundamentalism to a More Balanced Economy," *Annals of Public and Cooperative Economics* 80, no. 3 (2009): 345–60, p. 345.

29. Ibid., 348.

30. Quoted in Simon Johnson, "Paul Volcker Finds a Hammer," *New York Times*, December 17, 2009 (economix.blogs.nytimes.com/2009/12/17/paul-volcker-finds-a-hammer).

31. Paul Volcker, quoted in ibid.

32. Paul Krugman, "How Did Economists Get It So Wrong?" *New York Times*, September 6, 2009 (http://www.nytimes.com/2009/09/06/magazine/06Economic-t.html).

33. Umair Haque, "A User's Guide to 21st Century Economics," *Harvard Business Review Blog*, January 7, 2009 (blogs.harvardbusiness.org/haque/2009/01/a_users_guide_to_21st_century.html).

34. Russell L. Ackoff, "On Learning and the Systems That Facilitate It," *Reflections* 1, no. 1 (1999): 14–24, reprinted from The Center for Quality of Management, Cambridge, MA, 1996.

35. Brief Summary of the Dodd-Frank Wall Street Reform and Consumer Protection Act (http://banking.senate.gov/public/_files/070110_Dodd_Frank_Wall_Street_Reform_comprehensive_summary_Final.pdf).

36. For more on the GANs concept see Steve Waddell, *Global Action Networks: Creating Our Future Together* (Hampshire, UK: Palgrave, Macmillan, 2011); and Steve Waddell, "Global Action Networks: A Global Invention Helping Business Make Globalization Work for All," *Journal of Corporate Citizenship* 12 (Winter 2003): 27–42.

37. Ibid.

CHAPTER 12

1. IBM Global Business Services, *Capitalizing on Complexity: Insights from the Global Chief Executive Officer Study* (Somers, NY: IBM Global Business Services, 2010) (http://www-935.ibm.com/services/us/ceo/ceostudy2010/index.html), 3.

2. Ibid.

3. Ibid.

4. Robert Kegan, *In Over Our Heads: The Mental Demands of Modern Life* (Cambridge, MA: Harvard University Press, 1994).

5. Michael J. Mazarr, *Global Trends 2005: The Challenge of a New Millennium* (Washington, DC: Center for Strategic and International Studies, 1997).

6. Joseph A. Raelin, *Creating Leaderful Organizations: How to Bring Out Leadership in Everyone* (San Francisco: Berrett-Koehler, 2003).

7. For example, Marc Gunther, *Faith and Fortune: How Compassionate Capitalism Is Transforming American Business* (New York: Three Rivers Press, 2005); and Kent Greenfield, "New Principles for Corporate Law," *Hastings Business Law Journal* 1 (May 2005): 87–118.

8. Corporation 2020 website, http://www.corporate2020.org/.

9. See, for example, *World Business Council for Sustainable Development, Vision 2050: The New Agenda for Business* (Geneva: WBSCD, 2010) (http://www.wbcsd.org/DocRoot/dhxR1BWYVPX3e6wr0vZQ/Vision_2050_FullReport_040210.pdf).

10. Jared Diamond, *Collapse: How Societies Choose to Succeed or Fail* (New York: Penguin, 2005).

11. William McDonough and Michael Braungart, *Cradle to Cradle: Remaking the Way We Make Things* (New York: North Point Press, 2002). See also Paul Hawken, Amory Lovins, and L. Hunter Lovins, *Natural Capitalism: Creating the Next Industrial Revolution* (Boston: Little, Brown, 1999).

12. Janine Benyus, *Biomimicry: Innovation Inspired by Nature* (New York: Harper Perennial, 2002).

13. For example, James F. Moore, *The Death of Competition: Leadership and Strategy in the Age of Ecosystems* (New York: HarperBusiness, 1997).

14. On plenitude, see Juliet Schor, *Plenitude: The New Economics of Real Wealth* (New York: Penguin, 2010).

15. Joseph E. Stiglitz, Amartya Sen, and Jean-Paul Fitoussi, "Report by the Commission on the Measurement of Economic Performance and Social Progress," undated, ca. 2009 (http://www.stiglitz-sen-fitoussi.fr/documents/rapport_anglais.pdf).

16. Ibid.

17. Ibid., 12 (italics in original).

18. Ibid.

19. Ibid., 14–15.

20. Schor, *Plenitude*.

21. This topic is discussed at length by Robert D. Putnam in *Making Democracy Work: Civic Traditions in Modern Italy* (Princeton, NJ: Princeton University Press, 1993); also see his articles, "Bowling Alone: America's Declining Social Capital," *Journal of Democracy* 6,

no. 1 (January 1995): 65–78; and "The Strange Disappearance of Civic America," *American Prospect* 24 (Winter 1996) (http://epn.org/prospect/24/ 24putn.html).

22. For example, Steve Waddell, *Global Action Networks: Creating Our Future Together* (New York: Palgrave Macmillan, 2011); Maria M. Seitanidi, *The Politics of Partnership: A Critical Examination of Nonprofit-Business Partnership* (London, Springer, 2010).

23. See, for example, Sandra Waddock, *Not by Schools Alone: Sharing Responsibility for America's Education Reform* (Greenwich, CT: Praeger, 1995).

24. See, for example, Sandra Waddock, "Understanding Social Partnerships: An Evolutionary Model of Partnership Organizations," *Administration and Society* 21, no. 1 (May 1989): 78–100.

25. Joseph A. Schumpeter, *Theory of Economic Development* (Boston: Harvard University Press, 1934).

26. Peter M. Senge, *The Fifth Discipline* (New York: Currency Doubleday, 1990).

27. See Russell L. Ackoff, "On Learning and the Systems That Facilitate It," *Reflection* 1, no. 1 (1999): 14–24, reprinted from the Center for Quality of Management, Cambridge, MA, 1996. See also Karl E. Weick, "Educating for the Unknowable: The Infamous Real World" (presentation at the Academy of Management, Chicago, IL, 1999.)

28. Ackoff, "On Learning," 16 (italics added).

INDEX

2011 Carbon Nation, 222

3M Corporation, 261

AA 1000 AccountAbility Principles Standard, 196

AA 1000 Assurance Standard, 196

AA 1000 framework, 190, 196

AA 1000 Stakeholder Engagement Standard, 196

Acción International, 217

accountability, 2, 16, 30, 33, 48, 51, 69, 94, 98, 109, 117, 133, 143, 171–72, 178, 183, 185–89, 196–97, 212, 214, 235, 244, 252–53, 257, 265–26, 289–90, 293, 296, 302

AccountAbility, 185, 196, 214

Accredited Certification International, 197, 200

Ackoff, Robert, 60, 111, 288, 304, 308

AFL-CIO, 143

Agenda 21, 40, 94–95, 255, 257

American Apparel Manufacturers Association (AAMA), 249

American Management Association, 119

American Recovery and Reinvestment Act of 2009, 143

Annan, Kofi, 1, 94, 191–92, 264

anti-corruption, 4–6, 19, 94–95, 191–95, 244, 251–54, 262

Argyris, Chris, 62

ARTS of responsible management (accountability, responsibility, transparency, and sustainability), 109, 293, 302

Asian Business's "Asia's Most Admired Companies," 220

Auger, Pat, 123

B Corporations, 281

Baidu, 96

Bailon, Franz, 67

Baldridge Quality Award, 151, 170, 176–79, 185

Ballinger, Jeffrey, 125, 198

BANG technologies, 285–86

Barber, Benjamin, 283

Bear Stearns, 32–33

Belenky, Mary, 102

Bernays, Edward, 165

Berra, Yogi, 272

Berry, Michael, 230, 232

Bodwell, Charles, 171–72

boycott, 96, 123–24, 170, 234, 244

Brandeis, Louis, 214

Bretton Woods, 8, 31, 290

BRIC nations, 14, 284–85, 305

Brundtland Commission, 45

Bruyn, Severyn, 293

Buddhism, 93

Built to Last, 56–57, 72, 113. *See also* Collins, James; Porras, Jerry

Burns, James MacGregor, 83

Business Alliance for Local Living Economies, 291

California Public Employees' Retirement System (CalPERS), 212

Calvert Funds, 206, 209, 218–19

Calvert Social Investment Foundation, 209

Calvert's Social Venture Capital Fund, 218

Canton, James, Dr., 286

capitalism, 12, 21, 27–30, 37, 75, 132, 242, 260, 262, 281, 299

Capitalizing on Complexity, 294

Capra, Fritjof, 16, 222

carbon dioxide and toxic emissions, 9, 11, 36, 73, 219, 224, 235–36, 239–40, 261, 273–74, 279, 285–86

Carson, Rachel, 38

Carter, Craig, 123

Catalyst, 121

Caux Roundtable Principles for Business, 194, 263

Cavanagh, Gerald F., 9, 100, 102

Cemex, 164–65

Center for Strategic and International Studies (CSIS), 281

certification bodies, 197–98

chaebol, 103

Champy, James, 89

Chemical Manufacturers Association, 256

Chicago School, 28

child labor, 46, 94, 100, 123–24, 170, 176, 182, 189, 193, 206, 249, 280

China, People's Republic of, 14, 16, 47, 95–97, 103–4, 161, 174–75, 191, 239, 273, 284, 286

Christensen, Clayton, 229

Citizens United case, 28, 33, 159

citizenship, 4, 7, 76–78, 94, 141, 178, 191, 228

city planet, 284

civil society, 6–11, 15–25, 41–43, 47–48, 83, 127, 137, 157–58, 192, 240–42, 245–46, 252–53, 265, 271, 285, 293, 303–4, 308

Clean Clothes Campaign, 248

climate change, 1, 8–9, 189, 208, 240, 243, 277, 285. See also carbon dioxide and toxic emissions

Coalition for Environmentally Responsible Economies (CERES), 19, 256–60

Coca-Cola, 68–70

codes of conduct, 5, 84, 112, 123–25, 156–57, 176, 181–82, 185, 187, 190–93, 198, 248, 254, 266

cognitive development: 59–74, 83, 85, 98, 226, 275, 285, 295; conventional reasoning in, 61; postconventional reasoning in, 62; preconventional reasoning in, 61

Collins, James, 56–57, 72–74, 83, 89, 97, 113–14, 235

Commission on the Measurement of Economic Performance and Social Progress, 31, 300

commitment, 18, 56–57, 69–70, 77–78, 83–84, 91–93, 97–99, 110, 113, 138, 141, 146–53, 165, 171–72, 176–81, 194–95, 200–1, 222, 227, 237, 247, 257–60, 279

Communication-on-Progress Report, 192

Communications on Progress (CoPs), 192, 203

community, 2–4, 7, 12–15, 18, 21–25, 32, 37–38, 41–43, 50, 57–59, 68–70, 75–81, 86–88, 91–92, 94, 97, 99, 103, 109, 112–13, 117, 125, 131, 134–41, 147–48, 154, 157, 163–69, 173–74, 178–79, 184–88, 200, 205, 209–11, 216–19, 222–23, 235–37, 240–42, 248, 259, 263, 275, 280, 293–94, 306–7

Community Reinvestment Act (CRA), 209

competition, 16, 20–21, 29, 31, 36, 38, 57, 65, 73, 84–92, 95, 97, 115–17, 121, 124, 127, 132, 149–56, 160, 163–65, 170–73, 188, 200, 210, 219–20, 222, 227, 234–35, 240–42, 249, 254, 260, 262, 272–73, 283–84, 291–94, 299, 303, 308–9

completeness, 82, 202. See also wholeness

consciousness, 12, 15, 37, 59, 75, 170, 226, 295, Conservation International, 10–11

Consumer Protection Act, 34, 144, 289

conventional reasoning, 61. See also cognitive development

core ideology, 56–57, 73, 84, 114. See also Collins, James; Porras, Jerry

corporate citizenship: elementary, engaged, innovative, integrated and transforming stages of, 76–78

Corporate Knights and partners, 219

corporate mission, vision, and values statements, 81, 83–85, 96, 133, 136, 168, 208, 281, 306

Corporate Responsibility Index, 207

Corporation 2020, 296–98

Corruption Perception Index, 95, 253

Costco, 114–15

crisis management, 161–62

Danone, Groupe, 49–50

Davies, Gary, 220

Davos, Switzerland, 191

DDT, 38, 45

Declaration of Fundamental Principles and Rights at Work, 176, 191

Deepwater Horizon, 162

Dees, Gregory, 48

deforestation, 2, 10–11, 35, 40, 44–45, 70, 108, 167, 215, 223, 241, 255, 259, 279, 290–91

Deming Prize, 185

Deming, W. Edwards, 89, 152, 169–70, 185

developmental theory, 60–67, 76, 228, 275, 295

Devereaux, Mary O'Hara, 104

Devinney, Timothy, 123

Diamond, Jared, 298

distributive justice, 101

Dodd-Frank Wall Street Reform and Consumer Protection Act, 34, 37, 143–44, 289

Domini Social Funds, 206

Donaldson, Thomas, 64, 93–94, 190, 245
Dow Chemicals, 162
Drucker, Peter, 111
Dunfee, Thomas, 64, 93–94, 190, 245

Eaarth, 238
Earth Charter, 81, 84, 133
Eckert, Robert, 175
ecologizing, 23–25, 95
ecomagination, 78
economizing, 23–25, 29, 42, 85, 90, 108, 111,
    121, 127, 149, 156, 164, 202, 238, 249, 251,
    254, 308
Edge Economy, 288
Edmans, Alex, 119
efficiency, 21–25, 29, 37, 50, 69–70, 85–87, 108–
    13, 121–27, 144–46, 136, 212, 227, 252, 254,
    259–61, 273–74, 283, 287, 292, 299
Einstein, Albert, 295
elementary stage, 76–77. See also corporate
    citizenship
Elfenbein, Hillary, 116
Emerson, Jed, 107
emotional development, 59–61, 66–67, 71–75,
    83, 85, 226, 291, 294–95
emotional intelligence, 61, 66–67
empathy, 66, 70–71, 75
employee stock ownership plans (ESOPs), 48
empowerment of others, 71, 84, 125, 173, 199,
    222, 239, 278, 283, 293
engaged stage, 76–78. See also corporate
    citizenship
enterprise strategy, 17, 87–88, 93, 99, 176
entrepreneurship, 26, 31, 35, 48–51, 58, 86, 99,
    148, 216–19, 241–42, 281, 291, 308
environmental, social, and governance (ESG)
    issues, 35, 107–9, 118, 145, 171, 184–85,
    188, 200–8, 233, 264, 267, 289, 291, 302
Equator Principles, 193, 263–64
Esty, Daniel, 235
Ethical Trading Initiative (ETI), 197, 251
ethics, 2, 15, 24, 59, 61, 64–66, 72, 81, 89, 91–
    103, 106, 117, 123, 132–33, 137, 157–58, 178,
    189–90, 197, 205–6, 251–53, 263, 285, 297
European companies of American parentage
    (ECAPs), 158–59
European Quality Award, 170, 185
European Social Investment Forum, 208
Exxon Valdez, 256

Fair Labor Association (FLA), 197, 249
Fallon, Tip, 146

Far Eastern Economic Review's "Review 200,"
    220
Federal Deposit Insurance Corporation
    (FDIC), 209
Federal Reserve System, 31, 286–87
Financial Times's "Europe's Most Respected
    Companies," 220
Firms of Endearment, 72, 75, 97, 114
Fitoussi, Jean-Paul, 300
Fombrun, Charles, 220
Ford, 36
Foreign Corrupt Practices Act, 254
Forest Stewardship Council, 10–11, 35, 290–91
Fortune magazine's "reputation index," 140,
    220
foundational values, 93–95, 171–72, 175–76,
    186, 189–90
Frederick, William, 23–25, 29
freedom of religion, 100
freedom of speech, 91, 94, 98, 100, 245
Freeman, R. Edward, 87–88
Friedman, Milton, 28, 76, 132, 288
FTSE KLD 400, 117
FTSE4Good, 207
Fundamental Principles and Rights at Work
    (FPRW), 176, 191

Gaia hypothesis, 20
Gap, The, 79
Gardner, Howard, 61
Garten, Jeffrey, 87
General Electric, 78
General Motors, 36
generally accepted accounting principles
    (GAAP), 200–1
Genuine Progress Indication (GPI), 108–9
Ghoshal, Sumantra, 127
Gifford, Kathie Lee, 87
Gilbert, Dan, 87–88
Gilligan, Carol, 65–66, 102
Giscard d'Estaing, Olivier, 263
Gladwin, Thomas, 15, 45–46
Glass-Steagall Act, 287
GlaxoSmithKline, 36
Global 100 Most Sustainable Corporations in
    the World, 219
Global Action Networks, 290
Global Business Network, 284
Global Compact. See United Nations Global
    Compact
global financial crisis of 2008, 30–36, 108, 142,
    211, 227, 278, 286, 289

Global Footprint Network, 43, 223–25
Global Principles of Accountable Corporate Governance, 212
Global Reporting Initiative, 18, 35, 133, 185, 189–90, 200–2
GlobalWork, 104
glocal, 241
goals, 2, 19, 43, 57–59, 70, 73–74, 83, 86, 88–90, 109, 138, 144–45, 151–52, 157–58, 166, 172–80, 185–86, 199, 203–5, 215, 221, 236, 243, 255, 258, 261–62, 265, 277–81, 292, 300, 302
Goleman, Daniel, 66–67, 71
Googins, Bradley, 76–78
Google, 47, 95–97, 276, 305
governance, 9–11, 16, 21–22, 27, 35, 107, 109, 118, 133, 142–44, 203–4, 211–14, 223, 253, 267, 280, 285, 290–92, 301
Grameen Bank, 49–50, 165, 188, 216–18
Grameen Knitwear Limited, 217
Grameen Shakti, 217
Grameen Shakti/Education, 217
Grameen Telecom, 217
Graves, Sam, 125
greenhouse gas emissions. *See* carbon dioxide and toxic emissions
Greenpeace, 166,
Greenspan, Alan, 286–87
Gross Domestic Product (GDP), 25, 108–9, 300–1
Gross Happiness Indicator, 300
groupthink, 148
Guge, 78
Gunther, Marc, 4

Hammer, Michael, 89
Hammond, Allen, 26
Handy, Charles, 6–7, 30, 135, 142
Happy Planet Index, 108
Haque, Umair, 288
Harris Poll-Reputation Institute, 219
Hart, Stuart, 228–29
Hawken, Paul, 260–62
Hawley, James, 214
Healthy Cities Movement, 291
Henderson, Hazel, 239
HIV/AIDS, 35–36, 279
holons, 3, 14–15, 82
honesty, 24, 60, 81–84, 91–92, 99, 127, 144, 164, 173
human rights, 4, 5, 19, 37, 65, 81, 85, 87, 94, 96–97, 124, 137, 160, 170–71, 176, 180, 189, 191–93, 195, 201, 207–8, 244–49, 252–53, 262, 286, 298
Human Rights Watch, 96
Hurricane Katrina, 44
hypernorms, 64, 93–94, 175, 190–91

IBM Corporation, 294–95
An Inconvenient Truth, 222
individual or civil rights, 3, 37
Industrial and Textile Employees (UNITE), 249
Initiative for a Competitive Inner City (ICIC), 210–11, 215
Inner City 100 ratings, 210–11
innovation, 48–49, 58, 76–78, 89, 92–93, 99, 110, 124, 127, 149, 153, 155, 157, 164, 171–72, 178, 183–84, 186, 223, 227, 237, 242, 257, 261, 281, 283, 286, 288, 304
innovative stage, 76–78. *See also* corporate citizenship
Innovest Strategic Value Advisors, 111
Institute for Global Futures, 286
institutional corruption, 33–35, 43
integrated stage, 76–78. *See also* corporate citizenship
intellectual capital, 127–128, 135, 146, 149–50, 276–77
intellectual property rights, 36
Interfaith Center on Corporate Responsibility, 213, 249
Intergovernmental Panel on Climate Change (IPCC), 44
International Integrated Reporting Committee (IIRC), 203–4
International Labour Organization, 39, 94, 98, 100, 133, 176, 191, 248
International Monetary Fund, 8, 290
international nongovernmental organization (INGO), 252
International Truck and Engine Corporation, 230
Internet, 8, 95–97, 128, 151, 166–67, 170, 208, 243, 289
Isaacs, William, 63
ISO 14000, 200, 256–60
ISO 26000, 190, 199–201
issues management, 157, 160

J.P. Morgan Chase, 32
Jensen, Michael, 144
Johannesburg Stock Exchange, 207
Johansen, Robert, 104

Johnson & Johnson, 181
Juran, Edward, 170
justice, 34, 65, 81, 101–3, 133–34, 148, 256
JustMeans.com, 166

Kant, Immanuel, 98
Karnani, Aneel, 26
Keefe, Joe, 118
Kegan, Robert, 62–83, 80, 275, 295
keiretsu, 102
Kelley, Marjorie, 297
Kelly, Eamonn, 284–86
Kempen Capital Management, 207
Keynes, John Maynard, 126, 288
Kiernan, Matthew, 111
Kit Kat, 166–67
KLD Research and Analytics, 207
Kohlberg, Lawrence, 61–66
Korten, David, 299
KPMG, 204–5
Krugman, Paul, 288
Kuttner, Robert, 31
Kuznets, Simon, 108
kyosei, 263

labor rights, 19, 48, 87, 94, 98, 124, 140, 171,
    175–76, 180, 191, 197, 244, 249–50
learning: general purpose of, 18, 24, 67, 79, 85,
    91–92, 162, 166, 169, 175, 177, 222, 271, 276,
    292, 308; the learning organization, 13, 89,
    123–24; learning systems, 171–72, 183–84,
    186; social entrepreneurship and, 47–48
learning organization, the, 13, 89
Lee, Darren, 118
Lehman Brothers, 32–33, 287
Leisinger, Klaus, 126, 194–95
Lessig, Lawrence, 34
Liedtka, Jeanne, 89–93, 119, 228
life-cycle accounting, 228–35, 260
Life-Cycle Impact Analysis (LCIA), 232
Life-Cycle Interpretation, 232
Life-Cycle Inventory (LCI), 232
Ligteringen, Ernst, 205, 243
Living Planet Index, 223–24
living wage, 210, 249–51
Liz Claiborne, 248
Locke, Richard, 125
Lovelock, James, 20–21, 239
Lovins, Amory, 260–61
Lovins, L. Hunter, 260–61
loyalty, 7, 42, 57, 64, 83, 92, 99, 115, 120–23,
    144–52, 164, 167, 220, 249

MacIntyre, Alisdair, 89
Mackey, John, 131, 139
Management Today's "Britain's Most Admired
    Companies," 220
margolis, Joshua, 116
Marine Stewardship Council, 290
market value added (MVA), 118
Mattel, Inc., 161, 174–75
Maturana, Humberto, 59
Matzlon, Kurt, 67
Mazarr, Michael, 281–83, 296
McKibben, Bill, 238
McLaughlin, Andrew, 96
metanoia, 226, 306–8
Microsoft, 96–97
Millennial Generation, 146, 284
Millennium Development Goals (MDGs), 2,
    19, 215, 277–78
Millennium Project, 281–83, 295
Milstein, Mark, 228–29
mindfulness, 60, 69, 80, 105–6, 307–9
Minnesota Center for Corporate
    Responsibility, 263
Mintzberg, 90
Mirvis, Philip, 76–78
Moberg, Dennis, 100
modal values, 83–84
Monitor Group, 284
Montreal Protocol, 279
Mooradian, Todd, 67
moral development, 59–67, 71–74, 82–85, 94,
    98, 100–2, 226, 275
Morningstar, 207
motivation, 56–57, 63, 66, 70, 98, 115, 177, 240,
    273
MSCI ESG, 207
Mulder, Herman, 263
multiple intelligences, 61, 66–67

Nahapiet, Janine, 127
National Labor Committee, 248
natural environment, 1, 4, 12, 18, 21–22, 43–47,
    60, 81, 85, 88, 109–13, 131, 135–36, 171–73,
    177–79, 191, 205, 222–26, 237–38, 242, 260,
    273, 275, 282, 293–94, 298
neoclassical economic model, 28–32, 132, 211
neoliberalism, 28, 288–90
Nestlé, 166–67, 244
network capitalism, 242
New Economics Foundation, 218, 220
New Economics Foundation's Social Venture
    Capital Fund, 218–20

Nike, 79, 124–25, 155, 248
NLC, 87
NLC Report, 87
Nobel Peace Prize, 49, 216
Noddings, Nel, 24
nongovernmental organizations, 10, 16, 23, 38, 41, 75, 137, 173, 182, 188, 192, 197–99, 203, 208, 215, 237, 252, 265, 285, 303–4
Not for Sale Campaign, 248
Novartis, 194–95
Novartis Foundation, 126, 194–95
nuclear power stations, 162, 206–7

Occupy Wall Street, 43
OECD, 84, 95, 193, 213–14, 254, 262–63, 266
OECD Convention on Combating Bribery of Foreign Officials in International Business transactions, 95, 254
OECD Guidelines for Multinational Enterprises, 84, 193, 262, 266
okyakusama, 173
optimism, 66, 70, 285, 308
Organisation for Economic Co-operation and Development, 84, 95, 193, 213–14, 254, 262–63, 266
Organisation for Economic Co-operation and Development Convention on Combating Bribery of Foreign Officials in International Business transactions, 95, 254
Organisation for Economic Co-operation and Development Guidelines for Multinational Enterprises, 84, 193, 262, 266
organizational culture, 57, 83, 85, 90, 93, 97, 103–5, 110, 138, 147–50, 157, 160, 163, 176, 242, 247, 251, 277, 282, 304, 308,
organizational learning, 123, 186
organizational norms, 42–43, 57, 64–65, 93–94, 100, 133, 138, 147, 161, 175, 190–91, 201, 215, 225, 242, 277, 283, 291, 303
outsourcing, 9, 123–24, 146, 154–56, 183, 189, 198, 229–30, 240, 244

Palmisano, Samuel J., 295
Patagonia, 121
Patrimonio Hoy program, 164–65
Pattberg, Philipp, 11
PAX World, 118
performance, 57
Perrow, Charles, 162
Pfeffer, Jeffrey, 118, 120, 149
philanthropy, 4, 6–7, 12, 76–77, 108, 163, 182, 188, 209, 215

Philips Electronics, 263
Philips, Frederick, 263
Phillips-Van Heusen, 248
PhRMA, 36
Piaget, Jean, 61–63
policies, 4–6, 8, 15, 21–23, 34–41, 46–47, 57, 72, 77, 84, 87, 96, 109, 112, 119–11, 132–33, 140, 145, 147, 153, 159, 161, 165, 170, 182, 191, 195, 214, 235, 246–47, 253, 255, 257–58, 260, 265–66, 274, 279, 287, 290–91
political action committees (PACs), 27, 158–59
political rights, 3, 245
Pollution Prevention Pays, 260
Polman, Paul, 237
Porras, Jerry, 56–57, 72–74, 83, 89, 97, 113–14
Porter, Michael, 210, 240–42
Post, James, 135
postconventional reasoning, 62. See also cognitive development
practices, 4–6, 11, 16–18, 27, 29, 42–43, 56–57, 60, 62, 74, 78–128, 133, 137–39, 144, 147–53, 156, 161, 166–201, 205–6, 208–13, 219–21, 226, 228–30, 233–35, 240, 243–44, 246–48, 251–54, 256–58, 260–61, 264, 281–82, 287, 289, 292, 294, 297, 306, 308
Prahalad, C. K., 26, 229
preconventional reasoning, 61. See also cognitive development
Preston, Lee, 34, 135–36,
Principles for Responsible Investment, 193, 264, 289
Principles for Responsible Management Education, 193
privatized governance, 10–11
procedures, 57, 67, 84, 132, 148, 153, 180–81, 183, 189, 246, 254, 259–60
process approaches to management, 91–92
Procter & Gamble (P&G), 73–74
productivity, 9, 11, 21, 26, 29, 56, 69, 78–79, 81, 86, 107–12, 115, 119, 144, 146–47, 149–50, 153, 160, 183–84, 200, 261, 275, 284, 286
property rights, 46
Protect, Respect, and Remedy Framework on Business and Human Rights, 19, 85, 245–46
Purpose: beyond profits, 6–7, 27, 131–32, 136, 288; economizing as, 23; social, 50; and sustainable development, 243, 263, 292, 297–98, 306–8; uncivil 41; vision and, 56–60, 64–67, 71–74, 79, 83, 87–88, 91, 97–98, 106, 114, 139, 146–48, 158, 199–200, 205

Raelin, Joseph, 58
Rawls, John, 101
Reagan-Thatcher revolution of 1980, 31–32
recycling, 68–70, 73, 232–35, 259
Redefining Progress, 109
Reebok, 248
reengineering, 90
Reich, Robert, 30, 37, 106
Reinhardt, Forest, 234
remediation, 172, 186
renewable energy, 43, 73–74, 217, 223, 259, 274, 301
responsibility management (RM), 169. *See also* total responsibility management
Responsible Care initiative, 234, 256–58
Ricardo, David, 28
rights: human, 4, 5, 19, 37, 65, 81, 85, 87, 94, 96–97, 124, 137, 160, 170–71, 176, 180, 189, 191–93, 195, 201, 207–8, 244–49, 252–53, 262, 286, 298; individual or civil, 3, 37; intellectual property, 36; labor, 19, 48, 87, 94, 98, 124, 140, 171, 175–76, 180, 191, 197, 244, 249–50; political, 3, 245; property, 46; society and social, 3; women's, 282
Rio Declaration on Environmental and Development, 40, 191
Romis, Monica, 125
Rondinelli, Dennis, 230, 232
Royal Dutch Shell, 272–73
Ruggie, John, 245–48
Rugmark, 290
Russell 3000, 207

S&P 500, 114, 117–18, 143, 207
SA 8000 Workplace Standards, 196
Sachs, Jeffrey, 239
Sandoval, Ricardo, 164
Sarbanes-Oxley Act, 27, 37, 143
Save the Children, 216
Schor, Juliet, 262, 302
Schumpeter, Joseph, 305
self-awareness. *See* self-consciousness
self-consciousness, 59, 66–67, 74–75
Sen, Amartya, 300
Senge, Peter, 13–15, 55, 67, 71, 89–90, 226, 262, 307
September 11, 2001, U.S. terrorist attacks, 41
Shakti Doi, 49
Sheth, Jagdish, 72–74, 89, 97, 114
Silent Spring, 38
Sinegal find last name, 115
Sisodia, Rajendra, 72–74, 89, 97, 114

Slow Food, 291
small and medium-sized enterprises (SMEs), 5–6, 188, 265, 306
Smith, Adam, 28, 287
SNS Asset Management, 207
Social Accountability 8000, 10, 18, 183, 190, 192, 197–98, 201
Social Accountability Accreditation Services (SAAS), 197
Social Accountability International (SAI), 197
social capital, 7, 41–43, 110, 123, 12–28, 152, 154, 163, 216, 218, 242
socially responsible investment (SRI) index, 117, 119, 207, 267
society and social rights, 3,
Society for Human Resource Management, 119
Society of Environmental Toxicology and Chemistry, 231
Southwest Airlines, 121, 203
SPICE (Society, Partners, Investors, Customers, Employees), 75
spirituality, 12, 15, 56, 59, 61, 85, 90, 92, 284, 307, 309
Srivastave, Amit, 68
stakeholder capitalism concept of the firm, 132
Starbucks, 121
Sternin, Jerry, 216
Sternin, Monique, 216
Stiglitz, Joseph, 31–32, 287, 300–1
strategy, 4, 17, 26–27, 29–30, 47, 57, 73, 76–81, 85–90, 93, 97, 99, 113–15, 121–22, 124, 126, 133, 142–44, 150, 155–56, 159, 171–73, 176–81, 184, 194–95, 203–13, 217, 221, 227–29, 234–36, 243–44, 256, 286–88, 294, 297, 303–4, 306
supercapitalism, 30, 37
supply chain, 5, 15, 48, 70, 79, 124–25, 151, 154–56, 170, 175–76, 180–83, 187, 189, 193, 196–98, 207, 244, 261, 277, 290, 303
SustainAbility, 36
Sustainability Development Group, 236
Sustainability Living Plan, 236
sweatshops, 39, 123–24, 170, 189, 248–50
Synthesis Report, 44
Systems thinking, 1–47, 55–61, 64–65, 77, 80–101, 108, 119–20, 126–28, 139, 148, 162–63, 169–73, 179–90, 196, 199, 210, 216–17, 222, 228, 230–38, 240–44, 249, 252–55, 258, 261–62, 265–67, 273–75, 286–307

Teachers Insurance and Annuity Association-

College Retirement Equities Fund (TIAA-CREF), 213

Tellus Institute, 133, 297

The Fifth Discipline, 13–14, 55

The Natural Step (TNS), 44–45, 257

The Union of Needletrades, 249

The Web of Life, 222

third-way thinking, in Buddhism, 93

Timberland, 166

Toffler, Alvin, 276

Toffler, Heidi, 276

Tomorrow's Company, 298

Torbert, William, 62–63

total quality management (TQM), 89, 153, 169–96, 228, 231, 260–61

total responsibility management (TRM), 169, 171–72, 177–79, 182–83, 186–87, 189, 227, 243, 265

transforming stage, 76–78. *See also* corporate citizenship

transparency, 2–4, 16, 19, 36, 77, 95, 109–10, 125, 127–28, 133, 143, 166, 170–72, 178, 184–92, 196–200, 213–14, 227, 244, 252–53, 267, 277, 281, 285, 289–90, 293–94, 297, 302–3

Transparency International, 19, 95, 252, 290

Trillium, 206

Tripartite Declaration of Principles concerning Multinational Enterprises and Social Policy, 176

Troubled Asset Relief Program (TARP), 143

trust, 2–3, 7, 36, 42, 58, 64, 66, 80, 82, 88, 94, 104, 110, 123, 125–27, 134, 149–55, 164–66, 174, 186, 189–90, 193, 216–17, 236, 242, 252, 283, 289

Tylenol, 181

U.S. Forum for Sustainable and Responsible Investment (US SIF), 117, 207–8

U.S. Supreme Court, 28, 33, 87, 159

UN. *See* United Nations

UN Conference on Environment and Development, 11

UN Convention Against Corruption, 94, 191

UN Convention against Corruption, 191, 254

UN Economic and Social Commission for Asia and the Pacific (UN ESCAP), 253

UN Global Compact. *See* United Nations Global Compact

UN Global Compact Leaders' Summit, 126

UN Universal Declaration on Human Rights, 94, 191, 245

Unilever, 79, 236–37

Unilever, 79, 236–37

Union Carbide, 162

United Nations, 1–2, 40–41, 70, 84, 93–94, 100, 133, 176, 191, 203, 215, 217–18, 253, 255, 264, 290

United Nations Conference on Environment and Development, 11

United Nations Convention against Corruption, 94, 191, 254

United Nations Economic and Social Commission for Asia and the Pacific (UN ESCAP), 253

United Nations Global Compact, and corporations' social missions, 133; general description, 1, 5–6, 18, 84, 126, 176, 190, 203, 264, 278, 290, 298; and human rights, 94–95, 245, 247; at Novartis, 194–96

United Nations Global Compact Leaders' Summit, 126

United Nations Universal Declaration on Human Rights, 94, 191, 245

United Students against Sweatshops, 248

Universal Declaration of Human Rights, 94, 191, 245

utilitarianism, 100, 101

Varela, Francisco, 59

Vasella, Daniel, 194

Veiga, John, 118, 120, 149

Velasquez, Manuel, 100

vision 2050, 20

visioning, 70, 79, 291

Volcker, Paul, 31, 287

Waal, Frans de, 59

Wackernagel, Mathis, 223

Waddell, Steve, 291

Waddock, Sandra, 49, 125, 171–72

Wal-Mart, 78–80, 115, 234, 248

Wall Street Journal, 219

Walsh, James, 116

Walton, Samuel, 86

Water Conservation Pledge, 69

Web 2.0, 109–10, 165–68

Wheatley, Margaret, 15

White, Allen, 297

Whole Foods, 131, 138–40

wholeness, 81–82, 127

Whose Keeper?, 42

Williams, Andrew, 214

Winston, Andrew, 235